PLAN & BOOK
AILOR-MADE TRIP

CHILE   ECUADOR

TRIPS & UNIQUE EXPERIENCES CREATED BY LOCAL
EXPERTS AT INSIGHTGUIDES.COM/HOLIDAYS

has been inspiring travellers with high-quality travel content for
As well as our popular guidebooks, we now offer the opportunity to
e private trips completely personalised to your needs and interests.
g with one of our local experts, you will directly benefit from their
ocal know-how, helping you create memories that will last a lifetime.

OW INSIGHTGUIDES.COM/HOLIDAYS WORKS

STEP 1

Pick your dream destination
and submit an inquiry, or
modify an existing itinerary if
you prefer.

STEP 2

Fill in a short form, sharin
details of your travel plans
and preferences with a lo
expert.

STEP 3

Your local expert will create
your personalised itinerary,
which you can amend
until you are completely
satisfied.

STEP 4

Book securely online. Pac
your bags and enjoy your
holiday! Your local expert
will be available to answe
questions during your tri

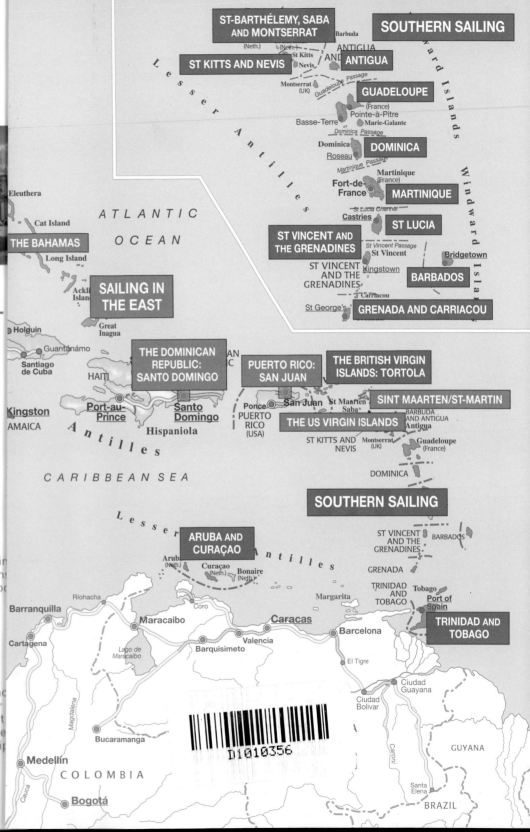

YOUR T

BRAZIL

INSIGHT

CARIB
CRUIS

TAILOR-MADE
TRAVEL

Insight Guides
over 45 years.
book tailor-ma
By connecti
expertise and

BENEFITS OF PLANNING & BOOKING AT
INSIGHTGUIDES.COM/HOLIDAYS

PLANNED BY LOCAL EXPERTS

The Insight Guides local experts are hand-picked, based on their experience in the travel industry and their impeccable standards of customer service.

SAVE TIME & MONEY

When a local expert plans your trip, you save time and money when you book, even during high season. You won't be charged for using a credit card either.

TAILOR-MADE TRIPS

Book with Insight Guides, and you will be in complete control of the planning process, from the initial selections to amending your final itinerary.

BOOK & TRAVEL STRESS-FREE

Enjoy stress-free travel when you use the Insight Guides secure online booking platform. All bookings come with a money-back guarantee.

WHAT OTHER TRAVELLERS THINK ABOUT TRIPS BOOKED AT
INSIGHTGUIDES.COM/HOLIDAYS

DON'T MISS OUT
BOOK NOW AT
INSIGHTGUIDES.COM/HOLIDAYS

CONTENTS

PRIVATE CRUISE ISLANDS

FURTHER READING

Travel tips

PLANNING THE TRIP

LIFE ON BOARD

A–Z WESTERN SHORES

A-Z EASTERN CARIBBEAN

A-Z SOUTHERN CARIBBEAN

Maps

LEGEND
◯ Insight on
◯ Photo story

THE BEST OF CARIBBEAN CRUISES: TOP ATTRACTIONS

△ **The Panama Canal**. Transiting this waterway, considered one of man's greatest 20th-century achievements, on a cruise ship is a fascinating and educational experience. See page 146.

△ **The Pitons, St Lucia**. The ultimate Caribbean landmark, the twin peaks of Petit Piton and Gros Piton are spectacular whether seen from land, sea or the air. See page 266.

▽ **Montserrat Volcano Observatory**. Watch steam and lava spewing from Montserrat's active volcano and get a first-hand glimpse of nature's devastating power. See page 228.

△ **Brimstone Hill Fortress, St Kitts**. A World Heritage Site, the well-preserved 17th-century fortifications afford a tremendous view to neighboring islands. See page 237.

△ **Whale watching**. Humpback whales are best seen at breeding time, January to March, in Samaná Bay, Dominican Republic; but Pilot, Brydes, Spinner and other whales and dolphins can be seen anytime off Dominica or throughout the Caribbean. See pages 192 and 246.

△ **Carnival in Trinidad**. A riot of exuberance and color, this is the best Carnival in the Caribbean – probably the world – with costumed revelers dancing to soca and steel pan. See page 296.

▽ **Colonial Zone, Santo Domingo**. The first city founded by the Spanish in the Americas, with the first cathedral, the first fortress, the first university and the first court, now a World Heritage Site. See page 188.

▽ **Kurá Hulanda Museum, Curaçao**. The region's best anthropological museum, whose private collection includes a moving permanent exhibit on the slave trade and the predominant cultures of Curaçao. See page 305.

▽ **Havana, Cuba**. Cuba is opening up to cruise visitors, drawn to the crumbling 16th-century architecture, vintage cars, Hemingway heritage, music and mojitos of the atmospheric capital. See page 183.

△ **Nelson's Dockyard, Antigua**. The last surviving Georgian dockyard in the world, beautifully preserved and still attracting sailing craft into the harbor, is brimming with character. See page 233.

THE BEST OF CARIBBEAN CRUISES: EDITOR'S CHOICE

The clear waters of Trunk Bay in the US Virgin Islands.

BEST BEACHES

Maria La Gorda, Cuba. Stretches for miles and is completely undeveloped, with spectacular underwater life close to the shore. See page 233.

Half Moon Cay, Little San Salvador. A lovely, curved bay of white sand on a Bahamas private island, See page 176.

Trunk Bay, St John, USVI. Can't be beaten for its underwater snorkeling trail in crystal clear water. See page 204.

Colombier Beach, St-Barthélemy. Reached by boat or a 30-minute hike – one of St-Barths' many unspoilt beaches. See page 226.

Maracas Bay, Trinidad. Spectacular, with rolling waves entering the horseshoe bay, and good for trying local food. See page 294.

Englishman's Bay, Tobago. Blissful, with an offshore reef. See page 295.

Cayman Islands diving.

TOP ADVENTURES

Waitukubuli National Trail, Dominica. A network of 115 miles (185km) of cleared trails used by slaves and farmers through forest and along coastline, and across mountains and valleys. See page 243.

Canyoning in Dominica. A great way to explore the rivers, cascades and waterfalls. See page 244.

Zip-lining in St Lucia. For an unbeatable adrenaline rush, swing through the trees or plummet down a ravine in the forest. See page 269.

Scuba diving in the Cayman Islands. Here, drop-offs, walls and wrecks attract marine life of all shapes, sizes and colors. See page 157.

Windsurfing and kitesurfing in Aruba. It's the strong, offshore wind over the shallow water that makes this the setting for international contests. See page 303.

Surfing in Barbados. The Atlantic waves rolling ashore at Bathsheba make for an exhilarating experience. See page 276.

Sailing in the Grenadines. This chain of tiny volcanic islands formed the backdrop to the movie *Pirates of the Caribbean*. See page 281.

Hiking in Saba. Trek up Mount Scenery through cloud forest and epiphytes in the hope of cloud-free views from the summit. See page 227.

BEST MARKETS

Castries, St Lucia. Central Market and the Vendor's Arcade opposite offer a pleasant mix of tourist souvenirs together with flowers and produce brought to town by farmers. See page 264.
Fort-de-France markets, Martinique. A kaleidoscope of color, not just for the fruit, vegetables and flowers, but also the traditional clothes made of Madras cotton worn by the vendors. See page 251.
Nassau Straw Market, Bahamas. A bustling, if touristy place, packed with baskets, mats and any conceivable item that can be woven from straw. See page 175.
St George's market, Grenada. Heady with the perfume of nutmeg, mace, cinnamon, cloves, cocoa and vanilla. See page 285.
Ocho Rios craft market, Jamaica. The place for hats, T-shirts, sarongs and all manner of souvenirs – but you'll need to be firm and polite to get a good bargain. See page 162.

Craft market painting.

BEST HANDICRAFTS

Molas. The patchwork-type embroidery of the Kuna people, on the San Blas islands, is exquisite, sewn onto blouses or cushion covers.
Basketwork. The basketwork of the Kalinago on Dominica is delicate, intricate, varied – and ultimately, useful.
Jewelry. Golden amber and pale blue larimar from the Dominican Republic can be bought as polished stones or set in silver jewelry.
Batik. Colorful batik clothing from Caribelle Batik on St Kitts is made using the soft Sea Island Cotton.
Earthworks pottery. This Barbadian pottery produces bright ceramics for the table, in unusual designs.
Organic chocolate. The Grenada variety is to die for, made using locally grown cocoa and so pure it won't melt on the way back to the ship.

Breakfast on deck with Regent Seven Seas.

ON-BOARD HIGHLIGHTS

Your private balcony. Soak up the sun on a day at sea; relax with a good book and not a thing to do.
Children's Club conservation lessons. Prepare them for shore trips to vulnerable islands and their fragile eco-systems. See page 54.
Sunset sailaways. Chill out after a busy day on shore with cocktails on deck to the sound of a steel band. See page 85.
Adults only. Splash out on a pass to the peaceful, adults-only deck space. Most ships have these, with squashy loungers, iced fruit kebabs, and bar service.
See page 79.
Watching dolphins race the ship at sunrise. Seeing them wild, free and full of fun is a magical moment. See page 54.
Dinner on deck. Choose a ship that offers al fresco dining and watch the stars come out as you eat.
Yoga at sunrise. Caribbean cruises often provide opportunities for an early morning workout on deck. See page 82.
Movies under the stars. Many ships have big screens on deck. Lie back on a sunlounger with your favorite cocktail and watch movies in the moonlight.

Dominican baskets.

BEST ARCHITECTURE

The Magnificent Seven, Port of Spain. Opulent Stollmeyer's Castle is just one in this Trinidadian line-up of very fine (if partly dilapidated) colonial buildings, dating from around the end of the 19th century, which gives Maraval Road its flair and elegance. See page 293.

Chattel houses, Barbados. These shacks were once home to plantation workers, who constructed the wooden 'sleeping boxes' – which were easy to dismantle – with mobility in mind. Painted in primary colors and pastel shades, and with intricate fretwork around the windows, they often double as craft shops. See page 278.

Dutch colonial houses, Curaçao. Santa Anna Bay, the narrow channel which divides Willemstad in two, is flanked by fine examples of pastel-tinted, traditionally gabled Dutch houses, in an echo of Amsterdam. See page 302.

Musée de St-John Perse, Guadeloupe. Housed within a beautifully restored colonial building, the museum commemorates the life and work of the island's Nobel Prize-winning poet (1887–1975) who idealized the Caribbean in his writings. See page 257.

Rose Hall Great House, Jamaica. Probably the best known of Jamaica's plantation Great Houses is Rose Hall, the 18th-century home of alleged 'white witch' Annie Palmer, which is grandly sited on a ridge. See page 161.

Palacio de los Capitanes Generales, Havana. Now housing the City Museum, this massive baroque structure with its thick mahogany doors served as the Cuban government's headquarters in the late 1790s. See page 185.

Going Dutch in Willemstad, Curaçao.

Orchid in El Yunque, the Caribbean National Forest, Puerto Rico.

BEST NATURE VENTURES

Reserva de la Biósfera Sian Ka'An, Mexico. Divided into three distinct coastal zones, this 1.3 million-acre (526,000-hectare) nature reserve contains broad savannahs, dense mangroves, tropical forests and many different types of marine habitat. See page 141.

Queen Elizabeth II Botanic Park, Cayman Islands. The marked trails in this oasis guide visitors past 600 species of indigenous plants; interpretive exhibits; rare, endemic Cayman blue iguanas; and much more. See page 156.

RESCQ (Restoration of Ecosystem Services and Coral Reef Quality), Saba. Aims to make an impact on coral reef health in the Saba Bank National Park, one of the largest protected marine areas in the Caribbean. The project raises new coral colonies in nurseries which are then used to repopulate denuded reefs. Visitors can help by joining one of the regular coral nursery maintenance dives conducted by local scuba outfitter Sea Saba. See page 197.

Asa Wright Nature Centre, Trinidad. More than 100 different species of bird, including several rare hummingbirds, can be observed amongst the vast amounts of tropical flora and fauna. See page 294.

BEST VIEWS

From your cruise ship. Sailing through the **Grenadines archipelago**, past bottle-green islands ringed by enticing beaches; nearing the pretty anchorage of **Iles des Saintes**, colorful wooden houses strung out around a half-moon bay; dropping anchor outside **Gustavia, St-Barths**, flanked by the sleek megayachts of visiting oligarchs. See pages 281, 255 and 225.

From the top of Chichén Itzá, Mexico. Views over the Yucatán from the Maya ruins of this fabled city. See page 140.

El Morro, Havana. Views over the harbor and the Malecón esplanade from the Morro fortress. See page 183.

Paradise Point, St Thomas. Ride the cable car up to the viewing platform. See page 201.

Shirley Heights, Antigua. 360° views over Nelson's Dockyard to Montserrat and Guadeloupe. See page 233.

Boiling Lake Trail, Dominica. Trek up into the Morne Trois Pitons National Park for rare vistas over Guadeloupe and Martinique. See page 246.

Jardin de Balata, Martinique.

BEST GARDENS

Botanic Gardens, St Vincent. Founded in 1765 to propagate spices and medicinal plants, these are the oldest botanic gardens in the western hemisphere. See page 281.

Andromeda Gardens, Barbados. On a rocky hillside, the garden harbors tropical plants collected from around the world, with a splendid example of a bearded fig tree. See page 276.

Diamond Botanical Gardens Mineral Baths and Waterfall, St Lucia. In the middle of a splendid garden, the area's steamy, restorative springs stream from the ground into tiled basins. See page 266.

Jardin de Balata, Martinique. Blessed with a grand view, these gardens also have a stunning anthurium collection. See page 252.

Shaw Park Botanical Gardens, Jamaica. Set around a natural waterfall and within handy walking distance of the cruise port. See page 163.

Maya ruins at Chichén Itzá.

MONEY-SAVING TIPS

For a general tour of an island, a local taxi driver is usually as good as, if not better than, an organized coach tour and will cost less for 3–4 people. Most will be a fount of local information, history and gossip, and able to suggest a nice place for lunch, or a snack at wherever he/she would normally eat. Agree the price before you set off, though.

Shore excursions and activities can also be booked direct via companies like www.cruisingexcursions.com and www.viator.com and are even cheaper if there's a small group of you. Don't have enough people for a group? Before you cruise, check out popular cruising forums like those at www.cruisecritic.com and hook up with others who are on the same trip as you. A lot of cruisers find taxi-shares this way. If there's a market at your port of call, look around for where the vendors and office workers eat their lunch. It will be typically local food, filling and cheap, tasty and interesting. Eat early, though, or it will all be gone.

If there are shops at the cruise terminal, buy your day's supply of mineral water there, as it's invariably cheaper than buying it on board. Take some back to the ship, too.

The Freedom of the Seas docked at Labadee, Haiti.

Beach larks on the US Virgin Island of St John

Grab a paddleboard in paradise

Catching some rays by Paradise Island.

ISLAND HOPPING

Douglas Ward, the world's leading authority on cruise ships, considers why many people choose to cruise the Caribbean.

Hitting the surf in Cozumel, Mexico

White sandy beaches, deep blue waters, bougainvillaea and passion flowers, tropical fruits, glowing sunshine, vibrant music and friendly, laid-back people place the islands of the Caribbean among the world's most popular holiday destinations. And there is no better way to experience the Caribbean, certainly for first-time visitors, than on a cruise. Cruising enables visitors to be as lazy or as active as they wish, combining the pleasures of life in a luxury, floating hotel with the enjoyment of well-organized shore excursions.

The Caribbean basin contains thousands of islands, stretching from Bermuda in the north to the coast of Venezuela in the south, Barbados in the east, and Costa Rica in the west. With most cruises beginning in Florida, much of this huge area is accessible on relatively short trips by sea, and the value for money is unbeatable.

The pitons of St Lucia

Cruising has come a long way since the 'booze cruises' of the 1930s, designed chiefly to escape Prohibition laws in the United States. The industry launched the revival of fortunes for many islands in the Caribbean, but World War II intervened and it was only in the 1960s that cruising was reborn, with passengers being flown to embarkation ports.

Since then, the worldwide cruise industry has grown enormously; while the concept hasn't changed much, it has been vastly improved, refined, expanded and packaged. Some ten companies operating large ships (loosely defined as ships carrying between 2,500 and 5,400 passengers) dominate the market, but smaller vessels (carrying fewer than 700 passengers) also have a place, and are capable of entering the uncrowded harbors where their larger sisters cannot venture.

These days, cruising is not just for the elderly or for the wealthy – passengers come from all age groups and walks of life, and cruises are designed to suit many different needs. Read on, and see if you would like to join them.

THE CARIBBEAN CHARACTER

Centuries of foreign domination, slavery and migration have forged local cultures that are strong, proud and creative.

Arrive in any Caribbean port, from the Bahamas down to Trinidad, and the first thing you will see will probably be a fortress. Havana's harbor mouth, for instance, is guarded by three formidable castles, the oldest of which was completed in 1630. The seaward approach to Martinique's capital, Fort-de-France, is watched over by the grim-looking Fort St Louis, continuously occupied by the French military for almost four centuries. Even a tiny island like St Kitts, no more than a dot on the map, has nine impressive forts, one of which proved so impregnable it was dubbed the 'Gibraltar of the West Indies.'

These scattered vestiges of military power, some ruined and others restored, remind us that the Caribbean has always been fought over. Its history is, to a large extent, one of conquest and conflict. Its landscapes are marked not only by fortifications, but by the memory of battles, uprisings and massacres. Not only did competing European nations go to war over this rich and desirable region, but pirates preyed on its ports, and enslaved Africans rose up in violent bids for freedom. Only in more recent times has this archipelago of islands discovered peace and left behind its turbulent history.

EARLY INVADERS

The first invaders were the people who gave their name to this part of the world. The Caribs arrived

Columbus lands on Watling Island, the Bahamas.

in around AD 1000, pushing up the island chain from their homelands in the Amazon Basin and conquering each territory they reached. Their victims were the peaceful Taínos, the first people to settle in the region, who also originated from South America. Fierce, fearless and reputedly inclined to cannibalism, the Caribs overwhelmed the Taínos, killing men and capturing women.

The Carib invasion may have been violent, but it was mild in comparison to the horrors inflicted by the first European invaders. Believing himself to be somewhere near China, Christopher Columbus landed on a flat, scrubby island in the Bahamas on October 12, 1492, unleashing the conquest of the New World by the Old. The Genoese adventurer, backed by the Spanish

The Caribbean Sea has borne witness to countless naval engagements and its waters conceal a wealth of competing nations' sunken warships and rusting cannons.

monarchy, made a first permanent settlement in what is now the Dominican Republic, founding a fledgling colony among the normally placid Taínos on the island he called Hispaniola.

Such was the brutality inflicted by the colonists on the Taínos, as they forced them to search for gold, that the indigenous people revolted. As uprisings were followed by reprisals and the Taínos succumbed to European diseases, a community of 300,000 on Hispaniola was reduced to a mere handful within three decades.

islands had only limited supplies of gold, the emphasis shifted to a new form of wealth: sugar.

KING SUGAR

It had been discovered that sugar cane, brought by Columbus on his second expedition in 1493, flourished in the fertile Caribbean soil. So began the reign of 'King Sugar,' the cruel ruler of the Caribbean economy for five centuries. But sugar plantations required labor, and with the Taínos almost extinct and the Spanish disinclined to sweat in the fields, a workforce was needed.

Slaves working in the fields in Cuba.

From this unpromising foothold, the Spanish empire strengthened and spread. Cuba, Puerto Rico and Jamaica were conquered, and *conquistadores* set sail from Santo Domingo to seize the vast territories of Mexico and Central America. The smaller Eastern Caribbean islands, sighted and named by Columbus, were not colonized, largely because of the presence of the ferocious Caribs. When it became apparent that the Caribbean

> When on-shore, pirates grilled their meat over boucans (a Carib word) or barbecues, from which the name 'buccaneer' derived.

The colonists accordingly turned to the African slave trade, which had been practised since the 1450s. The first slaves arrived in 1518, but soon the trickle turned into a flood.

Other European nations watched the expansion of the Spanish Caribbean with keen interest. Protestant England claimed religious motivations for its hostility towards Catholic Spain, but money and military competition were equally important grounds for animosity. Pirates from England, France and Holland began to prey on Spanish galleons and ports. Sir Francis Drake attacked and occupied Santo Domingo in 1585, destroying the pride of the Spanish empire. In response, the Spanish fortified their towns and protected their treasure fleets with warships. Gradually, other

European nations began to settle in the region, choosing the smaller islands of the Eastern Caribbean, which the Spanish had claimed but not occupied. The English claimed St Kitts in 1624 and Barbados in 1627. The French took Martinique and Guadeloupe in 1635. The Dutch took possession of islands such as Curaçao and Sint Maarten between 1630 and 1640.

Throughout the 17th and 18th centuries, the European powers fought among themselves for control of the Caribbean and its rich sugar industry. The British took Jamaica from the

'great houses' and fantastically rich West Indian planters. Fabulous fortunes were made, both by planters and manufacturers and by traders in Europe. But the system also carried the seeds of its own destruction. Huge plantations became breeding grounds for resistance and revolt among the slaves, who had nothing to lose but a life of overwork and cruelty. Uprisings ravaged almost every island and, although bloodily repressed, caused terror among the white minority.

The single event that changed the course of Caribbean history was the slave revolution of

Proclaiming emancipation to slaves on a sugar plantation.

Spanish in 1655 and from then on did their utmost to weaken the Spaniards' dominance of the larger islands. At the same time, conflicts between the British, French and Dutch reflected wider hostilities in Europe. No sooner were peace treaties signed than a new outbreak of fighting shook the region. Between 1660 and 1814, the island of St Lucia changed hands between the British and French 14 times. Throughout this period, millions of enslaved Africans were brought to the islands to ensure the flow of sugar to Europe was not interrupted.

SEEDS OF DESTRUCTION

The heyday of the sugar industry was the second half of the 18th century, the age of luxurious

The wealth generated by sugar and slavery fuelled the industrial revolution first in Britain, then in the rest of Europe, and this, ironically, led to the downfall of the colonial plantation system.

1791–1804, which destroyed the French colony of Saint Domingue and created the independent republic of Haiti. Here, in 13 years of civil war and foreign intervention, an army of ex-slaves beat Napoleon's military machine and freed themselves by force. Men such as Toussaint Louverture and Jean-Jacques Dessalines turned their fellow slaves into a lethal

PIRATES

For almost 200 years, from the 16th century, pirates, privateers and buccaneers terrorized the Caribbean with spectacular brutality.

Henry Morgan, the fearsome Welsh buccaneer who became the Governor of Jamaica.

Fiction has been kind to pirates, painting them as dashing desperadoes, but the truth was rather different. For the most part, they were driven by a mixture of religious hatred and greed as they wreaked havoc among the Spanish treasure fleets, earning notoriety for their spectacular brutality. Tolerated and even supported by European governments hostile to Spain, they were eventually banished by those same governments after they had outlived their usefulness.

ROYAL PATRONAGE

The first pirates were independent operators, mixing attacks on Caribbean shipping and harbor with smuggling and slave-trading. Soon they were sponsored by their rulers at home (and known as privateers rather than pirates), with Queen Elizabeth I of England a staunch supporter of Sir Francis Drake. He and others attacked shipping and towns throughout the Caribbean and Central America, forcing the Spanish to build expensive fortifications and reinforce the

fleets that carried gold and silver from South America back to Europe. Yet all these precautions couldn't stop Piet Heyn, a Dutch privateer, from capturing 31 bullion-laden ships off the coast of Cuba in 1628.

As wars raged between European nations in the 17th century, deserters, shipwrecked sailors and escaped slaves formed runaway communities in the Caribbean. The favorite haunts of these buccaneers were isolated Tortuga off Haiti and the empty cays of the Bahamas. They enticed ships onto reefs or attacked them from their own long canoes, capturing cargoes and murdering crews.

Life was short and brutish, with violent death or disease ever present. They lived in basic shacks, wore rough clothes of cotton and rawhide and were reportedly filthy with the blood of slaughtered cattle. Even so, the buccaneers developed deep bonds of affection among themselves and even entered into a sort of same-sex marriage, called *matelotage*, although this was probably a means of dealing with an individual's assets in the event of his death. In return for weapons, tobacco and rum, the buccaneers traded hides and meat with the passing ships that they did not choose to attack.

THE TIDE TURNS

The heyday of the pirates came in the 1680s, when Port Royal in Jamaica achieved infamy as the 'wickedest town in Christendom,' a decadent boomtown of taverns, brothels and gambling dens. It was here that Henry Morgan, fiercest of all seafarers, ruled as lieutenant-governor after a bloody career raiding Spanish ports. In 1692 Port Royal was destroyed by an earthquake and tidal wave in what many deemed an act of divine retribution.

Around that time, European leaders were tiring of their former pirate friends, as they now had their own Caribbean possessions. Some pirates retired gracefully, others were hunted down. The golden age of Caribbean piracy was over by the end of the 17th century, even though a few, such as Edward 'Blackbeard' Teach, carried on into the next The ruins of Port Royal give an idea of what life was like.

Under the sea, however, lie literally hundreds of wrecks, many the result of pirate attacks. Are they full of gold doubloons? Crowds of treasure hunters, professional and amateur, who flock to the islands think so.

fighting force, capable of beating the French and British. The other Caribbean societies watched with horror as the region's richest colony disintegrated.

Another blow to King Sugar came with the development of a rival beet sugar industry in Europe. European farmers and manufacturers began to compete with the vested interests of the old 'plantocracy.' Within the islands themselves, grotesquely unequal societies were increasingly under strain. A small minority of white landowners, backed by military force,

many continued to work for paltry wages on the plantations, while others left, establishing small farms or seeking work in the towns.

Abolition spelled the downfall of the Caribbean sugar industry, although vestiges of it clung on for many islands. Contract laborers arrived from India and other countries to fill the gaps left by the departing slaves. But the industry went through hard times, and gradually the European powers lost interest in their Caribbean possessions, turning instead to imperial adventures in Africa and Asia.

The French and patriots battle in Haiti (1802–04).

lorded it over a mixed-race population and a much greater number of black slaves. Hatreds ran deep, and conflict was commonplace.

ABOLITION

Slavery ended in the mid-19th century (it took longest to disappear in the Spanish colonies) through a combination of economic and political pressures. In short, the system was costly and inefficient as well as barbarous. Planters feared a repeat of the Haitian revolution, while liberals at home in Europe campaigned for abolition. Eventually, slavery was outlawed, the planters were compensated for their losses, and the slaves found themselves faced with freedom – of a sort. Few options were open to them and

⊘ INTERNAL CHANGES

While the post-slavery Caribbean islands slipped off the map as far as Europe was concerned, it was a period of great social change. The power of the white minority dwindled, although Europeans still remained firmly in control. The contrast between their lifestyles and those of the black and colored communities encouraged the latter to seek improvements through education and social reform. Churches of all denominations were active in redressing old inequalities and providing new opportunities. The Moravian church (a Protestant sect that originated in Bohemia) was particularly insistent that people of all races should receive education.

THE AMERICAN CENTURY

The 20th century was the American century in the Caribbean. The new superpower was opposed to any remaining European interference in its 'backyard' and moved to fill the void left by the colonial forces. In 1898, the US ousted the Spanish from Cuba and Puerto Rico, ending 400 years of Hispanic rule. There were subsequent interventions in Haiti and the Dominican Republic, where political chaos and economic mismanagement irritated Washington. The completion of the Panama Canal in

A cartoon depicts Uncle Sam using the American flag to shield a woman labeled 'Cuba Libre' from 'Insurgent' men.

1914, together with hostilities against Germany in World War I, made the US especially protective of its strategic interests in the Caribbean.

What most of the Caribbean islands wanted was independence. Haiti had led the way in 1804, but had been plagued by instability and poverty. The Dominican Republic finally threw out the Spanish in 1864; as mentioned, Cuba and Puerto Rico followed suit in 1898. But American influence remained strong, creating resentment among those who wanted to be free of outside interference. Afraid of communism, the US supported conservatives, including such unsavory dictators as Rafael Leonidas Trujillo, who ran the Dominican Republic like a

family business from 1930 to 1961. Washington's worst fears were realized when another dictator, Fulgencio Batista of Cuba, was ousted in 1959, and replaced by the revolutionary government of Fidel Castro – which has remained in power ever since, now under the leadership of his brother Raúl.

INDEPENDENCE

In most instances, independence took a more peaceful form. In the British colonies, greater self-government and universal suffrage was followed by complete independence from the 1960s onwards. Jamaica, Barbados and Trinidad and Tobago all severed colonial ties with London after the failure of a short-lived federation of English-speaking islands. They were followed by smaller territories, from Antigua to St Vincent. But some islands preferred to maintain their links with Europe. In 1946, Martinique and Guadeloupe voted to become *départements* of France, while the Dutch islands formed a federation with the Netherlands. A few tiny territories, such as Montserrat and Anguilla, opted to remain British colonies rather than face the economic uncertainty of independence.

In many respects, the modern Caribbean is something of a success story. The region enjoys democratic government and a steadily growing standard of living, while human rights and a modest prosperity are now taken for granted. Barbados, for instance, has some of the best quality-of-life statistics outside Europe and North America, as does oil-rich Trinidad.

There are still social and political flashpoints. The deep-seated problems of Haiti – which remains politically volatile and stubbornly poor – seem no closer to a solution following the devastating earthquake in 2010 which caused thousands of deaths and the destruction of much of the capital's infrastructure. There is occasional trouble in the tough inner-city ghettos of Kingston, Jamaica. But, for the most part, the Caribbean is a region of stability and social tolerance, where people of all backgrounds live together. One of the biggest developments of the 21st century has been the thawing of relations between the US and Cuba, a program of normalization of relations between the two countries agreed by then presidents Barack Obama and

Raúl Castro. The Trump administration subsequently reversed some of the arrangements but cruise ship routes remain largely unaffected.

The threats facing the Caribbean are now more economic than political. As a cluster of small states, the islands are especially vulnerable to developments beyond their control. These range from the hurricanes that regularly ravage communities to the onward march of globalization and the threatened loss of export markets to cheaper producers around the world.

times, distinctly different influences become obvious. The smaller islands of the Eastern Caribbean, for instance, are a fascinating blend of French and British influences, where French-built Catholic churches rub shoulders with solidly Anglo-Saxon town halls. Towns like Castries in St Lucia or St George's in Grenada reveal a subtle blend of Gallic and British influences, reflected in the French-based, musical *patois* spoken by many islanders.

Elsewhere, a particular European model is dominant. Barbados, affectionately known as

A cane-fuelled steam train on a sugar plantation.

THE EUROPEAN HERITAGE

This history of colonialism and conflict has left an indelible mark on today's Caribbean. Four European languages (English, French, Spanish and Dutch) are spoken across the region, together with many local dialects and creoles – a mixture of European, African and other languages. Colonial rule has left behind the architecture, habits and the tastes of the European mother country, whether in the shape of croissants in Guadeloupe, cricket in Antigua or gabled roofs in Curaçao.

Each island bears the imprint of its colonial past, but often this past is as culturally mixed as the people it has produced. Where more than one European power ruled an island at different

⊘ THE RELIGIOUS MIX

The Caribbean is a place where religion is taken seriously and where religious values look back to the pivotal role played by churches in the post-slavery period. Christian churches of every sort co-exist with other religious faiths, mostly derived from Africa or India and transplanted with slaves and laborers to the Caribbean. In Haiti and Cuba, traditional African spirits are worshipped by followers of *vodou* and *santería*. In Trinidad and the French islands, Hindu temples and Muslim mosques are testimony to the importation of religious ideas from the Indian subcontinent, brought by the laborers who became the new workforce in the 19th century.

'Little England,' was never occupied by any other colonial power and exudes Englishness in its parish churches, cricket grounds and Victorian architecture. The great cities of Havana and San Juan, on the other hand, are unmistakably Spanish, with colonnaded streets, plazas and fountains. The warehouses of Willemstad, Curaçao, look like a canal-side section of Amsterdam, while small towns in Martinique are reminiscent of provincial France with their war memorials and *tricolores*.

remained strong despite attempts by white slave masters to drive out 'superstition.' The voodoo religion of Haiti, much maligned and distorted by outsiders for centuries, is the living connection between this Caribbean nation and the West African societies from which millions of slaves were forcibly removed. In agricultural techniques, in food and drink, in dance, music and ritual, almost every Caribbean island remains linked to the distant African point of departure.

In some instances, there is another strong

Mennonite children at play in the town of Spanish Lookout, Belize.

MIGRANTS AND SETTLERS

European heritage is only part of the story. Each Caribbean island is also the product of a long history of migration and settlement, in which Africa, Asia and the Americas have all played vital roles. In the Spanish Caribbean, there was always a greater tradition of European migration, and the descendants of migrants from Andalucia and the Canary Islands can still be seen in the lighter-skinned peasant farmers of Cuba and Puerto Rico. In these islands slavery was less dominant than in Haiti or Jamaica, where today's majority population is of African descent.

Where Africans arrived in great numbers, their cultural and religious practices connection. Trinidad, for instance, has a majority population descended from the Indian laborers who were shipped from the sub-continent in the second half of the 19th century to work on the sugar plantations. Today, parts of rural Trinidad resemble Hindustan, as *dhoti*-clad laborers tend buffaloes among coconut groves. In the towns, meanwhile, the sounds and smells of India are evident in contemporary *chutney* music and Trinidad's favorite fast food, the curry-filled *roti*. Elsewhere, in Jamaica especially, a strong Chinese influence is detectable. Throughout the region the descendants of migrant traders from the Middle East play an important role in retailing and finance.

Pompous politicians or overbearing bureaucrats are likely to face well-deserved mockery, often in calypso songs, which with their witty lyrics, are traditionally a comment on the state of the nation.

A CREOLE CULTURE

Jamaica's motto, 'Out of many, one people,' contains the key to understanding the Caribbean character. This is a part of the world, per-

wonderful music, literature and visual arts. For a relatively small area of fewer than 20 million people, the Caribbean has been disproportionately fertile in creating new artistic forms.

The region is the birthplace not only of reggae, calypso and salsa, but also of world-class writers such as Trinidad's V.S. Naipaul, Cuba's Alejo Carpentier and St Lucia's Derek Walcott. In painting, sculpture and dance, the Caribbean can confidently compete with any other part of the world. Its sportsmen and women, too, are often world-beaters, ranging from champion

Jamaican family life.

Barbadian dance performance.

haps more than anywhere else, where people and cultures from every continent have been brought together into hybrid and mixed societies. The mixture of European, African, Asian and American has created what is known as a creole culture, a cocktail of differing influences and traditions. The term 'creole' used to apply to a white individual born in the region, but now means the distinctive blend of the parts that make the Caribbean whole.

So what are the defining characteristics of 'creoleness'? Generalizations are dangerous, and clearly each island has its own particular traits, but firmly at the heart of the region's collective identity lies creativity. Creole culture is enormously inventive, producing some

Cuban boxers to Jamaica's Olympic sprinters.

Above all, the creole character is formed by a love of freedom and a respect for the individual. The Caribbean has undergone the traumatic experience of slavery and, in many cases, dictatorship, and this bitter history has taught its people to value freedom. Independence and self-reliance are valued qualities in a region where economic conditions are often harsh, and many people are deeply attached to a small patch of land that they can call their own.

There is little affection for authority in the Caribbean. Few people enjoy taking orders – perhaps another legacy of slavery – and that is why visitors are sometimes frustrated by what they view as inefficiency or insolence. The only solution is to recognize that taking one's time is not necessarily a bad thing, and that patience and a sense of humor go a long way towards breaking down barriers.

A CHANGING ECONOMY

A child born today in the Caribbean is more likely to end up serving drinks in a hotel or driving a taxi than cutting sugar cane or growing vegetables. Agriculture is still the lifeblood of many Caribbean economies, and King Sugar still holds some vestiges of power

A couple enjoy the romance of a cruise.

in Jamaica and several other islands, but the economic landscape is one that is now changing rapidly.

Sugar never really recovered from the downturn of the late 19th century and continued to decline throughout the 20th. Some governments looked for agricultural alternatives, and in the 1950s the banana industry was encouraged to displace sugar across the eastern Caribbean. The advent of low-cost air transport meant that fruits, flowers and other exotic exports could be flown fresh to New York or London. But many farmers simply gave up commercial agriculture and found work in towns, or migrated. Big estates sometimes prospered, but small farmers faced tough times.

The islands looked for other livelihoods. Some, like Trinidad, were fortunate in having natural resources such as oil and gas. Others built up light manufacturing, taking advantage of their proximity to the huge US market and cheap labor rates. The Caribbean soon began to develop a reputation for low-cost assembly plants, making everything from T-shirts to baseballs. With advances in technology came new opportunities such as data processing and offshore banking.

TOURISM

The real economic trump card has been tourism. Since Victorian times, the islands have attracted the wealthy from colder climates, who wintered in the first hotel resorts to be built in Barbados and Cuba. With Prohibition in the US came floods of thirsty Americans to Cuba and the Bahamas, in search of rum cocktails and a good time. From the 1950s onwards, jet planes transported growing numbers of tourists from Europe and North America to the region, and almost every island, from mighty Cuba to tiny Saba, developed a tourism industry.

The 1990s witnessed new peaks in Caribbean tourism as all-inclusive resorts and cruising became increasingly popular with holiday-makers. Large all-inclusive chains such as Sandals spread throughout the islands, offering a guaranteed price for an entire vacation but frustrating local restaurant owners and others who depend on tourists spending money outside their hotels.

From hubs in Miami, Puerto Rico and Mexico, cruise ships criss-crossed the region, bringing millions of visitors each year to the islands. There is no sign that this vibrant industry is liable to slow down, although governments and investors know that tourism is a notoriously fickle business.

The economic importance of tourism to the Caribbean cannot be exaggerated. Of all the regions in the world, the Caribbean is the most dependent upon tourism as a contribution to GDP, and the sector is the biggest employer after the public sector. For every 'official' tourism worker there are many others – taxi drivers, farmers, artisans – who depend on the influx of visitors. Also numerous, however,

Each port has been developed for today's needs in different ways, but all evoke a shared history of colonial battles for possession, maritime trade in goods and slaves, and bittersweet sugar wealth.

are those who resent the investment spent on tourism infrastructure when schools and hospitals are chronically underfunded. Unemployment, poverty, crime, drugs and alcohol are worldwide problems that are magnified in small island societies.

CARIBBEAN CRUISING

The attractions of the Caribbean need no introduction: a year-round warm climate, blue seas and some of the best beaches in the world, are just a few reasons to visit. Add to that impressive waterfalls and mountains, an eclectic range of architectural styles and some fascinating historic sites, and it is easy to see why people return time after time.

Cruise ships offer a particularly inviting way into this rich and varied part of the world. In a week, for instance, it is possible to explore half a dozen entirely different islands, getting a tantalizing taste of the Caribbean's diversity. In some cases, a day may be long enough to gain an impression of an island, especially if it's a small one. More probably, a brief visit will leave you wanting to see more. Many people return for a longer stay in a place they first visited, fleetingly, from a cruise ship.

The beauty of Caribbean cruising is that each day offers an entirely different cultural experience. At first sight, some of the islands may look similar, with wooded hills surrounding the harbor and mountains stretching into the interior. But on closer inspection, you will discover that each port, and each island, has its own distinctive identity and flavor.

There is no mistaking the French feel of Pointe-à-Pitre, Guadeloupe, for instance, where ships moor next to the bustling Place de la Victoire, with its cafés, war memorial and colorful market traders. But just to the north, you'll find Antigua, where memories of Admiral Lord Nelson, an Anglican cathedral and a cricket ground are all resolutely British in atmosphere.

Most Caribbean islands have done a great deal to upgrade and modernize their cruise terminal facilities, and visitors can normally expect an array of shops, bars and restaurants on shore – although it would be a mistake to stay in the terminal and not take a look at the island beyond.

THE HEART OF THE ISLANDS

With a few exceptions, cruise ships moor close to the center of the major Caribbean ports, such as in Havana, San Juan and Santo Domingo. In

Norwegian Getaway departs St Thomas.

the smaller islands it is normally only a brief walk or taxi ride from ship to town. This means visitors can quickly be at the heart of things, and in more ways than one, for the ports in themselves are the heart of Caribbean islands – usually the capital or main town, not to mention the commercial center, as they have been since the height of the sugar trade. As a result, they are full of historic interest, revealing ancient warehouses, colonnaded arcades and imposing buildings as well as the ubiquitous fortifications.

Take a taxi or bus to the surrounding countryside or nearby beaches, but remember that the history of the Caribbean islands, both good and bad, is most clearly seen in the streets and buildings around their waterfronts.

A poster promoting an early voyage – illustrating the SS Havana in 1910.

sta desde el Morro.
City from Morro Castle.

DECISIVE DATES

1835
Arthur Anderson co-founds the Peninsular Steam Navigation Company; by the 1840s it offers Mediterranean cruises and has become the Peninsular & Oriental Steam Navigation Company (P&O).

1900
Orient Line operates the first Caribbean cruises, round-trip from the UK.

1910
Cunard Line, which had been founded in 1840 to operate transatlantic services, introduces its first cruise ships, *Laconia* and *Franconia*.

1920–33
US Prohibition creates a demand for 'booze cruises.' Non-US ships head into international waters, where they can supply alcohol.

1965
Princess Cruises is founded and begins cruising from the US West Coast.

Thomas Cook, package holiday pioneer.

1966
Norwegian Caribbean Lines (NCL) is set up to operate *Sunward* out of Miami on the first regular, year-round Caribbean cruise program.

1969
Royal Caribbean Cruise Line is created by Scandinavian shipping companies I.M. Skaugen, Anders Wilhelmsen and Gotaas-Larsen to compete with NCL.

1972
Carnival Cruise Lines (CCL) is formed by Ted Arison after he leaves NCL. The first cruise of the *Mardi Gras* is a disaster as it runs aground.

1974
Arison buys loss-making CCL from AITS for US$1 and assumption of US$5m in debts. It becomes the most successful Caribbean cruise line. P&O buys Princess Cruises.

1975
US television show, *The Love Boat*, becomes the first soap opera set aboard a cruise ship. Princess Cruises' *Pacific Princess* stars in the show.

1979
Knut Kloster, owner of Kloster Redeerei, gambles on buying the decaying, laid-up SS *France* to convert into the *Norway* for Caribbean cruising.

1986
Seabourn Cruise Line (originally named Signet Cruise Line) is formed to provide luxury cruises, some in the Caribbean.

Holland America Line historical poster, 1949.

1988
P&O buys Sitmar Cruises and merges it with its Princess Cruises in North America. Carnival buys Holland America Line and Windstar Cruises.

1989
The Greek-owned Chandris Group creates a new, upmarket cruise brand, Celebrity Cruises. The Panama Canal celebrates its 75th birthday.

1996
Thomson Cruises is revived, operating ships on charter and winter fly-cruising from the UK to the Caribbean. The first-ever passenger ship to exceed more than 100,000 tons – *Carnival Destiny* – begins cruising; too large to transit the Panama Canal, it cruises the Caribbean year-round.

1997
Carnival Corporation and Airtours jointly buy the leading European operator, Costa Cruises (Carnival later buys out the Airtours share). In the same year Royal Caribbean

International (RCI) acquires Celebrity Cruises for US$1.3 billion.

1998
Carnival buys Cunard Line.

1999
Royal Caribbean's 137,300-ton *Voyager of the Seas* is launched for Caribbean cruising, the first ship to have an ice rink and a rock-climbing wall among the passenger facilities.

2000
Worldwide, the number of cruises booked tops 10 million for the first time. Nearly 7 million are from North America.

2002
SeaDream Yacht Club begins operating with two small, luxury ships calling mainly at small, off-the beaten-track ports when sailing the Caribbean.

2003
The Carnival Corporation merges with P&O Princess Cruises, forming the largest cruise company in the world, offering a variety of Caribbean cruises across its brands.

2004
A record 1 million Britons book cruises. Cunard Line launches the world's biggest passenger ship to date, the 150,000-ton *Queen Mary 2*.

2005
Hurricane Katrina devastates the city of New Orleans.

2007
Azamara Club Cruises is founded by Royal Caribbean as a two-ship line offering culturally immersive cruises, many of them in the Caribbean.

2008
Celebrity Cruises turns cruise ship interior design on its head with the launch of the contemporary, classy Celebrity Solstice, soon to be followed by four sisters.

2009
Royal Caribbean launches *Oasis of the Seas*, at 220,000 tons the biggest cruise ship ever, carrying 5,400 passengers. Its sister, *Allure of the Seas*, follows in 2010, 2 inches longer, beaten to the top spot in 2016 by *Harmony of the Seas*, and again in 2018 by the 228,081-ton Symphony of the Seas.

2010
High-profile crimes in the USVI and Antigua, in which two cruise passengers are murdered by local men, cause cruise lines to re-organize their routes. Both islands fight hard to regain their valuable cruise business.

2011
Jamaica opens an entire new port, Falmouth, built specifically to accommodate the new generation of mega-ships.

2012
The sinking off the coast of Italy of *Costa Concordia* prompts global reviews of cruise ship safety drills. Hurricane Sandy wreaks havoc as it tracks across the Caribbean to the East Coast

2014
Cuba surges in popularity, with cruise lines offering round-the-island voyages as well as overnight calls to Havana.

2015
Carnival opens Amber Cove, a new port and shopping complex on Dominican Republic, near Puerto Plata.

2016
Norwegian Cruise Line opens a 75-acre eco-hideaway, Harvest Caye, on two adjoining islands off the coast of southern Belize to serve as a private beach for its clients. Multi-billion dollar expansion project completed, allowing much bigger ships to transit the Panama Canal.

2017
Hurricanes Irma and Maria cause devastating damage to multiple Caribbean islands, affecting cruise schedules. Richard Branson's Virgin Group announces Virgin Voyages, with a 2,750-passenger ship, Scarlet Lady, to launch in 2020 in the Caribbean.

2018
Cruise ships return to areas affected by Hurricane Irma. Royal Caribbean opens futuristic new terminal at PortMiami as a home for its newest, biggest ship, Symphony of the Seas.

Jamaica's mega-ship port at Falmouth.

...ONE, LES ANTILLES
L'AMÉRIQUE DU NORI

PAR LE N.M.«MILWAUKEE» 10 JANVIER 1938 DE BOULOGNE
HAMBURG-AMERIKA LINIE

CRUISING THROUGH HISTORY

The pursuit began as a novelty and developed, after a number of setbacks, into one of the most popular ways of seeing exotic places.

Cruising really began in the early part of the 20th century as an adjunct to the steamship companies' main business, which was getting passengers, mail and other goods to their destinations on line voyages. As the Hollywood blockbuster *Titanic* demonstrated, these ships were unashamedly class-conscious, divided into as many as four classes depending on the ticket price paid.

It was not until the mid-1930s that people were able to travel on ships designed to reflect the revolutionary concept of the sea as a positive attraction. The enclosed liners were being opened up so that passengers could see the sea from inside as well as outside, and cruise itineraries were being geared to avoid rough seas and bad weather.

Before the 1930s, most early cruising was on ships built for line voyages, and the ocean was not seen as something to be enjoyed.

Tourists watch a boy playing a ukelele, 1931.

PROHIBITION

It was during the mid-1920s and early 1930s that cruising really took off, when itineraries from the United States were being devised for a very specific reason: Prohibition, in force from 1920 to 1933, created an exaggerated demand for alcohol. The shipping lines saw their opportunity. By cruising from New York into international waters, they could offer a legal way of circumventing the ban. 'Cruises to nowhere' were advertised and quickly became known as 'booze cruises.'

Prohibition played a major part in stimulating the initial post-World War I cruise boom, but it was the keen pricing, increasingly lavish on-board facilities and stylish way of life that soon enhanced cruising's popularity. Across a broad (and relatively prosperous) spectrum of US and British society, as the Roaring Twenties turned into the Depression-hit Thirties, cruising was established as a fashionable thing to do.

BIG SPENDERS

Value for money has always been a reason for cruising's continued popularity, but there has always been a place for conspicuous consumption, too. Thus, French Line (CGM) was only too happy to promote the 1938 New York to Rio cruise of its transatlantic liner, the *Normandie* (at 79,280 tons, the largest French passenger ship yet built), as the first 'million dollar cruise.'

The company arrived at that figure by calculating the revenue it received from the 975 passengers who paid between $395 and $8,600 for the 22-day round-trip.

The *Normandie*'s passengers timed their escapism well – the outbreak of World War II ensured that it would be another decade before cruising was back on the international agenda, with the arrival of the 'Green Goddess.' Cunard's *Caronia*, which got its name because it was painted in three shades of green to increase its heat resistance in the tropics, caught the imagination of high society

No expense was spared in order to keep the wealthy cruise ship passengers amused.

on both sides of the Atlantic and quickly became known as the 'millionaires' ship.'

Later, in 1955, the Greek Epirotiki Line scheduled its ship *Semiramis* for the first Greek islands cruises to start and finish in Greece – a formula that became hugely popular when sold as 'fly cruises' from North America and the UK in the late 1960s.

COPING WITH THE JET AGE

The 1960s were a time of tumultuous change for the shipping industry. The first commercial jet flight across the North Atlantic took off in 1958 and heralded the end of the transatlantic liner business. Only Cunard Line continues the tradition

> The *Normandie* was in New York when France fell in 1940, and was commandeered by the US navy. In February two years later it was gutted in a fire. The sunken wreck was righted and renamed, but was dismantled in 1947.

today with the 150,000-ton *Queen Mary 2*, which took over the transatlantic run from *QE2* in 2004.

Change was rapid. Speed mattered. Within a couple of years, airlines had the bulk of the transatlantic business and by the end of the 1960s, just one in every 25 transatlantic travellers was choosing to go by sea. With other liner business to the Mediterranean, India and Australia gradually going the same way, the shipping companies found themselves with fleets of ships but nowhere to operate them profitably. Inevitably, many of the vessels were switched to cruising, but they met with mixed success.

Cunard was one of the lines trying to move with the cruising times but, having tried and failed with the two *Queens* (*Mary* and *Elizabeth*), it had to lay them up, along with the *Caronia* and two other ships, in 1967–68. It had more success converting *Saxonia* and *Ivernia* into the cruise ships *Carmania* and *Franconia*, but the most successful and best-remembered British cruise ships of the period were *Andes* and *Reina del Mar*.

Towards the end of that decisive decade, the focus in cruising switched firmly to North America, where a number of developments coincided to spark a new boom. Here, a new style of cruising was emerging that would lead to an era of unprecedented growth – and the Caribbean was to be at the heart of it. Although there had been some cruises from New York, and later Miami, to the Bahamas, Cuba and other Caribbean islands since the 1920s, the Caribbean had not always been seen as an ideal area for sea cruises, considered too far away from big cruising base ports such as New York.

SCANDINAVIANS LEAD THE WAY

The innovators were the Norwegian shipping family, Kloster Redeerei, which branched out from tankers and cargo ships and ordered the construction of a vessel that would open up a route from the United Kingdom to Spain via

Gibraltar. By the time the *Sunward* was delivered, however, stringent UK currency restrictions had been imposed and Britain and Spain were at loggerheads over the status of Gibraltar.

Action had to be taken. Kloster's contacts included the Arison Group in Miami and, with its help, *Sunward* was positioned there to test the market for Caribbean cruises. It would be the first ship to operate regular weekly cruises from Miami to the Caribbean islands.

The hunch paid off and the operations of the company, now known as Norwegian Cruise Line

a couple of similar-sized ships to cruise in the Caribbean (*Cunard Countess* and *Cunard Princess*).

Initially, all the lines restricted their operations to one-week cruises. Then, as now, North Americans had a shorter holiday entitlement than Europeans, and few people could commit more than a week of that valuable time to this new, untried style of vacation.

TEETHING TROUBLES

After a disagreement with Kloster, the Arison Group's owner, Ted Arison, left and in 1972

Elegance was a must for an evening on board.

(NCL), expanded fast. Three more ships were built between 1968 and 1971 and became known as the 'White Fleet,' as their bright, white livery made *Skyward*, *Starward* and *Southward* stand out against the blue of the Caribbean sea and skies.

Almost immediately other Scandinavian companies saw the potential, and three of them grouped together to form Royal Caribbean Cruise Line (RCCL). It, too, swiftly built three ships, the *Song of Norway*, *Nordic Prince* and *Sun Viking*, all introduced in the early 1970s.

All six ships were about the same size, at 16,000–18,000 tons and capable of carrying between 700 and 800 passengers. They were all based in Miami, which suddenly became a leading cruise port to rival New York and Southampton. Cunard also built

set up Carnival Cruise Lines. This got off to an inauspicious start when its first ship, the *Mardi Gras*, went aground on its first 'shakedown' cruise carrying hundreds of travel agents.

After two loss-making years, Arison had to buy out the company from its original backers for a derisory US$1 plus the assumption of a $5 million debt, but it became profitable almost immediately. In its early days, though, its success was based on low-cost cruises operated on secondhand ships which their owners were selling off cheaply as the liner business disappeared. A dramatic policy change at the end of the 1970s was to change Caribbean cruising again and turn Carnival into the largest cruise company in the world.

In ordering new ships in the early 1970s, NCL and RCCL were followed by the new, worldwide cruise company Royal Viking Line (RVL). After that, however, there was a long gap to the end of the decade when no line dared to order any more. During much of that time, the oil crisis caused by OPEC disputes threatened the viability of much passenger shipping. But the demand for Caribbean cruising continued to grow and so RCCL compromised by 'stretching' two of its ships.

This was a not-uncommon procedure with cargo ships, but the 1978 stretching of *Song of Norway* was the first time a cruise ship had ever been cut in half and had a new center section added to increase its capacity by nearly 50 percent. *Nordic Prince* went through the same process in 1980 and all three RVL ships were stretched over the next three years.

But, by then, Carnival had surprised the industry by ordering *Tropicale* for delivery in 1981. This was not only the company's first new ship, but also the first for the industry in eight years. It marked a breakthrough, and the cruise industry, not to mention the Caribbean, has never looked back.

SIZE MATTERS

Almost immediately, RCCL ordered *Song of America* and Home Lines ordered the *Atlantic*. This new confidence was mirrored in Europe, where a couple of German ships were also under construction. Lines were not just ordering new ships, they were ordering them big.

The Carnival and RCCL ships were both about 37,000 tons – not an unusual size for a liner, but then considered huge for a purpose-built cruise ship. They were twice the size of the White Fleet and RCCL's first three ships, and carried double the number of passengers (1,400–1,500) that those first ships had been designed to carry.

The cost of these first mega-cruise ships – US$100 million for *Tropicale* and $140 million for *Song of America* – also showed that the lines were prepared to gamble that Caribbean cruising was here to stay.

NEW WAYS OF CRUISING

The *Norway*'s initial cruise pattern was typical of the classic one-week routes taken by Caribbean cruise ships over the next two decades. From Miami, it headed for the duty-free port of Charlotte Amalie on St Thomas in the US Virgin Islands. The next stop was Nassau in the Bahamas, and finally there was a call at a private island (Great Stirrup Cay) also in the Bahamas, where the ship anchored.

But Caribbean cruises were developing in different ways. There were short cruises, of three and four days, to the Bahamas. At first, these all started from Miami but gradually other Florida ports turned to cruising – Fort Lauderdale/Port Everglades, Port Canaveral, Jacksonville, Tampa and Palm Beach all became starting points.

Ships docked at Cozumel, Mexico.

⊙ THE LOVE BOAT

In the 1960s, Stanley MacDonald, a Canadian-born, Seattle-based entrepreneur, set up Princess Cruises to run winter cruises from the US West Coast to the Mexican Riviera and summer voyages from Vancouver to Alaska. In 1975, a year after it was bought by P&O, the company received a boost when the seagoing TV soap opera, *The Love Boat*, began. As the scripts had been started on board a Princess ship, the line was chosen for location filming. Not only did the popular nine-year series boost Princess Cruises, the popularity of cruising in the United States soared. Actor Gavin MacLeod, who played Captain Merrill Stubing, acts as a brand ambassador for Princess Cruises to this day.

The classic Eastern Caribbean itinerary operated by companies such as NCL could also include San Juan, Puerto Rico. Then the lines developed western Caribbean cruises, which included calls at the exotic Mexican ports of Cozumel and Playa del Carmen, as well as Grand Cayman and sometimes Jamaica.

The problem with operating just one-week cruises was that there was only so far into the Caribbean that ships could travel from Florida in that length of time. It was a logical move, therefore, to start home-porting ships in the Caribbean

arrived. Since then, all the major lines – Carnival, Princess, NCL and Royal Caribbean International (RCI, formerly RCCL) – have built even larger ships, which spend most of their time in the Caribbean region, the reality being that there are not many ports in the world that can accommodate them.

The ships are built in Europe and usually spend a maiden season cruising there before relocating to a new home in the Caribbean.

While views from outside the ships have been changing fast, the views inside have been undergoing even faster change, These are not

A performance of Broadway hit Chicago on Allure of the Seas, one of the first big-name shows to be staged on a ship.

itself: San Juan, Barbados, Sint Maarten and Guadeloupe have all become regular home ports.

LIFE ON BOARD

The 'mega-ships' of the early 1980s would be dwarfed by those now cruising the Caribbean. During the 1980s and 1990s, vessels grew larger and larger until the first 100,000-ton ship, Carnival Destiny,

Israeli businessman and Carnival Corporation founder Ted Arison died in 1999, and the company is now run by his son, Micky – ranked by Forbes magazine as the 94th richest person in the US.

just ships, they are entire resorts, the culmination of a process that began in the 1980s, when those first large vessels were created to resemble resort hotels, with the emphasis firmly on fun, food and endless entertainments.

NCL was the first to stage on-board versions of major Broadway musicals of the time. Now, it shows world-class Broadway shows including Million Dollar Quartet, After Midnight, and Legally Blonde, while Royal Caribbean is staging Hairspray and Grease on two of its newest ships.

Soon it became the norm for all cabins to have private bathrooms, televisions with interactive and then satellite programming. On new ships, all cabins have USB docks. Private balconies have been added to most cabins with outside views, and 'virtual balconies' now feature in inside cabins on new ships, with live-streaming on a big screen from outside webcams. Internet cafes have been replaced by super-fast WiFi, for which there is a charge. Apps and wearable technology have sped up the check-in process and on board, allowed cruise lines to track a passenger's spending habits and provide a more 'personalized' experience.

SOME SEAGOING STATISTICS

The number of vacationers taking a cruise was more than 27.2 million in 2018, up from 17 mil-

WiFi and personalized apps are standard on ships

lion in 2009. Around 12.3 million come from North America, 2 million from Germany, 1.9 million from the UK and 1.3 million from Australia.

The Caribbean remains the world's most popular cruise destination, with 35.4 percent of all ships deployed there, followed by the Mediterranean, at 15.8 percent.

YOUNGER CRUISERS

The age of cruise ship passengers has been getting progressively lower. In the 1970s, the average age was approaching 60; today, on short Bahamas cruises, the average passengers are 30-somethings while, for trips of one week or longer, the average age for Caribbean cruise passengers is the mid-40s. This is partly

> *The newest cruise ships are so vast that the ship has, in effect, become the destination. This said, whole new port facilities have been developed to accommodate Royal Caribbean's new mega-ships; Falmouth in Jamaica and Amber Cove in the Dominican Republic being prime examples.*

due to the increasing number of families taking cruises. Most of the mega-ships run fully supervised activity programmes for children, who have designated swimming pools, playrooms, gaming arcades, clubs and discos. Cruising is also becoming fashionable among millennials, with ships offering entertainment and décor aimed specifically at this cohort; MSC, Royal Caribbean, Carnival and NCL are particularly successful in attracting younger cruisers.

Carnival carries the greatest number of children (more than 500,000 annually), whileother lines big in the family market include Royal Caribbean, Celebrity Cruises, NCL, MSC, Princess Cruises, Disney Cruise Line and P&O Cruises.

CARIBBEAN PROS AND CONS

The bigger ships – and most of them are very big – have not always been popular within the Caribbean. There have been problems with hoteliers who are worried that cruise lines are stealing their business, and from island authorities, who have understandable anxieties about pollution and overcrowding. For their part, the cruise lines have for a long time resisted increases in charges levied by ports and complained about facilities at the terminals and services on some of the islands.

Increasingly, however, the Caribbean islands have come to recognize that the revenue and the jobs created on the islands by cruising are invaluable to their economies. The higher quality of technology on board the newest ships is also solving problems of pollution and waste disposal; and what is more, there is also clear evidence that passengers who like an island they visit briefly on a cruise often do return for longer holidays. The Caribbean therefore needs the cruise lines as much as the cruise lines need the Caribbean.

TALL SHIPS

The seafaring poet John Masefield once wrote, 'All I ask is a tall ship and a star to steer her by,' thus capturing the romance of tall ships.

If tall ships still tug at the heart, it is because they tap into the romance of the great age of sail, when tea clippers such as the *Cutty Sark* plied the seven seas. The quintessential tall ship is the clipper, which enjoyed mastery of the seas from 1850 to 1875. Compared with its rounded, low-masted predecessors, the sleek clipper had a long waterline and narrow design build, allowing it to sail faster and closer to the wind.

THE CLIPPER'S ENDURING APPEAL

In 1866 the *Thorbecke*, a fast Dutch merchant clipper, sailed from the Netherlands to the Dutch East Indies in a record 71 days. Braving the perils of shipwreck, pirates and enemy fleets, the clippers would transport cargoes of sugar, spices, rum and coffee from the Caribbean colonies to Europe. Although the clippers struggled to survive the age of steam and the opening of the fast Suez Canal route, tall-ship replicas still sail Caribbean waters today.

Set against the bleached Caribbean light, these square-rigged windjammers conjure up an era of buccaneers and buried treasure, exotic cargoes and distant ports of call. These latter-day tall ships, often lofty four-masted barquentines, make voyages similar to those by ships following the spice routes of several centuries ago, while other majestic replica clippers, such as *Stad Amsterdam*, can be chartered by wealthy modern adventurers.

LIFE OF THE LIMEY

The sense of seafaring continuity is most apparent in Antigua's picturesque English Harbour, where Nelson was based from 1784 to 1787 as captain of HMS *Boreas*, a three-masted, fully rigged frigate. In Nelson's day, life on board a tall ship was one of considerable hardship. While officers' quarters were acceptable, the crew slept in hammocks strung into netting around the deck; these formed a protective barrier during battle, and could be used as life rafts. On a typical tall ship's voyage, lunch was fish stew or salted pork or beef while supper consisted of weevil-infested biscuits and red worm-infested cheese. Depending on supplies, drink was beer, brandy or rum. To combat scurvy, the British sailors were given fresh fruit, lemon or lime juice, hence the nickname 'limeys' given to them by the Americans.

Sea Cloud Cruises operate replica clipper ships in the Caribbean.

In the British navy, the punishment for drunkenness was a flogging with the cat-o'-nine tails – a nine-tailed whipping device – a punishment abolished only in 1879. Since 12 lashes would normally remove the flesh from a man's back, the ship's surgeon was required to apply salt or vinegar as an antiseptic. For a serious offence, such as desertion or striking an officer, the seaman would be 'flogged around the fleet': after being tied in a crucifix position, the hapless culprit was flogged on every ship in the fleet.

TALL-SHIP CRUISES

A more romantic way of recalling the era of tall ships is to try a tall-ship cruise with Star Clippers or Sea Cloud Cruises, both of which operate elegant, replica clipper ships in the Caribbean, or to sail on a more contemporary vessel that has the look and feel of a sailing ship, including sails, but is powered by engines, such as the two Windstar Cruises ships based in the region. (see pages 92 and 97).

THE IMPACT OF CRUISING

Cruise ship passengers are essential to the economy of most Caribbean islands, but there are social and environmental problems that need to be addressed.

The Caribbean is the world's leading cruise destination. Many livelihoods depend on the ships' passengers and crews, in fact the industry is crucial to the region not just as an employer but also for the revenue it raises. However, there is sometimes a high price to pay.

For years the Caribbean Hotel Association (CHA) and some politicians believed that cruising was a rival rather than a key contributor to the tourism industry. This attitude began to soften after the terrorist attacks on the US in 2001, which resulted in a significant downturn in North American tourism to the region: as air-land tourism declined sharply in the years following the attacks but cruise tourism continued to grow, there was a re-evaluation of the industry's importance.

ECONOMIC IMPACT OF CRUISING

The cruise lines claim that their industry provides jobs, not just on the islands, but also on the ships.

Solar panels under the funnels on Celebrity Solstice.

Not enough, according to Caribbean trades union officials. But the number of jobs on the ships going to Caribbean or Central American nationals has increased over the years. These made up the majority of service staff when the industry first started to develop in the 1960s and 1970s, until issues surrounding crew retention saw a fall in the 1980s and 1990s. This is being addressed and there has been an increase in hiring from the region over the years, partly – but not entirely – because of the influx of new and much larger ships.

Tourism is one of the Caribbean's leading employers, supporting more than 13 percent of jobs. It also provided 15.2 percent of the region's Gross Domestic Product (GDP) in 2017, according to the World Travel and Tourism Council, and that figure is expected to rise to more than 17.8 percent by 2028. Cruise tourism supported 79,000 jobs in the Caribbean in 2017–18, according to the Florida-Caribbean Cruise Association, generating $903 million in wages to residents.

BIG SPENDERS

Despite the emergence of 'new' cruise destinations and trends, among them growth in Asia and a surge in expedition cruising, the Caribbean remains the world's most successful cruise destination, with more than double the deployment of its nearest rival, the Mediterranean. However, this success brings with it both benefits and consequences. It can be argued that business from cruise tourism is spread more widely around the region compared with air-based tourism, which can be skewed towards islands with large hotels, high-capacity airports and a developed infrastructure. Even large cruise ships can reach smaller, less-developed places.

Critics say that because the cruise ships provide everything for their customers there is no need for them to spend at the ports of call, but the Florida-Caribbean Cruise Association claims that the average passenger spends over US$103 at each port they visit.

ENVIRONMENTAL ISSUES

The impact of hundreds of thousands of tourists a year on a particular beauty spot is hard to measure, but it certainly creates challenges. Apart from the effect of cruise visitors on land, environmentalists have long drawn attention to the impact of the ships, especially the mega-ships now dominating Caribbean cruising.

Criticism has prompted the industry to clean up its act, something made easier by the introduction of new ships – an average of 10 per year since 1990. The bigger, modern ships have built-in waste management systems and recycling centers which conform to international law. All cruise lines, regardless of the age of their ships, have developed more stringent practices of recycling over the last few years. All the big cruise lines have announced commitments to reduce or eliminate single-use plastics on board. An example of paper-saving practice is the widespread introduction of electronic ticketing and wearable technology on board like bracelets and medallions. Cruise lines

have also invested in technology to make their ships more fuel-efficient, as well as all sorts of other innovations – from new ship designs like that of Celebrity Edge, which reduce drag through the water, to eco-friendly hull coatings, waste heat recovery and more efficient air conditioning. Many new ships are also fitted with solar panels.

Whatever the arguments on the benefits and costs, there is a growing recognition that land and sea must work together. A proper partnership will benefit everyone – the traveler included (see page page 321).

Whale-watching in the Dominican Republic.

⊘ CRUISING WITH A CONSCIENCE

Little by little, cruise lines are beginning to offer a more socially responsible product while getting the message across to the passenger. Saga Cruises offers guests the chance to get involved with the projects of the Saga Charitable Trust, which include everything from funding schools to community centers in developing countries. Crystal Cruises now only lists ethically-caught fish on its menus and offers one 'volunteering' excursion on each long cruise – which might be helping out in a local orphanage or working on a construction project. Other lines (Holland America Line, Princess Cruises) hold fundraising events on board, usually power walks, where guests raise money for the lines' chosen charities.

Cruise lines have also, in recent years, been among the first to bring aid to Caribbean islands when disaster strikes. Royal Caribbean delivered tons of supplies to Haiti – via Labadee, the private peninsula it leases on the island – after the 2010 earthquake, as well as contributing more than US$1 million in aid, while P&O Cruises was on the scene after Hurricane Tomas devastated St Lucia in October 2010, bringing supplies and holding fundraising events for its guests. Carnival Corporation, Royal Caribbean, NCL and its sister brand, Oceania Cruises, were all quick to make donations and help the relief effort after the devastating hurricanes Irma and Maria in 2017.

The mighty Queen Mary 2.

THE ART OF CRUISING

Old hands know how to get the best out of a cruise. Here are their top tips on how to stay ahead of the crowd.

Gazing out across the waves at sunset during the cocktail hour, the trials of everyday life drift away across the deep blue water. Life aboard a cruise ship is so much more civilized, congenial, elegant. So much more of what life should be. A cruise is a floating fantasy, and so great is the choice, it can be anything you want it to be. The ports of call and excursions may be memorable, but they are sideshows; the ship itself is just as important. Even travellers who visit every port, take every available excursion and shop until it's time to sail still spend about 60–70 percent of their voyage on board. So just as important as the route is the choice of cruise line, and which particular vessel offers the style most suitable for your taste.

SPOILT FOR CHOICE

At the upper end of the scale, dining standards compare well with the finest restaurants on land, with impeccable service and menus designed by celebrity chefs including Nobu Matsuhisa, Marco Pierre White and Jacques Pépin. After-dinner entertainment ranges from lavish productions straight from Broadway to intimate cabaret acts and even (on some Royal Caribbean International ships) spectacular ice shows. And in between, the accent is on fun – be it a quiz in the ship's pub or a sophisticated party in its champagne bar.

The biggest cruise ships are generally the best bet for family groups spanning several generations, as they offer lectures, craft classes, bridge and bingo for older folk; well-run children's programs to keep youngsters safely occupied; and spas, gyms, ball courts, sports bars – and sunbeds – for mom and dad to enjoy. People with money to splash often choose smaller, 'boutique' cruise ships, where

Capturing those dream holiday moments.

shore excursions are exclusive and in-depth, and the included restaurants are generally of higher quality. Those in search of a more unusual itinerary might try joining the Caribbean leg of an around-the-world cruise, while adventurers could pick up a voyage on an expedition ship as it repositions from Antarctica to the Arctic via the Caribbean, usually via the more out-of-the-way ports.For a first-time cruiser, the choice of ship is bewildering: the floating skyscrapers can be cavernous rather than cozy, while small ships could confine them to an uncomfortably small pool of passengers. The best option may be a mid-sized (600 to 1,600 passengers) ship with a touch of elegance and a wide range of activities, as such vessels have enough nooks and crannies for luxurious privacy but – with spas, pools, casinos, cookery schools and guest speakers – plenty to engage the mind.

Despite brochure promises, cruise lines do not guarantee visits to specific destinations. Ships are huge objects subject to wind, weather, mechanical surprises and passenger emergencies. There is a possibility that destinations will be deleted from the schedule with no obligation for compensation; as with all shipboard life, the captain's decision is final. If the Maya ruins of Mexico's Chichén Itzá are central to

carefully: Is a port small enough to allow you to enjoy wandering around on your own? And might a museum or an uncrowded beach be more easily (and cheaply) reached by hopping into a taxi rather than queuing for a tour bus?

Caribbean excursions can sound wonderful when you're reading about them in a cold climate. But book too many and you may find a crowded schedule wearing on both your body and your budget. On some full-day tours to major sites, assembly times can be as early as 6am (though 8–9am is more usual). And a

The tall ship Wind Surf docked in Virgin Gorda.

your dream, perhaps you should consider a fly/drive package instead.

The simple answer to the question 'How long should you go for?' is 'How long can you afford?' Cruise ships offer such a variety of activities that the first week can be spent running from spa to Pilates to wine-tasting class (living the same high-octane life you've spent money to escape). Many find that a 10-day cruise is ideal, mixing activities ashore with lazier days on-board, achieving the goal of the vacation –to relax and regenerate.

EXCURSIONS

The best excursions get snapped up quickly and savvy travellers research and book the shore tours online long before they embark. Think

long, hot ride in a coach can take the gloss off a visit to the most spectacular temple. Pack appropriately – such as combat-strength insect repellent, a hat, sunscreen and your driver's license if you're planning to take a jungle jeep safari.

There is a growing trend to book independent shore excursions and many local tour operators

Stay on board when the ship's in port and you'll experience a completely different atmosphere. The crew relax, and there are no lines at the buffet or competition for a poolside lounger.

willing to provide them at prices undercutting the cruise lines. They will pick you up and drop you off at the ship. The cruise lines will tell you that if you book an independent tour and are late back, the ship won't wait, which is true, but a reliable operator will always get you back with time to spare.

Do note, though, that the magic of a cruise is the cruise itself: a sense of losing touch with the outside world. Some shore excursions can wipe that equanimity right off the compass, and perpetual tour-takers miss out on one of

nights being a case in point, or Seabourn's 'formal optional'.

A word of warning, though: while cruise ship holidays are generally becoming more casual, certain standards still do (and should) apply. Keep swimwear and bare feet for the pool and cover up if coming indoors. Also, be advised that many big ships still hold captain's welcome and farewell gala dinners, so it's worth packing at least one or two smart outfits, particularly if you would like a formal portrait as a memento of your cruise.

A peaceful swim on Celebrity Equinox.

A formal evening aboard P&O Cruises' Britannia.

the most delightful benefits – a port day spent aboard ship when all is serene, and you can get cut-price spa treatments). For part of the day at least, you really feel as though it's 'your' private ship.

DRESS TO IMPRESS

Haute couture and the high seas were made for each other, and those who love to dress up will find cruise ships – particularly luxury vessels, or the more traditional lines like Cunard – provide the perfect glamorous setting. On the other hand, the lines defining dress code are blurring, which more emphasis now on looking stylish than conforming to a set of rules, Marella Cruises' 'dress to impress'

EMBARKATION

All the mainstream cruise lines now offer electronic ticketing and registration, which means that much of the information you'd previously have filled in on paper, at the port, is collected online, speeding up the check-in process. Royal Caribbean, for example, can at its new Miami terminal get you from curbside to cabin in less than 20 minutes, so efficient is the check-in procedure these days. With lines that are not so technologically advanced, there are still ways to speed up the whole process. Suite passengers, for example, can use priority check-in desks, as can top-tier members of the cruise lines' loyalty schemes. So it's worth checking out what loyalty program the line has to offer.

At the check-in desk, have all your embarkation forms filled in (if you haven't done it online) and your credit card to hand, as these are usually registered on arrival so that each passenger's on-board account can be activated. After this, all goods, drinks and services you have on-board can be signed onto your cruise card. Toward the end of the cruise you will get an interim bill for checking, and, provided all is in order, the final amount will be put on your credit card at the end of the trip. On some ships you can keep a running check on your account via

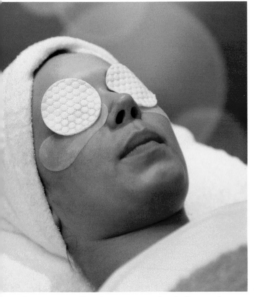

Spa facilities offered to guests tend to be impressive.

the in-cabin TV – useful if you want to keep tabs on expenses.

On arrival in your cabin, you'll usually find a small map of the ship. While you're waiting for your luggage to be delivered, grab it and go exploring. Not only will this help you orient yourself, it's also good to visit areas like the ship's library early, as veteran cruisers will head there first to bag the best choice of books. Keep an eye out for drinks promotions; cruise lines often offer wine packages, or soft drink packages on embarkation day which can be good value.

If your ship operates a two-seating dining system, this is also a good time to check out which table you've been allocated and that it suits you (there should be a card giving details of seating

and table number in your cabin). If there's a problem, alert the maître d'; even if it can't be sorted out there and then, they may be able to move you later in the cruise.

Remember, too, that the extra-charge 'alternative' restaurants usually work on a bookings-only system, so make your reservations online or on embarkation to avoid disappointment. Visit the spa to pick up a price list, but don't book too soon – unless you want a treatment at peak time, such as any days at sea – as discounts and multi-treatment offers are often flagged in the daily activities sheet and you can usually negotiate a special offer on port days.

LIFE AT SEA

The purser's office (also called reception) is the place to head for if you have a problem or need some information. It will also have spare copies of the daily activities sheet and port information (though these should be delivered to your cabin). Most ships also offer a daily British or American news digest and, again, you'll find spare copies at reception.

The shore excursions desk usually lies near the ship's main reception desk and, though it is only open at certain times, it should have port and shore excursion information to pick up.

Cruising has long been associated with romance. For crew members, fraternization with guests can lead to dismissal, so they generally socialize among themselves. But passengers travelling alone will find there is usually a 'singles party' held at the start of each cruise to introduce solo travelers to one another. Cruise lines also offer LGBTQ get-togethers, noted in the daily program as 'Friends of Dorothy', and on-board meetings of AA, known as 'Friends of Bill W.'

SHOPPING

Shopping is big business in the Caribbean (see page 79). Many lines have 'shopping advisors' who will brief passengers on what to buy and where to find the 'bargains' ashore – although it's important to remember that the main beneficiary of your shopping in recommended stores is the cruise line itself, thanks to a commission arrangement, so take advice from these people with a pinch of salt. On-board shops too are increasingly sophisticated, so it's worth

Reservations in the posh 'alternative' restaurant on board? You'll want to make the most of the fine dining, so be careful not to coincide a romantic dinner à deux with a day you've booked a long, exhausting shore excursion.

checking their prices for jewelry, clothing, cosmetics, crystal and other luxury goods before you head ashore.

forming, and also ensures that those with earlier flights make the airport in time. You'll then reclaim your bags in the cruise terminal, once they've been cleared by customs.

One hint for making disembarkation less soulless: some lines offer excursions on the final day of the cruise, ending at the airport. This can be a great way of combining a spot of sightseeing with the airport transfer and, in a way, feels as if you've extended your vacation a little.

Disembarkation day is also the time to settle your on-board account. You'll receive a

Colorful souvenirs on-shore in Dominica.

Be aware that if you buy alcohol or tobacco ashore, it could be confiscated and held in store for you until you get off the ship (to prevent you consuming it instead of drinking in the ship's bars).

DISEMBARKATION

To make departure as painless as possible, cruise lines ask you to pack on the last evening and place your luggage outside the cabin door. On a big ship, you'll be issued with color-coded luggage tags, which correspond with instructions in the daily program telling you what time you need to disembark. Although impersonal, this is the most efficient way of getting a couple of thousand people off a ship without huge lines

copy of your statement on the last night of the cruise, but it's a good idea to ask for a provisional copy the day before, so you can query any unexpected charges in advance of the long lines that always form on disembarkation morning. Remember, too, to reclaim your passport from the purser's office if it's been kept there for the cruise.

Finally, don't forget that, even on the last night, you're still on vacation! When you pack, keep a change of clothing and essential toiletries for the next day. Then, instead of feeling as though it's all over, head out on deck to watch the sunset, enjoy a delicious farewell dinner and revel in memories of a smooth and successful sailing.

THE CHANGING FACE OF CRUISING

If you want to learn ballroom dancing, sample gourmet food, try bridge, gaze at the stars or bask in a private retreat, there's sure to be a cruise to suit you.

What is a typical Caribbean cruise passenger? At one time, that would have been an easy question to answer – an older person, relatively wealthy, North American. But today it would be difficult to categorize typical cruise passengers, because they are as diverse as the world we live in.

They can be any age, from elderly, retired people to the toddlers who are brought along on family holidays. They may belong to any nationality or ethnic group or any kind of multi-cultural mix. They may be single, married or divorced; high-income executives or call-center employees; forecourt mechanics or professors of philosophy. They may belong to any faith on Earth – or follow no faith at all. Some wear orthopedic shoes, others sport tiny bikinis. They drink dry Martinis and bottled lager. They eat rare roast beef and grilled tofu burgers. They may have a disability that does not prevent them getting the most out of life. Some are straight, some are gay, some think this matters, others don't.

On the lookout for wildlife at the Tortuguero NP, Costa Rica.

An estimated 1 million children cruise every year, and cruise lines are going all-out to win their affection. You'll meet any number of well-known characters on Disney's ships, while Royal Caribbean even had Princess Fiona from Shrek name one of its ships.

PASSENGER STATISTICS

According to demographic studies conducted by Cruise Lines International Association (CLIA), there are a few statistics to consider. The average North American cruise passenger's age is 47, but one quarter of passengers are under 40. The average British passenger is aged 56. About 84 percent of North American cruisers are married, and more than a third have children under 18. On longer cruises – of three weeks or more – passengers are more likely to be older and wealthier, reflecting the amount of free time they have available, and fewer family demands on their income. On shorter cruises, of one week or less, passengers tend to be younger, with more diversity of income.

TRICKS OF THE TRADE

While they probably don't want clients to know this, many cruise lines divide their passengers – or prospective passengers – into market segments and then create advertising campaigns geared just toward them. Millennials, or Generation Y, is one of the most coveted cohorts, with a view to young people born between, roughly, 1981 and 1996 being the big-spending cruisers of tomorrow. Other loose market segments are 'family folks' – people described as family-oriented, traditional and cautious; 'baby boomers' – late-middle-aged professionals and youthful retirees who want to inject a sense of adventure into their everyday lives; 'luxury seekers' – people who take great pleasure in being pampered; 'want-it-alls' – people who are not necessarily wealthy, but have high aspirations and tend to spend beyond their means; 'consummate shoppers' – travelers who look for the best value, rather than the lowest price, when choosing a holiday; 'explorers' – well-educated, well-traveled people who are interested in the history and culture of the places they visit; and, last of all, 'ship buffs' – elderly, repeat passengers who just love being on cruise ships.

The J.N. 'Ding' Darling National Wildlife Refuge on Sanibel island, Gulf of Mexico.

⊘ GETTING CLOSE TO NATURE

Almost all of the Caribbean and Panama Canal cruises will feature some type of on-board lecture on local and natural history and the environment. However, if flora and fauna and the environment are of particular interest to you, pick a smaller ship on which you can get closer to the marine life, like Silversea Cruises' expedition vessels, or British line Noble Caledonia, which specializes in off-the-beaten-track itineraries. For specialty cruises, the Smithsonian Institution (tel: 855-330 1542; www.smithsonianjourneys.org) offers some wonderful nature-themed voyages on small expedition ships. And although it may seem an incongruous partnership, Carefree Birding (tel: 866-575 7764; www.carefreebirding.com) arranges birding cruises on Carnival and Celebrity Cruises ships, with group birdwatching, special excursions, quizzes, lectures and photography contests all part of the package. In addition to this, many of the large cruise lines offer scuba diving excursions in the Caribbean in conjunction with local operators.

Generally speaking, shore excursions are becoming more eco-friendly too. Avoid dolphin 'encounters' and shows, and if you take a whale- or dolphin-watching boat tour, always ask if the operator meets the criteria of the Whale and Dolphin Conservation Society (WDCS).

THEME CRUISES

As in other areas of society, consumers have become more demanding, and are seeking cruises that reflect their personal values and interests. In order to satisfy this, cruise lines have turned to specially designed theme cruises that cater to a huge range of interests, lifestyles, hobbies and niche markets. You name it and there's probably a cruise for it, from vampires and Goths' conventions to espionage buffs' cruises and hardcore boot-camp fitness.

In some cases, all the passengers on a ship participate in the particular theme; in others, only a proportion of them get involved. If two people travel together and one wants to take part in the theme activities while the other doesn't, that is quite feasible. Occasionally, theme cruises are connected in some way to the region they are sailing through, but most of the time they aren't. Best of all, theme cruises feature all the standard amenities of regular cruises and usually don't cost any more money.

Of the hundreds of theme cruises offered each year, only some are organized by the cruise lines themselves, while many are arranged by cruise organizers – individuals, small companies, special-interest groups and non-profit organizations that work hand-in-hand with the cruise companies to make it all happen. On some occasions, ships are chartered – or 'hired out' – by the cruise lines to the specific groups.

The most popular theme cruises today focus on food and wine, ranging from those that offer cookery demonstrations by acclaimed master chefs, such as Marco Pierre White and Jacques Pépin, to those with an emphasis on a regional cuisine, such as Taste of the Islands cruises that highlight French West Indian or Latin Caribbean food. Some of the better food-themed cruises include Crystal's Wine and Food voyages, in the company of big-name guest chefs.

Music is another major focus for theme cruises, with choices that include jazz, classical, opera, soul, salsa, gospel, country and western, Dixieland, 1950s retro rock'n'roll, and big-band orchestras. There's a growing trend for big-name entertainers to perform on cruise ships (as part of private charters): both Rihanna and Taylor Swift have done gigs on Royal Caribbean's ships, while Pitbull named and performed on NCL's *Norwegian Escape*.

Other theme cruises focus more on top-notch guest speakers. For instance, California-based InSight Cruises (tel: 650-787 5665; www.insight-cruises.com) offers genuinely in-depth cruises to the Caribbean and other destinations, featuring serious themes including astronomy and Mexican antiquities, presented by experts in a series of on-board lectures and shore tours. Cunard Line's ships have an ongoing cultural theme thanks to a stellar guest speaker program and hook-ups with the prestigious Juilliard School and the UK's Royal Academy of Dramatic Art; while Seabourn, Silver-

Use time on board to develop knowledge of marine life.

sea and Fred. Olsen Cruises also carry famous speakers from TV, radio, the arts and politics.

TAKING A HARD LINE

Cruise ships are becoming less and less tolerant of smoking. Most now allow no smoking at all inside the ship and more are banning smoking on balconies, as this is not only a fire hazard, but also an annoyance to non-smoking neighbors. Most cruise lines have cigar lounges, or smoking rooms, and several have created smoking areas on deck that offer shelter and seating (Royal Caribbean's Quantum class ships, for example). At the very least, smokers are allowed to smoke in one area of the outside deck, but if it's raining this can be pretty unpleasant.

CRUISE AND STAY

'Cruise and stay,' a term coined by the cruise lines for the practice of adding a land-based stay to a cruise, can offer the best of both worlds.

On the beach at Princess Cays in the Bahamas, with good connections to Miami and Fort Lauderdale.

From a traveler's point of view, the 'cruise and stay' might add up to the perfect holiday. It could mean combining active cruise itinerary with a spell on a beach; for example, a 12-night Panama Canal cruise might include Costa Rica, Nicaragua, the Panama Canal, Curaçao and the US Virgin Islands, plus a day in the Bahamas, which could be the only lazy beach day of the entire cruise.

In contrast, a 9-night western Caribbean cruise from Florida might include Grand Cayman, Jamaica and Cozumel; so a week's touring in Florida would make a good combination.

Alternatively, you could contrast types of accommodation. A spell on an enormous, glitzy ship might be followed by a hop from Miami to the Bahamas to chill out on a remote beach in the Out Islands.

Most cruise lines don't allow passengers to jump ship halfway through a cruise, so an extended holiday is easiest to plan around one of the Caribbean gateways, particularly for passengers from Europe;

Marella Cruises, for example, packages hotel stays in Barbados and Jamaica with its cruises, linked to its charter flights from the UK Often, cruise-and-stay packages are the initiative of travel agents or tour operators. One exception is Disney, which offers combinations of the theme parks in Orlando and its four ships. These operate cruises from three to eight nights from Port Canaveral in the same polished, Disney style as the parks.

BOOKING ACCOMMODATION

The main reason for booking land-based accommodation through a cruise line is financial, as many of them have set up good deals with hotels, and will also include transfers to the port. Passengers arriving from Europe will usually incur an overnight stay, which should be included in the cruise package and can be extended at low cost. There is a growing trend, too, for European tour operators to package cruises with flights and hotel stays, among them the UK's Virgin Holidays Cruises, which offers combinations on NCL, Royal Caribbean, Star Clippers, Carnival and Princess.

For the more adventurous traveler, there are endless opportunities for island hopping from Miami. A network of regional flights links most of the Caribbean islands, and many airlines – including American Airlines, Caribbean Airlines and LIAT – offer low-cost fares, although a private charter may be cost-effective if you are travelling as a group. Secure the services of a travel agent to help plan a trip like this.

OFFSHORE-BASED CRUISES

Miami and Fort Lauderdale work well as jumping-off points for the Bahamas, with plenty of flights to Nassau and onward connections to the Out Islands. Cruises that start and finish offshore are harder to find; it tends to be the smaller, more upscale lines that base themselves in Barbados (SeaDream Yacht Club, and some Silversea cruises, for example). NCL, Viking Ocean, and Royal Caribbean have programs out of San Juan, while Star Clippers and Windstar Cruises both operate out of Sint Maarten.

Barbados is an excellent base for touring the Windward Islands, just a short flight from St Lucia, St Vincent, the Grenadines and Grenada. San Juan, meanwhile, is close to the Virgin Islands.

A couple of lines still allow smoking in certain areas inside that are not smoking lounges. On Cunard's *Queen Mary 2*, smokers can light up in the G32 nightclub, while NCL's ships allow smoking in the casinos.

A new bone of contention is e-cigarettes. Although these cause no passive smoking harm, some cruise lines ban them nonetheless as they could be 'upsetting' to non-smokers. If smoking is important to you, check the individual policy of your chosen cruise line as the rules change all the time.

All the lines sailing in the Caribbean create festive holiday cruises for Christmas and New Year, complete with roving Santas, presents for children, and champagne and fireworks at midnight.

CRUISE TO HEALTH

The emphasis on health at sea nowadays goes a long way beyond non-smoking. There are specialty cruises devoted to yoga, bodybuilding, martial arts, meditation, stress reduction, aerobics, massage, tai chi and weight loss. Offerings might vary from gentle yoga and open-air sunset meditation on Star Clippers' yoga-themed cruises to running-themed voyages offered by companies like Marathon Expeditions (tel: 888 484 4441; www.runningcruise.com) with organized fun runs (some more testing than others) in every port.

Even if you don't go on a health-themed cruise, it's easy enough to keep the fitness levels up on board. All big ships have state-of-the-art gyms and some excellent classes (many of which carry a fee) that can rival your regular workout at home. If motivation is likely to be a problem, sign up on your first day for a course of five classes of, for example, spinning or boot camp. Or try something different, like the stretching and toning Kinesis Walls on Seabourn's ships. At the very least, if the gym really isn't your idea of a vacation, take the fresh air on deck and try to walk a couple of miles every day. Most ships have a promenade deck or a jogging trail.

Dieting on a cruise ship is actually easy if you're in the right state of mind, as you don't have to shop or cook, and there's so much choice. Most lines can cater to special diets, like gluten-free or vegan, if you warn them in advance, while all have healthier menu options such as low-carb, low-sodium and low-fat; these are more the norm than the exception nowadays. Portions are actually getting smaller, although no cruise line can control how many trips you make to the buffet!

The palm-fringed golf course by the sea at Gasparilla Inn and Club, Florida.

GOLF CRUISES

Sport is another magnet for themed cruises, with golf being one of the favorites. Golf cruises are offered by specialist tour operators such as Golf Ahoy (tel: 239-344-9187; www.golfahoy.com), which will hook up enthusiasts on board and arrange everything in port for a seamless golf vacation, or PerryGolf (tel: 800-344-5257; www.perrygolf.com). The Caribbean is particularly popular for golf cruises, thanks to its abundance of world-class courses such as Sandy Lane in Barbados and the Dominican Republic's legendary Teeth of the Dog at Casa de Campo.

NATURAL AFFINITY

Essentially, a cruise ship is the ideal meeting place for large affinity groups, whether they share a faith, a lifestyle or simply a common interest. A growing segment of the affinity market comprises cruises catering to African-American travelers. One company in particular, Blue World Travel (tel: 800-466 2719; www.festivalatsea.com), has earned a stellar reputation for its Festival at Sea Cruises. These cruises (usually on Carnival ships) run several times a year and feature lectures on African-American culture, Motown music nights and African-attire dinner parties. They also raise money for the United Negro College Fund, and donate thousands of children's books annually to Caribbean island libraries.

On a completely different tack, for free-spirited adults who want to feel the salty sea breezes on their skin and socialize with like-minded passengers, naturist cruises are offered by several groups, on a variety of privately chartered ships. One of the more established is Bare Necessities Tours (tel: 800-743 0405; www.cruisebare.com).

ROMANCE AT SEA

What could be more romantic than strolling on deck, hand-in-hand in the moonlight on your honeymoon? Well aware of the romantic potential of cruising, cruise lines compete with one another to offer wedding, honeymoon and renewal-of-vows packages, always at a price. The bigger lines have in-house wedding coordinators who will arrange everything from the flowers to the cake.

In terms of holding the actual wedding ceremony at sea, a lot of myth surrounds this. Essentially, this depends on where the ship is registered. Princess Cruises can hold weddings officiated by the captain, as can Celebrity Cruises, Carnival Cruise Line, P&O Cruises and Azamara Club Cruises. On other lines, you can bring your own celebrant on board, but you must hold the ceremony while the ship is in port. Some, but not all cruise lines offer same-sex ceremonies, Celebrity Cruises being one of the most LGBTQ-friendly.

Disney Cruise Line will allow couples to hold wedding ceremonies on the beach at Castaway Cay, its private island (although the official exchange of vows and paperwork must be done ashore, before the ship sails), while Holland America Line can arrange weddings at Half Moon Cay, its own private beach.

When it comes to honeymoons, cruise lines are quick to cash in on newlyweds' bliss, with all kinds of packages including champagne, flowers, breakfast in bed and couples' spa treatments. Consider all this carefully before paying, as it's sometimes cheaper to buy the individual elements separately.

A new trend is for cruise lines to offer gift registry services. Carnival, Princess Cruises and NCL all offer this, among others, which

Diving in the Caribbean can be very rewarding.

⊘ SOLO CRUISING

Although cruisers are predominantly couples, a ship represents a safe, friendly environment for single travelers. Most of the big lines offer singles' mingles most days, while the more traditional lines, including Cunard, Fred. Olsen Cruises, Crystal Cruises and Regent Seven Seas Cruises, have gentleman dance hosts to twirl single ladies round the floor. Solo passengers can ask to be seated at a big table at dinner – and indeed, the singles' tables are often the most riotous. More and more cruise lines are building ships with extra single cabins; check out NCL's Studio cabins on its newest ships, or the chic new single accommodation on Cunard's ships.

means your wedding guests can buy you gifts on board – chocolate-dipped strawberries and commemorative champagne flutes being, after all, more romantic than a new toaster.

CRUISING WITH PRIDE

There's a thriving market for LGBTQ cruise charters, which have become big business in recent years. So popular are these cruises that big organizers like Atlantis Events (tel: 310-859 8800; www.atlantisevents.com) and RSVP Vacations (tel: 310-432-2300; www.rsvpvacations.com) can fill

ACCESSIBILITY FOR ALL

Travelers with disabilities are welcomed on cruise ships and facilities for the less mobile are improving, although, inevitably, some things are overlooked. All new ships have cabins adapted to wheelchair users, albeit in varying degrees so check very carefully before booking. If you're uncomfortable walking long distances, consult the deck plans online if, for example, it's important to you that your cabin be located near the elevators, and avoid the very biggest ships – getting around these with a stick or walking frame

Relaxing in Suite Class on a Silversea ship.

the world's biggest ships for exclusive LGBTQ charters, featuring big-name entertainers and guest speakers, as well as a huge range of parties and excursions. Those exclusive charters aside, cruising is generally very welcoming to LGBTQ travelers who don't necessarily want the big party scene – the ships of Cunard, Seabourn, SeaDream Yacht Club and Star Clippers are especially popular, while among the big-ship cruise lines, Celebrity Cruises actively promotes itself as LGBTQ-friendly. Most of these have Friends of Dorothy gatherings on board, which are advertised in the daily program, but inclusivity nowadays is really more about the vibe on board, crew training and the use of inclusive language.

can be exhausting. Another tip when planning a cruise is to choose a voyage with as few tender ports (those where the ship anchors outside the port and guests are ferried ashore) as possible. It's much easier for the less able to get ashore down a gangway than by climbing onto a lifeboat that's bobbing up and down as the afternoon Caribbean winds get up.

Some of the best options include, for US cruisers, escorted Caribbean cruise packages for wheelchair users organized by Accessible Journeys (tel: 610-521 0339; www.disabilitytravel.com). Otherwise, most cruise lines have detailed sections on their websites advising on accessible cruising, or a good travel agent would be able to help.

CRUISE CUISINE

Every brochure will portray meal times as a gourmet extravaganza, but cruise cuisine can be very good, very bad or somewhere in between

It is possible to eat around the clock – and many do – hence the joke that you board as a passenger and leave as freight. Some passengers munch their way through a huge cooked breakfast, then it's mid-morning burgers on deck and a plate piled high from the lunch buffet. Next, a few cocktails by the pool, ice cream, afternoon tea with cakes, room service sandwiches, canapés at Happy Hour, full seven-course dinner and, the final nail in the coffin, the midnight buffet. Nowadays, though, this institution is more a case of snacks in the buffet restaurant as part of the big lines' 24-hour dining offers. With healthier cruising the trend now, the days of binge-eating at midnight are over. In fact, you could enjoy a bowl of fruit on deck at sunrise, a fresh salad for lunch and a perfectly grilled sea bass or lobster in the evening, interspersed with visits to the gym. Most ships include low-sodium and low-fat options on the menu, and a juice bar is as commonplace as a cake shop on today's cruising scene.

CHANGING STYLES

Cruising used to be one of very few types of holiday where guests would be assigned a specific table and dine at a fixed time every night. Happily for the gregariously challenged, the modern trend is towards open seating and multiple-choice dining. Modern 'floating resorts' have up to 10 à la carte restaurants apiece, ranging from French and Italian to Japanese and even Indian (service charges for these alternative restaurants vary from US$10 to US$35 a head, while some ships apply prices to individual dishes).

However, all ships still include a free-to-use main dining room for those who enjoy a traditional five-course dinner and like to make friends with their fellow passengers across the dining table. Several lines – such as Princess, P&O Cruises and Royal Caribbean – have made sections of their dining rooms open seating, whereby you turn up when you like for meals, while retaining a more formal two-sitting system for those who prefer this tradition. Pick the early sitting and you'll be able to enjoy a whole evening of entertainment and have room, if you are so inclined, for a late snack. American passengers tend to prefer this. Choose the late sitting and you can sunbathe until sunset, spend time

An eye for presentation.

Like restaurant food, cruise cuisine can vary greatly. In general, the maxim that you get what you pay for applies. A budget ship will serve bland food in generous portions, with endless buffets. On a big, modern cruise ship expect a choice of restaurants (some applying a service charge for the premier ones), together with a traditional two-sitting or eat-when-you-please main dining room with silver service and some themed evenings, for example, an Italian or French night. On ultra-luxurious ships, such as those of the all-inclusive Silversea Cruises, Crystal Cruises, SeaDream Yacht Club and Seabourn, champagne is available at any time and caviar on request.

dressing for dinner and still have time for a cocktail and the late show – which tends to be popular with Europeans and South Americans.

Other lines – NCL, Oceania Cruises, Viking Cruises and Azamara Club Cruises, for example, simply offer open seating dining.

Tables for two can be hard to come by on a cruise ship, so ask early if you wish to dine à deux in the main dining room. You may want to choose a big table if you're travelling alone. If you are unhappy with your table (or your dining partners), ask the maître d' to move you; a discreet tip will do the trick, provided the ship is not full.

WHAT TO WEAR

Although it is possible to cruise for a week without dressing up and cruising is becoming increasingly casual, most cruises will feature a mix of casual nights (smart casual 'resort wear'), informal nights (confusingly, this means cocktail dress and jacket and tie) and one formal night – full black tie. If you are invited to dine at the captain's table on the formal night, it should be regarded as an honor. There is no real knack to securing your place – invited guests include past passengers, VIPs, dignitaries and people celebrating a special occasion.

Dress code is interpreted very differently from ship to ship and has increasingly vague terms. Marella Cruises' 'dress to impress' can mean whatever you want, while Seabourn's 'formal optional' means that traditionalists sport black tie while others simply dress stylishly. Carnival and NCL passengers tend towards the casual, while guests on lines like SeaDream Yacht Club, Windstar and Star Clippers prefer a more chic look.

WHAT TO EXPECT

Given that the vast majority of Caribbean cruise passengers are American, the food on most ships will be geared to their tastes – generous portions, salads with rich dressings, a fair amount of meat and not much that reflects the region in which the ship is sailing. This means that you'll have no problem finding burgers or pizza, but a spicy Jamaican patty, a bowl of freshly made conch chowder or a snack of flying fish with chips will have to wait until you get ashore. Having said this, some of the specialty restaurants nowadays really are excellent; Umi Uma, Prego and the new Silk Kitchen on Crystal's ships are superb; while the Indian food in Atul Kochhar's Sindhu on P&O Cruises' ships

replicates some of the finest ethnic cuisine available in London, at a fraction of the price. On Oceania Cruises, you can feast on French classics, modern Asian and gourmet Italian at no extra cost.

Specialty restaurants aside, though, economies of scale dictate that most provisions are bought in bulk. Carnival Corporation, for example, keeps an entire county in Iowa in business, raising beef cattle for its ships. While you will find fresh local fruit and vegetables on the buffet, there is rarely more than a token dish or two to indicate that you are in the Caribbean. Even the mix for the rum punch may be from a can.

The Universe Dining Room, one of the four restaurants aboard the Carnival Destiny.

SPECIAL DIETS

Cruise lines are used to accommodating special diets, within reason. All cruise lines offer vegetarian dishes now and if you warn them in advance, can cater for gluten-free, dairy-free, nut-free and various other special diets. SeaDream even caters for raw food dieters, with a complete raw menu. Several lines keep a separate vegetarian menu from which you can order a day in advance, but do ask to see it as it's not always advertised. If you keep kosher, advise the cruise line before you sail. Kosher meals are usually bought frozen by the cruise line in advance of sailing.

Royal Caribbean has a Johnny Rockets burger restaurant on several of its ships.

THE SECRET LIFE OF A CRUISE SHIP

A good cruise should appear effortless, but an enormous amount of skill goes into making it seem so. Here's what goes on behind the scenes.

In a headlong rush to cruise around the globe, many passengers overlook the extraordinary floating world they are privileged to participate in. The occasional 'fly on the wall' documentary claims to present life behind the scenes of a cruise ship, but tends to sacrifice truth to sensationalism: rampant affairs, aggressive outbursts and sinking ships make better television than social harmony at sea.

The reality is that the crew, as diverse as a United Nations delegation, spend up to eight months at sea, sharing this potential powder keg with passengers. During a classic voyage, constellations of islands are visited and shipboard life runs like clockwork, from the delivery of thousands of meals to a dazzling array of on-board activities, culminating in dancing under the stars. It is an extraordinary achievement, and testament to the skill and professionalism of the crew that each voyage seems to pass so smoothly.

Many cruise lines predominantly employ Southeast and Southern Asian staff.

WHAT ABOUT THE WORKERS?

The days of crew being treated as galley slaves have long since gone. Company loyalty is paramount but, in such a highly competitive industry, there is a high staff turnover. The cruise industry faces an unprecedented demand for seagoing staff, with each new mega-ship employing a thousand-strong workforce. Since a contented staff provides better service and therefore encourages more repeat business, it is in the cruise companies' interests to recruit, train and retain the best crews.

As turnover can be as high as 80 percent in the hospitality business, the most successful cruise companies are delighted to have reduced staff turnover to around 25 percent. The marine department is less problematic since it comprises only 15 percent of the seagoing workforce. Moreover, the perceived glamour of sailing a passenger liner rather than a cargo ship means that there is no shortage of officers eager to clock up the nautical miles.

It is not uncommon to find over 40 nationalities working on a ship together. Hotel staff, who account for 70 percent of cruise personnel, could come from anywhere, although many cruise lines recruit extensively in Asia, hiring workers from Indonesia, the Philippines, India and Goa. North Americans, Canadians, Australians and English-speaking Europeans tend to be found on the entertainment or guest relations side, as well as in marine positions.

EQUAL OPPORTUNITIES

While all the cruise companies are equal-opportunity employers, certain nationalities gravitate towards similar positions. The cabin, dining and waiting staff are predominantly Asian and East European, selected for their strong service ethic. Exceptionally among major cruise lines, NCL recruits primarily from the Caribbean basin, even though the navigational officer class are mainly from Norway, reflecting the company's roots.

The cruise lines' junior officers are drawn from the best international marine academies, loyalty cannot be assured by anything other than constantly improving career prospects and conditions on board, as well as increased shore leave and varied itineraries. Seasonal deployment of cruise ships helps crews see more of the world, as does the option to switch to another ship in the fleet. In order to attract the best staff and crew, some cruise lines compete on pay, while others focus on working conditions and the total benefits package. A hotel director would receive greater rewards for managing a big resort, but is prepared to

Pre-service at Blu restaurant on Celebrity Equinox.

with other officers coming from cargo ships and ferries, and from rival cruise lines; it's not uncommon for lines to poach one another's top officers. All officers are chosen for their experience and ability to sail the ship, of course, but some job descriptions also make it clear that mingling with the passengers and entertaining at dinner are part of the brief. Some captains and senior officers have almost cult status and passengers will book a cruise according to who is on board.

ATTRACTING THE BEST

The high turnover of staff and the vast geographical spread of recruitment contribute to the cruise companies' headaches. Staff forego financial gain for the excitement and variety of a career at sea.

Crew retention is also helped by the provision of superior amenities, from free or discounted WiFi and staff gyms to shopping discounts, rental bikes and hire boats at various ports of call. Several cruise companies even offer staff a private pool and spa on board, as well as crew shore excursions. Another motivational factor is staff training for personal development and career prospects. With so many new ships being built, top crew on existing ships are usually transferred to the newest, and therefore most prestigious vessel to get the ship off to a good start. A transfer like this is seen as an honor.

One of the biggest challenges of keeping crew happy is to provide them with familiar food, so a big cruise line will often hire an Indian or Filipino chef for the crew mess. Unsurprisingly, there will still be complaints that it's 'not like at home.'

OFFICERS' PERKS

The entitlement to home leave is one of the clearest indicators of rank and seniority. A captain might be entitled to 13 weeks on duty, 13 weeks off, while a chief purser might receive four months on, followed by two or three months off. However, six months on and six weeks off, or eight months on, two months off is more usual for the lower ranks, including waiting staff and cabin stewards. Flexibility is required on both sides, but normally the constant juggling of home leave means that management has to cope with a 6–10 percent staff changeover every week.

Apart from enjoying more frequent leave, senior officers benefit from off-duty retreats to the public bars and restaurants. Since all crews work a seven-day week, with only a few hours off a day (depending on the shift), free time is sacred. However, given the space constraints aboard, the issue of access is crucial: to avoid swamping public bars with crew, and to discourage fraternization with passengers, only privileged staff are allowed to stray into public areas beyond their designated work space.

This policy also acts as a form of control, with access synonymous with the perks and privileges of seniority. The chief purser or hotel director will avoid staff scrutiny by disappearing to the Dog and Duck pub. Some cruise lines inject a more democratic note into proceedings. Carnival champions a single staff menu so that, in theory, the captain and the cleaner eat the same food. RCI, on the other hand, provides the officer class with a separate mess.

CREW FACILITIES

The absence of a crew mess bar is a controversial issue. In the interests of good working relations, some cruise lines favor private bars for the crew. Other, generally smaller, lines take the opposite view, fearing that excessive drinking could encourage rowdiness. On the principle that 'sailors will be sailors,' management prefers drinking to be confined to port. Some cruise lines have a zero tolerance policy to crew consumption of alcohol.

Fortunately, the new mega-ships and mid-sized super-liners have impressive purpose-built crew quarters, complete with television rooms, games rooms and sports facilities. Conversely, older or smaller ships provide more cramped crew quarters. Space on board is at a

Steering Sea Cloud.

premium, with rank determining the size of staff cabins. On older ships, four low-ranking crew may share an inside cabin. More common is a cabin for two or, on modern mega-ships, single cabins, even for junior ratings. Naturally, the captain and the hotel director enjoy spacious suites, often at the level of the bridge and usually doubling up as their office.

THE MASTER

The captain, respectfully known as the Master, exudes authority and calm, either courtesy of his or her role or by character. Many captains, especially those from Scandinavia, come from long-time seafaring families, speak good English, and tend to make speedy progress up the ranks.

The captain, rather like an ambassador, has to act diplomatically while ensuring the safety of the ship. For instance, maritime law dictates that the ship has to accept the services of a local pilot in each port. Although they supposedly bring a wealth of local knowledge to the task, the reality is that the pilots are rarely capable of handling a mega-ship – but the pretence of services rendered and gratefully received is maintained.

The captain is supported by the staff captain, his or her number two, and the first officer – both senior officers – who host tables on some ships

The vast majority of cruise ship captains are male, but women are starting to rise through the ranks. Royal Caribbean, Celebrity Cruises, P&O Cruises and Cunard all have female captains now, and several female senior officers.

and regale their dinner companions with nautical tales. They all have special radio headsets that can communicate between the bridge, the ship and the lifeboats in the event of an emergency.

EXPECTING THE UNEXPECTED

Facing the unexpected is a feature of life at sea. In the Caribbean, the captain is occasionally involved in rescuing boatloads of refugees, generally fleeing Cubans, who have to be supervised on board and deposited at the next port. More common are the challenges of the high seas, the hurricane season or the political situation, all of which can force a captain to change course and choose a different port of call from that on the itinerary. This is particularly true where passengers are transported to shore by tender (small boat), say in the case of Virgin Gorda or St-Barths.

KEY PERSONNEL

At some point in a cruise, the key personnel are introduced to passengers, often at the Captain's Cocktail Party. The hotel director is in charge of all non-marine affairs. As the person responsible for the largest department, he or she is usually an excellent administrator, linguist, mediator and troubleshooter. The post is often titled general manager in recognition of the responsibilities of the role: the incumbent is effectively in charge of a floating resort and responsible for the welfare of several thousand passengers and a thousand-strong crew.

It is invidious to select on-board roles that are more significant than others, but on the level of personality and entertainment value, passengers tend to be intrigued by the cruise director, the gentlemen hosts, the comedians and the ship's doctor. The cruise director is responsible for the smooth running of social activities and entertainment. Depending on the ship, they can be a holiday-camp figure of fun, a third-rate comedian or a slick showperson with

Captain Inger Klein Thorhauge, Cunard's first female captain.

⊘ THE BLUE BOYS

Generally dressed in blue overalls, the 'blue boys' are deckhands extraordinaire who can be seen all over the mega-ships performing anything from the most menial tasks to amazing aerial feats. These deckhands who are, indeed, usually male, are chosen for their agility and dexterity in performing tricky tasks.

Passengers looking up from their sunloungers are often astonished to see a couple of 'blue boys' washing vast wrap-around windows below the bridge; one may be suspended in mid-flight, nonchalantly chatting to an equally carefree colleague who has dispensed with his safety harness.

the charm to quell a piratical invasion. As the most high-profile member of staff, they are a character passengers tend to like or loathe. On small, international ships, cruise directors need to be multi-lingual. On some vessels they are in charge of excursions, or inviting local dignitaries on board, so diplomatic skills are required. Most, though, come from a showbiz background.

Blessed with problem-solving and public relations skills, the best cruise directors are adept at fine-tuning the entertainment in response to passenger reactions. If clients are tired, shows are

to ice sculpture, the Thai cabin attendant can improvise a temple dance.

The cruise director can be responsible for several hundred staff, including stage performers, sports personnel, social hosts (also known as cruise hosts) and the youth staff.

SOCIAL HOSTS AND COMEDIANS

The versatile social hosts, who have shipboard experience and a background in the entertainment and hospitality industry, may find themselves accompanying a shore excursion or, on a

Activity time for the kids.

timed to start earlier; if guests seem restless, an impromptu Latin dance session might be swiftly set up. The role also necessitates a fast response to changing events: if a tropical storm confines passengers to the public lounges, the director has to cancel their deck program and improvise new entertainment. If heavy swells cause the cruise ship to abandon tendering at St-Barths in favor of a safe berth at Antigua, the cruise director summons the guest lecturer to give an impromptu talk on the new port of call. In emergencies, every additional talent is exploited in the name of entertainment. The director knows the Brazilian waiter can play the guitar while concocting a Cuba Libre, the Mexican sous-chef can do a mean Elvis impersonation, the Filipino deckhand can turn his hand

more mass market ship, supervising the international belly-flop competition. Tireless youth staff may spend the morning teaching dinosaur survival skills to the under-fives, followed by games involving glow-in-the-dark slime. On another deck, their colleagues may be supervising basic army training and camouflage face-painting for a bunch of nine-year-olds or go-kart racing with manic 12-year-olds.

The largest mass-market ships employ comedians, entertainers who stroll through the ship, creating havoc in their wake. The cruise comics, professional clowns and stilt walkers are performers who also appear in the spectacular Disney-style evening parades on the biggest vessels. Some lines – Princess, for example – show

THE BIG TIME

With a schedule this demanding, flexibility and versatility are the names of the game when it comes to entertaining on the ocean wave.

3D flying space show on Symphony of the Seas.

For entertainers on a cruise ship, every night is show night. Ship-based singers, dancers, comics and musicians are likely to be called on to turn out shows in several different styles, seven days a week, although the bigger names in the Broadway productions on lines like Royal Caribbean and NCL have dedicated roles. Musicians could be playing calypso and reggae at the poolside during the day, providing smooth jazz at sunset, then dashing to the theatre for the song-and-dance spectacular. Come the midnight hour, they could well be the ones to get the disco started. A dancer will also be making quick changes – by day a salsa teacher, by night a member of the Jets in *West Side Story*.

THINK ON YOUR FEET

Ian Brock, former musical director for Celebrity Cruises, says, 'Players have to have a strong musical background and be able to sight-read music, but even more important is the ability to think on your feet. You have to adjust your style and tempo, sometimes even the key, to suit.' For dancers, the demands are even tougher. As well as turning out two or three shows a day, there is the small matter of a moving stage. Jumps are more adventurous on ship than they are on land as the stage is actually in motion. Dancers for a major show will rehearse for several weeks in shoreside venues, then two weeks on board before leaping into the footlights.

Increasingly, a job in a show on a cruise ship carries real prestige in the entertainment world. Performers are often recruited from original London or Broadway casts, or from touring versions of big shows. Big names are aligning themselves with cruise ships, for example, songwriter Sir Tim Rice, whose career is profiled on a popular music and dance show on board Seabourn's ships. Guest performers no longer see a stint on a ship as a sign of being on the way out; many are honored to be invited.

PERKS TO LIGHTEN THE LOAD

Being an entertainer on board comes with several perks. There are no bills to pay; food and accommodation are included; there's usually a bar and gym strictly for the crew. On some ships, you'll see the dancers training in the passenger gym, easily distinguishable from the guests by their extreme slenderness and bendiness.

To keep a freshness to the shows, a cruise line may move headline performers from ship to ship every few weeks, meaning that entertainers tend to live out of suitcases. Like so many who work for cruise lines, they either get hooked by life on the waves or quit after as short an engagement as possible.

All show-folk insist that they have been forced to become more flexible than when performing on shore. Weather conditions are checked daily, even hourly, with the captain. If a ship is heading for stormy waters, dancers may have to rethink their steps, and a magician may have to replace the juggling section of his act. In moderate weather, the band may strike up *Singing in the Rain*, but in a hurricane, they may have to play a part in soothing the passengers. As the *Titanic* went down in those freezing waters, the band in the ballroom really did continue playing, heroically taking the spirit of 'the show must go on' about as far as it's possible to go.

> *Remember that, however dashing the ship's doctor is, and however charming he or she may be over dinner, there are hefty charges involved in any consultation.*

vignettes of the evening entertainment in the main atrium, which creates a lively buzz all day.

One stand-up comedian from the north of England covers the world every year, beginning

cruising, conceivably running a dance school, or enjoying early retirement in sunny climes.

Apocryphal tales abound as to the additional services provided by the dance hosts. One dance host recounts how a cruise high-roller paid him several thousand dollars to keep his wife amused all night, in a bid to discourage her from returning to the marital stateroom until dawn. Even so, while the illusion of romance is part of the appeal of a cruise, a dance host caught indulging in any improper behavior can expect to be unceremoniously deposited at the next

Beginning a formal dinner aboard a Cunard ship.

in the Caribbean before moving on to the Amazon and the Baltic, and is skilled at adapting his patter to suit the differing audiences and routes.

THE GENTLEMAN HOST

The 'gentleman host,' also known as the dance host, is a feature on the more traditional cruises such as Cunard, Crystal, Silversea, Holland America and Fred. Olsen. Personable single men in their 50s and 60s are required (but often not paid) to act as dancing partners to unaccompanied women, or those whose companions don't dance. More single women cruise than their male counterparts, and often select a cruise specifically for the ballroom and Latin dancing. The hosts rarely choose to work full-time as they have a life outside

port of call. The reality is that the hosts are very democratic in how they divide up their time on the dance floor, to avoid showing favoritism.

DOCTOR AT SEA

Given that a typical cruise covers a wide cross section of society and ages, the ship's medical officers are kept busy. Most medical emergencies are linked to elderly passengers who have pre-existing conditions or who are simply too frail to undertake a long voyage. According to one doctor, a classic response to being diagnosed with a terminal illness is to book a Caribbean cruise. Naturally, doctors are reluctant to reveal that deaths occur on board, but on cruises with a high proportion of vulnerable passengers, one or two deaths is not exceptional. One doctor attributes some heart attacks to the elderly 'who decide to discover the treadmill for the first time in their lives.' Then again, curiously enough, these deaths often occur on the final or penultimate night, perhaps linked to cumulative exertion, a reluctance to return home or simply over-indulgence at the Captain's farewell dinner.

Helicopter transfers to airlift a passenger off a ship are rare, but the captain, when advised by the doctor, is empowered to do whatever is deemed to be in the best interests of the patient.

By and large, ships' doctors have the same record of success in treating illness as their colleagues ashore and, in terms of expertise, they claim that, within the Caribbean, only the island of Barbados can provide standards similar to those which are typically available on board.

MARITIME MISADVENTURE

A 'man overboard' emergency happens occasionally but the passenger is usually rescued safely, unless suicide is the intent. More often than not, there is no man overboard, but a

The How to Train Your Dragon ice show on-board Allure of the Seas.

⊙ MEET THE MAÎTRE D'

The ship's maître d'hôtel, normally a master or mistress of diplomacy and tact and an assiduous 'meeter and greeter' has usually worked his or her way up from assistant waiter to wine waiter or captain waiter. He or she has an unenviable role, particularly at the start of those cruises that don't offer open seating, when he will often be inundated by requests for changes to seating plans.

The less glamorous side of this challenging job involves daily briefings, in-service training and supervision of the dining staff, from the wine waiter to the fruit-juice maker. If most passengers come back late from an excursion, the dining staff has to allow some

leeway for mealtimes, which eats into their limited free time. On some ships, the maître d' liaises with the executive chef and the ship's chandler, who is responsible for provisions, including the selection of fresh seafood and fruit at key ports.

The maître d' is also one of the key figures involved in assuring standards of cleanliness. Hygiene on board needs to be stringent as common viruses can spread quickly among such a tight-knit community. The dining staff may even be called upon to stay up all night to give the restaurant a total spring clean and should a norovirus outbreak reach serious proportions, a 'deep clean,' involving widespread disinfecting of surfaces.

passenger has merely spotted something in the water and raised the alarm. This causes great disruption as the ship has to be slowed down and the coastguard called, if the vessel is near land.

Statistically, neither suicide nor death by misadventure should be regarded with surprise, given that ships are floating resorts of several thousand people and sometimes, a hotbed of grievances. Fortunately, murders aboard ship are as rare as deadly hurricanes. Even so, a family cruise off the island of Sint Maarten provided the setting for a marital murder and has become the stuff of maritime legend: an American footballer allegedly murdered his wife and tossed her body onto the pool deck. The FBI was dismayed that the ship's crew had then trampled all over the murder scene in an amateurish attempt to help.

PERSONAL RELATIONS

The best cruise ships are characterized by an easy camaraderie and the mingling of different nationalities, roles and ranks. Some cruise lines encourage married couples to work together while others frown upon such entanglements, fearing that any potential estrangement could jeopardize their work performance and disrupt the smooth running of the ship. The more charitable view is that coupledom promotes happiness and harmony on board, and liberal cruise lines do their utmost to keep couples on the same ship. Relationships with passengers, meanwhile, are regarded with suspicion: the crew are allowed to 'socialize but not fraternize' – although only blatant transgressions are punished.

Those who cope best with separation and homesickness tend be the young and single, or older staff with grown-up families. Crew members who suffer the most are parents with young children, particularly Asian women, a long way from home and cast in the role of main breadwinner. By entrusting their children to the care of grandmothers or aunts, they sacrifice their own happiness on the altar of economic prosperity, despite the management's blithe dismissal of their sacrifice as 'cultural tradition.'

Given the constraints of life aboard, the crew is always delighted to let off steam in port. Cruise lines do their best to encourage camaraderie and strengthen team spirit with watersports, football and basketball, barbecues and beach parties. However, the most poignant sight is of crew members sitting in the cruise terminal, Skyping the families they may only see six months hence. The advent of free WiFi in many of the world's ports is a real blessing for crew, who on board must pay for internet access.

TIME TO GO HOME

The end-of-cruise crew show is where the upstairs-downstairs worlds come together. The show reveals the hidden talents of the motley crew, whose range might embrace Thai dancing, Spanish flamenco, Filipino acrobat-

Socializing on Royal Caribbean's Oasis of the Seas.

ics and Russian folk songs. However, when the crew let their hair down and tear up the musical score, passengers are even more delighted. Guests on ships often become very attached to their favorite crew members, and seeing them having fun, out of context, can be a delight.

The official Farewell Message from the Master encapsulates the best of cruising, the coming together of the two worlds, landlubbers and seafarers, passengers and crew. The captain usually pays tribute to all aboard with his farewell from the bridge: 'We trust you will have pleasant memories in reflecting on your sailing experiences. We have been friends and shipmates for 1,197 nautical miles. Godspeed.'

COME ABOARD!

Life on a cruise ship can be as action-packed or as relaxing as you choose. One thing's for sure: you'll never lack entertainment.

All the cruise lines are in the business of spinning dreams from scraps of seafaring history and promises of romance at sea. From the sleek mega-yachts to the mammoth floating resorts, the ships slip into their seductive sales pitches. Most cruise companies deliver the glamour and glitz, even if some go overboard on the latter. While subtlety sometimes slips out of the porthole, the sheer scale of the razzmatazz compensates for any churlish quibbles about quality. The Captain's Cocktail Party, the sail-away rituals, the spectacular carnival parades, the surreal themed evenings, the celebratory parties, the gala dinners – all form part of the 'showbiz at sea' approach that characterizes contemporary cruising on the biggest ships afloat. On the other hand, a Caribbean cruise could, if you wish, be the floating equivalent of a stylish boutique hotel, with low-key entertainment, impeccable service, exquisite cuisine and long, lotus-eating days on what feels like a private yacht. Everything depends on the ship you choose.

Honduras-ahoy on *Allure of the Seas*.

CONTEMPORARY DESIGN

By definition, a ship is neither a destination nor rooted in any culture, so ship designers have carte blanche to put their own stamp on a new ship. While the fashion used to be for glitz and kitsch galore, both of which are still widely available on older ships, the trend now is towards fitness, wellness, bringing the outside in and increasing the choice of activities on deck, particularly in ships designed to sail year-round in the Caribbean. Many ship designers have worked on five-star hotels or top restaurants, and new vessels today bear the colors, textures and hallmarks of private yachts, albeit enormous ones, with light-filled atria, muted shades and elegant fittings.

It's true that some ships, even new ones, still have an element of theming, whether it's a Vegas-style casino or a sporting 'hall of fame' encrusted with memorabilia, or a fake Irish pub. A cigar bar might be incongruously cast as an old-school English gentlemen's club, complete with creaky leather armchairs. But more and more, famous brands are being brought on-board, rather than these tacky interpretations. Take the outpost of the legendary Miami drinking den, Tobacco Road, on *Norwegian Escape*, for example, or Carnival's Fat Jimmy's C-Side Barbecue, both of which add authenticity.

EUROPEAN MOTIFS

Ironically, it's some of the European ships that sport the most outrageous interiors, rich with visions of Venetian gondoliers, French shepherdesses, Roman emperors or Greek gods. Some on-board spas and restaurants have Italianate Rococo ceilings inspired by Venetian palaces, scenes that clash with pastoral views of French châteaux and cavorting chatelaines. Often, an 'English pub' will be a designer's idea of what an English pub might be, bearing little resemblance to reality. Costa Cruises famously goes for the all-out glitz (although even this line has toned it down in recent years), while MSC Cruises new ships literally sparkle, with their dazzling Swarovski staircases. But this is the world of cruising, or, rather, one snapshot of it, and not all ships are the same.

THE UPMARKET VERSION

Premium cruise ships – which offer more space per passenger and (in some cases) better quality food than the mass-market mega-ships – offer

A captain toasts his guests.

⊘ THE CAPTAIN'S TABLE

Being selected to dine at the captain's table on formal nights is both a privilege and a potential source of friction. Some would argue that it's counterproductive, pleasing the dozen chosen passengers, but deflating the rest; however, as a high-profile exercise, this event has its place on most traditional cruise ships. In preparation, the maître d' and the captain study the passenger manifest and select favored VIPs, repeat passengers, high-spenders in the best suites, people perhaps celebrating a special anniversary and a sprinkling of personable officers in full naval dress. The captain may add one or two favorites he or she has met during the cruise. If you receive an invitation, consider

it an honor and reply immediately. Observe the dress code for the evening, too.

The dinner, often preceded by the Captain's Cocktail Party, involves making a grand entrance and being under the scrutiny of everybody in the dining room.

Over champagne and usually decent wines, the captain either regales his or her guests with nautical anecdotes or retreats into shyness, depending on mood and nationality. Some are born raconteurs while others are more at home with nautical manoeuvres than making small talk. Over coffee and petits-fours, one taciturn captain confessed that he would rather face a medical emergency at sea than make a speech.

Big name interior designers are affiliating themselves with today's most prestigious ships, for example, Kelly Hoppen, whose cool neutrals adorn the chic Celebrity Edge, and Adam D. Tihany, who has given Seabourn's new ships a sumptuous, yacht-like feel.

a more discreet and restrained style of interior design. Celebrity Cruises arguably started the trend for emulating yacht interiors with its sleek Solstice-class ships, taking the concept even further with its new Edge Class. With input from yacht designers and interiors experts behind some of the world's most lavish hotels and bars, the soft neutrals, sumptuous textures and relaxing spaces on these boutique-style ships was such a success that Celebrity Cruises has gone on to bring many of the design concepts onto its older ships when their time has come for a refit. Princess Cruises and Holland America Line, too, are known for their more restrained but tasteful interiors, while Cunard Line genuinely follows serious design concepts in its new ships, rather than cartoonish recreations: *Queen Victoria* has a Victoriana theme, while *Queen Elizabeth* is filled with beautiful Art Deco touches in its public spaces and ballrooms. A complete refit for Queen Mary 2 in 2016 brought a new, contemporary look without losing the line's Art Deco heritage.

Fake columns and swirly carpets have no place on the newest luxury ships, either. Seabourn completely rethought the layout of a ship with its quartet of vessels: *Odyssey, Sojourn* and *Quest, and the slightly larger Encore and Ovation.* Warm woods and calming neutrals provide a yacht-like feel, but the flow of passengers through the ship has changed too. The traditional concept of a reception area has been replaced with Seabourn Square, a café-lounge-library area where passengers can chat with a member of staff, sip a cappuccino, browse the internet or select a book. Seabourn Square has become the heart of the ships, rather than an area traditionally associated with standing in line and paying bills.

Oceania Cruises, too, has ripped up the rule book with the design of its newest ships, *Marina*

and *Riviera*. Although these are priced just below the luxury lines, tremendous thought has gone into the colors and textures of the design. The French restaurant Jacques, on *Marina*, features wood sourced from an ancient barn near Lyon, while the blue marble of the pool bar was personally selected from an Italian quarry by the chief executive. *Marina* was the first ship to have interiors by Ralph Lauren Home, and the suites feature cashmere throws, silver gilt mirrors, zebra-print chairs and decadent, black leather loungers.

Royal Caribbean's hit stage-show, Hairspray.

ON-BOARD ENTERTAINMENT

Entertainment, by day or night, is inextricably linked to the ship's category, size and cruising style. The bigger the ship, the more there will be to do, and on the newest ships, there is constant innovation.

The big cruise lines compete to offer the most high tech and spectacular distractions. Recent

British design firm Richmond International has wowed the critics with its interiors on P&O Cruises' Britannia and the new Iona, with natural colors and textures creating a contemporary look.

innovations include the Two70° lounges on Royal Caribbean's *Quantum*, *Anthem* and *Ovation of the Seas*; beautiful living spaces by day, flooded with natural light; and futuristic entertainment venues by night, complete with moving robotic and super-high definition screens that provide a dazzling backdrop to aerial acrobats, who later join the guests at a dance party. The ships also feature the Bionic Bar, the first outlets at sea to be tended by robots, and dancing ones at that.

Carnival is another big innovator. The new *Carnival Horizon*, like its sister, *Carnival Vista*, has

Helping out in the kitchen on a Princess cruise.

a SkyRide, a unique, pedal-powered aerial ride high above the sea, as well as the first IMAX cinema at sea and a tangle of massive waterslides.

Norwegian Cruise Line's newest, ships, *Breakaway*, *Getaway*, *Escape* and *Bliss*, place a lot of focus on entertainment after dark, with

> *Five ships belonging to Celebrity Cruises actually feature half an acre of living lawn on their top deck, a haven where guests can picnic, sunbathe and play boules or croquet. Each lawn is maintained by a full-time lawn-keeper.*

jazz clubs, stand-up comedy, big Broadway shows and genuinely cool, Ibiza-inspired dance parties on deck. Azamara Club Cruises, which operates three mid-sized ships, takes its entertainment ashore with an included AzAmazing Evenings event on every cruise – usually drinks and canapés in a beautiful venue that reflects the local culture. White Nights deck parties are held on deck, with the Caribbean the perfect setting. Viking's chic, ocean-going ships, meanwhile, each come with a plush little jazz club, Torshavn, the perfect venue for intimate, late-night music and dancing. Silversea's sumptuous *Silver Spirit* and *Silver Muse* also have a sultry cabaret club, Silver Note.

The entertainment on British-style ships tends to be less glitzy than their American counterparts, although there is no lack of imagination in the venues. A big hit on P&O Cruises' *Britannia* is the Limelight Club, an intimate supper venue where guests listen to big-name entertainers in close proximity. The most luxurious ships offer less in the way of gimmicks, focusing instead on on-board lecture programs, gorgeous surroundings and sumptuous spas. A night on a luxury ship might involve, simply, a drink on deck, or a spot of dancing under the Caribbean stars, which, for many, is entertainment enough.

TOPICAL TALKS

In these fast-paced times, even vacations are seen as an opportunity for learning and self-improvement, and cruises are no exception. On long, lazy days at sea, which feature on most Caribbean cruises, passengers will find a variety of lectures, classes and workshops at which they can discover a new interest or improve an existing talent.

Crystal Cruises, for example, has its own Creative Learning Institute, which allows guests to try anything from learning a language to mastering tai chi or studying wine. The line also offers arts and crafts workshops, book clubs, and cookery classes in anything from chocolate to sushi-making. Oceania Cruises has an Artist Loft on its two newest ships, with regular classes in sketching and watercolor painting, while Celebrity Cruises has a partnership with Apple and offers 'Celebrity iLearn' workshops with classes in Photoshop and sessions on web design.

Even better, passengers could find themselves learning something new from a celebrity. Seabourn's themed 'Conversations' bring big names on-board to discuss themes including the arts, current affairs, culture and science. Rather be a star in your own right? Then join an acting class – led by graduates of the Royal Academy of Dramatic Art – on-board Cunard Line's *Queen Mary 2*.

The best guest lecturers are not restricted to the most exclusive cruise lines. Curiously enough, although Disney Cruises panders to passenger expectations with lectures on film studies and the Disney legacy, the company also offers talks on weighty maritime themes such as navigation and ship-building, and even star-gazing at sea.

FOODIE HEAVEN

Regent Seven Seas Cruises is one of many cruise lines offering food, wine and cookery cruises but its Circles of Interest foodie sailings are more in-depth than most, and include a chance to join the ship's head chef at an early morning produce market. Crystal Cruises' Wine and Food Festival, which is spread across several themed sailings every year, is a red-letter event in the gourmand's cruise calendar.

There's also a growing trend for ships to have high-tech cookery studios on-board. Oceania Cruises' Bon Appétit Culinary Center, present on *Marina* and *Riviera*, offers a series of cookery classes, often under the guidance of expert guest chefs, with shopping in local markets part of the class. Holland America Line, too, has a Culinary Arts Center on-board its ships, offering

cookery demonstrations and classes with top chefs. Virgin Voyages' Test Kitchen will be part laboratory, part cookery school, part restaurant.

On most culinary cruises, distinguished wine authorities provide wine-tasting demonstrations of select vintages, and lectures devoted to the noble grape to go along with the gourmet food. On Holland America's newest ships, passengers can blend their own wines under the eye of an expert, while on Cunard vessels, enthusiasts can come away with a qualification from the Wine & Spirit Education Trust.

Be tempted by exquisite desserts.

Ø ART AUCTIONS

On-board art auctions are a popular activity, even if 'world-class art at a fraction of gallery prices' can be interpreted to cover original Disney cartoons and sports memorabilia. Park West Gallery, the market leader on cruise ships, claims 'the finest collection on the seven seas,' with lithographs and prints by Dali, Picasso and Chagall. Passengers are tempted by the offer of 'free fine-art prints,' complimentary champagne and the extension of a credit line. Billed as a 'fast-paced rock and roll auction' with bids opening at US$100, the entertaining event can also be accessed online, with silent bids entered from your cabin, if you wish. Are these auctions a good idea? The usual rules apply: If you

like it, can see it in your home and consider it worthwhile, then go for it. But don't kid yourself that these are investment pieces, or anything particularly unique; the art sold at auction is the same from one ship to the next. It's meant to be entertainment and a bit of fun.

Cruise ships are beginning to take art more seriously, though (see page 81) and some have simply scrapped the auctions. Others bring guest artists on-board who may auction off their work: Celebrity Cruises, for one, invited pop art icon Peter Max on-board to auction off a painting for the crew fund and even accept commissions from guests who wanted their portraits painted – at a cost, of course.

CRUISING WITH CHILDREN

Facilities for youngsters abound on modern vessels, as cruise lines vie to win over parents and their offspring – tomorrow's paying passengers.

Children won't fail to be excited by the splash park on Carnival ships.

Traveling with the family is child's play these days. Teen discos, virtual-reality games arcades and rides, indoor and outdoor play centers, child-only swimming pools, circus skills lessons, supervised activity programs and kids' mealtimes have become an intrinsic part of modern mega-ship cruising.

Carnival Cruise Line attracts more than half a million youngsters a year – and keeps them happy with their own pools and deck areas, playrooms, arcades and teen discos, as well as a Camp Carnival activity program which allows youngsters to indulge in face- and T-shirt painting, enjoy quizzes and treasure hunts, play educational computer games, learn about science in a fun way and even take backstage tours with ships' entertainers.

Royal Caribbean is Carnival's biggest rival and its ultra-modern ships have indoor and outdoor children's facilities, plus an age-group-related Adventure Ocean youth program starting with Royal Babies, from just six months old. The line's Quantum class ships have a spectacular sports arena, Seaplex, complete with dodgems, a circus school and a roller disco, in addition to a skydiving simulator and two surf simulators. An imaginative kids program from **Celebrity Cruises**, meanwhile, includes DJ skills, creating a vlog with a GoPro, coding, and building a camp on deck.

Norwegian Cruise Line ships feature a Circus at Sea, where children can learn juggling and clowning, as well as cool teen dance clubs and specially designed family cabins near the kids' clubs. The **Princess Cruises** all-day activities are divided into three age groups and sister company **P&O Cruises** has a night nursery for kids aged 6 months to 5 years, and age-related kids' clubs all day and evening, up to teens.

It's not just the mega-ship lines that are trying to meet their demands. Luxury operator **Crystal Cruises** has kids' clubs and in-cabin babysitting (for an hourly fee). Even **Fred. Olsen Cruise Lines** – traditionally associated with an older clientele – offers kids' menus and activities on selected family sailings, as does upscale **Regent Seven Seas Cruises**, while **Holland America Line** offers babysitting and kids-only excursions, including horseback riding on the beach at HAL's private Bahamian island.

POINTS TO CONSIDER

Once on-board, give your children a tour of the ship so they know where your cabin is and how to find reception in an emergency. Some ships offer pagers for parents, while others have apps with deck plans. In a real emergency, of course, the crew in the kids' club will take responsibility for keeping your children safe, provided they're in there at the time.

Before you book, check what the line offers for your child's age group – and whether it's available outside school vacations. Check, too, whether the kids' clubs operate when the ship is in port. Sometimes they don't, which means you have to plan your day differently.

Check the level of supervision for very small children; reputable lines will happily tell you the ratio of 'child counselors' to youngsters and outline required qualifications. Many lines insist one parent be present at all times if the child is very young – which means staying on-board if the child attends clubs on port days. You must bring (and administer) any medication yourself.

PORTS AND SHOPPING TALKS

The tradition of talks on ports of call is an essential element of cruising, and is useful if you're not familiar with the next destination. At best, a destination talk is an unbiased, informative briefing by an expert lecturer on how to make the most of the next day's port, combining practical information with personal anecdotes and recollections of the island in question, as well as touching upon its politics, economy and social life.

At the worst, it's a scaremongering talk by the cruise director or a 'shopping ambassador' warning passengers not to shop anywhere that is not approved by the cruise line, not to travel around independently and essentially, to approach local people, restaurants and taxi drivers with caution. Many cruise lines use their port talks to push last-minute shore excursion sales. Sadly, the commercial agenda added to the legacy of a handful of security incidents in Caribbean ports and the growing litigiousness of cruise passengers means these talks can come across as extremely negative.

When it comes to shopping in the 'recommended' stores, passengers benefit from knowing that they have a guarantee as to the quality of their purchases, and, in the unlikely event of shoddy goods, have some recourse. But the cruise company or its representative will take commission on passengers' purchases; so shopping advice, although sound, is not necessarily wholly independent.

So, should you attend these port talks? They're without doubt useful if you're not familiar with the port of call, but use your own judgement to decide whether the lecturer is offering genuinely good information or simply pushing a commercial agenda. If you miss the talk, or can't be bothered to attend, they are almost always repeated on the in-cabin TV. With the constant growth in social media, many passengers in any case do their own research, using the message boards and professional reviews of sites like Cruise Critic (www.cruisecritic.co.uk) to inform themselves on ports before they arrive.

CRUISING ACROSS GENERATIONS

Cruises are perfect for satisfying different generations at the same time and cruise lines are increasingly catering to multi-generational groups. A family can cruise together, amuse themselves separately and share stories over dinner. The best cruise companies manage a clever segregation of fun-loving families and privacy-seeking adults. Many ships, for example, have a quiet, adults-only deck where grandparents can escape the mayhem around the family pool. On Princess, it's called 'The Sanctuary', on P&O Cruises 'The Retreat' and on MSC Cruises 'Top 18'. Carnival, Norwegian and Disney also offer adults-only space.

The most child-friendly cruise companies, such as Carnival, Royal Caribbean, NCL, Prin-

Playing video games in pods at Vibe, the trendy crash-pad for teens aboard the Disney Dream.

cess Cruises and Disney Cruise Line, offer fully supervised children's centers, divided according to age group, giving parents and grandparents a chance to relax while their offspring are entertained. Even the most luxurious of lines are beginning to tap into the multi-generational market: during school vacations, luxurious Regent Seven Seas Cruises and Seabourn both lay on very discreet children's entertainment, as the generation these lines initially set out to attract now have kids of cruising age and parents well into retirement, who may already be experienced cruisers.

There are a few considerations to booking a multi-generational cruise. A suite may be more effective than two cabins, for example. NCL's The Haven offers wonderful family accommodation in larger suites, as does MSC Cruises' Yacht Club. Many cruise lines, including Carnival, Norwegian, Royal Caribbean, Disney and Celebrity Cruises, offer cabins sleeping five. Request a table in the dining room just for your family, and think about booking a private car or minivan for shore excursions if it's cheaper or if you have specific plans. Check the ship's activity program for things you can do together, for example, Carnival's family-oriented stand-up comedy shows,

> *Royal Caribbean is the first cruise line to offer sky diving at sea, on thrilling Ripcord by iFly simulators, no prior experience required.*

daily program. But it's not just the newbies who are catered for; the daily program will reveal just how diverse cruises are, offering social events for singles, bridge players, dancers, those in AA, gay guests, teens, gamblers and regular guests. You

Cruising can be an ideal trip for grandparents and grandchildren to enjoy together.

a cookery class or a line dancing class. Several ships offer family-themed shore excursions, too.

The best aspect of sailing as an extended family, though, is that cruising offers the chance to be together when it matters – but for individuals to do their own thing as they wish.

CATERING FOR EVERYONE

Cruise ships have broad appeal, attracting people from all walks of life, but a cruise can seem intimidating for a first-timer; there's a system on-board that the regulars know how to work, not to mention the fact that a huge cruise ship can seem like a floating city at first glance. Fortunately, cruise lines greatly value first-time cruisers and will often put ship tours and newcomers' social gatherings in the

can go to everything – or you can do nothing and simply soak up the Caribbean sun.

SPORT

Cruise ships offer a surprising array of sports, given the limited space they have. All the big ships have a sports court for basketball, volleyball and sometimes paddle tennis. Many have golf simulators, recreating some of the world's top courses. Several have mini-golf, and for some years now the largest ships have been fitted with climbing walls up the funnels. There's always a gym and a range of exercise classes – and there's always a pool.

So what's new in on-board activity? Royal Caribbean offers boxing rings, surf simulators, sky diving, roller skating and trapeze lessons.

Seabourn has Kinesis walls in its gyms, which are supposed to tone everything, while SeaDream Yacht Club carries a fleet of mountain bikes for guests to use in port, and Carnival and NCL both offer challenging high-ropes climbing courses. Crystal offers reformer Pilates and guided jogs in port. The smaller ships, like those of Ponant, Seabourn and Star Clippers' Royal Clipper, have watersports platforms at the aft, which can be lowered to create a launch pad for windsurfing, dinghy sailing and the core-toning sport of the moment, stand-up paddleboarding.

P&O Cruises is another big collector, commissioning everything from scratch for its new ships, using only British artists, while Silversea commissions an eclectic range of Italian art for its ships.

What's happening now is art collections at sea becoming so significant that cruise lines are beginning to showcase their collections as an activity guests can enjoy on-board. On Celebrity Cruises' ships, guests can download an app that displays the locations of each painting or sculpture, giving information on each work and its creator.

Blissful relaxation aboard Celebrity Solstice.

ART AFLOAT

A growing attraction of a big cruise ship is the often astonishing collection of art adorning the stairwells and corridors. The tradition of displaying fine art on passenger ships has been around for decades, the art originally belonging to the private collections of the ship owners themselves. Nowadays, cruise ship art has become big business, to the extent that ships are becoming veritable floating museums. Royal Caribbean alone has spent more than US$120 million on art for its ships over the last 15 years, while Celebrity Cruises owns more than 14,000 original contemporary pieces across its Solstice-class ships alone – making the cruise line one of the world's largest corporate collectors.

Holland America Line offers self-guided art tours on its newest ships, where the multi-million dollar collection reflects the line's heritage and its connection to New York. Meanwhile, Frank del Rio, president of Norwegian Cruise Line Holdings, personally curates the lavish art collections on the ships of Oceania Cruises and Regent Seven Seas Cruises, both of which are part of the NCL group.

Cunard was one of the first lines to introduce a proper art gallery on-board, with its three ships each featuring an outpost of Clarendon Fine Art. The English gallery – based in Mayfair, London –displays a huge range of work, from Art Deco paintings to pieces from Cunard's own collection. Some of the work is for sale, while

SPAS AT SEA

Today you can return from a cruise fitter rather than fatter by taking advantage of a huge range of fitness facilities, from trapeze lessons to jogging tours.

Hot stone massage on Royal Caribbean International's Navigator of the Seas.

Dedicated dieters will be appalled to learn that for every week's holiday aboard a cruise ship, the average passenger gains 5lbs (2.3kg) in weight. And in the old days – short of a sprightly walk around deck and the occasional game of deck quoits – there wasn't much you could do about it.

But on today's ships you'll find gyms, jogging tracks, ball courts, swimming pools, golf simulators and spas. You can even (for a fee) have your fitness level and body fat assessed and a health regime designed specifically for you, or hire a personal trainer to put you through your paces.

And you don't have to pound away on a treadmill or step machine; you can experiment with yoga, Boxercise, HITT, spinning or Pilates geared to different ages and ability levels – though while aerobics and basic stretch classes are mainly free, most ships now charge a fee of US$10 upwards for specialist classes.

Sea spas now rival land-based health facilities in terms of the services they offer, and you can not only treat yourself to facials and massages but also have your teeth whitened, consult an acupuncturist on-board or even have a Botox treatment. Some ships, among them those of Costa Cruises and Celebrity Cruises, offer special 'spa cabins' with features like mood lighting, enhanced bathroom goodies, passes to the spa thermal suite and discounts on treatments.

FROM SCENTED STEAM TO SNOW CAVES

Features like herbal steam rooms and tropical rain showers are fairly commonplace even on big mass-market ships like those of Carnival Cruise Lines, Royal Caribbean, Princess Cruises and Norwegian Cruise Line (though you must pay extra to use them). On Viking Ocean's ships, access to the thermal suite is free and if you need to cool off from the Caribbean sunshine, there's actually a snow cave with real snow.

Not surprisingly, luxury ships like those of Crystal Cruises, Silversea Cruises and Seabourn have spas to match, with in-suite treatments, or even private retreats that can be hired by couples for a day of hedonistic treatments, dining and relaxing.

Before you head off for some pampering, though, beware of therapists pushing pricey lotions, and of high-priced treatments. Expect to pay over US$120 for a facial, a 55-minute massage or a reflexology session. Check the daily news sheet for offers, and ask for a discount on port days.

So far, so heavenly. But you don't have to stay in a spa cabin – or break the bank with expensive treatments – to get fit on a cruise. While charges have crept in for on-board fitness classes, use of gyms and swimming pools is still free. Healthy low-calorie, low-sodium, low-cholesterol dishes are available on most main dining room menus, while shore excursions in the Caribbean in particular are a chance to try hiking, white-water rafting and kayaking.

the gallery's artists sometimes come on-board to give talks to the guests.

SPAS

The cruise ship spa industry has become a multi-million dollar one, dominated by the lavish spas operated by the giant Steiner Leisure company, essentially those on NCL, Carnival, Holland America Line, Princess Cruises and Royal Caribbean. Canyon Ranch is another big player, with spas on ships belonging to Cunard, Celebrity Cruises, Oceania Cruises and Regent Seven Seas Cruises. Small lines like SeaDream Yacht Club have their own Thai-style spas offering products from La Prairie and Thalgo, while Ponant's ships have chic, Parisian beauty house brand Sothys on-board. On Star Clippers, you can have an excellent Thai massage in a tent that's open to the sea breezes on deck. I you enjoy an al fresco massage, there are sometimes treatments available on cruise lines' private islands; Royal Caribbean, for example, has a shoreside spa on Labadee, its private beach.

Cruise lines like spa concessions because they make money. From a customer's point of view, this means that, although spa facilities are impressive, treatments cost more than they would ashore, as there is no competition. The same treatment may also vary in price from ship to ship; the spas charge what the market will bear. Having said this, the spas on ships are often gorgeous, relaxing havens with their own thermal suites where you can take a sauna, lie on a heated lounger or rest on a private deck. And you can find bargains, too; days when the ship is in a popular port are a good time to find discounted treatments and promotions, or simply study the daily program for tactical offers.

Cruise ship spa practitioners have gained a reputation for 'hard selling' costly products with scant regard for passengers' desire for peace and quiet and a brief respite from consumerism. The easiest way to deal with the former is to say, politely, 'I like to relax during a treatment so please excuse me if I meditate/doze/don't talk.'

CASINOS

According to inveterate gamblers, ships' casinos and the Caribbean-style casinos ashore are more laid-back than any heart-attack inducing

session in Las Vegas. The games move at a slightly slower pace, the rules may be slightly looser, and games are friendlier and more entertaining. Even so, casinos produce extreme reactions among many cruise passengers: For the Americans, gambling is a standard activity, while the British tend to have a more ambivalent attitude to it, on the one hand decrying it as vulgar, on the other relishing the fun and excitement generated.

Typically, passengers appreciate the chance to lay bets in a safe, welcoming environment.

Where the money sometimes goes...

Certainly, gambling is a feature of most of the mega-ships, with American and international-style lines generally outshining their European rivals with dazzling, Las Vegas-style facilities and – in some cases – free drinks for players. Most casinos provide gaming lessons to novices, as well as offering slot machines with 'unprecedented state-of-the-art features.

LET THEM ENTERTAIN YOU

Cruise ship entertainment has come a long way since the days of songs-from-the-shows medleys and sequinned dance routines. What's changed is that now, instead of medleys, you can see the shows themselves.

Royal Caribbean and rival Norwegian Cruise Line have gone head-to-head in staging the biggest hits in musical theatre on their newest ships. Norwegian has staged *Rock of Ages*, *Legally Blonde*, *Priscilla, Queen of the Desert* and *Jersey Boys* on its most recent launches, as well as the ballroom spectacular *Burn the Floor*. Royal Caribbean's big-ticket shows include *Cats, Grease, Hairspray, We Will Rock You* and *Mamma Mia*.

Princess Cruises has its own specially commissioned show, *Magic To Do*, a combination of

None of these, it could be argued, reflect Caribbean culture, but the entertainment should be seen as just one element of what there is to do on-board. All ships have a band playing on deck, dancing under the stars and open-air movies, all of which work perfectly on a warm Caribbean night.

MUSICAL OFFERINGS

Cruise ships are all about live music, and while the extent of cultural immersion into Caribbean genres may be limited to dancing round the pool

A variety of live entertainment awaits.

song, dance and illusion, composed by Stephen Schwartz, best known for his smash hits *Wicked*, *Godspell* and *Pippin*. Everyone from the costume designer to the director has major Broadway hits under their belts.

MSC Cruises, meanwhile, has a partnership with Cirque du Soleil, which has own purpose-built home on the newer ships in a super high-tech, 450-seat lounge that includes a restaurant, so guests will be able to have dinner and then watch the aerial acrobatics.

Carnival recruits big names on the stand-up circuit on both sides of the Atlantic for its Punchliner Comedy Club, which includes a family-friendly show every day and a more adult-orientated offering late at night.

as the band belts out *Feelin' Hot Hot Hot*, there are choices around any ship. There is nearly always a piano bar where a handful of musicians play mellow background music, or a jazz trio, or a mixture of dance venues, tailored to the age group on-board, offering anything from ballroom to current chart hits. The bigger the ship, the more music it will have. Big-name acts are flown in, too, from

Sail-away constitutes a genuinely special moment for many cruisers, an experience for which they'll make a point of being on deck, or on their balcony, to take in.

classical guitarists to singers, and local folklore groups are sometimes brought on-board.

Alternatively, join a theme cruise charter featuring your favorite bands. Some recent examples include Kool and the Gang on Holland America Line; heavy metal band Def Leppard on MSC; a techno and trance cruise on NCL; a soul cruise on Celebrity; and Carnival's sell-out Carnival Live series, for which big bands (for example, Journey, Gladys Knight and KC and the Sunshine Band) come on-board for a one-off gig – a great chance to see a famous name in a small venue.

Most cruises, however, leave the port of call at sunset, providing passengers with the nightly ritual that is sail-away. The official line is that a timely departure allows the ship to reach the next port on schedule, but the reality relates to ship revenues: the casino and on-board shops can only open once the ship is at sea.

SAIL-AWAY

Each cruise line treats sail-aways rather differently but the spectacle always raises the

Carnival's Dream gets ready for departure from St Marten at sunset.

AN EVENING IN PORT

The Caribbean is different from cruising in, say, the Mediterranean, in that it doesn't so much lend itself to a night in port, as a lot of entertainment is hotel-based. Some Caribbean cruises do offer the occasional late sailing, though, providing a welcome opportunity to dine or drink ashore and a break from the rhythms of life at sea. Azamara Club Cruises offers late sailings from ports like Philipsburg, Sint Maarten, and Gustavia and on most of its Cuba cruises, spends two nights docked in Havana. Bucking the trend among the big ships, Celebrity Cruises has overnights in Aruba, Bridgetown, Cartagena, Curaçao and Cozumel.

spirits, reminding one why cruising has the edge over conventional land-bound holidays. As the sun sets and the staff serve poolside rum punches, there is always an ideal spot from which to view the spectacle of the ship gliding out of port and to reflect on the new discoveries of the day. At its best, the sail-away party is one of the highlights of a cruise: the quayside lined with smiling Caribbean islanders waving goodbye to the ship; a small band of passengers dancing to the steel band on deck; and the rest sipping complimentary rum punches while lapping up the views, the sunset and the sight of the vessel's foamy wake as the captain sets a course for the next island.

Labadee is one of Royal Caribbean's private islands.

YOUR CARIBBEAN CRUISE

Which islands to visit? What kind of ship to choose? This roundup of who goes where and what's on offer will help you decide what suits you best.

So meteoric has been the growth of cruising that ships are now as varied as hotels and resorts on land, catering for travelers of every age, taste and budget. Some ships are like floating country houses, with substantial libraries, wood-paneled bars, elegant lounges and intimate restaurants; others are big, glitzy ocean-going resorts, with state-of-the-art spas, cool nightclubs, themed restaurants and spectacular show lounges.

You can learn the ropes and sleep beneath the stars on a sailing ship, or pretend you are a millionaire for a week or two on an intimate luxury yacht. And the good news is that ships of all types spend all or part of the year exploring the Caribbean, which is the true heartland of the cruise business – as you will soon realize if you stroll along the Miami harborfront and see the skyscraper-high ships lined up at the piers.

WHY CHOOSE THE CARIBBEAN?

The Caribbean islands are synonymous with sun and fun; even the occasional shower seems little more than a burst of liquid sunshine. With soft-as-talc beaches, hospitable people, a laid-back lifestyle and wonderful shopping, the calypso islands are the place to chill out, soak up the sun, swim, snorkel and forget the pressures of everyday life.

But they offer far more than that: you'll also find lavish plantations, gorgeous scenery, a rich

Reason enough to go – snorkeling in those turquoise Caribbean waters.

history, varied local cuisine and plenty of things to do – from undersea exploration in a submarine to enjoying a world-class round of golf, discovering the secrets of a rainforest, learning how rum is made or going on a deep-sea fishing expedition.

Some people prefer to stay longer on one particular island and get under its skin, but many travelers find this restricting, and that is where cruising comes into its own.

A typical seven-night cruise from Miami or Fort Lauderdale will visit four islands – and seven-day itineraries can be combined with island stays, or with a different cruise, to create a 14-night 'back to back' cruise offering a real insight into the region, and a chance to

December to March is an ideal time to explore the Caribbean. The hurricane season is from June to November. If tropical storms present a threat, some port calls may be changed, but it's rare for a cruise to be canceled due to bad weather.

sample the unique personalities of many different islands. This makes for a good introduction if you're planning a holiday on land at a later date but are unsure which island you would prefer.

Many big-ship lines also own or lease private islands or sections of beach where visitors can play Robinson Crusoe, enjoy a barbecue and take part in a variety of water sports.

FLOATING RESORT OR PRIVATE YACHT?

In the 1980s the cruise lines designed a generation of big ships as 'floating resorts,' with a range of facilities from vast casinos to multiple restaurants and health spas, akin to those of the all-inclusive resorts ashore. While this concept has continued to grow, to the extent that Caribbean regulars, ironically, may barely go ashore during their week's cruise, so distracted are they by the ship, it isn't the only style of cruising available in this region. There are small, luxurious ships that call at the harbors favored by the yachting set – Virgin Gorda, St-Barths and secluded spots in the Grenadines; while mid-sized ships, on which the emphasis is on the

Zip-line if you dare.

The Ropes Course on Norwegian Breakaway.

⊘ WHAT'S INCLUDED IN THE PRICE?

There's a growing trend for luxury ships to offer all-inclusive pricing. This means, essentially, that all drinks are included, as well as dining in most of the alternative restaurants, and all gratuities. Some lines, such as Regent Seven Seas Cruises, also include a selection of shore excursions. Silversea, Crystal, Azamara Club Cruises, SeaDream Yacht Club and Seabourn are all all-inclusive. Others include some drinks, for example, Noble Caledonia and Viking Cruises both offer wine with meals. Marella Cruises is a rarity among the more mainstream lines in that all its ships are all-inclusive. No line includes spa treatments, though. Always check what's included before you book.

destinations as much as what's on board, may roam the southern Caribbean, skimming the coast of South America or venturing down to the Amazon. Some ships operate under sail. Some are aimed at older passengers wanting a quiet life on board, while others target the party set.

LIFE ON BOARD A BIG SHIP

The leviathans are more like miniature cities than traditional cruise ships. With – literally – acres of space on board, they offer around-the-clock action and plenty of nightlife.

Pulsating nightclubs vie for attention with intimate piano bars. You can prepare for dinner with a visit to a champagne bar, and round it off with a nightcap in a cool cocktail lounge and a spectacular show. You can opt for a casual meal in a pizza parlor or enjoy an evening pint at an English-style pub.

During the day you can swim, jog, visit the golf driving range, work out in the gym with a personal trainer, or have a game of deck tennis or basketball on a full-scale court. If you prefer, indulge yourself in the spa with a massage or wallow in a thalassotherapy bath. Enthusiastic shoppers will be pleased to know that the outlets on board sell everything from sunblock to big-name designer labels.

except on the most luxurious ships, but the food is varied, and, as a rule, it is nicely presented and plentiful. Those so inclined can eat and drink all day, starting with early-bird coffee at 6am and ending with a midnight snack at a 24-hour café. Many modern ships have made room for specialty restaurants where – usually for a surcharge of between US$15 and US$50 – passengers can celebrate a special occasion, indulge their gourmet tastes, sample recipes prepared by a celebrity chef or simply take a break from the main dining rooms and try something different.

Working off some energy on the hoops court.

Best of all – if you're traveling with children – these ships offer extensive facilities for kids, with all-day supervision and activities geared to different age groups, so you can relax, or let your hair down, secure in the knowledge that your children are happy and safely occupied.

The big ships have a wide range of accommodation, from small, inside (windowless) single cabins to spacious suites with hot tubs and roomy balconies. Cabins, whatever their size, are furnished to a high standard and each will have an ensuite bathroom (with a shower in the lower-grade accommodation, and shower plus bathtub in higher grades) and a TV.

Meals, by and large, are of three- to four-star restaurant standard rather than haute cuisine,

PROS AND CONS OF MEGA-SHIPS

These huge ships are smart, well-equipped, lively and offer good value for money in terms of the basic fare, although watch out once you're on board and all the extras begin to pile up. Their comfortable cabins and varied facilities can

A 'home port' is industry jargon for the ship's base: the point at which it turns around between cruises. This turnaround is the day the ship refuels, re-provisions, offloads waste and embarks passengers for the next cruise.

make traveling around the Caribbean islands as interesting and enjoyable as visiting them – particularly if you have children in tow. On the downside, ships that carry more than 3,000 people are bound to feel crowded, especially when you are embarking and disembarking.

Multiple facilities mean that you will rarely encounter hordes of people in one place at a time, but on sea days (when the ship does not visit a port), sunbathing on deck can be rather a cheek-by-jowl affair, as can the buffet breakfast – so be prepared to queue. And, on some ships, the relent-

Waiter on a Silversea cruise.

less 'fun, fun, fun' atmosphere of pool games, fashion shows and public-address announcements can be wearing if you're trying to relax.

To win over first-time cruise passengers, the big-ship lines also tend to cram itineraries full of port calls, which does mean you get a lot of variety for your money. But with so many people on board, the process of disembarking and getting passengers off on tours is a major production. Some ships don't organize this as well as others, in which case the constant sound of passengers being summoned ashore makes a lazy lie-in out of the question.

As a rule, the bigger the ship, the longer the wait to disembark, and the sheer size of these vessels means they have to anchor off some

ports and ferry passengers to the quayside by tender – something to consider if you feel seasick in small boats or have mobility problems.

On the whole, families, the young, the sporty and sociable types will love these ships; they're also good for single travelers and for people who've never cruised before and fear they'll go stir-crazy if they don't have enough to do.

SMALL IS BEAUTIFUL

In contrast, a small or mid-sized ship, such as those belonging to Oceania Cruises, the smaller Holland America Line ships, or the upscale vessels of Seabourn or Silversea, offer a more restful experience. Waiters at the breakfast buffet will help carry your tray and fetch your coffee. Announcements will be kept to a minimum. There will be space for everybody by the pool and no blaring music or knobbly-knees contests. Getting on and off the ship is simple and guests will often be greeted with cold towels as they re-board at the end of a long, hot day. Dinners are slow, elegant affairs. On an all-inclusive ship, there are no bar bills to sign for, which creates an atmosphere of conviviality. Dining in the alternative restaurants is like eating out in a top shoreside restaurant.

The downside – and yes, there is one – is that smaller ships tend to be quieter. The casino may lack atmosphere and the shows may not be all-singing, all-dancing spectaculars. Nightclub? What nightclub? The most you can usually hope for is one lively bar in the evenings. There's not usually much on for kids and teens. And the disadvantage of having fewer passengers is that if the minimum numbers for shore excursions aren't met, which can happen on the very smallest ships, tours get canceled, which can be extremely annoying if you'd set your heart on something.

HOME PORTS AND DESTINATIONS

Most of the big ships are based at one of Florida's three main ports. Miami is home to many Royal Caribbean, Carnival, Celebrity and Norwegian Cruise Line ships; Royal Caribbean has its own futuristic terminal here, the new Terminal A. Fort Lauderdale/Port Everglades is the base port for several Holland America, Princess, Celebrity and Royal Caribbean vessels (a dedicated terminal accommodates Royal Caribbean's vast Oasis-class ships, as well as the biggest Celebrity Cruises ships) and is also a key turnaround port for lines whose ships only cruise the Caribbean occasionally, such as Cunard Line, Seabourn, Silversea and Regent Seven Seas Cruises. Port Canaveral is the home port for Disney Cruise Line and for some Carnival, Royal Caribbean and Holland America ships.

Florida-based ships mainly operate regular seven-day runs to the eastern Caribbean (the Bahamas, St Thomas, St John's, Haiti and Puerto Rico) or the western Caribbean (Mexico, Belize, Grand Cayman and Jamaica).

To gain easy access to southern Caribbean islands, including Dominica, St Kitts and Nevis, Grenada, St Lucia, Aruba, Curaçao and Martinique, some mega-ships have moved away from the traditional ports. San Juan on Puerto Rico is now home to several ships, while Barbados has attracted P&O Cruises, Windstar and Star Clippers, among others.

Cruise ships also reach the Caribbean from further afield. New York is an increasingly popular base for sailings to the Caribbean, with cruises on offer from Princess, Viking, NCL and Oceania. Ships also sail from ports including Jacksonville in Florida, New Orleans in Louisiana, and the Texan port of Galveston. For European or Australian fans of Caribbean cruising, this means more options for add-on drive packages allowing them to explore lesser-known parts of the US before or after their cruise.

Most British cruisers reach the Caribbean by air, for sailings with companies like P&O Cruises, Marella Cruises and Fred. Olsen Cruises, as well as lines like Saga and Noble Caledonia. Some lines (P&O Cruises, and Cruise & Maritime Voyages, for example) make the long crossing to the Caribbean to create a no-fly cruise; but for the cash-rich, time-poor traveler who only has 10 days or so to chase the winter sunshine, these three-week epics, including two Atlantic crossings, are not an option.

GETTING THE RATIO RIGHT

If you are attracted to 'floating resort' style cruising, be aware that there are two styles of mega-ship: Contemporary and Premium.

Catching the breeze in Sint Maarten.

⊘ WORLD CRUISES AND LONGER VOYAGES

One way of finding an unusual Caribbean itinerary is to check out the world cruises that operate every year from January to April. Instead of the round-trip Miami seven-night staples, ships on world cruises operate point-to-point voyages that can be booked as sectors, so you don't need to buy the whole world circumnavigation. For example, it might be possible to board in Panama City, sail through the Panama Canal, cruise the Caribbean for a couple of weeks and disembark in New York. Or joining a ship that's sailing south through the islands and down the coast of Brazil to the Amazon might be an option.

Lots of cruise lines operate world cruises or extended winter voyages, among them Cunard, P&O Cruises, Princess Cruises, Saga, Crystal Cruises, Regent Seven Seas Cruises, Silversea Cruises, Seabourn, and Viking.

Any UK passenger who longs to sail the Caribbean but prefers not to fly can still make the journey, as long-distance cruising from Britain is on offer from P&O Cruises, Cruise & Maritime Voyages, Fred. Olsen and Saga Cruises. You'll cross the Atlantic, spend a week or so in the Caribbean and return. This requires a commitment of three weeks or more, and would only appeal to someone who relished the thought of some 10 days at sea; but it does open a whole new world of discovery to anybody who, for whatever reason, would not be able to travel by air.

HOW TO BUY A CRUISE

If you're new to cruising, you can't beat the good advice of a specialist cruise agent – who will also ask questions you hadn't thought of.

Coming ashore.

A lot of cruisers will do their research online, but end up booking through a knowledgeable cruise agent. Having said that, it does help to start by knowing a little about what you want. You might want to consider the following criteria:

Route preference? If there are any islands on your must-see list, this will narrow down your choice of cruises. Other factors might be the departure port and whether you want a fly-cruise or are planning to drive to the port.

Size of ship? A big ship with masses of facilities, or a smaller one with a more refined atmosphere? Are there any facilities that really matter to you, for example a steakhouse, childcare, a casino?

Best time to travel? Bear in mind the US's spring break vacation, which many cruisers see as a time to avoid the mass-market ships. Hurricane season is June/July to November, which doesn't guarantee bad weather but increases its possibility (and is reflected in the price of Caribbean cruises). Europeans should note that Thanksgiving weekend is a great time to look out for bargains, as Americans tend to make this a family, at-home celebration rather than a time to travel.

Fellow passengers? Ships on world cruises, or very expensive voyages, will normally attract an older age group. Mass-market ships have a broader age range. Some are not suitable for children, for example Azamara Club Cruises, SeaDream and Saga (which is for the over-50s only). Virgin Voyages' new ship, *Scarlet Lady*, is over-18s. On Ponant's ships, a lot of passengers will be French, and on Hapag Lloyd's vessels, German. English is the main language on the cruises sold as 'international.'

Type of cabin? Some cruisers are content with an inside cabin as a place to crash, while others want the luxury of a private balcony. Families may take interconnecting cabins, or an inside for the kids and a balcony across the corridor for the parents. Larger families may even opt for a suite. Single travelers should get their agent working for the best possible single discount, so you don't pay double the fare.

Budget? Do you want to spend all your money on the cabin, in other words go for a top cabin on a cheaper ship, or is a more basic cabin on a more luxurious ship of importance?

FINDING THAT BARGAIN

And now for those elusive bargains. Booking late is disliked and discouraged by the cruise lines, but if you're flexible, it can snag a really good deal. Booking early is encouraged and can also bring discounts of 20–30 percent. Don't be fooled by 'brochure prices.' These are more of a token to make everybody feel as though they've found a bargain when they book for less. Booking online is only advisable if you know exactly what you want.

Specialist cruise agencies are a good source of bargains, as many cruise lines pass on spare capacity for them to fill. They are also adept at putting together no-hassle (and protected) fly-cruise packages. To find an accredited cruise specialist, visit the website of CLIA, Cruise Lines Industry Association, which is the main trade association globally. In the UK, it's www.cruiseexperts.org or on Twitter, @CLIAUK and in the US, www.cruising.org or @CLIAGlobal. Offers are also posted daily on review websites such as Cruise Critic (www.cruisecritic.com).

Virgin Voyages' new, adults-only Scarlet Lady, is promising to shake up the cruise industry, with drag shows, bottomless brunches, a tattoo parlour and a Korean barbecue. Oh, and no such thing as 'passengers'; they're called 'sailors.'

Contemporary ships are aimed at the mass market (and priced accordingly), while Premium-rated ships are higher-priced, carry fewer cruise passengers and offer a touch more class.

A quick way to discover whether the ship you're considering is Premium or Contemporary is to divide its tonnage by its passenger capacity to get the Passenger Space Ratio (PSR). This gives the clearest indication of how crowded you will find life on board a particular ship. For example, the 101,509-ton/2,758-passenger Contemporary ship *Carnival Victory* has a PSR of 36.8, while the 108,806-ton/2,600-passenger Premium ship *Golden Princess* has a PSR of 41.8. The higher the PSR, the less likely it is that you will feel hemmed in by your fellow passengers. But this serves only as a loose indicator of the quality of the ship. A smaller, older ship could offer the last word in luxury but a low PSR – the two vessels of SeaDream Yacht Club, for example, have a relatively low PSR and no balcony cabins, but offer some of the finest food, wine and service afloat. There are many other factors to bear in mind when choosing a cruise.

On nearly all the big ships that sail in the Caribbean, the majority of passengers are North American and the on-board currency is the US dollar. But you'll also come across Brits, South Americans, Mexicans, Australians, Germans, French, Scandinavians and Italians in the passenger mix, as cruising's appeal grows worldwide.

THE MEGA-SHIP OPERATORS

Websites are given below; for local telephone numbers, see listings in the Travel Tips section.
Carnival Cruise Line (www.carnival.com). King of the swingers and part of the world's most successful cruise company, Carnival has 29 Contemporary-rated ships, the majority of which are based in the Caribbean. They range in size from around 70,000 tons (and 2,056 passengers) to the big, new *Carnival Horizon*, 133,500 tons and carrying 3,954 passengers.

On-board style: bold, brash and buckets of fun – this is where American blue-collar workers let their hair down. Quality food and entertainment, though, and the kids' facilities are excellent.
Perfect for: party lovers of all ages, young families, singles on the razz.
Not for: those in search of a quiet life.
Holland America Line (www.hollandamerica. com) is also owned by Carnival Corporation. It is a Premium operator which currently has 14 ships. Vessels range from the medium-sized 55,451-ton/1,266-passenger *Maasdam* and

Enjoying the view from a Carnival stateroom balcony.

Veendam to the flagship, *Nieuw Statendam*, at 99,500 tons and 2,666 passengers.
On-board style: smart, fairly elegant and traditional – the on-board décor harks back to the line's Dutch origins and includes some genuine antiques.
Perfect for: older travelers, traditionalists.
Not for: party people or families outside school holidays (the line's older ships do not have many children's facilities).
Royal Caribbean International (www.royalcarib bean.com). Royal Caribbean's 26 ships range from the 24,077-ton/2,350-passenger *Majesty of the Seas* to the 228,081-ton/5,518-passenger *Symphony of the Seas*, with a slide that plummets through ten decks, surf simulators, a two-deck family suite, a zip-line and ice rink on board.

On-board style: attractive décor adds a touch of class to Royal Caribbean's mega-ships. The newest vessels have genuinely stunning features and have borrowed their yacht-like interiors from sister line Celebrity. Multiple dining options are available and Royal Caribbean's ships offer the fastest WiFi at sea.

Perfect for: families, sporty types, those who enjoy a lively atmosphere and anybody who enjoys big Broadway shows.

Not for: some older people, or the less mobile, who may find making their way round the huge ships a challenge.

'Central Park' aboard Oasis of the Seas.

⊘ CARGO VOYAGES

Many cargo ship lines keep a few cabins for passenger use, and these are worth considering as a really different way to sail around the Caribbean. You certainly won't be just one of a crowd; in fact, the ships carry so few passengers that you might feel more like a character in an Agatha Christie thriller. The downside is that the ships call at freight, not passenger, terminals (with few facilities) and sailing times are based on the rate at which cargo can be loaded and discharged – so there is no fixed schedule. London-based The Cruise People (tel: 020 7723 2450; www.cruisepeople.co.uk) is a market leader in this field, with worldwide contacts.

Celebrity Cruises (www.celebritycruises.com) is a sister brand of Royal Caribbean. It is a Premium line which has nine ships ranging in size from the tiny, 2,842-ton, 94-passenger *Xpedition* to the dazzling Celebrity Edge, 129,500 tons, carrying 2,900 people.

On-board style: elegance for big-ship lovers; the giant ships have top-grade suites and beautifully designed spas, while the older, smaller ships are less well equipped, but more cozy.

Perfect for: young(ish) high achievers who want to let their hair down; health fanatics; LGBT cruise fans

Not for: serious drinkers (as prices are high).

Princess Cruises (www.princess.com). This Carnival-owned, US-based line has 18 ships; its largest is the 143,700-ton/3,660-passenger *Sky Princess*.

On-board style: a British flair for organization combined with American pizzazz puts this Premium-class line a notch above. A clever buffet restaurant design means you rarely have to queue; the ships have a contemporary, sophisticated look; and a reputation for good food.

Perfect for: people who love the facilities of big ships but appreciate intimate spaces in which to hide away.

Not for: people who like to be spoon-fed (you'll be given a time and place for embarking on a tour, then it's up to you).

Norwegian Cruise Line (www.ncl.com). NCL operates 17 Contemporary ships ranging from the 75,338-ton/1,966-passenger *Norwegian Spirit* to the massive, 168,028-ton, 4,004-passenger *Norwegian Bliss*, launched in 2018.

On-board style: casual, relaxed and friendly, with a huge choice of lovely restaurants, attractive deck areas and good entertainment (including full-scale Broadway shows). Late check-out on disembarkation day is a rare – and real – boon to travelers facing transatlantic flights home. The lifestyle on board is casual, with no fixed dining times or strict dress codes, unless you still want to celebrate the more traditional style of cruising.

Perfect for: families, young couples, people who like to mix and enjoy big ships with style. NCL's newer ships have some of the best nightclubs at sea.

Not for: those who like formality.

Costa Cruises (www.costacruises.com). Another Carnival subsidiary, Contemporary-class Costa Cruises has 14 ships, ranging from the 53,000-ton/1,779-passenger *Costa NeoClassica*

to the 132,500-ton/4,947-passenger *Costa Dia-dema*. Costa ships have a distinctly European feel: the company was founded by Italians and has a strong following in Italy and other European countries. Costa offers a substantial range of winter Caribbean cruises, spanning eastern, western and southern routes.

On-board style: expect later meal times than on American-dominated ships, as well as livelier bars and cafés, lessons in Latino dances rather than the usual line dancing, and an international crew happy to let linguists practise on them (although English is the main on-board language).

Perfect for: Europhiles who enjoy a lively cosmopolitan atmosphere

Not for: those who like to dine in peace (Italian exuberance en masse can get *very* noisy); lovers of comedy – entertainment is dominated by magicians and singers, thus avoiding language problems with an international audience. Also, although there are children's clubs on board, Italian families rarely use them and the ships can get overrun with kids at busy holiday times.

Disney Cruise Line. The entertainment giant broke into cruising with the 83,338-ton/1,750-passenger *Disney Magic* in 1998, launching the sister-ship *Disney Wonder* a year later, followed by *Disney Dream* and *Disney Fantasy*. The ships are mainly Caribbean-based, sailing from Disney's own dedicated terminal at Florida's Port Canaveral, but also sail in Alaska and Europe. Cruises can be packaged to include stays at Disney's Florida resorts and – as you might imagine – children's facilities on board these floating theme parks are dazzling. However Disney has also gone all-out to attract child-free couples too, offering elegant restaurants and designating one swimming pool and particular areas of each ship as adults-only.

On-board style: elegance with a touch of Disney magic; the highlight of each ship is the Animator's Palate dining room, which goes from black and white to full-color as you dine.

Perfect for: families and Disney fans.

Not for: those not enamored of Mickey Mouse.

EUROPEAN LINES

US-owned ships may dominate the Caribbean but there are also plenty of options for travelers who prefer a more European feel.

MSC Cruises (www.msccruises.com) has become a major player. From small beginnings running older ships, the 18-ship line MSC has grown rapidly to operate some of the largest vessels afloat – such as the futuristic, 4,132-passenger MSC Seaside, with a new hull design featuring a broad promenade circling the ship for outdoor dining. All the newer vessels include an entire ship-within-a-ship in the Yacht Club: an exclusive area of suites, deck space and dining for those who want a big-ship atmosphere but the pampering of a luxury vessel. **Marella Cruises** www.tui.co.uk/cruise) operates six older, classic ships and features a decent Caribbean fly-cruise program in

Castaway Cay, the 1,000-acre (405-hectare) island that Disney Cruise Line guests can call their own.

winter, aimed exclusively at the UK market and using parent company TUI's huge charter airline to fly passengers from regional airports. Drinks are included on every cruise. **P&O Cruises** (www.pocruises.com) offers fly-cruises to the Caribbean on its two newest ships, *Azura* and *Britannia*, using Barbados and St Lucia as gateways (and therefore avoiding the necessary day at sea to reach the Caribbean islands from Florida) as well as round-trip cruises from Southampton on *Arcadia, Ventura* and *Aurora*.

Virgin Voyages (www.virginvoyages.com) is a new cruise line, backed by Richard Branson's Virgin Group, operating one ship, Scarlet Lady, with three more on order. Aimed at over-18s, the ship brings new meaning to cool and contemporary, with a tattoo parlor, multiple restaurants – all included in the price and one featuring a drag show – bottomless brunches, impressive gym and spa space and a promise of no buffets or set dining times.

CRUISES FROM UK PORTS

If you live in the UK and don't want to fly to an embarkation port, you'll find that some lines – including **P&O Cruises**, **Cunard Line** (www.cunard.com), Saga Cruises (travel.saga.uk) and **Fred. Olsen Cruise Lines** (www.fredolsencruises.com) have

The phenomenal sails needed to power the Star Clippers ships.

⊘ FIND YOUR ITINERARY

Different itineraries in the Caribbean suit different types. Lovers of swish yachtie bars and small ports should set a course for St-Barths, the BVI, the Grenadines or Martinique. Shopaholics can't go wrong in the USVI or Nassau in the Bahamas. Foodies will love Barbados, while golfers will enjoy any itinerary that takes in the Dominican Republic and Jamaica. For adventure and antiquities, the Central American ports are best. In the south and east Caribbean, Aruba has some of the loveliest beaches; Dominica is best for hiking and river tubing. For sheer dramatic scenery, the Pitons in St Lucia are hard to beat, while kids will love activities in Jamaica and the Cayman Islands.

sailings to the Caribbean from the UK, as does budget operator Cruise & Maritime Voyages (www.cruiseandmaritime.com), which operates long explorations to South America via the Caribbean. These cruises usually last at least three weeks, and so tend to attract a high proportion of retired people.

LUXURY SHIPS

If you have cash to splash on the finer things in life, try cruising the Caribbean aboard a luxury ship. Five-star operators include **Silversea Cruises** (www.silversea.com), **Seabourn Cruise Line** (www.seabourn.com), **SeaDream** (www.seadream.com) and **Regent Seven Seas Cruises** (www.rssc.com). All operate smallish deluxe vessels offering top-class cuisine and service, all-suite accommodation and all-inclusive prices. Also, the ships can usually get into the region's smaller, more exclusive ports.

Another five-star-plus operator is **Crystal Cruises** (www.crystalcruises.com), which offers similar service and facilities on somewhat larger ships. Expect spacious, elegant surroundings and a high standard of service. Crystal is the best of the luxury lines for families, with kids' clubs in the holidays.

Taking on the luxury lines from 2020 is the **Ritz-Carlton Yacht Collection**, with two ultra-luxury, all-suite yachts accommodating 298 passengers each. River cruise operator **Scenic** (www.scenicusa.com) has entered the luxury ocean cruise market, too, with a chic yacht, the 228-passenger *Scenic Eclipse*, complete with submarine and two helicopters.

Hapag Lloyd's Europa 2 (www.hl-cruises.com), one of the most luxurious ships afloat, also has a handful of 'international' sailings to the Caribbean, meaning that the language on board is English rather than German. The ship is stunning, with absolutely top-notch food, enormous amounts of deck space and beautiful cabins. It's not all-inclusive, though; you pay for drinks.

Oceania Cruises (www.oceaniacruises.com) is a Miami-based luxury operator pitched just below the ultra-luxury lines in price, focusing on the finest cuisine and in-depth exploration, but choosing not to go the all-inclusive route. Its six mid-sized ships have open-seating dining rooms and upmarket accommodation, and itineraries include some overnight stays. Oceania's big rival is Azamara Club Cruises (www.azamaraclubcruises.com), owned by Royal Caribbean and operating three ships from the same family as Oceania's smallest four, although completely different in style with a chic, contemporary look. Azamara also majors on destinations, with long stays in ports and an emphasis on fine food and wines, which are included in the price.

French-owned Ponant is a rapidly expanding line in the luxury market, with small, chic ships designed for expedition cruising, some of them based in the tropics. Infinity pools on deck and clever technology, such as an underwater viewing lounge and a retractable watersports platform, make these the ideal choice for anybody looking for an intimate environment with a French touch and an international passenger base.All these operators offer worldwide itineraries, including Caribbean sailings.

CULTURAL CARIBBEAN CRUISES

A handful of cruise operators fall into their own category, offering more in-depth exploration of the Caribbean region on mid-sized ships. Viking Cruises (www.vikingcruises.com) isbetter known for its river cruises, but has rapidly expanded from one ocean-going ship, *Viking Star*, to six. Viking's style is low-key, with beautiful, Scandinavian-influenced ships, smart spas, lovely deck spaces including infinity pools overlooking the stern, and excellent food. Wine is included, as are excursions in every port, and every cabin has a balcony, which is perfect for the Caribbean.

SAILING SHIPS

Windstar Cruises (www.windstarcruises.com), **Ponant** (www.ponant.com), **Sea Cloud Cruises** (www.seacloud.com) and **Star Clippers** (www.starclippers.com) all have sailing ships in the Caribbean for all or part of the year (although the Star Clippers and Sea Cloud ships are the only ones to genuinely sail – the others rely mainly on motor power). They are a popular option for people who want to be on the water but don't want the whole big-ship cruise experience. Star Clippers bases a ship in Cuba all winter, fulfilling growing demand for the island.

Windstar offers stylish, laid-back cruising on motor-assisted vessels, while on Star Clippers' tall-masted ships, passengers can learn the ropes by helping the crew hoist sails – only if they want to, of course. Similarly, the ultra-posh Sea Cloud attracts mainly Germans, but its gorgeous sailing ships also have an American following.

SMALL SHIP AND EXPEDITION VOYAGES

Although the Caribbean isn't the most likely part of the world for expedition cruising, a handful of lines operate very small, intimate ships, calling at islands overlooked by their bigger sisters. **Blount Small Ship Adventures** (www.blountsmallshipadventures.com) operates a couple of 96-passenger ships on some wonderful itineraries that take in the Out Islands of the Bahamas, or the smaller British Virgin Islands. British tour operator **Noble Caledonia** (www.noble-caledonia.co.uk) charters various ships and owns three, offering in-depth exploration of

The in-suite spa in Seven Seas Explorer's Regent Suite.

the region with no more than 116 fellow travellers. Wine with meals is included, as are all excursions. **Hurtigruten** (hurtigruten.com) offers a short season of Caribbean exploration on its expedition ships that are relocating from Antarctica to Europe for the summer.

REPOSITIONING CRUISES

While some ships spend all year in the Caribbean, others go there only for the winter months, spending the summer in the Mediterranean, the Baltic or Alaska. Joining them for what is called a repositioning, sailing to or from the Caribbean (flagged in the spring and autumn sections of brochures), is a good way to tour the region and enjoy a long-ish cruise on the cheap.

🔍 SHORE EXCURSIONS

Booking shore excursions will bump up the cost of your holiday, so it's important to understand the benefits and limitations of these brief snapshots of island culture.

One excursion in each port of call on a seven-day cruise could add more than US$500 to the overall cost of your cruise – so make sure you know what you're getting into.

Mexico's Chichén Itzá.

Shore excursions have improved dramatically as passengers become better traveled and more demanding. As the average age of the typical cruiser comes down, excursions have started to revolve more around activities – such as kayaking, hiking, mountain biking, horse riding and scuba diving. This type of 'soft adventure' is accessible to passengers of virtually all ages and fitness levels.

However, as Caribbean cruising typically involves big ships and big numbers, it is inevitable that you will feel regimented when 3,000 passengers pour down the gangway to a waiting fleet of coaches. If you want to travel at your own pace, mingle with the local people, sample street food and soak up the atmosphere, then you should do your own thing.

PROS AND CONS

Shore excursions are planned to give an overview of a destination or a taste of an activity, rather than a deep insight. You will travel by bus, usually (but not always) with an English-speaking group and guide, although some trips are by self-drive Jeeps – so remember to take your driving license.

Having to pre-book shore excursions before you depart, or as soon as you board the ship, takes away the spontaneity of visiting new places. Sadly, this is a fact of life; for the sake of logistics, numbers have to be finalized some days in advance. The daily on-board talks on shore excursions can be a heavy sell, but they do present an opportunity to ask questions.

The majority of cruise lines detail shore excursions on their websites, and you can book before joining the cruise. This means you'll get the tours you want, although there is no guarantee that they will operate, as a minimum number of participants has to be met. If a tour is canceled, you'll be accommodated on a different one, or your money will be refunded.

Sometimes, it is difficult to better a cruise line's excursion. Scuba diving is a case in point, as a diving tour will include all equipment and instruction, as well as transportation from the ship. Several lines now offer tailor-made excursions, including a chance to crew an America's Cup yacht in Philipsburg, Sint Maarten, in a mini-regatta; while the upscale lines have a concierge service to create individual excursions for those with deep pockets.

Some organized excursions, though, do seem pointless. At Nassau in the Bahamas, all the shops, most of the decent colonial architecture and the Straw Market are within easy walking distance of the port, yet cruise lines charge upwards of US$60 for a harbor cruise and tour of the grounds of the opulent Atlantis Hotel.

Dolphin 'encounters' are invariably disappointing. Typically, visitors find themselves standing waist deep in water while a solitary dolphin meanders around an enclosed area. A lot of beach excursions, too, are a waste of time, at up to US$50 for a morning on a beach – all you are paying for is the coach transfer.

Some of the better shore excursions in the Caribbean are the adventurous ones. Kayaking through the mangroves in Antigua, looking out for sea turtles and frigate birds; riding a horse across the highlands of Barbados; or hiking through the El Yunque rainforest in Puerto Rico. Perhaps the ultimate (and most expensive) trip is a descent to 800ft (240 meters) down the Cayman Wall in a research submarine (not to be confused with the tourist submarines, which dive to much shallower depths), to spot deep-water corals and deep-sea life. The excursion, offered by most of the big lines or bookable privately, costs several hundred dollars a head and must be arranged in advance since the sub only takes two people.

PLANNING YOUR OWN EXCURSION

When it comes to planning where to go, the shore excursion staff will be able to help, although they cannot be expected to have in-depth knowledge of every port. They will get their ground operator to arrange car rental, or a taxi or minibus with guide, and assist with itinerary planning. You can book cheaper excursions, too, with independent operators that mimic the cruise lines' offerings, among them Cruising Excursions (www.cruisingexcursions.com) and Viator (www.viator.com). Make sure you allow plenty of time to get back to the ship, as it won't wait if you are not on an official tour.

If your heart is set on something like tickets to a cricket match in Barbados, arrange it before you leave through a specialist operator. Don't be over-ambitious: You will have only a few hours and, if the ship is anchored outside the port, passengers on official excursions get priority for the tenders.

A taxi can make life easier. Always agree the fare before you depart and pay only when you are back at the ship. Don't misjudge the journey time back to the port. A ship will wait for a delayed tour bus, but not for a lost individual, and it is your responsibility (and expense) to rejoin the cruise at the next port.

Several Caribbean ports are perfect for self-guided tours. Take your own map as cruise lines often provide only rudimentary photocopies. In Bridgetown, Barbados, there are shops, galleries, markets and historic buildings a 15-minute walk from Deep Water Harbour, where ships moor up. The island is safe and easy to get around by car or Mini-Moke – but allow time for getting lost in the country lanes, and for the slow pace of traffic.

In busy, commercial St Thomas, hop onto a ferry to the beautiful beaches of St John. Grand Cayman is regarded as a model island in terms of safety, cleanliness and a hassle-free attitude. Curaçao's capital, Willemstad, with bright buildings and pavement cafés, is easy to explore on foot. Chic, celebrity-studded St-Barths can be explored in a day by hire car, or you can walk through the little town of Gustavia to beautiful Shell Beach, with no need for a car. In St Vincent, hike up Mount St Andrew, near Kingstown, for incredible bird life and views.

The fantastic scenery at El Yunque National Park, Puerto Rico.

Sometimes, though, DIY exploration is impractical. Car hire in Jamaica and St Lucia is expensive; distances are long and you may be hassled. If you don't want a coach trip, join forces with other passengers to book a minibus and enjoy the scenery rather than worrying about getting lost.

The coastline at Manzanillo, Costa Rica.

Watching the sunset, Caye Caulker, Belize.

INTRODUCTION

A guide to the most popular ports of call, with principal sites clearly cross-referenced by number to the maps.

Troupials, Curaçao.

The chain of islands that stretches from off the southern coast of Florida to the northern shores of South America is a diverse and fascinating place to visit. Add a warm climate cooled by trade winds and you have almost perfect cruising conditions. The proximity of the Caribbean islands to each other makes them ideal ports of call for cruise ships, many of which attempt to take their passengers to paradise and back in just seven days.

Whether you want to slap on the sun lotion, read a good book and bask in the sun, discover pristine coral reefs and shipwrecks, hike through a rainforest or explore Maya ruins, a Caribbean cruise can give you a taste of all of these things and more.

The Places section aims to cover the most popular ports of call which make up the three most typical Caribbean cruise routes: western, eastern and southern. The following chapters have practical advice about making the most of your time ashore and include attractions in the Caribbean as well as Bermuda and the Bahamas, Mexico and Central America, which are all often included on Caribbean cruise itineraries.

A western cruise route almost always begins in Florida and offers the ideal itinerary for reaching some of the best dive sites in the western hemisphere: in Belize, Honduras and the Cayman Islands. Dry-land excursions include the Maya ruins of Chichén Itzá in Mexico and Tikal in Guatemala.

View from Temple IV, panorama of Gran Plaza, Tikal, Guatemala.

An eastern itinerary takes travelers to the Bahamas, with its collection of private islands, and to Spanish-influenced Puerto Rico and the shopping hotspot of St Thomas.

The southern cruise route is where you'll find some of the best beaches as well as picturesque towns in the British Virgin Islands, dense rainforests and the dramatic Trafalgar Falls in Dominica, and the spectacular peaks that are symbols of St Lucia – the Pitons. Only the small ships can reach the 30 or so unspoilt islands and cays in the Grenadines. Often the final stop on this route is Aruba or Curaçao, just off the north coast of Venezuela, offering a taste of the Dutch colonial influences in the region.

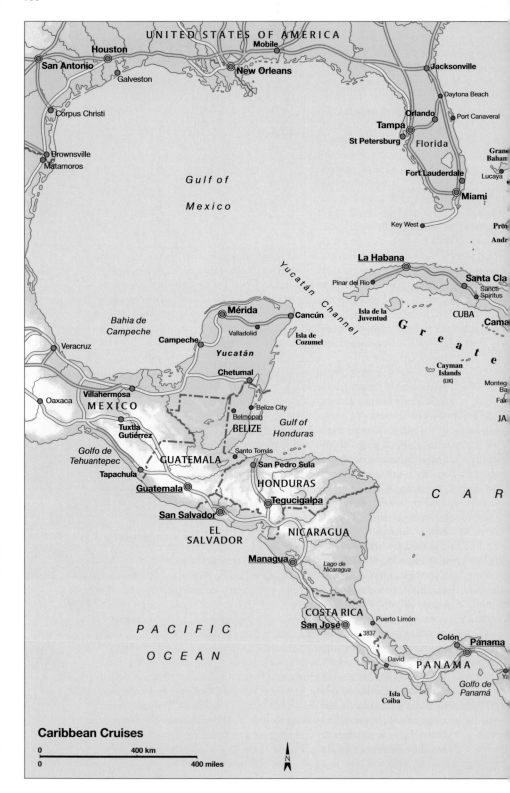

UNITED STATES OF AMERICA

Houston
San Antonio
Galveston
Mobile
New Orleans
Jacksonville
Daytona Beach
Corpus Christi
Orlando
Port Canaveral
Tampa
St Petersburg
Florida
Grane
Baham
Brownsville
Matamoros
Fort Lauderdale
Lucaya
Miami

Gulf of

Mexico

Key West
Proy
Andr

La Habana
Pinar del Rio
Santa Cla
Sancti-
Spiritus

Yucatán Channel

Mérida
Cancún
Isla de la
Juventud
CUBA
Cama
Bahia de
Campeche
Campeche
Valladolid
Isla de
Cozumel
Yucatán
G
r
e
a
t
e
Veracruz
Cayman
Islands
(UK)
Monteg
Ba
Chetumal
Fal
Oaxaca
Villahermosa
Belize City
JA
MEXICO
Belmopan
Gulf of
Honduras
Tuxtla
Gutiérrez
BELIZE
Golfo de
Tehuantepec
Santo Tomás
GUATEMALA
Tapachula
San Pedro Sula
Guatemala
HONDURAS
C A R
San Salvador
Tegucigalpa
EL
SALVADOR
NICARAGUA
Managua
Lago de
Nicaragua

COSTA RICA
Puerto Limón
San José
▲3837
Colón
Panama
PACIFIC
David
PANAMA
Ya

OCEAN
Golfo de
Panamá
Isla
Coiba

Caribbean Cruises

| 0 | 400 km |
| 0 | 400 miles |

N

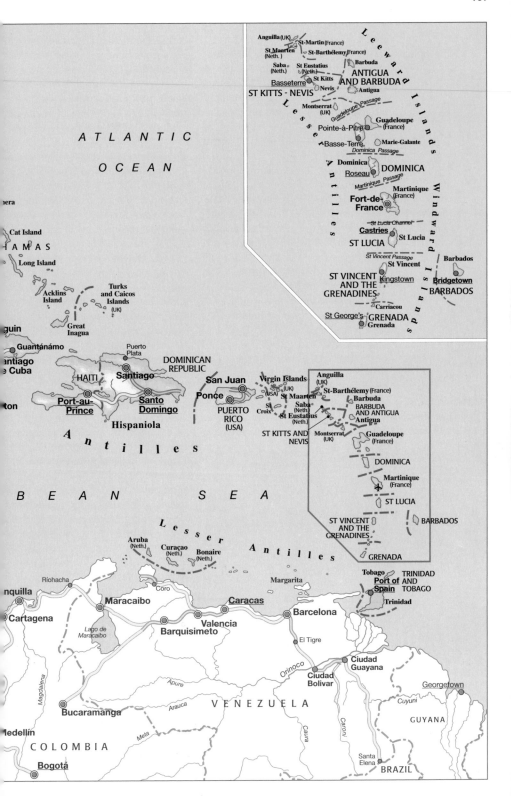

Anguilla (UK)
St-Martin (France)
St Maarten (Neth.)
St-Barthélemy (France)
Saba (Neth.)
St Eustatius (Neth.)
Barbuda
ANTIGUA AND BARBUDA
St Kitts
Basseterre
Nevis
ST KITTS - NEVIS
Antigua

Leeward Islands

Montserrat (UK)
Guadeloupe Passage
Guadeloupe (France)
Pointe-à-Pitre
Basse-Terre
Marie-Galante
Dominica Passage

Dominica
Roseau
DOMINICA

Martinique Passage
Martinique (France)
Fort-de-France

Windward Islands

St Lucia Channel
Castries
St Lucia
ST LUCIA

St Vincent Passage
St Vincent
Barbados
ST VINCENT AND THE GRENADINES
Kingstown
Bridgetown
BARBADOS

Carriacou
St George's
GRENADA
Grenada

A n t i l l e s
L e s s e r

A T L A N T I C

O C E A N

era

Cat Island

B A M A S

Long Island

Acklins Island

Turks and Caicos Islands (UK)

Great Inagua

guin

Guantánamo
Puerto Plata
DOMINICAN REPUBLIC

antiago e Cuba

HAITI
Santiago
San Juan
Virgin Islands
Anguilla (UK)
St-Barthélemy (France)

ton
Port-au-Prince
Santo Domingo
Ponce
(USA) (UK)
St Maarten
(Neth.)
Saba
(Neth.)
Barbuda
BARBUDA AND ANTIGUA
Antigua

Hispaniola
St Croix
PUERTO RICO (USA)
St Eustatius (Neth.)
ST KITTS AND NEVIS
Montserrat (UK)
Guadeloupe (France)

DOMINICA

Martinique (France)
ST LUCIA

ST VINCENT AND THE GRENADINES
BARBADOS

GRENADA

A n t i l l e s

B E A N   **S E A**

L e s s e r   *A n t i l l e s*

Aruba (Neth.)
Curaçao (Neth.)
Bonaire (Neth.)

Riohacha
Coro
Margarita
Tobago
TRINIDAD AND TOBAGO
Port of Spain

nquilla

Cartagena
Maracaibo
Caracas
Barcelona
Trinidad

Lago de Maracaibo
Valencia
Barquisimeto
El Tigre

Ciudad Guayana

Magdalena

Bucaramanga
Apure
Orinoco
Ciudad Bolívar
Georgetown

Arauca
Cuyuni
V E N E Z U E L A

Medellín
Meta
Caura
Caroni
GUYANA

C O L O M B I A

Bogotá
Santa Elena
BRAZIL

Cayman Island diving.

CHOOSING A ROUTE

The tastes and interests of cruise passengers are diverse and the choice of trips can be confusing. This chapter offers advice on how to identify the cruise itinerary that will suit you best.

If all you want to do is eat, sleep and indulge in the luxurious amenities found on most cruise ships, it doesn't matter all that much which route you take. But if your goals are more specific, the route you choose can matter a great deal.

Have you always dreamed of scuba diving along the Cayman Trench? Would you like to climb an ancient pyramid? Pay homage to Bob Marley's music? Mingle with the Carib Indians? Sprawl out on a deserted beach? See where Nobel Prize-winning authors Derek Walcott and V.S. Naipaul grew up? Swim with dolphins? Explore Dutch architecture? Sip afternoon tea on the veranda of a Great House? Ride jet-skis at full throttle? Attend services at the oldest synagogue in the Caribbean? Savor the exotic blooms of a tropical garden? Take in a cricket match? Wander around Empress Josephine's childhood home? Shop for a diamond-studded Rolex watch?

If any of these are on your list of things you'd like to do while on a Caribbean cruise, it's a good idea to read the glossy cruise brochures very carefully in order to determine which destinations are the most suitable.

Many companies and ships offer the same routes because they have already proved successful with millions of passengers. Logistically, most of these tried-and-tested itineraries make sense when you consider the geographic proximity of the islands involved. Even so, different cruises sailing on the same routes can vary enormously, and aside from specific activities or sites, there are a few important points to consider when choosing a route.

SPECIFICS TO CONSIDER

In an effort to pack more excursions into a shorter period of time, some cruise lines offer a different port of call

Canyoning in Jamaica.

The Adenium obesum, otherwise known as the desert rose.

Strolling in paradise, on the Grenadian coast.

every day. While these routes may be good for first-time visitors to the Caribbean who want to see as much of the region as they can, other passengers may find them overwhelming – if it's Tuesday it must be Trinidad, and so on. Although island-hopping like this can be stimulating and fun, it leaves little time to get to know a specific port of call. Memories of such a port-packed cruise can wind up being one big blur. They can also leave you feeling you need another week to recover from the trip once you get home.

How much time is spent in each port is an important factor. Does the shore excursion give a full day on the island, or just a few hours? If it's just a few hours and there's something you really want to see, you could wind up spending more time looking at your watch than at the sites in the port. Along with the number of hours allotted for the port, whether the ship actually docks at the pier or has to anchor offshore and ferry passengers to shore will affect the amount of time available for exploring the destination.

Once in the port, does the cruise line offer a decent range of excursions? Prearranged trips are headache-free and are the most efficient way to explore a port of call, but they can be expensive. Also, if you are going to sign up for a land excursion, you need to know if it includes some free time built into the schedule to allow you to wander around on your own, or to go to the beach.

Another good thing to ask is how many full days at sea the itinerary includes. Most Caribbean cruises have at least one day when you see nothing but the sea. A few have two or three full days at sea. For some people, spending a whole day and night at sea with no port diversions is a calm and relaxing experience. For others, it can seem monotonous, although in reality it's the best time to unwind under the Caribbean sun.

The type of islands the cruise visits is something else to consider. Do you want a route that takes in the smaller countries of the eastern and southern Caribbean, the larger ones of the

western Caribbean, or a little bit of both? Do you want a route that takes in the most popular and most visited ports such as Nassau, St Thomas and San Juan? Or do you want one that visits quirky, off-the-beaten-track islands such as Dominica, Bequia and Tobago?

Lastly, there is the most important question to ask yourself when deciding on an itinerary: What would you like to see?

BEST BEACHES

Trying to devise a 'best beaches list' often leads to heated debates, but there are a few gems that most people agree upon. On Eastern Shores cruises some of the prettiest stretches of sand include Gold Rock Beach in Freeport, Cable Beach in Nassau, Harbour Island near Eleuthera, Puerto Rico's Luquillo Beach, Trunk Bay and Francis Bay in St John, Orient Beach and Baie Longue in St-Martin, Buck Island in St Croix, and the beaches of Maria La Gorda in Cuba.

Western Shores favorites are Negril Beach and Doctor's Cave in Jamaica, Seven Mile Beach in Grand Cayman,

Smathers Beach in Key West, Labadee (which is Royal Caribbean and Celebrity Cruises' 'private' beach) in Haiti, Ambergris Caye in Belize, Playa San Francisco and Playa del Carmen in Mexico, and Key Biscayne in Miami.

On the southern routes, top spots include Grand Anse in Grenada, the Platinum Coast in western Barbados, Cane Garden Bay in Tortola, St Jean Beach in St-Barths, Half Moon Bay in Antigua, Anse Tarare in Guadeloupe, Grand Anse des Salines in Martinique, Palm Beach and Eagle Beach in Aruba, Pink Beach and Sorobon Beach in Bonaire, and almost all the pristine beaches in tiny Tobago.

TROPICAL GARDENS

Along with strolling on beaches, smelling the exotic floral scents of a tropical garden is another luscious treat, and several Caribbean islands have world-famous botanical treasures. Among the prettiest is Martinique's Jardin de Balata in the hills outside Fort-de-France, where footpaths meander around giant ferns, lotus ponds and sweet-smelling

Jardin de Balata, Martinique.

ylang-ylang trees. In Barbados, Andromeda Gardens is widely known for its variety of orchids, heliconias and cacti. St Vincent's Botanical Garden is said to be the oldest in the western hemisphere, and contains a breadfruit tree supposedly planted by Captain Bligh. Bath Garden in Jamaica dates back to the mid-1700s, when it was established by British colonials. The Bahamas has The Retreat in Nassau and Garden Groves in Freeport. And Puerto Rico's Jardín Botánico, just outside bustling San Juan, holds one of the most extensive collections of tropical plants in the world.

GREAT SNORKELING AND SCUBA SITES

You can do scuba diving on a cruise, sometimes from the ship on small-ship cruises although more often, on an excursion. When diving is offered, it's in conjunction with a local operator for the simple reason that they are experts in the area. If you intend to do a lot of diving in the Caribbean, it's much better to get certified before you leave

Choose the Cayman Islands for an unbeatable snorkeling experience.

home. Or you could content yourself with snorkeling; several cruise lines carry equipment on board and there is no shortage of opportunity.

Considered by many to be the best snorkeling experience not just in the Caribbean, but in the world – Grand Cayman's Stingray City is top of the list for cruise stops because of its easy-to-access shoal, surrounded by friendly rays. Grand Cayman also has hundreds of official scuba diving sites where the steep drop-off of the Cayman Trench, along with dozens of sunken ships, provide some fascinating underwater adventures.

Saba has some of the finest diving in the area with about 40 official dive sites marked by black coral, underwater lava flows and a vibrant assortment of marine life. Regularly voted one of the top dive spots in the world, the waters off of St Croix provide dramatic underwater trails full of brilliantly colored coral canyons. Nearby Trunk Bay on St John is also noted for its calm aquamarine waters and a 225yd (205-meter) snorkeling trail, where underwater signs explain the resident marine life.

Other locations that regularly make it onto lists of best Caribbean dive sites include Palancar Reef and the Chankanab Lagoon near Cozumel; Blue Hole off Belize; Mary's Place near Roatán in Honduras; Town Pier off Bonaire; the famed wreck of HMS *Rhone* in Virgin Gorda; the *Bianca C* wreck off Grenada; Pinnacles off St Lucia; Mushroom Forest off Curaçao; and Ambergris Caye off the coast of Belize.

Other excellent snorkeling sites include the calm waters that surround Antigua, the shallow waters of Buccoo Reef in Tobago, the entire French side of St-Martin, Coki Point Beach in St Thomas, the Curaçao Underwater Park, Shoal Bay East off Anguilla, and the Baths off Virgin Gorda. If your ship calls at Tobago Cays (confusingly, in the Grenadines), do not miss the opportunity to snorkel in some of the clearest water imaginable.

RETAIL THERAPY

If it's shopping opportunities you are after, several Caribbean ports are known for their mega-shopping malls with duty-free stores full of brand-name goods. Typical items on sale in these modern enclaves include fine jewelry, watches, camera equipment, nautical maps and antiques, china, perfume, linen, clothing, leather goods, woodcarvings, local art and crafts, cigars and alcohol.

American shoppers often favor the Virgin Islands since the US Government allows its citizens to bring US$1,600 worth of goods home tax-free (from other islands the amount is US$800). Puerto Rico is also a great place for American shoppers because it levies no taxes on goods taken into the US.

With more stores than any other Caribbean island, St Thomas is shopping heaven. In the capital, Charlotte Amalie, countless boutiques offer brand-name goods at discount prices (it's advisable to know the cost of things at home to ensure you are getting a good deal). When several ships are in at once, though, the atmosphere can be hectic, and the chances of negotiating lower prices are slim.

Shopping in Christiansted, US Virgin Islands.

⊙ Tip

Molas make great purchases. They are a kind of intricate patchwork made by the Kuna Amerindians of Panama.

Grand Cayman also has a good shopping district, with hundreds of first-rate stores surrounding the port. Although many of the products sold here are quite expensive, they are usually of excellent quality, and the country has no sales tax. In the Bahamas, Freeport's International Bazaar features over 100 shops with vendors from around the world. Aruba and Curaçao are noted for a wide assortment of Dutch products, and the Dutch side of Sint Maarten offers some of the best discounts on European products in the Caribbean. In Martinique and Guadeloupe, French wines, food products and perfumes are abundant. St Lucia has a big duty-free shopping center for cruise passengers at Pointe Seraphine in Castries, selling perfumes, crystal, china, jewelry, cigars and clothing, as well as wood carvings and other local arts and crafts in more than 20 stores.

If collecting locally made arts and crafts is one of your holiday goals, there are a few things to look out for. San Juan is noted for its colorful carnival masks that look great on walls,

and Haiti is good for metal sculptures and primitive paintings. Batik fabrics are plentiful in Jamaica and Martinique. The finest straw baskets and hats, laboriously plaited by hand, can be found in the Bahamas. The best wood sculptures are made in Jamaica. Miniature model boats with minute, detailed work are made in St Vincent and the Grenadines.

The Dominican Republic is the place to buy amber, the honey-coloured gem that is turned into jewelry and trinkets by local artisans, since it is one of the few places in the world with a natural supply. In Saba, an intricate thread-knotting technique produces Saba lace, a trademark souvenir of this tiny Dutch island. The San Blas Islands of Panama and the port of Colón near the Panama Canal are noted for bold and beautiful embroidered *molas*. And in just about any port in Mexico you will find Taxco silver jewellery, clay pottery, hand-painted tiles and dishes, embroidered blouses, wool blankets and naturally dyed textiles.

Remember that the cruise ships themselves also have duty free stores, so if you're after a particular style of jewelry or a watch, price it on the ship as well as ashore.

PRIVATE ISLANDS

If the idea of shoulder-to-shoulder crowds makes you cringe, choosing a route that visits a private island is the solution. Most cruise lines have at least one private beach, an environment free of the hassles found in most commercial ports. The advantage of a private island is that passengers have it to themselves and everything from food to watersports is laid on.

Just about all of the private getaways offer a beach, lounge chairs, swimming, snorkeling, volleyball, hire of sailing boats and jet-skis, children's play areas with supervised activities, ice-cold alcoholic drinks and a gourmet picnic lunch. Some also provide live calypso or

Disney's self-contained Castaway Cay.

reggae music and the opportunity to buy goods made by local vendors.

Mostly found on routes to the Bahamas and the eastern Caribbean, private island choices include Disney Cruise Lines' Castaway Cay in the Bahamas, Costa Cruises' Catalina Island off of the Dominican Republic, Royal Caribbean's Coco Cay in the Bahamas and Labadee in Haiti (shared with sister line Celebrity Cruises), Princess Cruises' Princess Cays in the southern part of the island of Eleuthera, and Great Stirrup Cay in the Bahamas, used by both NCL and Holland America. NCL also has a new private beach in Belize, called Harvest Caye.

One note of caution: Most private getaways are reached by tender, which means that they are occasionally skipped due to bad weather or choppy seas – be prepared for this possible disappointment.

HISTORY AND ARCHITECTURE

Although nature provides most of the best scenery on Caribbean cruises, there are destinations where history and man's mark on the landscape play the main roles in the local story. Some of the oldest and most dramatic sites can be found in Mexico, where the ancient Maya cities of Tulum and Chichén Itzá provide a vivid history lesson on pre-Columbian life.

Old San Juan in Puerto Rico and Santo Domingo in the Dominican Republic are the places to go for Spanish colonial architecture and history. Both have great bastions of defence in the form of old brick forts and arsenals, as well as grand Spanish-style mansions, relics from the age of Juan Ponce de León and Christopher Columbus, ancient cathedrals and excellent museums.

On the islands formerly colonized by the British, where sugar plantations once provided wealth for the settlers, many historic Great Houses still stand. Among the more interesting are St Nicholas Abbey and Sunbury Plantation House in Barbados, Rose Hall and Greenwood Great House in Jamaica, Montpelier Great House in Nevis, and Pedro St James in Grand Cayman. The French-colonized islands also have

Snorkeling is an activity offered by just about all of the private island getaways.

⊘ SAFETY AND SECURITY

While the vast majority of Caribbean vacations, on cruise ships and in hotels, pass without incident, there have been some high-profile tragedies in recent years: Cruise ship passengers were murdered in the US Virgin Islands and on Antigua, the consequence being that cruise lines pulled out of each destination, although they did return eventually. The crimes have raised all kinds of ethical questions about tourism in the region, and whether not all islanders welcome wealthy cruise passengers who flaunt their money and, in the opinion of locals, contribute little to their economy.

Does this mean that the Caribbean is dangerous? Not necessarily, although passengers should be vigilant in areas known for social unrest – the USVI murder came as a result of being caught in the crossfire of gang warfare, while Jamaica is also notorious for its social problems. If in doubt, stick to the cruise ship's tours, rather than going it alone in a taxi. It's also probably better not to stray alone from busy beaches, and to avoid ostentatious displays of wealth in areas that are clearly underprivileged. But keep these crimes in perspective, tragic though they are: hundreds of thousands of cruise passengers return from the Caribbean with very happy memories of their interaction with local people and of their time on the islands.

⊙ Tip

Don't forget to pack sturdy walking shoes and waterproofs if you plan to hike through a rainforest such as Puerto Rico's El Yunque. Take a pair of jeans for a horseback riding excursion, and hard-wearing sneakers to protect your feet if you want to climb Dunn's River Falls in Jamaica.

Great Houses – two of the most beautiful are Habitation La Grange in Martinique and Maison Zevalos in Guadeloupe.

Other enclaves redolent of past times include the buildings in the old city of Willemstad in Curaçao, which are reminiscent of Amsterdam; Nelson's Dockyard National Park in Antigua; the ruins of Port Royal in Jamaica; El Morro, the imposing fortress in Havana; and the ancient stone carvings – petroglyphs – executed by the Amerindians around AD 300 in Guadeloupe.

POPULAR SHORE EXCURSIONS

Trying to rate shore excursions is difficult as it is often a matter of taste and interests, but there are a few in the Caribbean that rate as universal favorites.

The Xcaret Ecological Park near Playa del Carmen, Mexico, is a Disneyesque destination in itself where you can fill a whole day with swimming, snorkeling, water rides, dolphin encounters and ancient Maya games. There is so much to do and see that passengers are often exhausted (but happy) when they return to the ship.

Excursions that offer rides on the Atlantis submarines – in Barbados, Grand Cayman, Aruba and St Thomas – are always thrilling, informative and fun. A tour of the Carib Territory in Dominica gives visitors a chance to interact with the only real 'natives' left in the Caribbean. Excursions to Puerto Rico's El Yunque rainforest, one of the most beautiful in the world, allow passengers to experience the lush, cool and extremely wet interior of a tropical island.

A trip to Jamaica's Dunn's River Falls, near the port of Ocho Rios, usually amazes visitors, giving them the best photo opportunity of their entire holiday. A side-trip to the town of Hell, in Grand Cayman, provides a good laugh and is the best place in the Caribbean from which to send postcards home or take pictures for Instagram.

Bicycle excursions in Bonaire, where the flat landscape is dotted with wild flowers and pink flamingos, are a delight for athletic nature lovers. Wandering around the Hato Caves in Curaçao, where there's a maze of grottos filled with stalactites, makes

Bonaire's striking pink flamingos.

a surprisingly offbeat Caribbean tour. In St Lucia, a visit to the world's only 'drive-in volcano,' near the city of Castries, affords passengers close-up views of a lava-filled crater and a thoroughly bizarre experience. Last of all, there are excursions that take passengers horseback-riding on a beach – in Jamaica, St Lucia, St Thomas, Barbados, Tortola, St Martin or Aruba – which is often the perfect land-based antidote to several days at sea.

LONGER VOYAGES/ ROUTE ROUNDUP

The exact cruise routes and ship allocations vary from year to year according to fashion, demand for destinations and the location of ships. Broadly speaking, this is how it works:

Winter is the busy season in the Caribbean, when practically all cruise lines have ships there. A large number of these leave in spring and cross the Atlantic for Europe, where they'll stay until October, or head through the Panama Canal, west and north to Alaska. Ships still sail in the Caribbean through the summer months, but as a rule, only those on the regular short hops that are operated year-round by the big lines.

Those lines with a year-round presence in the region include Carnival, Royal Caribbean, NCL and Disney, offering three- to seven-night cruises out of Florida (Miami, Fort Lauderdale, Tampa or Port Canaveral), calling at mainstream ports such as the US Virgin Islands, Nassau, Cozumel and Sint Maarten. The bulk of passengers are American, as well as Brits looking for bargain prices, as rates are keen in this low season.

From October/November onwards, it's a different story. Ships of all sizes are based in the region, sailing from the big Florida ports as well as smaller ones such as San Juan, Barbados or Montego Bay. Itineraries vary from the regular seven-night runs to long, detailed explorations of smaller islands, and point-to-point cruises (where you fly to one island and fly home from another – for example, Barbados to Aruba). There are also voyages that have come through the Panama Canal into the Caribbean, or start in Florida and do the Caribbean before heading for the Canal, or incorporate a few Caribbean ports into a South American itinerary. As winter is also peak season for South America, a lot of ships will work their way right round the continent, with Caribbean cruises at either end of their season there.

World cruises, too, often take in parts of the Caribbean, and you can book a sector on one of these. Because a ship on a world cruise has a lot of distance to cover, a Caribbean sector may not be as port-intensive as a seven-nighter out of Miami, so expect fewer islands and more days at sea.

Christmas and New Year is a busy time in the Caribbean, with many ships celebrating, decked out with decorations and even, in the case of Disney

Jamaica's Dunn's River Falls.

Yucatán birdlife.

Turquoise idyll, Turks and Caicos.

Cruise Line, fake snow falling on Castaway Cay, its private island. Some lines celebrate a more secular version of Christmas, while others (mainly the British ones) include carol singing, Santa visits and church services. Others have Hanukkah services. If you do book a Christmas cruise, expect to spend Christmas day at sea, rather than in port.

Other types of Caribbean cruise include repositioning voyages. When the seasons change – in April/May and October/November – and cruise ships move from their winter to their summer cruising areas (or vice versa) there are bargains to be had as these long cruises, with several days spent at sea, are less popular. You'll only get a couple of Caribbean ports at best, as the object of the cruise is to get from A to B as quickly as possible, but there are advantages.

Firstly, there's the price. Secondly, a repositioning from the Caribbean (as opposed to a port much further north, like New York) takes a long route across the Atlantic, meaning you'll get as much as two weeks at sea – a great chance to relax. Even more special is a transatlantic on one of the sailing ships, such as those of Star Clippers, when you really do get a sense of the vastness of the ocean once the balmy Caribbean waters have been left behind. Thirdly, thanks to the advantageous pricing, a repositioning could mean a fortnight on a ship far more luxurious than you would normally have considered. Finally, for quite a few people with time to spare, it's a way of creating a long vacation at a reasonable price: for example, book the repositioning from Europe and stay on board for the first cruise of the Caribbean season.

ROUND-UP OF THE ROUTES

A short, three- or four-day western Caribbean cruise from Miami, Fort Lauderdale or Port Canaveral would typically call at a couple of ports such as Key West and Cozumel, with a day at sea. Grand Cayman and Cozumel is another possible combination. Longer western Caribbean routes, from seven to nine days, would also normally include one of the Jamaican ports, or Costa Maya, or a combination of Belize, Roatán (Honduras) and the Cayman Islands.

A mini-cruise to the Bahamas from the same ports could reach Nassau, Freeport and the cruise line's private island – many of these are small Bahamian islands – in three or four days (mini-cruises usually have a day at sea to encourage passengers to spend money on board). Ships operating a Bahamas cruise from further north – Baltimore or New York, say – will spend longer at sea, usually two days, to reach the tropics.

The eastern Caribbean is further from the American home ports so tends to attract seven-day itineraries, which might include a stop in the Bahamas (Nassau or private island), the US Virgin Islands, San Juan (Puerto

Rico), Grand Turk (Turks and Caicos) and Sint Maarten. Longer cruises also reach Antigua and Tortola (BVI).

Southern Caribbean cruises need to be longer if they're departing from Florida ports, although many will embark in San Juan (Puerto Rico) or Barbados. Islands on the southern route include the USVI, the BVI, Dominica, St Lucia, St Kitts and Nevis, Sint Maarten (or, for smaller ships, the posh French side, St-Martin), St Vincent and the Grenadines. Some ships head further south still and skim the north coast of the South American continent, calling at Aruba, Bonaire and Curaçao, or Margarita island.

Longer cruises – 10 nights or more – from Florida or the southern US ports might circle the Caribbean, cruising south and east, taking in eight or nine islands.

It's important to remember, though, that, with so many Caribbean cruise permutations available, you can almost always find what you want. One of the increasingly popular no-fly cruises from the UK to the Caribbean will take around 23 nights. There will be one stop in the Atlantic in each direction – usually Madeira or the Azores – and then five days in each direction crossing the Atlantic. Typically, five or six eastern or southern Caribbean ports are included in these itineraries.

There's also a huge selection of 'roaming' Caribbean itineraries on the smaller ships – lines such as SeaDream, Fred. Olsen Cruises, Seabourn and more – which don't have a home base in the region, but operate point-to-point itineraries. These are often the most unusual and interesting, and may include Cuba, Guadaloupe (and Iles des Saintes), Martinique, St-Barths, the Dominican Republic and even Anguilla, Saba and Montserrat. What's more, ships on world cruises may include a Caribbean segment, which might allow you to board on the West Coast, transit the Panama Canal, sail around the Caribbean and fly home. For these more complex itineraries, the advice of a good travel agent is invaluable.

Gabled houses Dutch-style in Aruba's capital, Oranjestad.

Accessible on a mini-cruise – the Bahamas.

SAILING THE WESTERN SHORES

Western Shores cruises offer a fascinating first taste of the region – ideal for people to see if they'll enjoy cruising, or those who have time only for a short break.

Sailing through the Caribbean and the Gulf of Mexico, Western Shores cruises don't take in a great many countries, but the ones they do visit offer a condensed and varied introduction to the diverse cultures, histories and landscapes of the region. Occasionally, they also offer the added bonus of stopping at Central American ports of call, which can be a distinctly different experience from the traditional West Indian destinations of the eastern or southern Caribbean.

With departures from Miami, Fort Lauderdale, Tampa, Port Canaveral, New Orleans (which has undergone considerable redevelopment since being destroyed by Hurricane Katrina in 2005), and Galveston, western Caribbean cruises don't travel as far as the eastern or southern Caribbean ones, and so tend to last for a week or less. This makes them perfect for first-time cruisers who want to test the waters but don't have many days to spare – or who are concerned about possible seasickness. Luckily, the waters in this area are almost always placid and clear.

The western Caribbean itinerary tends to appeal more (although not exclusively) to American vacationers, because it takes in ports that are more developed, more commercial and have far more modern amenities than many of the smaller Caribbean islands. However, more developed and more commercial also means more Americanized, so west Caribbean cruises may not appeal to people wanting to get away from areas of mass tourism.

Another thing to take into account when choosing a western Caribbean route is that this route does not offer the French West Indian flavor found in places such as Martinique, Guadeloupe, St-Barths or St Martin. Nor does it have any Dutch Caribbean components. A few of the cruise lines – Royal Caribbean in particular – call into the Haitian port of Labadee, a private little beach usually

Diving at Key Largo.

Marking the spot of the southernmost point in the US, Key West.

described in brochures as being in Hispaniola (which contains both Haiti and the Dominican Republic). But Labadee is a protected and exclusive enclave leased by the cruise line, and doesn't offer much opportunity for interacting with the Haitian people or culture.

WESTERN DELIGHTS

The Western Caribbean still has plenty to offer, however: awesome Maya Indian ruins, a stunning barrier reef, breathtaking waterfalls, sugar-fine sand beaches, towering mountains, exotic gardens, colonial history, designer goods at duty-free prices, championship golf courses, funky tropical architecture, arts and crafts, the lilting rhythms of reggae, smooth Caribbean rum, potent Mexican tequila and a chance to mail a postcard from a tiny town called Hell.

KEY WEST

The specific routes described here are determined by which ports the ships depart from, but most Western Caribbean cruises take in very similar ports of call. Starting off in the US, at the

The Half Shell Raw Bar in Old Port, Key West.

southern tip of the Florida Keys chain, is Key West. Although it is not, of course, a Caribbean island, Key West has a definite Caribbean mentality and atmosphere. In fact, the city once jokingly tried to secede from the US and declare itself the Conch Republic of Key West. It provides a gentle introduction to the more foreign destinations soon to come.

With a modern port near the historic Old Town area, Key West is easy to explore and is full of offbeat museums, gingerbread architecture, literary history and eccentric characters. Aside from wandering around on foot, organized shore excursions of the city usually include a narrated trolley tour that stops at the Ernest Hemingway House, the Key West Aquarium, the Mel Fisher Maritime Heritage Museum – a brick fort dating back to the American Civil War – and the Key West City Cemetery, where several tombstones are proof that the local people have a sense of humor: one reads, 'I told you I was sick'!

The next stop across the sea from Key West is Cuba and the town has a great deal of Cuban history of its own. A

⊘ TEXAS AND LOUISIANA

Several companies, including Carnival, Royal Caribbean and Disney, offer cruises from the Port of Galveston (tel: 409-765-9321; www.portof-galveston.com) on the Gulf of Mexico. Itineraries usually include Mexico, Belize, Honduras, the Cayman Islands and Jamaica. Galveston is popular with American passengers who prefer not to fly to Florida to start their trip. Within walking distance from the port is the historic Strand District, with architecture listed on the National Register, and plenty of shops, restaurants and bars too. The Galveston Island Trolley is a good way to see the town: stops include the cruise terminal and the Silk Stocking Historic District. The Port of Houston has fared less well; as it's located inland, with a long canal journey to get to the open sea, and is often fog-bound, cruise lines dropped it altogether in the spring of 2016.

The Port of New Orleans (tel: 504-522 2551; www.portnola.com) is fully operational following extensive rebuilding to repair the damage caused by Hurricane Katrina. Carnival, NCL and Royal Caribbean base ships here. The Julia Street Cruise Ship Terminal is conveniently located within walking distance of the French Quarter. Most cruises head for the Western Shores, especially Mexico's Yucatán Peninsula; while river cruise lines head inland, up the Mississippi River.

wealth of art, antiques, maps and arti- facts relating to the island are on dis- play at the city's San Carlos Institute.

MEXICO AND CENTRAL AMERICA

About 500 miles (800km) southwest of Key West is the jewel in the crown of most Western Shores cruises – Mexico. The country's Yucatán Peninsula has several world-famous ports – Cozumel, Playa del Carmen, Costa Maya – that are extremely popular on this route. Along with the ancient Maya cities of Tulum and Chichén Itzá, where stone pyramids stand as somber reminders of this once great culture, ports of call in the Yucatán have excellent beaches, great shopping, several watersports theme parks, inter- net cafés and a lazy, laid-back lifestyle. Mexican ports also offer horse-riding trails, scuba diving and snorkeling excur- sions, botanical gardens, colonial archi- tecture, museums full of pre-Columbian artifacts, and a chance to see crocodiles and jaguars in the wild.

Directly south of Mexico are the tiny, English-speaking Central Ameri- can country of Belize and larger,

The Maya ruins at Tulum.

Spanish-speaking Honduras. Both are included on Western Caribbean cruises, and the main attraction is the barrier reef just offshore. Considered to be one of the best dive sites in the Western Hemisphere, the reef is a natural wonder marked by brilliantly colored coral. It also has several sunken ships and a variety of exotic marine life. In Honduras, ships sail right into the Bay Island of Roatán where the reef is within swimming distance of the port.

To access the reef in Belize, ships call into Belize City and offer passengers excursions by motorboat. Passengers on NCL's cruises can now experience Belize from Harvest Caye, the line's 75-acre private island, which, the cruise line said in the face of opposition from environ- mentalists at the time of building, would take the pressure off Belize City.

THE CARIBBEAN ARC

Another major highlight on this itin- erary is Grand Cayman, an English- speaking British colony known as a shoppers' paradise. Ships here sail into the capital city of George Town, where

Ocho Rios, Jamaica.

⊙ Fact

Jamaica's Falmouth port took four years to build and, after many delays, opened in the spring of 2011 at a cost of US$213 million, the bill shared between Royal Caribbean and the Port Authority of Jamaica.

an endless assortment of fine quality duty-free stores lures passengers. British, American and Canadian currencies are all accepted.

Easily arranged, excursions from George Town include snorkeling tours of Stingray City (see page 114), and visits to the Cayman Turtle Farm, Cayman Islands National Museum, Queen Elizabeth II Botanical Park and Pedro St James – a classic West Indian Great House with an important colonial history. One excursion that most cruise passengers take here is to the little town of Hell, where the urge to mail a postcard is almost impossible to resist.

Last on the list of Western Shores ports are Ocho Rios, the new port of Falmouth – developed by Royal Caribbean to accommodate its biggest ships – and Montego Bay, all on the English-speaking island of Jamaica. Much larger than Grand Cayman, Jamaica is a mountainous country with a clearly defined national identity.

As the most visited port on the island, Ocho Rios often has several ships in port at once and at times can feel as congested as a big northern city. Excursions here are usually to Dunn's River Falls, where passengers climb barefoot near the 600ft (200-meter) cascading waters. There are also horse-riding trips to Chukka Cove, rafting down the peaceful Martha Brae River, and bus tours to the grand plantation houses. If ships sail into Montego Bay, excursion options include the Rose Hall Great House, the Greenwood Great House and the Old Fort Craft Park.

DEPARTURES AND DURATION

While the specific routes and the number of nights that various cruise lines offer for Western Shores journeys change yearly, there are a few things to consider before booking. The first is to decide is which departure city – Miami, Fort Lauderdale, Tampa, Port Canaveral, Jacksonville, Tampa or Galveston– best suits your travel plans. Also, since most cruises leave in the late afternoon, a tour of the departure city itself can be incorporated into your vacation, so it's worth thinking about which of them you might like to see.

Another variable is how many and which ports the ships sail into. Some cruises make stops at all the above-mentioned ports; others stop only at two or three. A few – especially those departing from Miami and New Orleans – make a circular loop around the island of Cuba and on these a typical itinerary might be: Miami, Key West, Playa del Carmen, Grand Cayman, Ocho Rios, Miami. Others zigzag between destinations: Tampa, Grand Cayman, Belize City, Cozumel, Tampa. Naturally, the choice of the cruise line itself will influence the atmosphere of the trip.

Three- to five-night cruises on the Western route make for great long-weekend mini-escapes. The longer, seven- to 11-night cruises feel more like a real vacation. Available at all times of the year, the companies that offer Western Caribbean cruises include Carnival, Celebrity, Costa, Disney Cruise Line, MSC Cruises, Norwegian Cruise Line, Princess, Royal Caribbean, Holland America Line and Regent Seven Seas Cruises.

Only small turtles can be handled at Cayman Turtle Farm, Grand Cayman.

You won't miss this lifeguard hut on Miami's South Beach.

FLORIDA PORTS OF CALL

Art Deco architecture, old cigar factories, rockets blasting into space and Ernest Hemingway's favorite bar are just a few of the things to be found in Florida's five cruise ship ports.

With the largest cruise port in the world, handling over 5.3 million passengers a year, **Miami** is the main gateway for all types of Caribbean cruises. Only 8 miles (14km) from Miami International Airport, and easily reached from the I-95 highway, PortMiami (tel: 305-347 4800; www.miamidade. gov/portmiami) is a state-of-the-art facility with plenty of parking, a large staff of ground personnel, excellent security, luggage conveyer belts and convenient airline check-in counters capable of issuing boarding passes for flights home. Along with an ample supply of taxis, a fleet of shuttle buses designated specifically for cruise passengers is permanently stationed at the airport.

Many of the passengers who embark from here can't resist Miami's exotic, multi-ethnic atmosphere, and wind up taking advantage of the special 'cruise layover' packages offered by most major hotels in the city.

SOUTH BEACH ART DECO

A sprawling and intense metropolis of over two million people, Miami offers a vast and varied list of diversions to choose from. The one thing most tourists make a point of seeing, especially if they are only in town for a few hours, is **South Beach's Art Deco National Historic District** . At the southern end of Miami Beach, just a few miles east of the Port

of Miami, this dense little enclave contains over 800 Art Deco buildings and is one of the liveliest and most flamboyant neighborhoods in the US. The **Art Deco Welcome Center** (tel: 305-763 8026; www. artdecowelcomecenter.com; daily 9am–5pm, Thu until 7pm), on Ocean Drive, holds a wealth of information on the area and offers free maps and walking tours.

Along with the pastel architectural masterpieces that line the streets, South Beach is full of colorful characters – New York fashion models, Hasidic Jews, trendy locals, European

Main attractions
Miami Seaquarium
Vizcaya Museum and Gardens
Art Deco Welcome Center
Las Olas Riverfront
Merritt Island National Wildlife Refuge
Kennedy Space Center
Busch Gardens
Mallory Square
Hemingway House

Maps on pages 130, 133

South Beach's Art Deco architecture.

tourists, Cuban salsa singers, Haitian drummers and proud LGBT couples.

In addition to Ocean Drive and Collins Avenue, the **Lincoln Road Mall ❸** on South Beach is always bustling with locals and visitors. A pedestrian-only avenue jam-packed with outdoor cafés, boutiques and restaurants, Lincoln Road is home to the **South Florida Art Center** (tel: 305-674 8278; www.art centersf.org; Mon–Fri 12pm–6pm, Sat–Sun 1pm–6pm), a collective of more than 100 artists. Just a few blocks away is **Española Way ❸**, a stunning group of flamingo-pink Mediterranean Revival buildings that house more art galleries, cafés and shops.

Between South Beach and Downtown, check out the new Miami Design District (www.miamidesigndistrict.net), an ultra-cool neighborhood dedicated to art, architecture, dining and shopping; this is the place to come for Louboutins or a Hermes bag.

DOWNTOWN MIAMI

Closer to the port, **Downtown Miami** has several interesting spots all within walking distance from each other. **Bayside Marketplace ❸** (www.bayside marketplace.com; Mon–Thu 10am–10pm, Fri–Sat 10am–11pm, Sun 11am–9pm), a 16-acre (6.5-hectare) waterfront entertainment complex, is full of unusual shops and restaurants, and usually has free live music. Directly across the street is the peach-colored **Freedom Tower**, the Spanish-style 1925 building that once served as a processing center for immigrants. The city has a new cultural center, too, Museum Park, on the site of the old Bicentennial Park, housing the Perez Art Museum Miami (www.pamm.org; Mon–Tue and Fri–Sun 10am–6pm, Thu 10am–9pm, closed Wed) and the Frost Museum of Science, which features a planetarium and three-level aquarium as well as numerous changing exhibits, all family-friendly (www.frostscience.org; daily 9.30am–6pm).

FROM DOLPHINS TO DOMINOES

A few miles to the south is the **Miami Seaquarium ❸** (tel: 305-361 5705;

www.miamiseaquarium.com; daily 10am–6pm;), a popular attraction with dozens of marine exhibits and an active conservation program. Nearby is **Coconut Grove**, a one-time art colony turned upmarket neighborhood and home to **Vizcaya Museum and Gardens**  (tel: 305-250 9133; www.vizcaya.org; Wed–Mon 9.30am–4.30pm, closed Tue), a 70-room Italian Renaissance-style palace full of European antiques. A short distance west is **Coral Gables G**, an enchanting district with glorious old houses, the historic **Biltmore Hotel** and the lush lagoons of the **Venetian Pool** (call for hours, tel: 855-391-6903; www.biltmorehotel.com).

For a taste of the Cuban flavor that makes Miami such a rich experience, a trip into the neighborhood of **Little Havana** is in order. Along with the main commercial artery of **SW 8th Street** (Calle Ocho), where the scent of Cuban coffee permeates the air, other places of note include: the **Bay of Pigs Monument**, which pays tribute to those who lost their lives in the foiled 1961 invasion of Cuba; **Domino Park**, where elderly Cubans gather to play dominoes and talk about the lives they left behind; and **Woodlawn Park Cemetery**, where three former presidents of Cuba are buried.

FORT LAUDERDALE

About 35 miles (56km) north of Miami, the ultra-modern **Port Everglades** (tel: 954-523 3404; www.porteverglades.net) ranks after Miami as the third-busiest cruise port in the world, but is far less congested than its neighbor to the south. Equipped with plenty of parking spaces, taxis, curbside baggage handlers and comfortable waiting areas, Port Everglades is 2 miles (3km) from **Fort Lauderdale/Hollywood International Airport** and just a few minutes' drive from Fort Lauderdale's popular attractions. World famous for its silky 2-mile (3km) beach, 300 miles (480km) of navigable waterways, and wealthy yachting community, **Fort Lauderdale ❷** is one of the most cosmopolitan cities in Florida.

Dedicated to the good life, the city's persona is most evident along **Las**

Scarlet macaws at Fort Lauderdale's Butterfly Gardens

The Seminole Hard Rock Casino.

⊘ SNOWBIRDS TO PARTIERS

The postwar migration boom that transformed Florida into the thriving center of the American Sun Belt has cooled in recent years, but the natives and new arrivals to be encountered in its five cruise ports remain part of a dizzying, diverse pageant. Senior citizens who maintain second homes in the state, known as 'snowbirds,' are estimated to cause as much as a 20 percent population bump in Florida during the winter months. However that doesn't mean that the stereotype of the elderly-filled Sunshine State holds true – the median age is 30-something in South Florida, as well as the counties of Pensacola and Tampa, and anyone who experiences first-hand the rollicking nightlife in those cities can attest to the energetic spirit of its local young people.

Rocket Park,
Cape Kennedy.

Atlantis with a Hubble
Space Telescope replica
at the Kennedy Space
Center Visitor Complex.

Olas Boulevard, a red-brick street with old-fashioned gaslights, horse-drawn carriage rides, outdoor cafés, antique shops and art galleries. Towards the western end of Las Olas, a series of footpaths known as the **Riverwalk** leads past several historic sites on the banks of the **New River**. Not far from Las Olas Boulevard are several attractions. Housed in a rustic 1905 inn, the New River Inn Museum of History (tel 954-463 4431; Mon–Fri noon–4pm; Sat–Sun 9.30am–4pm) contains exhibits on the area's history, including Indian artifacts, historic photos and fine antiques. The plantation-style winter home of the late art collector Frederick Bartlett, **Bonnet House** (tel: 954-563 5393; www.bonnethouse.org; Tues–Sun 9am–4pm), is a grand estate filled with unusual art and artifacts from around the world. The **Museum of Discovery and Science** (tel: 954-467 6637; www.mods.org; Mon–Sat 10am–5pm, Sun noon–6pm) offers educational hands-on exhibits for children. Finally, the small **Museum of Art**, located at Nova Southeastern University (tel: 954-525 5500; www.nsuartmuseum.org; Tue–Sat 11am–5pm, Thu until 8pm, Sun noon–5pm), display European and American art.

PORT CANAVERAL

Catering mostly to the three- and four-day Caribbean cruise market, **Port Canaveral ❸** (tel: 321-783 7831; www.portcanaveral.com) may not be as busy as Miami's or Fort Lauderdale's ports, but it is a first-rate facility nonetheless. And because of the location, about 50 miles (80km) east of Orlando, cruises departing from here often offer special pre- or post-cruise packages to Walt Disney World and other central Florida attractions.

What is also desirable about Port Canaveral is its proximity to Kennedy Space Center and the Merritt Island National Wildlife Refuge. Sprawling over 140,000 acres (57,000 hectares), the peaceful **Merritt Island National Wildlife Refuge** (tel: 321-861 5601; closed prior to shuttle launch) has hundreds of species of water birds, alligators, manatees and loggerhead turtles living on its salt marshes – all oblivious to the rockets taking off nearby.

At the northern boundary is NASA's **Kennedy Space Center** (tel: 855-433 4210; www.kennedyspacecenter.com; daily 9am–6pm, closed some launch days; extra attractions during launches), a theme-park-style attraction great for adults as well as children. It features an authentic space-ship control room, an IMAX theatre and regular bus tours that explore the launch pads, launch control center and training facilities. A little to the north of the Space Center is **Canaveral National Seashore** (daily 6am–6pm), a protected barrier island beach strewn with sea grapes, sea oats and cabbage palms. Marked canoe trails inside the park meander through a lagoon almost always bustling with egrets, ibis, cranes, terns and herons.

TAMPA

On Florida's Gulf Coast, Port Tampa Bay, with its 30-acre (12-hectare) Garrison Seaport Cruise Terminal (tel: 813-905 7678; www.tampaport.com) specializes in cruises to Mexico and other destinations in the western Caribbean. Thoroughly updated in 1998, the terminal contains the enormous Channelside, an entertainment complex with dozens of shops, bars, cinemas and an aquarium.

A fast-growing and very modern city, **Tampa ❹** has several interesting attractions for those who want to add a few days onto their cruise holiday. **Busch Gardens** (tel: 813-884-4386; www.buschgardens.com; call for opening times), one of the more popular theme parks in the state, is world-famous for its thrilling rides and excellent wildlife exhibits.

More formal attractions include the **Henry B. Plant Museum** (tel: 813-254 1891; www.plantmuseum.com; Tue–Sat 10am–5pm, Sun noon–5pm), a former luxury hotel built by a Florida railroad magnate in the 1890s, and the **Tampa Museum of Art** (tel: 813-274 8130; www.tampamuseum.org; daily 10am–5pm, Thu until 8pm), housing ancient Greek and Roman artifacts and 20th-century American art.

Established in 1886 by a Cuban cigar factory owner, **Ybor City** is an historic neighborhood of old buildings, colorful Spanish-style tiles and wrought-iron gates, whose old cigar shops and factories have largely been turned into swish restaurants, bars, antique shops and boutiques. The **Ybor City Museum** (tel: 813-247 6323; www.ybormuseum.org; Wed–Sun 9am–5pm) does a good job of elucidating the history of the cigar-manufacturing community.

KEY WEST

The southernmost city in the continental US, **Key West ❺** (pop. 25,500) has a flamboyant, anything-goes atmosphere that has made it a tropical refuge for many offbeat characters. Barely 4 miles (6km) long by 2 miles (3km) wide, it is truly a great port of call and welcomes about 700,000 cruise passengers each year. It's a small city, easily explored on foot, and full of gingerbread

Lolita the killer whale at Miami Seaquarium.

architecture, literary legacies and interesting nooks and crannies.

Passengers disembarking in the **Port of Key West** (tel: 305-809 3790) do so at the main pier near **Mallory Square**. Right in the heart of **Old Town**, the square is by the bustling marina that hosts the **Sunset Celebration** every evening. Jugglers, mime artists, musicians, dancers and animal tamers put on a free show with the orange setting sun as their backdrop.

Departing from Mallory Square, the venerable **Conch Tour Train** (tel: 888-916 8687; www.conchtourtrain.com; daily 9am–4.30pm) has been taking visitors on narrated treks through the city since 1958 and provides lots of juicy history along with the fun, open-air ride. A tribute to the late treasure diver after whom it is named, the **Mel Fisher Maritime Museum** (tel: 305-294 2633; www.melfisher.org; Mon–Fri 8.30am–5pm, Sat–Sun 9.30am–5pm) displays a bounty of treasures – coins, jewels, silver bars – that have been salvaged from sunken ancient Spanish galleons found in the waters offshore.

Setting out the attractions of Mallory Square, Key West.

There's more shipwreck-themed fun at the Key **West Shipwreck Treasure Museum** (tel: 305-292 8990; www.key westshipwreck.com; daily 9.40am–5pm). Through actors and interactive exhibits, visitors hear swashbuckling tales of the notorious pirates who raided ships off this coast during the 1700s. The **Little White House** (tel: 305-294 9911; www.trumanlittlewhitehouse.com; daily 9am-4.30pm), which chronicles the many holidays that US President Harry S. Truman took here during the 1940s, is another popular attraction.

HEMINGWAY HOME

While there are many historic homes in Key West, the one that draws the crowds is **Hemingway Home** (tel: 305-294 1136; www.hemingwayhome.com; daily 9am–5pm), on the corner of Whitehead and Olivia streets. It was here, in this beautiful Spanish colonial mansion, that the Nobel Prize-winning author spent his winters during the 1930s. Perfectly preserved, the house is filled with Hemingway's antique furniture, art, old books and hunting trophies. Down the road is **Sloppy Joe's**, a boisterous old saloon with peanut shells covering the floors and said to be Hemingway's favorite bar. Other famous watering holes in the city include the **Hard Rock Café**, **Captain Tony's Saloon** and the **Margaritaville Café**, owned by singer Jimmy Buffet.

Adding more oddness to this already delightfully odd place is **Ripley's Believe It Or Not! Museum** (tel: 305-293 9939; www.ripleys.com/keywest; daily 10am–8pm), a bizarre repository of antique diving gear, authentic shrunken heads and a hurricane tunnel complete with gusts of gale-force winds. Dating back to the 1800s, Fort East Martello (tel: 305-296 3913; daily 9.30am-4.30pm) is an old red-brick fort, in which a history museum houses objects from the Spanish-American war, as well as exhibits on Florida's Native Indians and the many writers who have called Key West home.

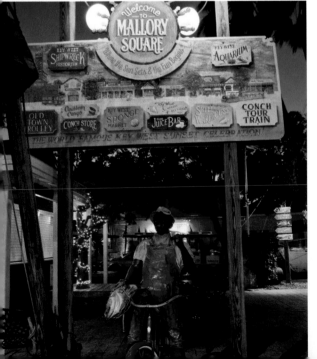

MEXICO AND CENTRAL AMERICA

Maya ruins, a wealth of wildlife, colonial cities, and islands where the traditional Kuna culture remains unchanged all present a great contrast to the engineering marvel of the Panama Canal.

Full of ancient Maya ruins and ripe with strong national identities, ports of call in Mexico and Central America offer rich experiences not found in most small Caribbean islands. Routes in this area vary greatly and are often determined by the size of the cruise ship. While some companies feature three- or four-day itineraries, more often than not cruises here last for 10–14 days, and some include a transit through the Panama Canal.

THE YUCATÁN PENINSULA

Jutting out into the Gulf of Mexico and the Caribbean Sea, Mexico's **Yucatán Peninsula** was always destined to become a major cruise destination. Just 500 miles (800km) from the Florida coast, it is blessed with white-sand beaches, calm turquoise waters, a vibrant arts and crafts tradition, and pyramids left behind by the Maya Indians who lived here long before colonial times. It is also an efficient and well-managed place with every modern amenity imaginable.

Topping the list of most loved and most visited ports is the small island of **Cozumel** ➊. In the 1980s, only a handful of ships docked but it now draws so many that some have to tender passengers to land, usually into **San Miguel** ➋. Those lucky enough to dock do so at the **International**

Pier or **Puerto Maya Pier**. Just a few miles from town, both piers are modern facilities with information booths, international phone access and plenty of taxis (tel: 987-872 0236) and rental cars (tel: 987-115 5284).

EXPLORING SAN MIGUEL

Across from the pier is the **Plaza del Sol**, the main town square where locals and tourists gather. The nearby seaside promenade, the **Malecón**, is jammed with craft and souvenir shops, as is the busy **Rafael Melgar Avenue**.

Main attractions
Cozumel
Tulum
Chichén Itzá
Cockscomb Basin Wildlife
  Sanctuary & Jaguar
  Preserve
Tikal
Parque Nacional Cahuita
San Blas Islands
Panama Canal

Maps on pages 138, 140

Cozumel, a favorite port of call.

Also on Melgar is the **Museo de la Isla de Cozumel** (Cozumel Island Museum; tel: 987-872 0833; Mon–Sat 9am–4pm), a former luxury hotel that now contains exhibits on pre-Columbian and colonial history, maritime artifacts and displays on indigenous endangered animals. Tours of the museum are in English and Spanish.

About 2 miles (3km) south of San Miguel, at the Casa del Mar Hotel, is the home base for **Atlantis Submarine Tours** (tel: 987-872 5671; www.atlantissubmarines.travel). Ideal for non-swimmers who want to see the world below the water's surface, the 48-passenger Atlantis submarine offers a delightful tour of the offshore reefs.

RUINS AND BEACHES

A few miles inland from San Miguel is **El Cedral**, a small collection of Maya ruins; close to the central area of Cozumel is **San Gervasio**, another Maya site. Both sites are well preserved, but seem almost insignificant when compared to the size, scope and historic value of other Maya cities on the mainland.

At the southwestern end of the island is **Playa San Francisco**, a 3-mile (5km) beach dotted with restaurants and water sports operators. Other good beaches are **Playa del Sol**, **Playa Plancar** and **Playa Bonita** – the latter is one of the most secluded beaches on the island. But the pride and joy of Cozumel is the beach at **Parque Nacional Chankanaab** (Chankanaab Beach National Park; tel: 987-872 9760; Mon–Sat 8am–4pm). Along with a beautiful soft sand beach, the park contains a landlocked natural pool connected to the sea by an underground tunnel. It also features a botanical garden with 800 species of plants, a small natural history museum and a swim-with-dolphins program.

In Cozumel, as in other ports of call in the Mexican Caribbean, the most popular shore excursions are to the Maya ruins of **Tulum** ❸ (daily 8am–5pm). Costing about US$120 per person, this day-long trip is worth the time, money and effort. Perched on a cliff, the walled city of Tulum is the only Maya site that fronts the sea. Most

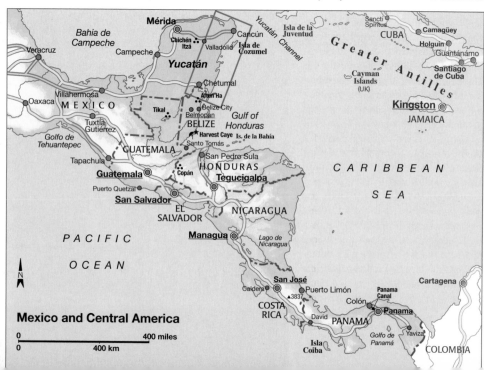

Mexico and Central America

of it is flat and easy to explore, but for those who have difficulties with walking there are small buses running from the main entrance to the center of the site. Beautiful beaches complete with cafés and restaurants just below the ruins offer a pleasant way to wind up the tour, which includes time for relaxing after the visit.

Other excursions from Cozumel include horseback-riding tours, jeep trips through the jungle-like mangroves of the island and ATV tours including a visit to the cenotes – or water-filled sinkholes – that form a honeycomb underground.

PLAYA DEL CARMEN

On the mainland a few miles west of Cozumel is **Playa del Carmen ❹**, one of the busiest cruise ship ports in Mexico. Cruises with Playa del Carmen on their itinerary have several options: they can anchor off the coast and ferry passengers to shore here; they can dock at Cozumel and ferry passengers from there to Playa; or they can dock at the **Puerto Calica Cruise Ship Pier**, about 8 miles (13km) south of Playa del Carmen, and bus passengers to Playa. Many local operators and taxi services offer customized tours of the area, but be warned: passengers booked on ship-organized excursions sometimes take priority over tenders ferrying people to land, so you should check this out in advance.

Twenty-odd years ago, Playa del Carmen was a sleepy fishing village with no electricity but today it's a pulsating port of entry for American cruise passengers, and a favorite getaway for young European travelers who get here by land. Full of old clapboard houses, Playa hasn't lost its counterculture, rustic atmosphere, despite its popularity. At the heart of town is **Avenida Cinco** (Fifth Avenue), a busy street full of inexpensive restaurants, bars with potent margaritas, internet cafés, and shops selling silver jewelry and crafts.

XCARET

One of the more popular excursions from Playa is to **Xcaret ❺** (tel: 998-883 3143; www.xcaret.com; daily 8.30am–10.30pm), a uniquely designed ecological and archeological theme park. The Yucatán's answer to Disney World, Xcaret (pronounced *ish-car-et*) is a stunningly beautiful and thoroughly modern attraction with myriad diversions including palm-lined beaches, a snorkeling lagoon, botanical garden, sea turtle nursery, replicas of Maya ruins, water rides, horseback riding and a chance to swim through underground rivers. While it is very commercialized, Xcaret can provide an entire day's worth of activities and is great fun for children.

Offering similar experiences to Xcaret are two other theme parks, **Xel-Há** (tel: 984-883 3143; www.xelha.com; daily 9am–6pm), pronounced *shell-hah*; and **Xpu-Há** (tel: 984-133 6701; www.laplayaxpuha.com; daily 10am–6.30pm), pronounced *ish-poo-hah*. Both have snorkeling, scuba diving and other watersports.

Maya craftsmanship in Chichén Itzá.

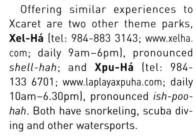

Playa del Carmen.

Cozumel and
Costa Maya

0   20 miles
0   20 km

CHICHÉN ITZÁ

The most spectacular excursion in this area, however, is a full-day trip to the Maya ruins of **Chichén Itzá** (daily 8am–4.30pm), about 150 miles (240km) inland from the coast. While it is costly (more than US$160 per person), time-consuming and tiring, a trip to Chichén Itzá is the highlight of any Yucatán holiday. Among the best-known ruins in Latin America, the fabled ancient city provides a fascinating picture of Maya life in the 10th century. Covering 4 sq miles (10 sq km), the site contains the towering **Pyramid of Kukulkán**, several temples, an observatory, ball courts, steam baths, a sacrificial well and a council house. Local guides offer excellent tours in English and there's an on-site restaurant for refreshments. In the evening, Chichén Itzá puts on an impressive **sound and light show**.

COSTA MAYA

The newest Mexican Caribbean port of call, **Puerto Costa Maya**, is located about 175 miles (280km) south of Playa del Carmen, near the border with Belize. North of **Majahual ❻**, the purpose-built port can accommodate up to three cruise ships. It's a small port compared to others in Mexico, yet packed with opportunities for exploring, relaxing, activities, entertainment and shopping.

A small coastal settlement with a pretty beach and a few shops and restaurants, this area is known more for its natural beauty than for modern, man-made attractions. The best excursion here is a snorkeling or scuba trip to the impressive **Parque Nacional de Chinchorro Submarino ❼** (Chinchorro Reef Underwater National Park). About 30 miles (48km) long and 9 miles (14km) wide, this atoll is one of the last virgin reefs in the region and has areas that drop to depths of 3,000ft (900 meters). Surrounded by an intricate maze of coral heads, it is nearly always teeming with exotic tropical fish, and has over 30 sunken ships to explore. Enormous leatherback turtles are often spotted by snorkelers here, as are numerous dolphins, who love to mingle with visitors.

Another favourite tour from Costa Maya is to the **Reserva de la Biósfera Sian Ka'an** ❽ (Sian Ka'an Biosphere Reserve; tel: 984-141 4245), a 1.3-million-acre (526,000-hectare) nature preserve about 50 miles (80km) north of the Costa Maya port. Divided into three distinct coastal zones, the Sian Ka'an contains broad savannas, dense mangroves, lush tropical forests and many different types of marine habitats. It is home to pumas, jaguars, spider and howler monkeys, ocelots, white-tailed deer, tapirs, crocodiles, loggerhead turtles and manatees. Along with numerous flamingos and brightly colored parrots, it contains and protects over 300 species of birds. Be warned: The mosquitoes can be fierce so cover up well and wear repellent.

BELIZE

A tiny, English-speaking country with a stunning Caribbean coastline, **Belize** is noted for its breathtaking barrier reef – the second largest in the world. While small cruises tend to anchor at Belize's offshore islands, most large cruise ships call at Belize City, anchor offshore and use tenders to transport passengers to the **Fort Street Tourism Village**, where there are shops, restaurants and taxis.

Although it has a weathered, run-down, Caribbean atmosphere, Belize City (pop. 95,000) contains a few points of interest that can be explored by taking a city tour excursion or hiring a local taxi. Towering over the harbor is the **Baron Bliss Lighthouse and Park**. One of Belize's greatest benefactors, Baron Bliss was a wealthy British yachtsman who took ill and died while in port. At his request, his body was entombed in front of the lighthouse, and his money used to build local schools and hospitals.

Not far from the harbor is **St John's Cathedral** (daily 6am–6pm), the oldest Anglican Church in Central America, built in 1812. Across the street is **Government House**, a beautifully preserved colonial mansion; and a block away is the **Yarborough Cemetery** with gravestones dating back to the 1700s. On North Front Street, the Belizean Handicraft Market Place (Mon–Sat 9am–5pm) is a market place that sells Belizean crafts, pottery and woodcarvings. The **Great House Hotel** on Cork Street houses the **Smoky Mermaid** (tel: 501-672 4759; www. smokymermaid.com; daily 6.30am–10pm), an outdoor restaurant that serves wonderful local seafood dishes.

Rather than spending time in Belize City, many cruise passengers prefer to take day-long excursions to the **Crooked Tree Wildlife Sanctuary, Cockscomb Basin Wildlife Sanctuary and Jaguar Preserve**, the **Belize Zoo** or the Maya archaeological sites of **Xunantunich** and **Altun Ha**. There are also excursions that take passengers for **inner tube river rides** through a series of caves; on snorkeling trips to

Playful signage at the Belizean Arts Gallery, Ambergris Caye.

Fisherman and his canine companion, Tobacco Caye, Belize.

Central America's bounty of pre-Columbian gold is on display at the Museo de Oro, San Jose, Costa Rica.

the strikingly beautiful coral reef at the **Hol Chan Marine Reserve** on Ambergris Caye; and to **Lamanai**, a secluded ancient Maya ceremonial center surrounded by rainforest on the New River. Local water taxis run by the Caye Caulker Water Taxi Association (tel: 501-223 572) operate services daily from the Belize Marine Terminal to **Ambergris Caye** and **San Pedro Island**.

GUATEMALA

Located just to the south of Mexico, **Guatemala** shares a border, as well as a rich Maya history, with its northern neighbor. Almost 60 percent of the local population here are indigenous, with roots traceable to the ancient Maya. Guatemala is also rich in nature with more than 600 species of orchid and 300 species of bird.

Although it doesn't have pretty beaches and isn't a major destination for Caribbean cruises, two Guatemalan ports are often included in Panama Canal itineraries: **Puerto Quetzal** on the Pacific Coast and, on the Caribbean Coast, **Santo Tomás**. Built a century

ago as a company town for the United Fruit Corporation, Santo Tomás serves as the headquarters of the Guatemalan Navy, and is the more interesting of the two towns.

Both ports, however, are used as jumping-off points for day-long excursions to the Spanish colonial city of **Antigua**, the capital **Guatemala City**, **Lake Atitlán**, and especially the Maya ruins of **Tikal** (www.tikalpark.com; daily 6am–6pm). The largest and most impressive of all the classic Maya sites, Tikal contains over 500 excavated structures including the **Temple of the Giant Jaguar** and the **Lost World Complex**, a recently discovered group of pyramids. There are two on-site museums and well-trained guides who offer excellent historical tours explaining the architecture, customs and lifestyle of the Maya people. Excursions to Tikal cost several hundred US dollars per person, and involve both a plane and a bus ride. However, it is one of the best Maya sites and definitely worth a visit for an understanding of the Maya's grand designs.

HONDURAS

Like Guatemala, **Honduras** has many spectacular Maya ruins in the interior, but it also has a cluster of offshore islands, the **Islas de la Bahía** (Bay Islands), which attract Caribbean and Panama Canal cruises. The main islands are **Utila, Roatán** and **Guanaja**. The largest and most visited of these is Roatán (pop. 109,000), a lush, 25-mile (40km) -long strip of land that is world-famous as a dive destination and has a long history as one of the best boat-building enclaves in Latin America. Most of the people here speak English rather than Spanish, and the island has several small hotels, restaurants and dive operators who take passengers out to the coral reef. There are also bikes for hire and taxi services available near the cruise ship pier.

Anthony's Key Resort in the **Sandy Bay** area of Roatán serves as the home for the

A margay at Belize Zoo.

Roatán Institute for Marine Sciences (tel: 504-9556 0212; www.roatanims.org), a conservation group that conducts environmental tours of the island. Visitors to the Institute can also interact with dolphins at the dolphin encounter sessions.

Along with Roatán, a few expedition cruise ships also call in at **Puerto Cortés**, a palm-fringed bay on the Caribbean coast that bustles with commerce. Excursions here (by plane and bus) are to the Maya ruins of **Copán** (daily 8am–6pm) at the southern limit of the Maya empire. The most important archeological site in Honduras, the ruins of Copán consist of a sprawling collection of pyramids, ceremonial courts, temples and altars said to date back to AD 464. Adjacent to the ruins is the colonial town of Copán, with cobblestone streets and red-tiled roofs. The archeological park is home to **Copán Sculpture Museum** (Daily 8am–4pm), an impressive repository of sculpture and artifacts from the site.

COSTA RICA

A peaceful and dramatically beautiful country, **Costa Rica** is often called the Switzerland of Central America. With its tropical rainforests, pounding rivers and glorious beaches, it does not disappoint visitors. While a few ships stop at the Pacific port of **Caldera**, an ideal jumping-off point for excursions to national parks in the mid-Pacific area, the majority of Caribbean cruises stop at **Puerto Limón**. Columbus landed here on his final voyage declaring the place a rich coast – *costa rica*.

Limón is a palm-fringed city with a mountain backdrop and an atmosphere that is more Afro-Caribbean than Latin American – many residents here speak English. Far less congested than San José, the capital, it is a lively but slightly run-down city with a sprinkling of old wooden houses painted in bright pastel colors.

Not far from the port is the Chinese Cemetery, where many Chinese immigrants who worked on the local railroad are buried. At the center of town, next to the old harbor, is **Parque Vargas**, a bustling promenade dense with tropical trees and plants.

Ferried ashore by tender, passengers have several excursions to choose from. Popular choices are white-water rafting trips to nearby rivers and visits to **Parque Nacional Cahuita** (Cahuita National Park; daily 8am–4pm), where glass-bottomed boats offer views of the coral reef and hiking trails wind through lush rainforest. Local tour operators also offer specially designed birdwatching, turtle watching and eco-tours.

For passengers with a whole day to spend, bus tours can be taken to **San José**, about 70 miles (112km) inland. In the heart of the country, San José is home to almost one million people, and visiting it can be an intense experience. Founded in 1737, it is dotted with Spanish colonial architecture, and has several splendid museums. Among the best are the **Museo Nacional** (National Museum; www.museocostarica. go.cr; Tue–Sat 8.30am–4.30pm, Sun

The Jammin' restaurant, Puerto Viejo, Costa Rica.

Portrait of Kuna Indian Daniel Lopez, the island village chief, who has the power to grant or refuse permission to outsiders who wish to visit the island.

Four women of the Indigenous Kuna people proudly display their traditional, handmade costumes.

9am–4.30pm), where the history of the country, from pre-Columbian days to the present, is explained; the **Museo del Jade** (Jade Museum; www.museodel-jadeins.com; daily 10am–5pm), which displays the world's largest collection of pre-Columbian jade jewelry and artifacts; and the newly renovated Museo del Oro Precolombino (Pre-Columbian Gold Museum; Tue–Sun 9.15am–5pm), which contains the most comprehensive collection of pre-Columbian gold artifacts in Central America.

For shopping and snacking, **El Pueblo Shopping Centre** (daily 24 hours) is a purpose-built 'village'– where a number of cobblestone streets and adobe buildings contain dozens of shops selling Costa Rican arts, crafts, coffee, rum, cigars, embroidered blouses and woodcarvings.

If you don't have enough time for a drive to San José, a smaller and funkier town is **Puerto Viejo de Limón**, about 15 miles (24km) down the coast from Limón. An eclectic mix of surfers, Rastafaris, expats and world-weary travelers gathers here and the party atmosphere is contagious.

PANAMA

Although transiting the canal (see page 146) is the main tourist attraction of this small Central American country, Panama has worked hard in recent years at wooing Caribbean cruises to its city of **Colón**. Located near the Panama Canal's Atlantic entrance, the **Port of Colón** underwent a US$45 million expansion in 2000, and now the modern facility caters to mega-cruise ships and their passengers.

A sprawling glass and marble complex known as **Colón 2000**, the port includes a duty-free shopping mall, cultural center, information booth, several restaurants and an internet café. Adjacent to the port is the **Radisson Hotel**, complete with an on-site casino (daily 24 hours). Although the port itself is very pleasant, there's not much else to see in Colón and most passengers take excursions to nearby sites.

The most popular excursion (for those whose cruise doesn't include a canal crossing) is a ferry trip organized by **Aventuras 2000** (tel: 507-209 2000; www.aventuras2000.com) the port's

on-site tour company, which sails through portions of the Panama Canal then continues with an eco-tour of the area, as well as offering half-day trips to Panama City

There are also half-day bus tours to the Canal's **Gatún Locks**, as well as excursions to **San Lorenzo Fort**, the **Barro Colorado Nature Preserve** and an **indigenous Embera Indian village** on the banks of the Changres River. A few tour operators allow passengers to go for a swim in the Panama Canal from the shores of the **Gatún Yacht Club**, and helicopter tours of the canal are available.

SAN BLAS ISLANDS (GUNA YALA)

Just off the northeast coast of Panama in the indigenous province of Guna Yala are the 378 **San Blas Islands**. Here it is not engineering wonders that draw visitors, but a simple Indian lifestyle that has managed to hold tight to centuries-old traditions. The autonomous home of the **Kuna Amerindians**, the San Blas are beautiful Caribbean islands without the razzle-dazzle of development.

Spread out over 60 islands, there are about 50,000 Kunas still living here.

As cruise ships sail into the waters, the Kunas paddle out in their dugout canoes to greet passengers and hawk their wares; after that, tenders bring passengers ashore. Once they have arrived on land, visitors are often dumbstruck by the simplicity of it all. Most of the Kuna speak only their native language, rather than Spanish, and live in bamboo huts without electricity or running water. Fishing, farming and making *molas* are their means of survival. An intricate, patchwork-type embroidery using a reverse appliqué technique done on black fabric, *molas* make an irresistible souvenir. Boldly beautiful, the embroidered pieces are sometimes sewn onto blouses and shirts, and are also used for place mats and as cushion covers.

Every year in late February, the Kuna commemorate the anniversary of the **Kuna Revolution**, and these bucolic little islands come alive with celebrations and ceremonies conducted by local chiefs.

○ **Fact**

The best time to be in Cahuita is from February to April, and in the second week of October for Carnival.

Playa Uvita, Punta Uvita, Costa Rica.

○ THE BURGEONING MAYA WORLD

Visiting the sparsely populated Yucatán, it's entertaining to imagine how it might have been in Maya times. The massive pyramid of Chichén Itza, the stunning setting of Tulum, the sheer size of Tikal: these Maya cities represented the pinnacle of a complex society. Thousands of smaller settlements exist with archeologists continually piecing together the complexities of a Maya world that stretched from the Yucatán south through Belize, Guatemala, Honduras and El Salvador. Across this immense area competing hereditary rulers governed, goods were traded and wars were fought. The history of the Maya is engraved in stelae found at Tikal, Copán and countless other sites, the smaller sites providing insight into food production, water storage, a religion of multiple deities, astrology, and a complex and accurate calendar system.

The Maya emerged around 2000 BC. By 800 AD the population had peaked at around 1800 inhabitants per square mile (equivalent to the average population density in London, England, today). The area would have been packed – this was one of the highest population densities in human history. Wandering slowly around the Maya structures provides a brief glimpse into the region's past, into a time that must have been dynamic, wonderfully chaotic and a world away from the sleepy encounters of today.

THE PANAMA CANAL

One of the Seven Wonders of the Modern World, well over one million ships have transited the Panama Canal since it first opened in 1914.

It may not have the natural beauty of some Central American sights, but the Panama Canal boggles the mind with its colossal engineering ingenuity – so it's not surprising that it's now one of the highlight destinations for many Caribbean cruises.

A 50-mile (80km) -long ribbon of water, the canal connects the Atlantic and Pacific with direct passage through Central America, thus avoiding the 8,000-mile (12,800km) journey around South America. Approximately 40 vessels travel through the original canal each day, with a growing number using the new, bigger Aqua Clara locks that opened in 2016.

Steam Shovel Trains Excavate the Canal in 1913

POLITICAL WRANGLES

Although it was marred by political undertones, the building of the Panama Canal is considered one of the greatest human accomplishments of the 20th century. After a failed attempt by the French in the late 1800s, construction was turned over to the US government in 1903. At the time, the Republic of Panama was struggling to gain its independence from Colombia, and the deal it cut with the US government – US$10 million up-front and US$250,000 per year afterwards – was its ticket to freedom. Desperate for economic development, Panama also granted the United States the administration rights to the canal in perpetuity. By 1906, more than 25,000 people were employed in the massive undertaking. And when it finally opened, seven years later, it did indeed bring a boom to the area.

In 1977, US President Jimmy Carter agreed to revoke the original treaty, and worked out an arrangement that would grant Panama control of the canal by 1999. Today, the canal is managed entirely by Panama and represents 10 percent of its GNP, bringing in about US$500 million per year.

The lowest fee ever charged for a crossing was 36 cents, when adventurer Richard Halliburton swam the canal in 1928.

For the majority of cruise passengers, a trip through the canal stands out as an amazing experience. While it is always being maintained, the majority of the canal is still in its original condition. It usually takes about eight hours to sail through, although the overall time is longer as much of it is spent waiting in line with dozens of other ships.

ENGINEERING MARVEL

The beauty of the canal lies in its prodigious engineering. At over 100 years old, the canal is still broadly the same as it was when originally built. French efforts to build a canal in the early 1890s crumbled, hobbled by a high death toll that saw more than 22,000 workers lose their lives and by a failure to maintain the technical expertise and equipment necessary to complete the task. Later, the US construction project would require medical advances to minimize the spread of deadly mosquito-borne diseases, in particular malaria and yellow fever. The Panama Canal Railway was created to shift the hundreds of millions of tonnes of material removed from the canal cuts, while beyond the railroad, new equipment was developed for the task, including pneumatic power drills, rock crushers and cement mixers – all common equipment in modern construction. The canal was completed in 1914, two years ahead of schedule.

In October 2006, a US$5.25 billion project was approved to expand capacity and maintain the role of the canal in global maritime routes. A new lane and a new set of locks were created, finally opening in June 2016, meaning much larger ships, known as post-Panamax, could fit through the channel. The expansion has created 30,000 jobs and rocketed Panama's GDP growth rate into one of the highest in the world, despite delays on the project of more than two years. When a cruise ship makes a transit, engineering experts, as well as Central American history specialists are on board to offer a blow-by-blow account of the proceedings. Surrounding the canal and visible from the ships is the Panama Canal Zone, a small city full of schools, homes and churches that cater to canal employees.

COMPLICATED PROCESS

While being towed through the canal, ships enter a series of three locks – the Miraflores, Pedro Miguel and Gatún (or the new Aqua Clara locks for post-Panamax ships – which are connected by artificial lakes and canals. The locks are like giant aquatic elevators that raise the ships up over the land and then gently lower them down to sea level. Standing on deck of a big ship, it's almost possible to touch the sides, while if you make the transit on a small vessel, there's a sense of wonder as your ship is dwarfed in a lock by a giant freighter. Once the ships pass through, the locks empty their water and fill back up again, ready for the next ship.

Each time, millions of gallons of fresh water from nearby lakes is used (saltwater would damage the machinery). For safety reasons, cruise ships always pass through the canal during daylight hours, while cargo and private vessels pass at night with bright lights guiding the way.

Whether sailing from the Caribbean to the Pacific or vice versa, most Panama Canal cruises are one-way trips. For most passengers, it's a fascinating experience, all the more so with the spectacular scale of the expansion works.

Aurora transitting the Panama Canal.

Fort Louis overlooking Marigot Bay, St-Martin.

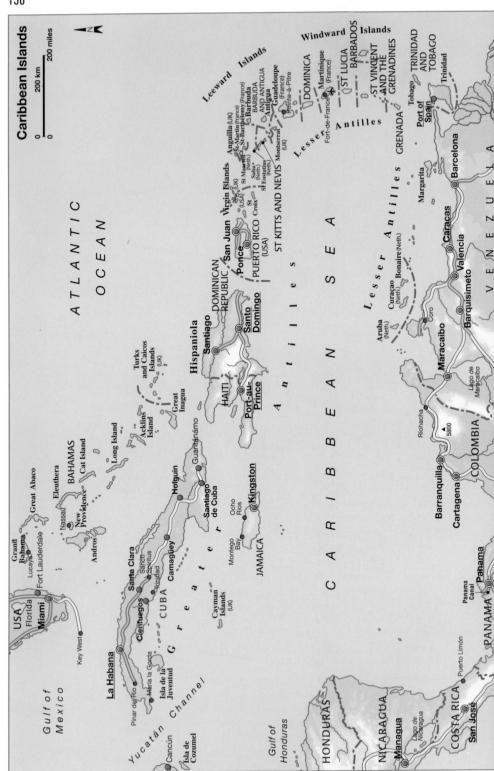

Caribbean Islands

0   200 km

0   200 miles

ATLANTIC OCEAN

USA
Florida
Miami
Key West
Fort Lauderdale

Gulf of Mexico

Cancún
Isla de Cozumel

Yucatán Channel

Pinar del Río
María la Gorda
Isla de la Juventud
La Habana

CUBA
Santa Clara
Cienfuegos
Sancti Spíritus
Trinidad
Camagüey
Holguín
Santiago de Cuba
Guantánamo

Greater Antilles

BAHAMAS
Grand Bahama
Lucaya
Great Abaco
Eleuthera
Nassau
New Providence
Andros
Cat Island
Long Island
Acklins Island
Great Inagua
Turks and Caicos Islands (UK)

Cayman Islands (UK)

Ocho Ríos
Montego Bay
Kingston
JAMAICA

HAITI
Port-au-Prince

Hispaniola

DOMINICAN REPUBLIC
Santiago
Santo Domingo

San Juan
Ponce
PUERTO RICO (USA)

Virgin Islands
St Croix (USA)

Anguilla (UK)
St-Martin (France)
St-Barthélemy (France)
St Maarten (Neth.)
Saba (Neth.)
St Eustatius (Neth.)
ST KITTS AND NEVIS
Montserrat (UK)

Leeward Islands

BARBUDA
ANTIGUA
ANTIGUA AND BARBUDA
Guadeloupe (France)
Pointe-à-Pitre

DOMINICA
Martinique (France)
Fort-de-France

ST LUCIA
BARBADOS

ST VINCENT AND THE GRENADINES

Windward Islands

GRENADA

Tobago
Port of Spain
TRINIDAD AND TOBAGO
Trinidad

Lesser Antilles

CARIBBEAN SEA

Margarita
Aruba (Neth.)
Curaçao (Neth.)
Bonaire (Neth.)
Coro
Barcelona
Caracas
Valencia
Maracaibo
Lago de Maracaibo
Barquisimeto

VENEZUELA

Riohacha
5800
Barranquilla
Cartagena

COLOMBIA

Gulf of Honduras

HONDURAS

NICARAGUA
Managua
Lago de Nicaragua

COSTA RICA
San José
Puerto Limón

PANAMA
Panama Canal
Panama

THE CARIBBEAN ARC

Like a necklace of precious stones, these diverse island nations stretch almost from the Gulf of Mexico to South America.

A Bananaquit on Dominica.

The islands of the Caribbean are, physically and culturally, places of distinct difference. From the Greater to the Lesser Antilles, each country has its own character and atmosphere shaped by its history and the variety of its people. The region has more depth than the stereotypical images of sun-kissed beaches and friendly people would have us believe.

Here the topography reveals nature at work, from the lush rainforests of Dominica, St Lucia and the other Windward Islands, where rain falls freely, to the limestone caves and thorny scrubland on arid Aruba, Bonaire and Curaçao. The mountainous Greater Antilles reach for the sky at Pico Duarte in the Dominican Republic, the highest peak in the Caribbean, while underwater the deepest known point is the seemingly bottomless Cayman Trench.

During a shore excursion you are likely to hear French, Dutch, Spanish and English, as well as infinite combinations of creole and patois. A Latin flavor awaits visitors to Puerto Rico, the Dominican Republic and Cuba, formerly part of the Spanish empire and now leaders in music, rhythm and dance. On St Martin you can experience two cultures in one trip: the island is Dutch on one side and French on the other, but English is widely spoken and there is a

Sampling some Cayman coconut.

noticeable leaning to the US. French-African culture prevails in Martinique and Guadeloupe, but chic St-Barths is the French Riviera transplanted to the tropics. The British influence is unavoidable in Barbados, where a statue of Admiral Nelson still stands in Bridgetown. There is even Irish heritage present on Montserrat.

Further south you can explore Grenada, the Spice Island, known for its aromatic nutmeg, organic cocoa and lush vegetation, and Trinidad, a land famous for its special brand of bacchanalia – Carnival. This island combines a big-city attitude with a serene pastoral landscape, abundant wildlife and, as elsewhere in the tropical region, a seamless mix of diverse cultures.

The reef around the North Sound.

THE CAYMAN ISLANDS

A tiny island with a sweet mixture of Caribbean heritage, British sensibility and American modernism, Grand Cayman is a major port of call that attracts more than one million visitors a year.

Breathtaking dive sites are what usually come to mind when thinking of **Grand Cayman**. But this peaceful little paradise is also an affluent and sophisticated place with the highest standard of living in the Caribbean.

Grand Cayman (population 63,000) is a British Overseas Department with a modern and well-managed infrastructure that gracefully coincides with an old-fashioned sense of values. The island has no inner-city slums, no poverty in the countryside and no street vendors harassing tourists. Nor are there any casinos – conservative Christian churches hold a great deal of sway here.

Only 28 miles long and 7 miles wide (45 by 11km), Grand Cayman is the largest and most developed of the Cayman Islands chain, which includes **Cayman Brac and Little Cayman**. With a population of 2,100, Cayman Brac is a rugged limestone island with about a dozen hotels that cater mostly to scuba divers. Also for divers, Little Cayman is even tinier, with a resident population of about 150 and a handful of rooms offering accommodation. Both are accessible by commercial planes from the capital, George Town, and by private yacht.

Just 480 miles (770km) south of Miami, Grand Cayman is the only one of the three islands that accepts major cruise ships. In an effort to maintain its quiet atmosphere, it allows up to four ships in port at any one time and requires them to anchor offshore and ferry passengers to the dock via tenders.

Debarkation takes place in the capital city of **George Town** ❶, at either the **North Terminal** or the **South Terminal**. Located just a few hundred yards apart, both are modern, well-maintained facilities and within walking distance of several interesting spots in the city. Small and compact, George Town is dense with commerce

⊙ **Main attractions**
George Town – Fort George, Elmslie United Memorial Church
Cayman Islands National Museum
Hell
Turtle Farm
Stingray city
Pedro St James Historic Site
Queen Elizabeth II Botanic Park

Map on page 154

Footprints in the sand on Seven Mile Beach.

Bold stained-glass windows adorn Elmslie United Memorial Church, known locally as Grand Cayman's 'cathedral.'

and classic Caribbean architecture and is easy to explore on foot. For other points of interest outside the city, large air-conditioned buses offer excursions and taxis are available.

TOURING GEORGE TOWN

Right on the waterfront alongside the terminals, **Fort George** is the first thing most passengers notice. Built in 1790 as defence against the Spanish, the original fort was made of solid coral rock with walls 5ft (1.5 meters) thick. While not as large as many other Caribbean forts, it was strategically positioned and has warded off many attacks.

During World War II it was used as a watchtower to spot the German submarines that often patrolled the coast. To make way for construction, most of the fort was demolished in 1972, and three small portions of the wall, two long cannons, and a lookout hut remain.

Across the street from Fort George on Harbour Drive is the **Elmslie United Memorial Church** (www.elmsliechurch.

org.ky; Mon–Fri 9am–5pm, Sun 9am–noon, services on Sundays 9am and 10.30am).

Named after a Presbyterian minister who served here from 1846 to 1863, the church is an impressive structure with a timber roof shaped like an upturned schooner hull, brightly colored stained-glass windows and sleek mahogany pews. The grounds surrounding it contain several memorial plaques and old stone grave markers.

NATIONAL TREASURE

Further along Harbour Drive stands a neat white colonial building with green hurricane shutters and a bright red roof. This is the **Cayman Islands National Museum** (tel: 345-949 8368; www.museum.ky; Mon–Fri 9am–5pm, Sat 10am–2pm), a treasure trove of artifacts that serves as the country's collective memory. One of the finest in the Caribbean, the museum opened in 1990 in the city's Old Courthouse, which dates back to the 1830s. It is the second-oldest surviving building in Grand Cayman and a fine example

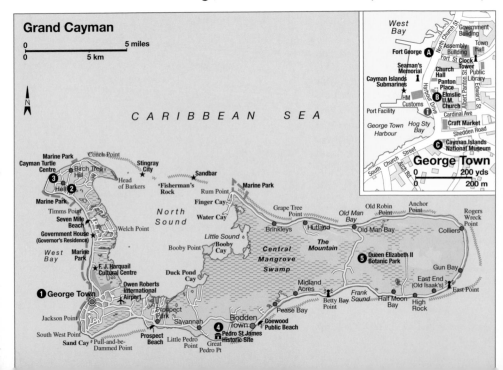

of classic Caymanian architecture. The first floor is constructed of wattle and daub, and the second floor – complete with veranda – is of framed timber. Along with a 10-minute film in an air-conditioned theatre, the museum's many exhibits include a three-dimensional depiction of the undersea mountains and canyons that make up the Cayman Trench, scientific displays of the island's natural habitats, and a collection of locally made furniture, tools, nautical antiques and artwork. Every morning a conch horn is blown and the flag is raised to signal the opening of the museum. Conch horns were traditionally blown to announce the arrival of a ship in port.

PLEASURES ABOVE AND BELOW WATER

Across the street from the museum, Cayman Islands Submarines operates day and night submarine dives to 100ft (30 meters) below the surface, as well as tours of the shallower reefs on the Seaworld Observatory, a glass-bottom boat (tel: 345-949 7700; www.caymanislandssubmarines.com; departure times fit in with cruise ships schedules).

On the submarines, views from the portholes of the comfortable, airtight ship are stunning – coral formations, sponge gardens and marine creatures in various tropical colors.

If your ship is in port for the evening and the moon is new, take a pontoon boat tour or a kayak trip with Cayman Sea Elements (tel: 345-936 8687; www.caymanseaelements.com) to admire the mangroves in the moonlight and the curious bioluminescence in the water, which glows green when disturbed.

Other points of interest nearby are the **Cayman Islands National Archives**, the **Farmers' Market** at the George Town Cricket Pitch (Mon–Sat, 7am–6pm) for local fruit, spices, juices and art, and the **Craft Market** – a favorite stop for visitors shopping for island-made souvenirs. And at the

intersection of Fort and Edward streets is the **Clock Tower**. Built in 1937 in honor of King George V, it is just one of many monuments on the island representative of the Caymanian allegiance to Britain. Also on Edward Street is the **Public Library**, well stocked with books on island history and culture. Scattered throughout the town are duty-free shops selling the usual goods and gold coins, china, crystal, Irish linen, leather goods and the locally produced Tortuga Rum.

POSTCARDS FROM HELL

A few miles from George Town, Grand Cayman becomes more tranquil. Tropical cottages painted in bold Caribbean colors dot the landscape, and the pace of life is slow. After passing the high-rise hotels that line **Seven Mile Beach**, north of town, a tiny sign points the way to **Hell ❷**. The entire town consists of a petrol station, a post office and a few quirky gift shops. A touristy but fun geological site, it got its name from the surrounding acres of pock-marked limestone rocks that look like

☉ Shop
One thing to look out for while shopping in Grand Cayman is caymanite. A semiprecious stone found only in these islands, caymanite ranges in color from beige to pink to brown, and makes beautiful jewelry.

Horse riding on Barker's Beach.

Turtles at the Cayman Islands Turtle Farm are usually fed in the early morning and late afternoon.

A face-to-face encounter with a stingray.

the charred remains of an inferno. A wooden platform leads to an observation deck above the eerie landscape. A statue of the devil stands guard, and several signs warn: The Removal of Hell Rocks is Prohibited.

A popular stop is the **Hell Post Office** (Mon–Fri 8.30am–5pm, Sat 9am–12.30pm), from where visitors can mail a postcard home from Hell.

STINGRAYS AND SEA TURTLES

On Boatswain's Beach (pronounced Bo'sun's) is the **Cayman Turtle Centre ❸** (786 Northwest Point Road, West Bay; tel: 345-949 3894; www.turtle.ky; daily 8am–5pm). Founded in 1968, it has successfully implemented a breed-and-release program that has introduced over 31,000 tagged turtles to the wild. The facility is, though, a working commercial turtle farm, selling meat for local consumption. Turtle meat and shells are banned in the US and Europe, so do not take home turtle souvenirs. A major tourist attraction, visitors can see and touch the lively creatures that range in size from

6lb (3kg) babies to fully mature ones weighing about 600lbs (272kg), and swim in a salt water lagoon with turtles and other marine life.

Another favorite attraction is **Stingray City**, often called the best 12ft (3.5-meter) dive spot in the world. Off the northern end of the island and accessible only by tour boat (which can be arranged at the port), this is a shallow, sheltered bay consisting of a barrier reef, a sandbar, calm water and hundreds of stingrays. Equipped with raw squid, visitors are dropped into the waters and the stingrays eat right out of their hands.

COLONIAL HOMES AND GARDENS

To the east of George Town, in **Savannah**, is one of the most important historic sites on the island. **Pedro St James Historic Site ❹** (tel: 345-947 3329; www.pedrostjames.ky; daily 8.30am–5pm) is a magnificently restored manor house with formal English gardens, perched on a limestone cliff. It was here, in 1835, that the Declaration of Emancipation was read, freeing local slaves from bondage. Built in 1780 by slave labor, the house is the oldest stone structure on the island and offers a realistic view of Caribbean colonial life. With a glistening gabled roof, exterior staircase and wrap-around veranda, it is furnished with antiques. A colonial-style visitor's center contains a multimedia theater that shows a 20-minute video of the site and Caymanian history on the hour from 10am until 4pm.

A few miles inland from Pedro St James is **Queen Elizabeth II Botanic Park ❺** (tel: 345-947 9462; www.botanic-park.ky; daily 9am–5.30pm), a 65-acre (26-hectare) nature preserve and one of the finest botanical gardens in the Caribbean. This oasis is equipped with trails that guide visitors past 600 species of indigenous plants, interpretive exhibits, a pond and dozens of rare, endemic Cayman blue iguanas.

⌕ THE DEEP SEA

Whales, dolphins, sharks, turtles and stingrays – all manner of impressive creatures inhabit the nourishing waters of the Caribbean.

The Caribbean islands have established a number of marine parks, from the Cayman Islands to Bonaire, all swarming with rainbow shoals of wrasse, grouper, snapper, angelfish and barracuda. Sea turtles, stingrays, mantas, reef sharks and even whale sharks also lurk in these waters. Most cruise lines organize marine-life excursions, from snorkeling or scuba trips and submarine voyages to big-game fishing and whale and dolphin safaris.

Whale-watching excursions are a popular attraction, with a classic whale and dolphin safari offering a 90 percent success rate in spotting both creatures. Samaná Bay in the Dominican Republic has the most accessible whale watching in the Caribbean. Humpback whales come here in January–March to give birth in the warm waters and it is common to see a mother and calf close to the surface, or a 30-tonne male showing off his athleticism, soaring out of the water before diving below the boat.

Excursions involving frolics with dolphins are a feature of the Mexican and Costa Maya itineraries, as well as off the coasts of St Lucia and Dominica. Bottle-nosed dolphins surf the seas in search of food, leaping out of the waves like faulty torpedoes. Six dorsal fins may swim into view before the dolphins arch out of the water, dancing backwards on their tails, spinning into the distance. These boisterous, inquisitive creatures love games and attention, so greet every new cruise-load of passengers with unabated affection.

Hawksbill, leatherback and Green turtles are endangered and protected, but can be seen throughout the Caribbean. Covering huge distances on their migrations, they return to the islands' sandy beaches to lay their eggs. Scuba divers and yachtsmen often see them in deep waters, while swimmers and snorkelers frequently encounter them around Bequia or Barbados. Stingray City on Grand Cayman is an opportunity for tame, velvety-skinned stingrays to get fed by fish-wielding cruise passengers.

FROM SCUBA DIVES TO SUBMERSIBLES

If serious diving appeals, then the Cayman Islands, Grenada, Tobago and Bonaire represent some of the best sites in the Caribbean. Exhilarating dives visit historic shipwrecks or dramatic drop-offs. The 1977 film *The Deep* was shot around the wreck of the Rhone off the British Virgin Islands. Today, the wreck, which sank in 1867, is part of a marine park, home to tropical fish and humpback whales who calf here between January and March. Several islands offer submarine (or semi-submersible) trips: Aruba, Curaçao, Barbados and Grand Cayman are popular. St Thomas provides a memorable marine experience: Delicate corals and rainbow-colored fish are visible from a submarine and an underwater observatory.

As for sharks, they received unequivocal support from Jean-Michel Cousteau, son of the late Jacques Cousteau, during a visit to the British Virgin Islands. In his capacity as trustee of the marine park, Cousteau defended the killers: 'Sharks have been around for 360 million years and humans for 3 million. The sharks' job is to clean up the seas of sick and wounded marine life,' and should not be blamed for 'mistakenly identifying a flapping white human for food.' So there: simply accept your place in the great food chain of life.

Sperm whales around Dominica.

JAMAICA

You can go to Jamaica for the reggae and Red Stripe, but other attractions include river rafting, birdwatching, exotic botanical gardens and the colonial Great Houses.

Jungly hills and ravines, the misty Blue Mountains, powdery beaches and vibrant coral reefs are reason enough to visit Jamaica, named Xaymaca (land of wood and water) by the Taíno Indians who first settled here. The island's irrepressible spirit is another: scruffy towns resounding with the deep bass tones of the ever-present reggae music; a rusting Red Stripe sign swinging in the breeze, promising deliciously strong, ice-cold beer; or a roadside shack selling spicy patties and jerk pork.

It is true that Jamaica has had highly publicized security problems, and there have been instances of tourists being robbed at gunpoint and even kidnapped, but these incidents should be kept in proportion. Gangland violence occurs in Kingston, not on the north coast where cruise ships call. A more common problem is the relentless hassle from street traders pouncing on cruise passengers as they emerge from their ship, making shopping, or simply walking around town, an exhausting experience.

In spite of this, a trip to Jamaica can be a rewarding experience and warrants in-depth exploration. Don't hire a car – the roads are potholed and the local driving haphazard, at best. Distances between the main north coast resorts are large, so it is advisable to get around by taxi and stay within the vicinity of the port, be it Montego Bay, the main tourism center; Falmouth, which receives the biggest ships; Ocho Rios, which attracts the majority of ships; or smaller Port Antonio in the beautiful east.

MONTEGO BAY

The island's second-largest town (after Kingston) and the main center for tourism, **Montego Bay** ❶ sprawls around a jagged, semicircular bay towards the western end of the north coast. The part of most interest to visitors, containing the shops, bars and restaurants, is located east of Sam

Main attractions
Montego Bay
Rose Hall Great House
Falmouth
Ocho Rios
Shaw Park Botanical
  Gardens
Dunn's River Falls
Harmony Hall
Rafting on the Rio Grande

Maps on pages
160, 163

Margaritaville, a lively Montego Bay hangout.

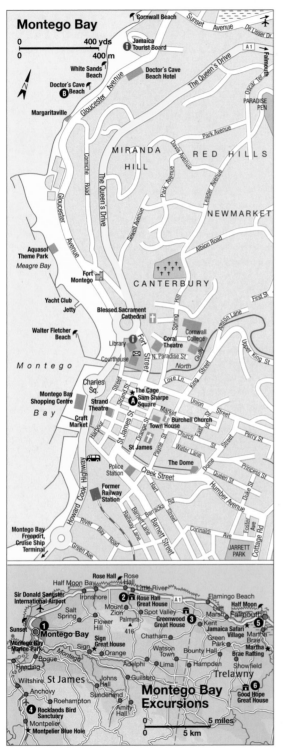

Montego Bay

Sharpe Square and along the waterfront. Cruise ships dock at the multi-million-dollar Freeport complex, on reclaimed land to the west of the bay, 1 mile (1.6km) or so from the center.

There is little of real interest here apart from the **Montego Bay Freeport Shopping Centre**, a good source for gemstones, watches, cigars, rum and designer labels. Most ships run a shuttle service covering the 10- to 15-minute journey into town; failing this, there will be a long line of willing taxi drivers waiting outside the terminal.

Historians claim that 'montego' comes from *manteca*, a Spanish word meaning lard, which was made from the fat of the wild boars that inhabited the area in the 16th century and shipped abroad by the Spanish. Today, local people simply refer to the town as MoBay.

A poignant reminder of the misery of slavery is the stone **Cage**, once used to contain drunks or errant slaves, in **Sam Sharpe Square A**, named after Sam 'Daddy' Sharpe, who led slave revolts during the winter of 1831–32. The British authorities responded harshly, hanging Sharpe in The Parade in 1832 and also killing 500 of his associates. The square has a memorial sculpture to Sharpe. Otherwise, apart from a smattering of Georgian buildings in the streets around the square, there is little else of historic interest in Montego Bay, a place given more to partying than to heritage.

HIP STRIP

The Montego Bay Shopping Centre, the Craft Market and a long line of bars are all located along the beach on Gloucester Avenue, otherwise known as the 'Hip Strip', ending at **Doctor's Cave Beach B** (daily). The beach was made famous in the early 1900s by Dr Alexander McCatty, whose claim that the water here had curative powers brought rich Americans flocking in their hundreds. The strip of fine sand, with good beach facilities, still attracts visitors today. There are coral gardens close to the shore, as well as a lively bar, a food court and a cyber cafe.

If you stroll along Gloucester Avenue you can enjoy some harmless, if mindless, fun at **Margaritaville**, a noisy, action-packed beach bar serving Jamaican food and *fajitas*. There is a choice of 52 varieties of margarita with which to wash the food down, or you can be entertained in the bar's hot tubs and on water trampolines and a monster water slide. Alternatively, try the outdoor **Pork Pit**, a local institution, which sells sizzling, peppery jerk pork and chicken accompanied by ice-cold Red Stripe beer.

Montego Bay also hosts the Reggae Sumfest in a variety of venues around town. This is a massive annual music festival held in August, with bands playing round the clock for five days. The event attracts thousands of visitors from all over the world, drawn by the island's musical culture.

GREAT HOUSES AND BIRD-WATCHING

Behind the mass commercialism, Montego Bay has a colorful history and several Great Houses still stand on large plantations. **Rose Hall Great House ❷** (www.rosehall.com; daily 9.15am–5.15pm), the 18th-century home of alleged 'white witch' Annie Palmer, is the best known. It lies on a ridge east of the city past Ironshore and Half Moon Bay.

Nearby, heading eastwards, is **Greenwood Great House ❸** (www.greenwoodgreathouse.com; daily 9am–6pm), which was built by relatives of the poet Elizabeth Barrett Browning in 1800. Greenwood contains several antiques and the largest collection of rare musical instruments and books on the island.

Bird lovers can head inland, southwest of Montego Bay, taking a taxi to Anchovy and the **Rocklands Bird Sanctuary ❹** (http://rocklandsbirdsanctuary.info, tel: 876-952 2009; daily 2–5pm). This is a bird reserve, established in 1958, where visitors can experience excellent sightings of various attractive indigenous species, including the wonderful, tiny, colorful hummingbirds.

⊙ Tip

Blue Mountain Bicycle Tours organizes guided cycling trips down the 1,500ft (460 meters) from Murphy Hill to Dunn's River Falls (tel: 876-974 7075; www.bmtoursja.com; Mon–Sat 8am–5pm).

The dining room at Rose Hall Great House.

⊙ LIGHTNING BOLT

Jamaica has long been known for producing world-class athletes, but every so often the world is outclassed by a Jamaican. Usain Bolt, born in 1986 in Trelawny, stood 6ft 5ins (1.96 meters) by age 15 and had already started to win medals. At his first World Junior Championships in 2002, he was so nervous that he put his shoes on the wrong feet, but he won the 200-meter race, becoming the youngest-ever World Junior gold medalist. Teenage wobbles and injuries interrupted his progress, but Bolt was recognized as an exceptional athlete. He holds three Olympic and four World titles in the 200-meter event, and has won numerous awards for sportsmanship. Bolt retired from athletics in 2017.

FALMOUTH

Some 22 miles (35km) east of Montego Bay is **Falmouth ❺**, home of the newest cruise ship port in Jamaica, which can receive the biggest cruise ships. The pier is triangular and has been developed as an 18th-century concept town with cobbled streets, shops, boutiques, restaurants, bars and shady parks.

The Georgian town of Falmouth used to export sugar and rum and is the best example of its type in Jamaica, with a fine colonial courthouse, St Peter's Anglican church, and pretty 18th-century houses with wrought-iron balconies. The Jamaica National Heritage Trust has declared the whole town a National Monument. Much of the town center is now pedestrianized, including the central Water Square. Tram cars and horse-drawn carriages take visitors on tours around town.

MARTHA BRAE

Excursions from Falmouth include rafting on the **Martha Brae** (tel: 876-952 0889; www.jamaicarafting.com; daily 8.30am–4.30pm), a beautiful river with a colorful legend of a Taíno witch who lured Spanish gold hunters to a cave where they hoped to find treasure, but were never seen again. A guide expertly punts you downstream on a 30ft-long bamboo raft for two. It takes about an hour to travel the 3 miles (5km) to Martha's Rest at the mouth of the river, about 2 miles (3km) from Falmouth. Overlooking the Martha Brae is the **Good Hope Great House ❻** (daily), a fine example of a Georgian plantation house, furnished with antiques and with a commanding view over the surrounding countryside. Tours are available around the house and estate, with its old water wheel, kiln and other sugar-mill ruins. All sorts of adventure activities are available on the estate, from ziplining to river tubing and ATV tours.

OCHO RIOS

In the northern county of Middlesex lies the parish of St Ann, and at its heart is **Ocho Rios ❼**, known locally as Ochi. The coastal town is backed by scenic hills with coconut palms and fruit plantations, while its soft, sandy beaches are protected by coral reefs. Contrary to popular opinion, the name Ocho Rios does not come from the Spanish for eight rivers, but is a corruption of the original name *Las Chorreras*, 'the waterfalls,' of which there are several, creating a perfect environment for some of the island's most spectacular vegetation.

The cruise ship terminal, on the edge of town, has telephones, toilets, an information desk and a taxi rank. If you want to venture out on your own, getting around independently is relatively easy since taxis can be picked up at the terminal. Be sure to use only the licensed JUTA taxis, which publish fixed fares, and agree on a price in advance.

It is easy to walk around town from the terminal, but on a hot, humid day, the temptation to take an inexpensive taxi ride is hard to resist. There is no

DJ-cum-record stall owner at the Olde Craft Market.

shortage of retail opportunities. For wood carvings, batik, fashion jewelry, toys, hats and T-shirts; visit the **Olde Craft Market.** . All the prices are inflated, particularly in the markets, and haggling is expected – be bold but polite and enjoy it. Jamaicans generally have a great sense of humor, but good manners are considered very important and politeness will usually pay off.

Highlights of the Jamaican calendar include pre-Lent Carnival, with parades and bands in the main towns; the Ocho Rios Jazz Festival in June; and Independence Day on August 6, a public holiday with street parades and concerts.

FOREST AND GARDENS

On a journey around the town, ask the taxi driver to head inland for a trip through **Fern Gully**, a lush, hardwood rainforest where the road is overhung with giant ferns and lianas. In the past more than 60 species were recorded here, but the fern population has dwindled slightly as a result of hurricane damage and possibly pollution, including increased car fumes. However, the winding road bordered by the trees and vegetation is still worth seeing.

Ocho Rios has two excellent botanical gardens. **Shaw Park Botanical Gardens** ❸ (tel: 876-974 2723; daily 8am–4pm) comprises of 25 acres (10 hectares) of tropical trees and shrubs set around a natural waterfall and is within walking distance of the cruise terminal. Nearby, **Konoko Falls** ❹ (tel: 876-974 6235; www.konokofalls.com; daily 8am–4.30pm) is a serene water garden that surrounds a small building containing rare Taíno artifacts.

Art for sale, Olde Craft Market.

RIVER FALLS, HORSE RIDING AND ZIP-LINING

On a hot day, **Dunn's River Falls** ❽ (www.dunnsriverfallsja.com; daily 8:30am–4pm, cruise ship days from 7am), five minutes' drive from the port and 2 miles (3km) west of the town center, is irresistible. Dunn's River cascades for 600ft (180 meters) down a series of limestone shelves through the dappled shade of the rainforest. Official guides lead chains of visitors up the slippery rocks, stopping for photos in

Fern Gully.

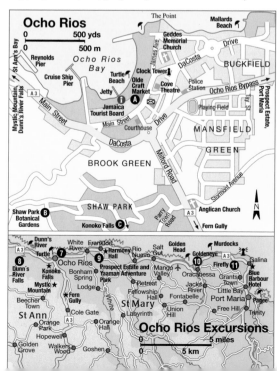

Feed the ostriches at Prospect Estate.

the freshwater pools; get there early to avoid the rush, especially if more than one cruise ship is in port (it can take three at a time). The guide will expect a tip. It is possible to climb independently, but the rocks are slippery and the water is powerful enough in places to make you lose your footing. Wear rubber-soled shoes or hire shoes at the falls, and prepare to get soaked.

Nearby is **Mystic Mountain** (tel: 876-974 3990; www.rainforestadventure. com; daily 8am–5pm), a thrill-seeker's dream, complete with a dramatic bobsled ride (on a track, there being no snow), ziplining and the Sky Lift chairlift that carries you 700ft over the rainforest, with views of the coast.

Seven miles (11km) west of Ocho Rios is **Chukka Cove** (www.chukka.com; tel: 876-979 8500; daily), which organizes horse-riding excursions. The 3-hour beach ride meanders through two of the island's oldest sugar estates before stopping at Chukka Cove's private beach for a swim. Chukka Cove is also known for its polo, and international tournaments take place here

during March and April. Alternatively, sign up zip-lining at Cranbrook Rainforest Gardens, or river tubing on the White River, both thrill rides that actually require no skill at all.

A TASTE OF PLANTATION LIFE

A short drive east of Ocho Rios is **Yaaman Adventure Park**, on **Prospect Estate** (tel: 877-344 3385; www.yaamanadventure. com, daily, 9am–5pm), one of the best examples of a working plantation, where you will find bananas, sugar cane, coffee, pimento (allspice), coconuts, pineapples and cassava cultivated over 1,000 acres (400 hectares). There are tours of the plantation on horseback, or by camel, Segway or tractor, up to the **White River** gorge and owner **Sir Harold's Viewpoint** overlooking the coast. On site, there's a cookery school, too, where you can learn to prepare Jamaican specialities.

Combine a visit to the plantation with a stop at the pretty, gingerbread-house **Harmony Hall** (tel: 876-975 4222; www.harmonyhall.com; Tue–Sun 10am–5.30pm; free), nearby. Formerly a Methodist Manse, built in the mid-1800s, it is now an art gallery showing the work of some 100 established and upcoming Caribbean artists. Alongside the paintings and sculpture on display there is an interesting gallery shop, and an elegant restaurant on the ground floor.

SOPHISTICATED PLACES

Ocho Rios has several decent beaches ideal for a day of sun-worshipping and splashing about in the sea. **Mallards Beach**, at the eastern end of town, will be busy, but a 20-minute taxi ride further east, out of Ochi and past Rio Nuevo, lies **Oracabessa Bay**. This is the location of **Goldeneye** , which was once the home of novelist and former British Naval Intelligence officer Ian Fleming (1908–64), the author of the James Bond adventures. The building is now a hotel (www.goldeneye.com), owned by legendary music producer Chris Blackwell, head of Island Outpost. Alongside is **James**

Rafting on the Martha Brae River.

Bond Beach, location of a two-story, open-air beach bar Moonraker, or five minutes away by car, the quieter Reggae Beach is preferred by locals.

Just outside Port Maria, down the coast from Oracabessa, you will find **Firefly ⓫** (tel: 876 725 0920; www.firefly-jamaica.com; daily, 8am–6pm), the former home of Noël Coward (1899–1973), now managed as a museum by Island Outpost on behalf of the Jamaican National Trust. The house has breathtaking views of the north coast and offers a fascinating insight into the colorful past of the multi-gifted and popular actor, composer and playwright, who entertained the likes of Errol Flynn, Sean Connery and Elizabeth Taylor, among others. It is, however, showing its age and the whole museum project is currently under review.

PORT ANTONIO AND THE EAST

Cruise ships also call at Port Antonio, at the foot of the Blue Mountains, a dramatically beautiful part of the country. This is the county of Surrey, the wettest on the island, but also the greenest, where the forest meets the turquoise sea and fishing villages dot the coastline. Port Antonio dates from 1723, but its prosperity dates from 1871 with the start of banana shipments to Boston in the US, which were an immediate success. The town became the banana capital of the world, and the banana boats brought the first tourists to Jamaica. Although these glory days are gone, there is a thriving marina and there are plans to develop the town further for tourism. Navy Island, offshore, once owned by Errol Flynn, is awaiting redevelopment.

The **Rio Grande**, just west of the town, is the largest river in Jamaica. Bananas were once floated down it on rafts but then, in the 1940s, Errol Flynn organized raft races and developed the attraction for tourists. Rafting on the Rio Grande (tel: 876-715 1111; www.portantonio.com; daily 9am–4pm) on bamboo rafts is the best in Jamaica, with the ride from Berridale to Rafter's Rest taking 2–3 hours through a lush tropical rural landscape. There are opportunities to stop en route for a snack or a walk.

⊙ **Fact**

The White Witch, an 18-hole championship golf course, is part of the luxurious Ritz-Carlton Rose Hall Hotel in Montego Bay (tel: 888-767 3425). Two other local courses are the Half Moon (tel: 876-953 2560) and Tryall (tel: 876-956 5660).

Port Antonio marina.

Ships anchored at Nassau cruise port.

San Geronimo Fort, San Juan.

SAILING IN THE EAST

The eastern Caribbean is ideal for seven-day cruises that take in a culturally diverse range of islands, including a few tiny spots that are exclusive to the cruise lines.

First, one needs to define what the eastern Caribbean consists of – in cruising terms, at least. The main islands covered on eastern Caribbean tours are the Bahamas, Puerto Rico, the US Virgin Islands, Sint Maarten, Dominican Republic and Cuba. A quick look at a map might suggest that the British Virgin Islands should be included in this list; they are, in fact, usually part of the cruise lines' southern itineraries.

The majority of the major lines cover these eastern ports of call. Because the region is fairly close to the United States, most of the cruises begin in Florida – at Miami, Fort Lauderdale or Port Canaveral – from where they can comfortably cover quite a lot of nautical miles in seven days – the usual length of a trip.

One of the joys of these itineraries is that they visit islands that are culturally so different. The Bahamas has strong British influences combined with all the color of the Caribbean; Puerto Rico may be part of the USA, but the port of San Juan is an archetypal Spanish colonial town; St Thomas combines excellent duty-free shopping with fantastic beaches; while Sint Maarten/St Martin is a pleasing mixture of Dutch and French cultures. The Dominican Republic, meanwhile, is attracting a growing following of golfers who cruise as well as offering plenty of soft adventure activities.

CRUISING OPTIONS

Available options range across the spectrum, from the largest ships, carrying 5,000 passengers or more, to the smallest boutique vessels. Most of the cruises include two or three full days at sea, as it's a long haul south from Florida to the Caribbean, to give passengers a chance to enjoy the facilities they offer on board. A typical itinerary sailing from Miami might visit San Juan (Puerto Rico), Philipsburg, Sint Maarten, Charlotte Amalie on St Thomas, and Nassau.

Carnival Splendor at Half Moon Cay in the Bahamas.

The clubbing scene in St Maarten.

Several of the cruise lines' 'private islands' are in this region. All have wonderful beaches and, after being welcomed ashore with a chilled rum punch and the rhythms of a steel band, passengers spend their time swimming, sailing, water-skiing, and enjoying a sizzling barbecue. Princess Cruises owns Princess Cays in the Bahamas, while Royal Caribbean owns an island, Coco Cay, not far from Nassau in the Bahamas, and Labadee, a peninsula on the secluded north coast of Haiti (sometimes included on eastern itineraries). Disney's Castaway Cay is one of the best, with a long sliver of white sandy beach, bars and bicycles. Opinions about these islands are mixed, as they are lacking in Caribbean culture and you will be sharing your 'private' spot with fellow cruise passengers.

THE BAHAMAS

Even though the Bahamas is actually in the Atlantic, it is invariably included in Caribbean tours, and for that reason we have covered it in this book. In fact, a visit to **Nassau**, capital of the Bahamas,

Fun on Castaway Cay, Disney's private island paradise.

is among the highlights of an eastern Caribbean cruise. The cruise terminal, Festival Place, has all the facilities a visitor could want. Passengers disembark right in the heart of Nassau, and schedules allow time for a guided walk around the historic capital of this ex-British colony. If your ship docks in **Freeport** on Grand Bahama Island, a range of outdoor activities are on offer, from a visit to the Lucaya National Park to a chance to swim with dolphins.

SAN JUAN, ST THOMAS AND ST JOHN

San Juan, in Puerto Rico (which also acts as a home port for ships venturing further south; see page 195), offers a different kind of experience. Most cruise ships dock at Calle Marina, just to the south of the lovely old Spanish colonial town, and the majority of people are content to spend their day soaking up the atmosphere. El Yunque rainforest is not far away.

The US Virgin Islands are something else again. Ships dock at **Charlotte Amalie**, in St Thomas, which has a lovely harbor and is known as the duty-free shopping center of the Caribbean. The nearby island of **St John**, two-thirds of which is an unspoilt national park, is reached by a short, inexpensive ferry ride.

Cruise ships calling at Sint Maarten usually dock at the main port, **Philipsburg**, and allow passengers time to visit **Marigot** in St Martin (a port which was unfortunately badly damaged by Hurricane Irma in 2017), thus giving a flavor of both Dutch and French sides of the island in one brief visit.

Cuba is enormously popular now with US passengers, despite the tightening of the rules by the Trump administration. American citizens can, however, visit as part of a 'cultural exchange' and several lines take passengers on cruises that comply with the regulations, among them Silversea, Azamara, Holland America Line and Regent Seven Seas Cruises.

PRIVATE HIDEAWAYS

Soft breezes, sun-drenched beaches, aquamarine seas, marinas brimming with luxury yachts – the rich are amply rewarded in the Caribbean.

Said Voltaire of the Caribbean, 'You go to heaven if you want, I'd rather stay here.' Owning a private island is the ultimate fantasy, best embodied by Necker Island, a millionaire's playground in the British Virgin Islands. Richard Branson, founder of Virgin, bought it in 1979 for personal use, but now accepts paying guests, including many A-listers. The island, a smooth green lump ringed with sand, is designed as an exclusive Balinese-style estate. A constant supply of home-cooked food, butlers and speedboats ensures that guests are happy.

Cruise passengers are tempted to think that they, too, can enjoy a private island for a day, but it is shared with thousands of others.

Celebrity hideaways couldn't be further removed from the cheerful inclusiveness of the cruise lines' private ports of call. Each island has its own fashionable following, with Mustique, St-Barths and Barbados among the most select. Mustique, put on the map by Princess Margaret in the 1960s, has been offering sanctuary to the stars ever since. From Mick Jagger and the late David Bowie to David Beckham and Tommy Hilfiger, celebrities appreciate the privacy symbolized by a secluded pastel-pink villa and manicured lawns.

St-Barths is where the rich like to play poor, but vintage Veuve Cliquot may well accompany the baguette on the beach. The pared-down chic of St-Barths has much to do with the cheek of the French in daring to transform this arid rock into St Tropez. As a haunt of Rockefellers and Rothschilds, European royalty and international celebrities, St-Barths feels more Côte d'Azur than Caribbean. When you're in port, play the mega-yacht game. Check out the vast private yachts, some so huge they can't fit into Gustavia's harbor, Google them, and then try to spot the famous owners and their glamorous guests.

Barbados, as anglicized as St-Barths is Gallic, represents an equally exclusive haunt for celebrities, who relish the re-creation of a colonial grandeur that never quite existed, typified by the luxurious Sandy Lane Hotel.

Not that these islands have a monopoly. Antigua is home to Eric Clapton, while Oprah Winfrey also has a residence on the island. Parrot Cay in the Turks and Caicos is the most over-hyped hideaway, a colonial-style resort framed by coral reefs and cactus groves. Bruce Willis, Barbra Streisand and Britney Spears are all fans. There have been reports that the actor Leonardo DiCaprio has bought part of the tiny island of Blackadore Caye. The island, which is a short boat ride from the Belize barrier reef, is slated for development as an exclusive eco-resort. Meanwhile, Nicholas Cage, Johnny Depp and Julia Roberts all allegedly own islands in the Bahamas, as do Lenny Kravitz, Faith Hill and Jim McGraw.

Jamaica has its fans, too. After being 'discovered' by Noël Coward, Jamaica appealed to Ivor Novello and Charlie Chaplin, Clark Gable and Errol Flynn. Ian Fleming, creator of James Bond, built Goldeneye, his winter retreat, here. Now owned by Chris Blackwell, the founder of Island Records, it remains a bolthole for stars such as Michael Caine and Harrison Ford, Pierce Brosnan and Sting, who penned *Every Breath You Take* while ensconced on the bamboo sofa.

The port of Gustavia, St-Barths.

THE BAHAMAS

Learn about Bahamian history in Nassau, see how the rich have fun on Paradise Island, and use Freeport as a starting point for visiting botanic gardens and swimming with dolphins.

When it comes to cruising the Bahamas, all eyes are on the two main ports: Nassau, the national capital, on New Providence Island, and Freeport, on Grand Bahama. The two islands are truly a study in contrasts, but both offer something for short- and long-stay visitors: from colonial architecture to glitzy casinos, from white, sandy beaches to opportunities to encounter dolphins.

New Providence, roughly 20 miles (32km) in circumference and 8 miles (13km) wide, is home to almost a quarter of a million residents. Nassau is situated on the north shore of the island, approximately 180 nautical miles southeast of Miami, and, for many people, this commercial hub *is* the Bahamas. It is certainly a more atmospheric town than Freeport, the nation's second city, which was created in 1955, but the latter is a jumping-off point for an island that has much to offer, from limestone caves to lush exotic gardens.

The Port of Nassau's **Prince George Wharf** Ⓐ has all the facilities that cruise ship passengers need. **Festival Place** (Mon, Tue, Fri and Sat 8am–8pm, Wed, Sun 9am–2pm, Thu 8am–5pm) on the wharf is a two-story, colonial-style village of brightly painted little shops and kiosks selling

souvenirs. There is an information office for tours, attractions, maps and leaflets where you can also buy water-taxi tickets for Paradise Island. There is also a post office, a communications center for phone calls and internet access, hair braiding and live music on some days, in the indoor plaza. As you emerge on to Bay Street, you can pick up a horse-drawn carriage tour or a taxi tour, or hop on a shuttle bus. There are scooter rentals to your right as you come out and further along are the tour boats and ferry boats. The

Ⓞ **Main attractions**
Festival Place, Nassau
Pirates of Nassau
  Museum, Nassau
Half Moon Cay, Little San
  Salvador
Rand Nature Center,
  Grand Bahama
Lucayan National Park,
  Grand Bahama

Ⓞ **Maps on pages 174, 176**

Costumed guide at Pirates of Nassau Museum.

A sunny day on Princess Cays' sandy beach, Eleuthera.

port can accommodate 12 cruise ships at a time and they all berth directly by the pier, so tenders are not needed. Passengers literally walk off the ship, through Festival Place and onto Bay Street, in the heart of the city and central shopping area, a few hundred yards away.

GETTING TO KNOW NASSAU

There are dozens of ways to enjoy Nassau if you have only a day in port. The Bahamas Ministry of Tourism can match up visitors looking for genuine cultural exchange and enrichment with a local ambassador via the People To People program, which costs nothing; apply in advance via www.bahamas.com.

There's plenty to see in town, too. As you pass the 19th-century **Public Buildings** **B**, just off Bay Street, you will probably learn a little about the islands' history. They became English colonies in 1629, briefly fell under Spanish rule in 1782 and, after years as a dependency, became the independent Commonwealth of the

Bahamas in 1973. Immediately south of these government offices are the Supreme Court building and the quaint octagonal **Nassau Public Library** (Shirley Street; tel: 242-322 4907; Mon–Thu 10am–8pm, Fri 10am–5pm, Sat 10am–4pm), built in 1797 as a jail, which contains, among other things, a small collection of Amerindian artifacts in one of the cells.

The library stands on the corner of Parliament Street, where you will see some lovely historic buildings, mostly dating from the mid-19th century. Prominent among them is **Jacaranda House**, with wide, latticed verandas, privately owned but hosting jazz in the evening of the first Sunday of every month. Not far away stands **St Andrew's Presbyterian Church** **C**, known as The Kirk, a pleasant, welcoming building; the Trinity Methodist Church; and Christ Church Cathedral, with a beautiful stained-glass window above the altar. From The Kirk you go over George Arch (also known as the Gregory Arch) to **Government House** **D** (Blue Hill Road and Duke

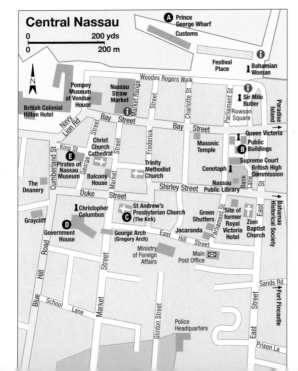

Central Nassau

Street; tel: 242-322 1875), a pink and white building that has been the official residence of the Governor-General since 1801.

A glitzy new resort development, Baha Mar, is now fully open at Cable Beach, a short drive from the dock. The complex comprises three luxurious hotels, operated by Rosewood, Grand Hyatt and SLS, which between them offer over 40 bars and restaurants, lavish spas, an 18-hole golf course and one of the largest casinos in the Caribbean. As yet, day passes are not being offered to cruise passengers but you could always have lunch in one of the restaurants, or try your luck in the casino.

PIRATE PLEASURE DOME

A shuttle bus transports cruise ship passengers from the dock to the **Pirates of Nassau Museum E** (tel: 242-356 3759; www.piratesofnassau.com; Mon–Sat 8.30am–5.30pm, Sun 9am–2pm), just a few blocks away, opposite the cathedral. At this intriguing interactive museum,

visitors board a full-size replica of the pirate ship *Revenge* and enter the world of cutlass-wielding, bloodthirsty pirates. You are encouraged to 'walk among them as they eat, drink, sleep, gamble, plot and pillage,' and in the process, learn about Bahamian history and some of the world's notorious buccaneering characters.

A pirate pub serves lunch and dinner, and next door to it 'Plunder!', a pirate-themed gift shop, tempts you to buy. On the 10-minute walk back to the ship you could stop at the **Straw Market** to buy souvenirs – baskets, dolls, table mats, hats – made from plaited thatch palm. Vendors will try and sell you anything and everything.

PARADISE ISLAND

At Prince George Wharf, ferryboats wait to take passengers to **Paradise Island**, across Nassau Harbour. This resort island (formerly and less glamorously known as Hog Island) is a very swish place indeed. Among its expensive pleasures are the Atlantis Resort; the Hurricane

Junkanoo festivities, including street parades, take place the day after Christmas and again on New Year's Day.

Atlantis Hotel on Paradise Island in Nassau.

A local guide leads a tour through the Lucayan National Park.

Souvenir dolls on sale in Lucaya, Grand Bahama.

Hole, a haven for luxury yachts; the Versailles Gardens, complete with 14th-century cloisters, brought from France and reconstructed, stone by stone, surrounding the exclusive Ocean Club, A Four Seasons Resort; and the 18-hole championship Ocean Club Golf Course. There is also a slender crescent of white sand called Paradise Beach. There are organized tours to Paradise, or you can just get on a ferry and go independently.

PRINCESS CAYS, ELEUTHERA

This is a private cay used exclusively by Princess Cruises and P&O Cruises, with 1.5 miles (2km) of beachfront at the southern tip of lovely Eleuthera, one of the Bahamas' out islands, east of Nassau. There is shade from palm trees, hammocks to lie in and a coral reef offshore. Watersports equipment is available to rent, as well as a beach barbecue, a bar, a boutique and a small section where local vendors sell souvenirs and braid hair. Numerous tours are

sold based around the resort, among them cycling, clear-bottom kayaking, dune buggy safaris, stingray encounters and snorkeling. When a ship is in, there's a colorful Junkanoo (carnival) procession at lunchtime.

HALF MOON CAY, LITTLE SAN SALVADOR

This stunning private island, a former pirate hideout, is visited by Holland America's ships during most of their Caribbean and Panama Canal itineraries. About 100 miles (160km) from Nassau, just southeast of Eleuthera and west of Cat Island, only 45 acres of the island's 2,400 acres (971 hectares) are developed; the rest is a bird sanctuary. Activities include a nature trail, kayaking, horse-riding, Aqua-trax tours, deep sea fishing, glass-bottomed boat tours, swimming with stingrays and the Aqua Park with lots of water toys. Available for rent are air-conditioned, beachfront cabanas which each come with a fridge stocked with cold drinks, fruit and snacks, to help you relax on the

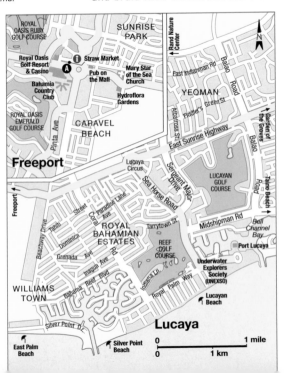

beautiful arc of white sand with shallow, turquoise water.

BERRY ISLANDS

Lying north of Nassau and south of Grand Bahama, this collection of tiny islands is a dream for fishermen and divers. **Great Stirrup Cay** was the first private island to be developed for cruise ships and is now used by the Norwegian Cruise Line. Bertram's Cove has white sand, offshore coral reefs and shade from palm trees. You can rent snorkeling equipment, foam floats, inflatable rafts, pedalos, kayaks and small sailing boats for the day. Limbo dancing and beach games are organized with a lunchtime barbecue. There's also hiking (you can walk to the lighthouse that dates from 1863) or you can just lie in a hammock and watch everyone else.

Royal Caribbean's newly developed **Coco Cay**, originally named **Little Stirrup Cay**, in the Berry Islands, is a strip of sand with its own cruise ship pier about 50 miles (80km) from Nassau. There is a rumor that the grave of the pirate Blackbeard is located here. There is a sunken plane and a shipwrecked replica of *Queen Anne's Revenge*, Blackbeard's flagship that sank off North Carolina in 1718. Activities include rides in a tethered balloon; the tallest waterslide in North America; plush overwater villas; and the Caribbean's largest freshwater pool.

CASTAWAY CAY

Located 175 miles (282km) east of Miami and just west of Abaco, Disney Cruise Line has its own private beach, Castaway Cay, formerly **Gorda Cay**, also with its own pier. Passengers are transported around by tram, with Disney characters in abundance.

There are three beaches: one for families, one for teens and one for adults only. The latter includes a bar and hammocks, and beach massages are offered. The teen beach has volleyball. Activities and facilities include paddleboats, waterslides, kayaking, snorkeling for sunken treasure, tubes

> **⊘ Fact**
>
> Jazz fans will be pleased to find Count Basie Square in Port Lucaya, complete with bandstand. Born in New Jersey, Basie made Freeport his adoptive home.

Colorful wooden stalls at night in Count Basie Square, Freeport.

and rafts. There's even a post office and a shop on this island.

GRAND BAHAMA

Grand Bahama, which is three times the size of New Providence, sits at the northern end of the Bahamas chain, and has just over 51,000 residents. The emphasis here is on the outdoors – from nature walks to full-fledged eco-adventures, all available on organized tours.

The **Lucayan Harbour Cruise Facility** lies 65 miles (105km) east of West Palm Beach and 80 miles (128km) northeast of Miami. Covering 1,630 acres (668 hectares), it can accommodate the largest cruise ships in the world. The total berth length of over 6,000ft (1,800 meters) accommodates both cruise ship and day ferry berths.

The massive terminals have everything cruise passengers could wish for. The area has a tropical-landscape design and encloses a huge, Bahamian-style retail and entertainment village center and marketplace, where most of the standard excursions organized by the cruise lines begin.

Golfing comes with a view in the Bahamas.

The harbor lies to the west of central Freeport. If you are going to explore alone, there are taxis to take you to the International Bazaar or to Port Lucaya.

THINGS TO DO IN FREEPORT

Most of the attractions of Grand Bahama lie a little way outside town; Freeport is pretty enough but it's mainly a business center. The **Straw Market**  offers some local color, as does the Fruit Market (buy the local spicy red pepper sauce here).

The main hub of the action though, is Lucaya, east of Freeport, where there are two big beach hotels and the Port Lucaya Marketplace, packed with souvenir shops, boutiques, craft stores, places to eat and drink, and live music. There's also golf and gambling for those who want it, and all manner of watersports from the stunning white sand beach.

NATURE TRAILS

There is a fascinating excursion to be made to the **Rand Nature Center** (tel: 242-352 5438; www.bnt.bs; Mon–Fri 9am–4pm), to the north of Freeport. Run by the Bahamas National Trust, this 100-acre (40-hectare) national park has some interesting nature trails, a flock of West Indian flamingos (the national bird of the Bahamas) and well-informed guides to talk you through it all.

To the east of Freeport and Lucaya lies the **Garden of the Groves** (tel: 242-374 7778; thegardenofthegroves.com; daily 9am-4pm), spectacular, landscaped botanical gardens with waterfalls and a lush fern gully (a popular spot for wedding parties). Children will enjoy the petting zoo, and visitors of all ages should love the African pygmy goats, Vietnamese pot-bellied pigs, and colorful peacocks, macaws and cockatoos. Alligator feeding time is always popular, too. There is also a Bahamian arts and crafts market, a café and a children's party area. The garden is named after Georgette and Wallace Groves, who created this lovely spot. Groves also founded the Grand Bahama Port Authority and Freeport itself in the 1960s.

There is also a guided nature tour through the **Lucayan National Park** (tel: 242-352 5438; daily 9am–4pm), about 13 miles (21km) east of the Garden of the Groves. Led by knowledgeable local guides, you can explore the caves that form one of the largest charted underwater cave systems in the world. The park has an extensive figure-of-eight system of paths that take you into two caves, in one of which were discovered artifacts and bones relating to the island's first inhabitants, the Lucayan Amerindians. Above ground, the 40-acre (16-hectare) park has trails through forests rich in tropical vegetation – cedar and mahogany trees – and mangrove lagoons that support a wealth of birdlife.

THE DOLPHIN EXPERIENCE

Among out-of-town excursions, a perennially popular one is to the **Dolphin Experience** at Sanctuary Bay, a 9-acre (4-hectare) lagoon a short ferry ride from the UNEXSO (Underwater Explorers' Society; tel: 800-992 3843; www.unexso.com) dock at Port Lucaya. The tour takes approximately 2.5 hours and includes informative talks about these intelligent mammals. You can have various kinds of in-the-water encounters with wild dolphins that inhabit Sanctuary Bay, a natural lagoon, including swimming or even snorkeling with them; rates vary, depending on what you want to do. Certified divers can also join shark encounter dives.

OTHER ALTERNATIVES

Other cruise ship excursions include snorkeling and kayaking trips and beach parties on the lovely Lucayan Beach and Taino Beach (the latter about 2 miles/4km) from Port Lucaya.

The **Sea Safari Snorkel Adventure** is also popular, and organized cruise ship tours are run twice daily. It's a two-hour foray among Grand Bahamas' tropical fish and living corals, at Rainbow Reef and the surrounding area. It's only minutes away from the dock, and also has a rock-climbing wall and two water slides. All gear is provided and there is professional instruction and supervision.

A diver swims with a captive bottle-nosed dolphin at the UNEXSO dive site.

The wave-thrashed Malecón.

A taxi glides past the Capitolio.

CUBA: HAVANA

After years of isolation, Havana has once more become a tourist hotspot. This vibrant city offers culture, colonial architecture and ever-present, irresistible music, all within a compact area.

The largest of all the Caribbean islands (population: 11.2 million), Cuba was the most-visited country in the Caribbean during the 1950s, but when Fidel Castro came to power in 1959, the tourism boom ended. Thirty-two years later, following the breakup of the Soviet Union and the loss of revenue it represented as a trading partner, Cuba again turned to tourism for its economic salvation. Today, the island is a popular destination once again, with newly developed infra-structure and bright prospects ahead for further tourism.

Sultry, exotic, romantic and rich with Latin music and colonial history, the island has a gorgeous landscape of lush mountains, powdery beaches and tropical greenery. A shore excursion offers an eye-opening glimpse of the complex realities of the embattled economy of this socialist island. Cuba is a remarkably safe country, especially considering the poverty of many of its inhabitants, and it puts a great deal of effort into making visitors feel welcome.

Although the island has eight ports of entry, the majority of cruises come ashore in the capital city of **Havana** at the **Terminal Sierra Maestra**, an odd blend of old colonial-style architecture, modern chrome-and-glass and hardwood floors, and has an antique Dodge

The cigar is a symbol of Cuba.

car propped up on display. Located on **Avenida San Pedro**, it is packed with modern amenities, including a snack bar and gift shop, and disembarks its passengers onto **Plaza de San Francisco**, a small square centered around a lion fountain, right in the heart of Old Havana where tour buses and taxis await.

The first thing passengers spot when sailing into the harbor is the impressive fortress, **El Morro** (daily 10am–7pm) on one side of the entrance and the smaller **Castillo de San Salvador**

⦿ Main attractions

El Morro, La Cabaña and
  la Punta fortresses
Palacio de los Capitanes
  Generales
Plaza de la Catedral
La Bodeguita del Medio
Museo de la Revolución
Museo Nacional Palacio
  de Bellas Artes: Arte
  Cubano
Capitolio
Tropicana Nightclub

Map on page 184

Eating ice cream on Obispo Street.

de la Punta on the other. Built in the 1500s, both structures provided Cuba with a defence against French and British invaders during colonial times. A heavy chain linked the two fortifications and was raised at night to keep out pirates. At the tip of El Morro is a lighthouse that has guided thousands of ships into port with its sweeping beam of light since it opened in 1845. Alongside El Morro is the imposing 18th-century **Castillo de San Carlos de la Cabaña** (daily 8am–11pm), where every evening at 9pm, the cannon are still fired to commemorate the former practice of closing the city gates. Both El Morro and La Cabaña contain some interesting museums and it is worth a trip across the bay to visit them.

HABANA VIEJA

A typical day-long excursion in Havana usually includes a city tour in an air-conditioned bus, a stop for lunch and a walk though **Habana Vieja** (Old Havana) – a Unesco World Heritage Site packed with beautiful Spanish colonial buildings, many with brightly tiled, plant-filled courtyards. English-speaking guides usually accompany groups at all times. While some cruise companies insist that their passengers take an organized tour, others allow them to explore on their own. If you do this, you will find there is plenty to see within walking distance of the terminal.

The **Plaza de Armas** is the city's oldest square, dating back to around 1520. One of the busiest public places

in Havana, the plaza is a meeting place for local people by day and night. In the center stands a statue to Carlos Manuel de Céspedes (1819–74), a Cuban hero who fought unsuccessfully against Spanish rule; and a mass of stalls selling fascinating secondhand books and prints lines two sides of the square.

Several historic buildings sit around the plaza, including the **Palacio de los Capitanes Generales** Ⓒ, a massive Baroque structure with thick mahogany doors that served as the headquarters of the Cuban government in the late 1790s. Today, it houses the **Museo de la Ciudad** (City Museum; Tacón 1 between Obispo and O'Reilly; tel: 53-7-861 5062; daily 9.30am–6.30pm, last tour 5pm), a repository of paintings, sculptures, artifacts, military uniforms and documents pertaining to the city's history, with a special collection devoted to the Cuban wars of independence.

A few doors down is the **Castillo de la Real Fuerza** Ⓓ (tel: 53-7-864 4490; daily 9am–6.30pm), the first fortress constructed by the Spanish in Cuba. Surrounded by a muddy water moat, it was built by the explorer Hernando de Soto in 1538, destroyed by the French a few years later and then reconstructed in 1558.

LEAVING THE SQUARE

To the west lies the beautiful **Plaza de la Catedral** Ⓔ, dominated by the Baroque 18th-century **Catedral de La Habana** (Empedrado corner of San Ignacio; daily 9am–5pm; Sun Mass at 10.30am; free, but small charge to go up the tower). Among the Spanish colonial buildings around the square, the **Palacio de los Marqueses de Aguas Claras** is perhaps the most splendid. It now houses the El Patio restaurant; this is quite expensive, but the tables set outside are a great place for a rest and a drink, and there's usually a band playing.

Opposite the cathedral is the **Palacio de los Condes de Casa Bayona**, built in 1720 for Governor-General Chacón but now housing the **Museo de Arte Colonial** (Colonial Art Museum; San Ignacio 22, corner Empedrado; tel: 53-7-862 6440; daily 9am–6.30pm). Packed with artifacts from centuries of colonial rule, most rooms are furnished to represent the lifestyle of a wealthy Havana family in the 19th century.

One of the most-visited spots in Old Havana is **La Bodeguita del Medio** Ⓕ (Empedrado 207; tel: 53-7-867 1374; daily noon–midnight). This 'little store in the middle of the block' is packed with pre-revolutionary history and full of Ernest Hemingway memorabilia. A classic Cuban tavern, the Bodeguita's walls are covered with messages written by satisfied customers from around the world. Along with Hemingway, who downed numerous *mojitos* (a rum, mint and lime-juice cocktail) at the wooden bar, other notables who have imbibed here include Graham Greene, Errol Flynn, Gabriel García Márquez, Salvador Allende and Fidel Castro himself.

Decorative objects from past times at the Museo de Arte Colonial.

With live Latin music most nights and some lunch times, the bar is always busy. The traditional Cuban food is a bit pricey because this place is a tourist hotspot.

Another world-famous bar, and a lunch stop on most Old Havana tours, is **El Floridita** (Obispo 557, corner Monserrate; tel: 53-7-867 1300; www. floridita-cuba.com; daily noon–1am). Also a Hemingway hangout, the Floridita is where the Nobel Prize-winning author came to drink daiquiris, which were supposedly invented here. Modernized in recent years to accommodate tourists, the Floridita has lost some of its old Bohemian charm; the food is pricey, but it still serves excellent daiquiris.

A FEW MUSEUMS

The **Depósito de los Automóviles** ⓖ (Car Museum; Oficios 13 corner Justiz, tel: 53-7-863 9942; Tue–Sat 9am–4.30pm, Sun 9am–1pm) contains a collection of beautifully preserved old cars, one of which belonged to the revolutionary hero Che Guevara. Many

Floridita, self-proclaimed cradle of the daiquiri.

more cars from the 1950s can still be seen on the streets. Just south of the cruise ship terminal is the interesting **Museo del Ron** (Rum Museum; Avenida del Puerto 262 between Sol and Muralla; tel: 53-7-861 8051; daily 9am–5.30pm; guided tours), with a tour that takes you through the whole process of rum production and ends with sampling in the bar and an opportunity to buy. The highlight for many people is the extensive model railway running around a model of a sugar refinery.

Between the two main thoroughfares, Avenida de los Misiones and Agramonte, on Refugio, is the **Museo de la Revolución** ⓗ (Museum of the Revolution; tel: 53-7-862 4091; daily 10am–5pm). It holds a wealth of material on the Cuban revolution – including some wonderful photographs and torn and bloodstained garments – the years of struggle that preceded it, and its accomplishments.

Attached to the museum is the **Memorial Granma**, where the *Granma*, the motorboat that brought

Fidel Castro from Mexico to Cuba at the start of the revolution, is displayed in a glass case. Outside, a bullet-pocked delivery van, used for an attack on the Presidential Palace, and remnants of a U2 spy plane shot down over Cuba in 1962, are watched by military guards.

Heading back towards the palm-fringed Parque Central, you will find the huge and airy modernist building housing the **Museo Nacional Palacio de Bellas Artes: Arte Cubano** ❶ (National Museum of Fine Arts; Trocadero between Zulueta and Monserrate; Tue–Sat 10am–6pm, Sun 10am–2pm), which holds the largest collection of works by Cuban artists in the country. The 20th-century section includes pieces by Wifredo Lam, Carlos Enríquez, René Portocarrero and Eduard Abela. It is generally considered to be the best museum in the city. Its sister museum on the east side of the Parque Central, **Museo Nacional Palacio de Bellas Artes: Arte Universal** (tel: 53-7-861 0241), contains an extraordinary international collection of paintings, by artists ranging from Velásquez to Canaletto, as well as the works of Cuban painters, and Greek and Roman statuary.

The grandiose, domed building at the far side of Parque Central is the **Capitolio** ❶ (Paseo de Martí between San Martín and Dragones; tel: 53-7-861 0261; daily 10am–5pm), reopened in 2018 after eight years of restoration work. Originally built in the 1920s as the presidential palace and modeled on the Capitol in Washington, it now houses the Academy of Sciences. Tours are available or you can wander around on your own. Next to it stands the flamboyant **Gran Teatro**, where national ballet and opera companies perform.

NIGHTLIFE

If a cruise ship is in port during the evening, excursions usually include a prearranged trip to the famous **Tropicana Nightclub** (www.cabaret-tropicana. com; Calle 72, 4504, between 43 and 45, Marianao; tel: 537-267 0110; Tue–Sun 8.30pm–3am). Known for its live salsa bands and sexy floor shows, the Tropicana delivers a once-in-a-lifetime treat. Beneath an open-air canopy of palm trees, the high-energy, ostentatious Tropicana ballroom features over 200 performers in each cabaret show. The shows are fantastic, but the cost of an evening here can be steep, with tickets at US$70–90, depending on your seat and the age of your rum.

The Tropicana, however, is not the only hot nightspot in town. In a city where music seems to seep out of every nook and cranny, there are numerous clubs, bars, cafés and dance halls where the local acts are first-rate – and far less expensive than at the Tropicana. An equally popular evening out is the various tributes to the Buena Vista Social Club, in smaller venues, with rum included and often, ending the evening dancing on stage with the band.

A refreshing Havana Club mojito, perfect with a sprig of mint.

Havana is synonymous with the sound of music.

THE DOMINICAN REPUBLIC: SANTO DOMINGO

The oldest town in the New World, Spanish colonial Santo Domingo is well worth exploring, but trips to Dominican Republic's stunning beaches and other attractions in the east are also options.

Main attractions

Catedral Basílica Menor
de Santa María
Fortaleza Ozama
Museo de las Casas
Reales
Museo Mundo de Ambar
Jardín Botánico Nacional
Altos de Chavón
Amber Cove

**Maps on pages
189, 193**

Whether your cruise ship docks in **Santo Domingo ❶** or east of the city at La Romana, a visit to the historic quarter of the capital is worth putting on the agenda. The old town, known as the **Zona Colonial**, although somewhat edgy, is packed with architectural gems, cobbled streets and historic museums, churches and palaces within what is left of its fortified walls. First founded in 1496 on the eastern bank of the Ozama River, it was moved across the river in 1502 after a hurricane destroyed the original wooden buildings. It flourished in the 16th century as the Spanish conquistadores used it as a base for their voyages of discovery and conquest, but an attack by Sir Francis Drake in 1586 nearly destroyed the city when his men pillaged and burned the buildings. Much of the old quarter has been carefully restored and preserved and is now a Unesco World Heritage Site, notable for having the first cathedral, first university, first royal court and first coinage in the Americas.

There are two cruise ship terminals either side of the river. The Sans Souci terminal on the east bank is the larger and can accommodate large cruise ships. There are duty free stores, an information center, internet access and buses and taxis outside. The Don Diego terminal on the west bank is nestled just under the Fortaleza Ozama, and also has information, internet access, currency exchange and shopping. Cruise ships also call at the new port of Amber Cove, just west of Puerto Plata on the north coast, although this is too far from the capital for a day trip.

CITY OF FIRSTS

If you are disembarking at the Don Diego terminal, head up the steps into town, where you will find yourself on **Calle El Conde**, a pedestrian boulevard lined with shops that runs across

Museo de las Casas Reales.

the old town to the former entrance gate, Puerta El Conde. Cross **Calle Las Damas**, the first-ever cobbled street, where the ladies of the court used to promenade, and one block further on is **Parque Colón**, with the **Cathedral**  on your left. The Catedral Basílica Menor de Santa María (Primada de América; Mon–Sat 9am–4.30pm, Sunday for services), was the first cathedral built in the Americas, after the first bishop complained to the Spanish emperor that he 'had no roof over his head.' Dates of its construction differ, with some saying Diego Colón laid the foundation stone in 1514, while others claim it wasn't started until 1521, but all agree that it was dedicated in 1542. Much altered over the centuries, it is now has three aisles with a raised nave and 14 chapels.

Return to Calle Las Damas to visit the **Fortaleza Ozama** (tel: 809-686 0222; Tue–Sun 9am–5pm), the oldest fortified structure in the city. The inner courtyard is dominated by the **Torre del Homenaje** (Tower of Homage), built in 1503 and used as a prison for centuries. The fortress was the largest and most important of the 20 defensive positions built along the walls of the town, with a commanding view of the mouth of the river.

COLONIAL MANSIONS

Calle Las Damas contains some of the most important colonial mansions. Note the huge arcaded inner courtyard of the **Casa de Bastidas**, once occupied by the royal tax collector, Rodrigo de Bastidas, who went on to colonize Colombia. The **Casa de Francia** once housed the conquistador, Hernán Cortés, before he left to conquer Cuba and Mexico. The luxury hotel **Hostal Nicolás de Ovando** is named after the governor of the island from 1502 to 1509, and has some delightful courtyards overlooking the river, and elegant rooms. The building opposite was originally a Jesuit church but was converted in the 1950s by the dictator Leonidas Trujillo into the **Panteón Nacional** (tel: 809-686 2453; Tue–Sun 9am–5pm), and now contains the mortal remains of the country's heroes and many of its presidents.

⊙ Fact

Christopher Columbus' bones were brought to Santo Domingo for burial in 1540 after his death in Spain in 1506, but later peregrinations to Cuba and Spain brought confusion over whether tombs uncovered in the cathedral in the 19th century were those of Columbus, his brother or his son. His presumed remains now lie in the Faro a Colón, inaugurated in 1992 to commemorate the 500th anniversary of his landing.

Fortaleza Ozama.

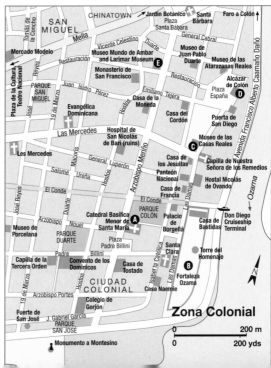

Zona Colonial

0   200 m
0   200 yds

Exclusive Casa de Campo.

Trujillo built himself an ornate tomb, but after his assassination in 1961, he was not given the honor of being interred here. A massive complex of buildings from the early 16th century used for royal administrative purposes is now the **Museo de las Casas Reales** ⓒ (tel: 809-682 4202; Tue–Sun 9am–5pm). The museum documents the nation's development from conquest to independence. Two highlights are an 18th century pharmacy and a collection of weapons.

Calle Las Damas heads north to **Plaza España**, from where there are lovely views over the river. Old warehouses have been restored and converted into brasseries, bars and souvenir shops and at night there is often music and folk dancing in the square. On the east side of the plaza is the **Alcázar de Colón** ⓓ (tel: 809-686 8657; Tue–Sun 9am–5pm), the fortified residence of the first viceroy of the New World, Columbus' son Diego Colón. Built without any nails by 1,000 Taíno slaves, it is an impressive two-story structure with arched colonnades

on both floors. It is now a museum with colonial works of art and furniture.

From Plaza España, walk along Restauración to the junction with Arzobispo Meriño. On the far right-hand corner you will see the fascinating **Museo Mundo de Ambar** ⓔ (Arzobispo Meriño 452 corner Restauración; tel: 809-686 5700; www.ambermuseum.com-daily 8am–6pm). Amber is found in the mountains along the north coast of the island, near Puerto Plata, and this museum has a stunning display of fossilized insects trapped in the resin. The guided tours (not obligatory) are very informative and staff will help you to distinguish real amber from fake. There is a workshop where you can watch jewelry being made, and a well-stocked shop.

MARKETS

Just north of the Zona Colonial on the other side of Avenida Mella is the new **Chinatown**, built at the end of the 1990s. There are a growing number of Chinese-owned businesses, including restaurants and supermarkets, mostly selling goods imported from China. Two traditional Chinese gateways guard the entrances along Avenida Duarte. Further west on Avenida Mella 505 is the more local **Mercado Modelo**, a covered market where you can find handicrafts, paintings, food and other souvenirs. Bargaining is acceptable here, as most prices have been marked up to account for it.

BOTANICAL GARDENS

The **Jardín Botánico Nacional** is a taxi ride northwest of the Zona Colonial, off Avenida J.F. Kennedy (entrance on Avenida Jardín Botánico; tel: 809-385 2611; www.jbn.gob.do; 9am–6pm). Covering an area of 180 hectares (450 acres), it contains plants endemic to the Dominican Republic, 300 types of orchid and a beautiful Japanese garden. A tractor-drawn 'train' allows you to rest your feet and keep out of the

sun, taking you past palm groves and through exotic tropical vegetation.

CITY SIGHTS EAST AND WEST

The Zona Colonial makes up only one percent of the total area of the sprawling city of Santo Domingo and while the old city can be toured on foot, you will need a taxi or organized tour to visit other sights. The harbor promenade known as the Malecón, or Avenida George Washington, heads west for 7.5 miles (12km) to the western city limits. Carnival parades and other festivities are held here and several of the city's top hotels are located here, although it is in need of some beautification and repairs to infrastructure. Inland from the Malecón there are several cultural places of interest, including the **Palacio de Bellas Artes**, the **Teatro Nacional** and the **Plaza Cultural** where the major museums are grouped in modern buildings.

East of the Ozama River in the Parque Mirador del Este is the monumental **Faro a Colón** (tel: 809-591 1492; Tue–Sun 9am–5pm), or Columbus Lighthouse. In 1923, a group of Latin American countries agreed there should be a project honoring Columbus and in 1929 a British architectural student, J. Cleave, won the commission. The 'recumbent cross'-shaped concrete structure, eventually built in 1986–92, is based on his design. Inside is the marble tomb of Christopher Columbus, permanently under guard. At night, a laser beam is capable of lighting up the clouds in the shape of a cross, but electricity shortages make this a very rare event. Tours to this side of the city usually include the **National Aquarium** and **Los Tres Ojos**, pools in limestone caverns once used as bathing spots by the Taínos.

BEYOND SANTO DOMINGO

Many cruise ships call at other ports in the Dominican Republic, east of the capital, and only offer Santo Domingo as an excursion. **La Romana** is one of the most popular, although the sugar-exporting town has little of interest to tourists. It is, however, within easy reach of some worthwhile excursions

> ### ⊘ Fact
>
> Pico Duarte in the Cordillera Central, at 3,087 meters (10,128ft), is the highest mountain in the Caribbean, but only just exceeds the height of its neighbor, La Pelona, which reaches 3,082 meters (10,112ft).

A game of chess in the centre of the Zona Colonial, the historical district of Santo Domingo.

> ### ⊘ LABADEE (LABADIE)
>
> Labadee is a private beach resort, leased to Royal Caribbean International, surrounded by breathtaking mountain scenery on the northern coast of Haiti. Enclosed by a security fence, passengers may not leave the property and only a select few Haitians are allowed in.
>
> RCI contributes a huge amount to the Haitian economy, paying the government a levy per tourist, employing 300 workers and allowing another 200 or so to sell to passengers. After the devastating earthquake in 2010 that caused severe damage to homes and infrastructure in Haiti, RCI donated US$1 million to the relief effort and its ships ferried supplies and personnel to the stricken country.
>
> Labadee is divided into seven 'neighborhoods,' each offering different activities: from Adrenaline Beach, with its own coaster ride and the Dragon's Breath Flight Line, the world's longest over-water zip-line; to Barefoot Beach, a VIP area for suite guests featuring cabanas. There's a family beach, a whole area dedicated to watersports and a 'town square' housing a market, shops and places to eat. No private island would be complete without its own cocktail – here it's the rum-laced Labadoozie.

Altos de Chavón, the quirky artists' village above the Rio Chavón.

Cayo Levantado.

and it is only 63 miles (102km) from Santo Domingo, along a good road. Just east of La Romana is **Casa de Campo**, the premier tourist resort in the country, an enclave built in the 1970s and covering 7,000 acres (2,800 hectares), with private villas, a marina, tennis club, riding school with polo, and three world-class golf courses. Celebrities appreciate the privacy and the guest list is impressive.

From the marina, boat tours go up the Chavón River to **Altos de Chavón ❷**, an international artists' village built by an Italian in mock-Italian style, on a hilltop above a gorge. A strange combination of art college and tourist attraction, it also has the **Church of San Estanislao**, containing the ashes of the patron saint of Poland, which was consecrated by Pope John Paul II. There is an amphitheater seating 3,000, which has seen performances by Frank Sinatra, Gloria Estefan and Julio Iglesias, and an interesting archaeological museum (daily 9am–5pm) which features Taíno exhibits.

BEACH EXCURSIONS

The Dominican Republic has some of the Caribbean's most beautiful beaches; those in the east of the country have glorious stretches of white sand, backed by palm trees, gently sloping into the clear blue sea. A 20-minute boat trip from La Romana is **Isla Catalina ❸**, also called **Serena Cay** by some cruise ships. There is no development on the island, which is dry and flat, but visitors come in their thousands during cruise ship season. The beach here is protected by a reef, which provides interest for divers or passengers in glass-bottomed boats, and plenty of water sports are on offer.

About 15 miles (25km) east of La Romana is the former fishing village of **Bayahibe**, its beaches now developed for tourism with several all-inclusive hotels and hostels for dedicated divers. It sits on the edge of the **Parque Nacional del Este**, where archaeological discoveries have been made dating human habitation of the area to 2000 BC. Offshore, but still part of the National Park, is **Isla Saona**, visited by catamarans and speedboats for a few hours on pristine beaches. A feature of this trip is the *piscina natural*, a natural swimming pool of waist-deep water formed by a sandbar, where boats stop for you to swim.

SAMANÁ PENINSULA

On the northeast coast of the Dominican Republic, the Samaná Peninsula was once an island, but in the late 18th century the narrow channel separating it from the mainland started to silt up and join the two together. During the 20th century transport to the peninsula was difficult and the beautiful beaches here were enjoyed by comparatively few people, who stayed in small inns and guesthouses. Now, with a modern international airport and better roads, its popularity has soared and hotel construction has mushroomed. Nevertheless, the green, forested hills and sandy bays remain unspoilt and it is always possible to escape the crowds.

From January to March, the highlight of any trip to the Samaná Peninsula is **whale-watching**. During this time, some 3,000 humpback whales migrate from the north to mate and calve in **Bahía de Samaná ❹**, a National Marine Mammal Sanctuary. Watching these gigantic creatures is a majestic sight, the young males showing off their acrobatic skills while mothers with calves glide gently along close to the surface. This is one of the best places in the world for whale watching, with strictly regulated and organized boats taking care not to disturb their activities. Seasickness pills are distributed on the best boats, but if this isn't for you, there is a whale-watching observatory on land at Punta Balandra, about 250 meters/yds along a trail on the tip of the peninsula (charge).

Cruise ships coming in to Samaná offer a beach excursion to the little island of **Cayo Levantado**, sometimes dubbed Bacardi Island because it once featured in a company ad. The center of the island is taken up by the Luxury Bahía Príncipe Cayo Levantado all-inclusive hotel, but at one end there is a romantic sweep of sand and palm trees.

AMBER COVE

In 2015, Carnival Corporation opened an ambitious new port project, Amber Cove, on the north coast of the island, near Puerto Plata. The new port, which can accommodate 10,000 cruise passengers, is now used by all Carnival's brands, among them Holland America Line, Costa and P&O Cruises.

Amber Cove is a resort in itself, with shops, beaches and watersports equipment as well as a giant waterpark, colonial-style buildings, old forts and rainforest safaris. It's a pleasant day trip and although Puerto Plata is only a short drive away, many cruise passengers are unlikely to stray very far from their own custom-built entertainment complex.

At Puerto Plata itself, one of the main attractions is **Ocean World**, a complex of pools where you can swim with dolphins, have a 'sea lion encounter' and get in the water with sharks (tel: 809-291 1000; www.oceanworld.net; daily 9am–6pm).

The Samaná Peninsula still provides an opportunity to escape the crowds.

The honor guard at the tomb of Christopher Columbus.

PUERTO RICO: SAN JUAN

Concentrate on the lovely Spanish-colonial old town if you have a one-day stop in San Juan, or take a trip to El Yunque rainforest. For extended stays, rent a car and go exploring.

San Juan is ideally placed as a home port for cruise ships heading into the southern Caribbean, and it is also superbly sited for passengers coming ashore when ships are paying a visit to Puerto Rico. The port acts as the unofficial gateway to Old San Juan. Dating back to 1521, this is the most attractive part of the city and one of the most fascinating historic areas in the Caribbean.

The vast majority of ships dock at Calle Marina, just to the south of the old town. New berths for mega-ships have been added and the cruise terminal upgraded with more facilities (shops, ATMs etc.). San Juan is, however, the busiest cruise port outside the US mainland, especially at weekends, so there are times when ships have to use berths in other parts of the city – usually at the Pan American Dock. These are some distance from Old San Juan (certainly not walkable), but ships usually provide a free shuttle service to the old town to make up for this inconvenience.

EXPLORING THE OLD QUARTER

If you are one of the majority who disembarks at Calle Marina, turn left past the tourist and post offices in Plaza Marina into Paseo de la Princesa and start up the gentle incline that is Calle San Justo. You are now in **Old San Juan** (El Viejo San Juan) – and it

The cathedral, San Juan.

shows. Puerto Rico may have been a US territory for over a century, but little here appears to have changed since the days of Spanish rule. The narrow, cobblestone streets are lined with 16th- and 17th-century Spanish colonial houses, with plants hanging from the balconies.

San Juan is one of the hottest places in the Caribbean, but don't let the heat deter you from walking – there is plenty of shade in the old town's streets. The traffic is pretty terrible, especially later in the day. There are

Main attractions
Castillo San Felipe del
  Morro
Castillo de San Cristóbal
Museo de Pablo Casals
Catedral San Juan
  Bautista
El Yunque National Forest

Map on page 196

plans to pedestrianize the old town. You'll overtake the tourist coaches if you walk, and you see a lot more. There are frequent, free open-air trolley buses, too, which you can hop on and off if you get tired. Their rattling progress over the cobbles and loud, guided commentaries ensure you can always hear them coming.

The best way to organize a tour of the old town is to make an early start from the ship and head straight for the 16th-century fortress, El Morro, the town's focal point, and then meander back through the streets, taking in the other sights. It is an easy 30-minute stroll to the fortress, which stands in glorious isolation facing out to the Atlantic in the far northwest corner of Old San Juan.

The most scenic route is to follow Paseo de la Princesa along the old city walls, stopping off at the impressive **La Fortaleza** Ⓐ, a 16th-century fortress which became a lavish mansion for the governor of San Juan. It still serves that function today, but part of it is open to the public for guided tours.

Alternatively, you can take Calle San Justo or any of the streets leading up from Paseo de la Princesa where it meets Plaza Marina, then turn left at the top from where **Castillo de San Felipe del Morro** Ⓑ (daily 9am–6pm) and Calle del Morro, the access road through its extensive grounds, are clearly visible. There are official US National Park guided tours of the fortress every hour, but it is more fun to take off on your own. It is a hugely atmospheric place – the walls are 20ft (6 meters) thick in places, and inside them is a maze of medieval nooks and crannies, dungeons, lookouts, courtyards, ramps, hidden staircases and gun turrets. There is a small museum that gives some information on the fort's history, but the whole site is a living museum.

FAMOUS CONNECTIONS

Leaving El Morro, turn left at the end of Calle del Morro along Calle Norzagaray, and a 15-minute walk will take you to the 17th-century **Castillo de San Cristóbal** Ⓒ, which is larger than El

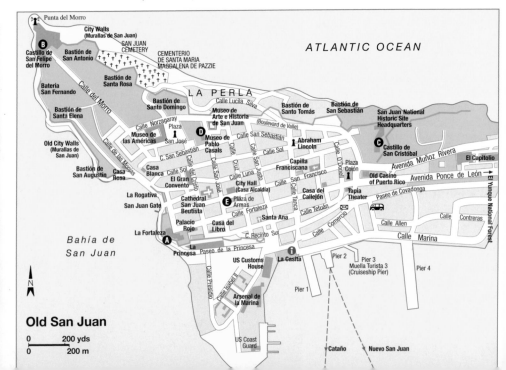

Old San Juan

Morro but not as impressive. Alternatively, take a right turn from Norzagaray into Plaza San José, one of several attractive, Spanish-style squares. In the center, there is a huge statue of Juan Ponce de León, the founder of the first settlement in 1508 and the first governor of Puerto Rico.

The most interesting site, however, is the **Museo de Pablo Casals** ❼ (Tue–Sat 9.30am–4.30pm), which illustrates the life and some of the works of the Catalan cellist who lived in San Juan for more than 20 years.

Head south from the plaza and you come to the heart of the old town shopping district, which lies along Calle Fortaleza, San Francisco and Cristo. San Juan used to have a reputation as a cheap duty-free shopping port, especially for gold jewelry. There are still plenty of fancy jewelers, but if your cruise is going to St Thomas it's better to wait, as prices are generally better there. On Calle Cristo, there is a favorite Old San Juan watering hole – the El Convento Hotel. It was originally a 17th-century Carmelite convent and much of its architecture remains intact, but it has long been operating as a classy hotel. Enjoy lunch in its Patio del Nispero or have a drink in the delightful courtyard.

If you prefer something less touristy, though, the old town is full of small, unpretentious cafés serving authentic Puerto Rican cuisine – a variation on traditional Spanish food, with rice and beans the staple dish.

El Convento is right opposite the city's **cathedral**, Catedral San Juan Bautista (Calle del Cristo 151–153; tel: 787-722 0861; www.catedralsjb.org; daily 9am–5.30pm) – the final resting place of Ponce de León. From here, the attractive main square, **Plaza de Armas** ❺, is just a short walk south, and it's on the way back to the ship. If you are running out of time, you can hop on a trolley, as they stop right by the cruise piers.

EXCURSIONS OUTSIDE SAN JUAN

The most popular shore excursion outside San Juan is to **El Yunque National Forest** (tel: 787-888 1880; www.fs.usda.gov/elyunque; 7.30am–6pm; free, small charge for El Portal Rain Forest Center). This 27,000-acre (11,000-hectare) area of rainforest is home to about 250 species of trees and plant life, plus hundreds of frogs and tropical birds, including colorful Puerto Rican parrots. The forest was badly damaged by hurricanes Irma and Maria in 2017 but is recovering, although nature will take time to repair itself in some areas. It makes a half-day organized tour, including a photo-stop at **El Luquillo Beach**, the most attractive on the island. However, it is a relatively easy place to reach independently by taxi or even by bus (there is a bus station on Calle Marina near the dock), and easy to explore as there are many marked trails.

Another popular tour is to the **Casa Bacardi Visitor Centre** (tel: 787-788

An artist captures the mood of the old town.

Orchid and canopy at the El Yunque National Forest.

8400; www3.bacardi.com; Tue–Fri 9am–4.30pm, Sat–Sun 9am–4.30pm) at Cataño, across the bay south of the old town. If you want to go alone, a ferry leaves every 30 minutes from a berth next to the cruise ships (the fare is just 50c one way). Entrance to the distillery is free – the hope is that you will buy what you taste there after your 45-minute tour.

EL CONDADO

El Condado, where there is a line of four- and five-star high-rise hotels on a sandy beachfront, is a long, hot walk from town and the beaches can be pretty crowded in the high season (winter). There is usually the option of organized ship's excursions that include lunch at one of the hotels and time on the beach, but you can easily take a taxi or a bus.

There are numerous casinos in San Juan, several of which are open 24 hours. The one at the La Concha Resort, a short taxi ride from the dock (tel: 787-721 7500; www.laconcha resort.com).

If your ship is in overnight or at least until late in the evening, there will be excursions to the Las Vegas-style shows at one of the largest hotels. It is better to take the tour than to book independently; the cruise lines have been good customers over many years so their passengers are given the best seats.

San Juan, linked by causeways and bridges to the rest of Puerto Rico, is the main jumping-off point for southern Caribbean cruises, which means that passengers have an overnight stay before joining the ship or may choose to stay longer, with maybe a week at one of the hotels along El Condado beach strip.

BEYOND SAN JUAN

If you are staying on, it is worth renting a car and exploring. At 100 miles (160km) long and 40 miles (64km) wide, Puerto Rico is one of the larger islands in the Caribbean and has one of the largest populations – nearly four million.

Your first stop could be **Ponce**, a Spanish colonial town towards the south coast. There is a good direct (toll) road so it only takes about 90 minutes. Further southwest, near La Parguera, is **Phosphorescent Bay**, so-called because its microscopic marine life lights up at night when disturbed by larger fish or boats. There is a similar phenomenon on **Vieques**, one of three tiny islands off the east coast. But to see that, or the sea turtle nests on the island of **Culebra**, you need to book a tour locally.

For snorkeling, head for a beach east of El Condado along the Atlantic coast – Ocean Park, Isla Verde or the palm-fringed and coral reef-protected Luquillo (see page 197). For golfers, the best courses are about an hour from San Juan. Advance notice is necessary, so book an organized trip from the ship or contact one of the clubs directly to book a round.

Parque De Bombas, the Victorian Fire Station, Ponce.

Colorful houses in Wharfside
Village, Cruz Bay, St John.

THE US VIRGIN ISLANDS

St Thomas is known for its retail therapy, but also has an interesting port to explore. A ferry ride away lies St John, mainly a national park, while St Croix hides its secrets underwater.

US Virgin Islands

Caribbean Sea

St Thomas is the duty-free shopping hub of the Caribbean, a fact you'll notice the moment you step ashore. Although a few ships anchor in the bay and tender passengers into the heart of the capital, Charlotte Amalie, most come alongside at Havensight Dock, just over 1 mile (1.6 km) east of town.

But this wasn't close enough for the local shopkeepers, so they created Havensight Mall. Every major duty-free retailer has an outlet here and in the capital's shopping center, and boxes of the duty-free drink and cigarettes that are delivered to the ships in huge quantities all day. Cruise staff aren't joking when they say that ships leave lower in the water after a day in St Thomas. The mall development does mean that it's hard to see the port for the shops, but it also means you can fit your shopping in quickly and conveniently before you go off exploring the rest of the island. If the Havensight Mall is too much, try the Yacht Haven Grande Marina, also within walking distance of the pier, with more upscale shops. For duty free booze, the Lockhart Gardens Kmart is the best bet.

Crown Bay, on the other side of the harbor, about twice as far from the capital as Havensight, is also used on busy days. The port area has a replica sugar mill and other facilities, but the

shops at Crown Bay Center are not as extensive as at Havensight. The ferry to **Water Island**, the fourth US Virgin Island, leaves from Crown Bay Marina.

CHARLOTTE AMALIE

The first-time visitor will want to see **Charlotte Amalie ❶**. It is the capital, after all, and also has one of the most attractive harbors in the region, especially when the sun sets behind the sails of the yachts that usually fill the bay.

There are always scores of taxis waiting by the dockside – not all official, but

◎ Main attractions
St Thomas: Charlotte Amalie shopping, Frenchtown, St Peter Greathouse and Botanical Gardens, Coral World Ocean Park.
St John.
St Croix: Frederiksted, Christiansted, Buck Island Reef National Monument, Salt River Bay national park.

Map on page 202

A diver looks through a crevasse in the USVI's clear waters.

⊙ Shop

Genuine bargains can be found in the shops (particularly drinks and cigarettes in A.H. Riise, and jewelry in Cardow), and there are guarantees that the goods (and the discounts) are bona fide. The retailers know that if they rip off passengers, the cruise lines will stop recommending them – and that would spell disaster for their sales figures.

all operating on a shared basis, and most of them of the large 'people mover' variety. There is a fixed rate into Charlotte Amalie, but you will join a slow-moving line of traffic that could take more than 20 minutes. It is better to walk into town and use a taxi to come back. To do this, go through the mall, turn left out of the dock gates and follow the road; it takes 15–20 minutes and there is a good view out to sea for most of the way.

Fort Christian, now a museum (tel: 340-776 4566; Mon–Fri 9am–4pm), marks the start of the town center. Built by the Danes in 1680, it is the oldest building in continuous use on the island and is a National Historic Landmark. Right behind is Emancipation Garden, overlooked by the local tourist office, the Grand Hotel and the post office.

This is the start of Main Street, the main shopping area, which runs parallel with the waterfront with endless alleyways connecting the two, each with its own mini-shopping mall. At the entrance to each shop will be some out-of-work actor or comedian using magic tricks and jokes to sweet-talk people inside. There are also outdoor bars and cafés, which sell snacks and exotic cocktails at high prices.

HISTORICAL SURPRISES

Although it is richer in shops than it is in conventional sights, Charlotte Amalie does have a few places of historical interest that are worth a detour. Turn right by the tourist office instead of left, and walk in the other direction along Main Street, which becomes Norre Gade. Almost immediately there is a flight of steps cut into the hillside, which leads up to Kongens Gade. Turn right to **The 99 Steps** (although, if you count them, you'll find there are actually 103). Near the top is what's left of **Blackbeard's Castle** (www.blackbeardscastle.com; currently closed for post-hurricane renovation; check website for details), built by the Danish government but used (allegedly) by Blackbeard – the pirate, Edward Teach – as a lookout. And who could blame him, as there is such a splendid view over the harbor.

Near the foot of The 99 Steps, along Crystal Gade, is **St Thomas Synagogue** (Mon–Thu 9am–4pm, Fri 9am–3pm). Constructed in 1796, but rebuilt three times since, it remains the second-oldest synagogue in the Caribbean (the oldest is in Curaçao).

Back on Norre Garde stands the impressively large 18th-century

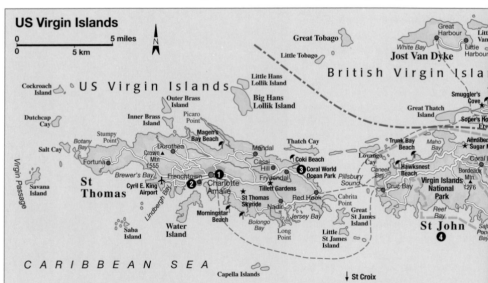

Frederick Lutheran Church (still under-going repairs from the 2017 hurricanes) and, nearby, Government House, which is a more recent building (1867) of less interest, but with a spectacular view of the harbor. A surprising find is in the middle of the shopping frenzy in Main Street: on the right as you come from the dock, at No. 14, is the place where artist Camille Pissarro was born in 1830. Upstairs houses the **Camille Pissarro Art Gallery** (Mon–Sat; free).

FURTHER AFIELD

If you have only one day in St Thomas (which is probably the case), you should allocate at least half of it to exploring beyond the capital, on an organized excursion or on your own. The majority of the excursions are water-based – trips on sailboats, catamarans or kayaks for swimming, snorkeling and scuba-diving. In fact, as the US Virgin Islands continue to rebuild after significant damage caused by two hurricanes in 2017, most of the cruise lines' offerings are water or beach based. The offshore waters are remarkably clear and, as well as umpteen coral reefs, several old shipwrecks (including a mail boat that went down in 1967) have become popular dive sites since they are home to some colorful marine life.

The cost of half-day trips is between US$50 and US$100, depending on what's on offer. Tours include seaplane and helicopter trips that offer spectacular views of the island, but they are fairly brief (from 25 to 40 minutes) and quite expensive. You could try a cheaper alternative, the Paradise Point Tramway – a 7-minute cable-car ride that takes you up 700ft (210 meters) to a viewing platform from where the views are just as good. The tramway station is just across the road from Havensight Mall.

GETTING AROUND

Taxis trips around the island or to particular beaches can be arranged through your ship or independently (which is cheaper). Renting cars and bikes is easy and the roads are good, but, although this is not a huge island (12 miles long by 3 miles wide/20km by 7km), there's a surprising amount of traffic congestion, especially in and out of town, so allow plenty of time to return to the ship. Taxis are probably the best bet as the drivers know journey times. Competition is so fierce, they all stick to official fixed rates so you don't need to haggle.

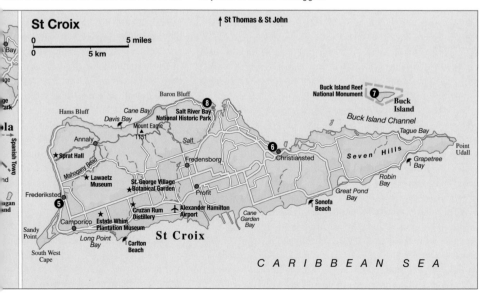

The Emancipation Garden, between Tolbod Gade and Fort Christian, has a bronze bust of a slave blowing a conch shell. It marked the 150th anniversary of emancipation celebrations.

Places to avoid include Bluebeard's Castle – not to be confused with Blackbeard's. Taxi drivers will suggest it, but it's just a hotel (currently under reconstruction following hurricane damage) beside a stone watchtower around which developed a dubious legend about the pirate Bluebeard. Equally dubious is the claim made for Magen's Bay (on the north coast) as one of the world's top 10 most beautiful beaches. This was true once but the beach has fallen from grace, partly because of overcrowding. There is also a small charge to use it. There are far better beaches on the east coast – Sapphire and Secret Harbor – and on the south coast – Brewer's and Morningstar.

Apart from those excellent beaches, where should you head? There's **Frenchtown ❷** for a start, just the other side of Charlotte Amalie from Havensight (head out along Veterans' Drive). The original community was set up by French émigrés from St-Barths, and this fishing village still has some French style, especially in the eateries. **Coral World Ocean Park ❸** (tel: 340-775 1555; www.coralworldvi.com;

Nov–Mar daily 9am–4pm last admission 3pm, times may vary by season), by Coki Point on the island's northeast coast, is easy to reach independently as it is only a 15-minute drive from Havensight. The centerpiece is a three-level underwater observatory from which to view an enormous range of marine life. But the highlight is watching the divers from the observatory when they come to feed the sharks, moray eels and stingrays in the predator tank. There is also a Nautilus semi-submersible – an enhanced glass-bottomed boat tour – or Sea Trek, where you don a special helmet to follow a trail along the seabed with no need for any scuba experience. 'Encounters' can be booked with sea lions, sharks and turtles.

ST JOHN

It may seem strange to land on one island, then take a trip to another, but a visit to the neighboring island of **St John ❹** is one of the most popular excursions, either organized or done independently. Two-thirds of St John is an unspoiled national park (gifted to the US by the Rockefellers) with 110 different types of tree affording a habitat for hordes of birds and butterflies. It also has more than 40 beaches and coves. Caneel Bay is the most popular, but Trunk Bay, with its underwater snorkeling trail, is probably the best.

There are regular (and cheap) ferries across from Charlotte Amalie (a 45-minute journey) and from Red Hook, which is about 25 minutes from Havensight on the east coast, from where they are cheaper, more frequent and shorter at only 20 minutes. Do leave enough time to get back to the ship.

ST CROIX

Large cruise ships arrive at **St Croix** in the port of **Frederiksted ❺**, which offers little for the visitor beyond a handful of shops by the pier entrance. Sights include the renovated

⊘ SAILING IN THE VIRGIN ISLANDS

The archipelago of the US and British Virgin Islands are the most popular sailing waters, blessed with endless anchorages and the comfort that nowhere is too far from anywhere else. Hundreds of islands face one another across Sir Francis Drake Passage, which separates the American and British islands. Successions of secluded coves conceal eccentric beach bars which have acquired a loyal yachtie following.

Enhanced by a reputation as a sophisticated playground, the BVI have more sailing schools, bareboat yacht-charter companies and flotilla sailings than anywhere else in the Caribbean. The range of watersports on offer simply confirms the islands' appeal to visiting sailors, from windsurfing and sea kayaking to swimming in quiet coves, snorkeling in eerie caverns or diving to explore wrecks. For some, however, leisurely pottering around the islands, stopping off at watering holes, is a poor substitute for the adrenaline rush gained by sailing a boat at speed, and the first few months of the year see numerous regattas and subsequent rum-fueled celebrations. The BVI Spring Regatta and Sailing Festival based at Nanny Cay, Tortola, and the Rolex Cub Regatta at the St Thomas Yacht Club both attract hundreds of competitive sailors and spectators from around the world.

18th-century Fort Frederik, with its museum and art gallery, and the Caribbean Museum Center for the Arts (tel: 340-772 2622; www.cmcarts.org; Thu–Sat 10am–5pm, later on cruise ship days), promoting regional art. The island's other port, Christiansted, is the capital and has far more in the way of welcoming shops, bars and restaurants, but only the smaller ships can get in there.

However, there is much more to the island than immediately meets the eye. At 82 sq miles (212 sq km), St Croix is larger than St Thomas, but it is generally much less developed, and far less crowded with people and traffic. Some of the most popular places to visit are only a short coach or taxi ride from Frederiksted (agree the taxi fare in advance: there are no meters). Interesting sites include the Cruzan Rum Distillery (tel: 340-692 2280; www.cruzanrum.com; tours Mon–Fri 10am–2pm), the St George Village Botanical Garden (www.sgvbg.com; Mon–Sat 9am–3pm, Sun 9am–1pm) and the Estate Whim Museum, the only sugar plantation in the US Virgin Islands (Wed–Sat and cruise ship days 10am–3pm). Some of the best beaches – and St Croix is rightly known for its beaches – are equally close: Sandy Point, Cane Bay and Davis Bay.

Some ships organize shuttle buses from Frederiksted to **Christiansted ❻**, about 30 minutes away. If yours doesn't, take a taxi; licensed taxis wait at the dock (price depends on the number of passengers but budget US$24 for 1–2 people). Although the architecture still shows clear signs of Christiansted's 18th- and 19th-century Danish heritage (visit the Steeple Building, a local history museum), there has been some rebuilding following serious hurricane damage. The most striking is the King's Alley complex of shops and boutiques, but shopping here is nowhere near on the scale of that on St Thomas.

UNDERWATER TREASURES

Christiansted is the embarkation point for boats to 850-acre (344-hectare) **Buck Island Reef National Monument ❼** (www.nps.gov/buis). This underwater national park has its own marked underwater trails, 12ft (3 meters) down among the coral reefs, which teem with exotic fish and other marine life. There will be organized excursions from your ship, but dive shops all along the waterfront at Christiansted sell scuba-diving and snorkeling trips to the island, so it's easy to go off on your own. If you leave the ship straight after breakfast, there's time to reach Buck Island independently, enjoy two or three hours of scuba diving there and get back for departure time.

Salt River Bay National Historic Park ❽, on the north coast, is of particular interest to US visitors. The site of a Columbus landing – the only one on US territory – and a battle between his men and the Carib Indians, it has a huge mangrove forest and an underwater canyon, which is ideal for scuba diving.

Ⓞ Tip

St Croix has two 18-hole golf courses, The Buccaneer (www.thebuccaneer.com) and Carambola (www.golfcarambola.com), which was designed by Robert Trent Jones and is particularly attractive, as well as challenging enough for players visiting St Thomas to fly across just to play.

The stairway known as The 99 Steps was built by the Danes in the 1700s. There are similar steps cut into almost every hillside in St Thomas.

📷 TROPICAL BOUNTY OF THE ISLANDS

Flowers of the forest, fruit of the trees, vegetables from the ground – under the blazing sun there's a treasure trove of color, dazzling greenery and food.

Like the people of the eastern Caribbean, the flora of the region is a great melting pot. There were plants that were here before man, plants brought by the Caribs in their canoes when they paddled from South America, those which came from Africa during slavery and those brought from all over the world by the adventuresome Europeans.

For visitors to the region from North America or northern Europe, familiar only with expensive house-plants nurtured in a centrally heated room or the exotic fruit and vegetable section in the supermarket, the sudden sight of these magnificent plants growing naturally in a tropical landscape is intoxicating.

MARKET DAY

Venture into a local market in the rainier, more mountainous islands and explore the unfamiliar: the knobbly soursop (it makes an excellent juice); the pale green christophene or cho-cho of the squash family; tiny green and red peppers, some fiendishly hot. Drier islands will not have such a range, but there will be 'ground provisions' – the root vegetables, such as yams, which are part of the staple diet. And there are the cut flowers: the amazing red or pink gingers, artificial-looking anthurium and dramatic torch gingers. Everyone grows something somewhere.

And while there are the formal botanical gardens, and gardens of former estate houses to visit, don't forget to admire the ordinary backyard garden growing an amazing range of vegetables, fruit and exotic flowers, often in just a tiny space.

The delicate hibiscus grows all over the tropics. Its flower lasts only one day but can be made into a refreshing red drink called sorrel, flavored with spices, sweetened with sugar, and popular at Christmas.

The coconut tree is one of many useful varieties of palm which grow throughout the Caribbean. The fronds are used for thatch and the trunks for building houses; while the coconut provides drinking-water when unripe and a calorie-rich milk inside tasty flesh when ripe.

The exquisite torch lily, also called the wax rose, torch ginger or ginger lily, are found from Costa Rica to Barbados; the statuesque plant is a favorite in botanical gardens and ornamental flower displays.

Vanilla stems climb a coconut tree near the water.

Spice and all things nice

There is a sweetness in the Caribbean air which romantics might attribute to spice, and in particular to the vanilla plant, a straggly plant from the orchid family, with an exquisite-smelling flower that opens only for a few hours in the morning. Pollinating is done by hand and the resulting pods give the much sought-after vanilla flavor.

Although spices such as vanilla and nutmeg were once an important export crop, most arrived in the Caribbean in the 18th century from the Far East 'spice islands.' Once, Grenada grew some 25 percent of the world's nutmeg. You can still see the warehouses at Gouyave on the west coast where the spice is sorted. The outer lacy red covering is ground down into a powder and becomes mace. Visit local markets throughout the region for supplies of nutmeg and cinnamon (dried strips of bark), pale gold rhizomes of ginger, black pepper (grown on a vine) and cloves (dried flower buds).

Nutmeg, once stripped of its red lace covering of mace and the outer shell, can be ground for use in cooking or as an essential oil in perfumes and pharmaceuticals.

startling flower of the shaving bush tree, or Bombax
oticum, native to Mexico but grown in Florida and the
ibbean.

tropical fruits of the Caribbean have been delighting
ors for centuries. 'None pleases my tastes as does the
', wrote George Washington of the pineapple during a
to Barbados in 1751.

Colonial buildings in Philipsburg.

SINT MAARTEN/ST-MARTIN

You can experience three different cultures in one day – remnants of Dutch colonialism in Philipsburg and French chic in Marigot, both infused with Caribbean flair.

Sint Maarten, the Dutch side of the island and St-Martin, the French side, sustained terrible damage in the 2017 hurricanes, Irma and Maria. Some 95 percent of buildings in St-Martin were completely destroyed. Rebuilding took more than 18 months, including the complete reconstruction of Princess Juliana Airport in Sint Maarten; the French side, at the time of writing, is making a much slower recovery. If you haven't visited for a while, expect a lot of change, as the island is now stronger and better prepared, but the same charms that the island has always offered: duty free shopping, gorgeous beaches and, on the French side, reminders of St-Martin's European heritage, not least in the food.

Convenience is the key to Philipsburg's appeal as a cruise stop. Tendering into this port from a big ship is an advantage, as tenders will take you to the Little Pier in the main town; if you berth, you will be out at Pointe Blanche's cruise terminal which – although it has shops and other facilities – lies 1 mile (1.6km) away from the center of town. Taxis proliferate, however, and a multi-passenger minibus (a better option, as taxis are expensive) will get you into the center for about US$3 a head.

AROUND TOWN

Once in **Philipsburg** ❶, the going is easy, although you should be prepared

for crowds. The town curves around Great Bay Beach and a boardwalk makes this a pleasant stroll. The compact little port can be explored easily in less than an hour and, since the main shopping streets are called Front Street (Voorstraat) and, running parallel, Back Street (Achterstraat), it's not hard to find your way around.

Old Street lies at the end of Front Street and here you will find al fresco restaurants and the Old Street Shopping Center, a small mall with more than 20 shops as well as grill and pizza

⊙ **Main attractions**

Philipsburg
The Butterfly Farm
Marigot
Baie Orientale beach

◉

Map on page 211

Sint Maarten Carnival.

⊙ Tip

If you visit the island on a small- to medium-sized ship (such as one of the Star Clippers vessels), you could well call at Marigot – the French capital – instead of Philipsburg.

restaurants. Good places for lunch are Antoine's on Front Street and The Greenhouse, nearby, for catch-of-the-day specials.

First, though, you should head for **Wathey Square**, which has a late 18th-century courthouse and some beautiful old buildings decorated with traditional West Indian 'gingerbread' fretwork. A lively market, a selection of restaurants and plenty of shops make this a magnet for visitors, but it's also worth wandering around the *steegjes* (the little lanes connecting the main streets), which conceal some lushly planted courtyards lined with more boutiques and cafés.

Among the best buys is jewelry, which is reasonably priced (as it is throughout the Caribbean); Colombian Emeralds, a chain with a good reputation among cruise passengers, is represented in Philipsburg. There are also shops selling Gucci and other designer goods as well as alcohol and leather products at duty-free prices – although not as low as they are in St Thomas.

But for a real taste of the West Indies, call in at one of the small local stores crammed with spices, cane sugar, batik clothing, hand-woven hammocks, local craft wares and guava-berry liqueur – the local rum-based firewater which, although an acquired taste when drunk neat, gives a cocktail considerable kick.

A short drive inland is the **Rockland Estate**, a new eco-adventure park. Its star attraction is the Flying Dutchman, the world's steepest zipline, which whizzes you 2,800ft down a mountainside with an average gradient of 42 degrees four abreast, so you can 'race' your friends. The Soualiga chairlift provides a less adrenalin-inducing ride and still delivers wonderful views down over the countryside and the coast and beyond to the islands of St-Barths, Anguilla and Saba. There's a second zipline, Sentry Hill, and the Schooner, another thrill ride, closer to the ground, as you slide down a specially built track in a big inner tube. The 'eco' element of the whole place is the maintenance of the estate itself, an 18th-century plantation;and the thrill rides have been designed to minimize impact on

Baie Orientale.

the surrounding nature. You can also visit the Emilio Wilson Museum on the site, telling the story of Trace Wilson, who was born here into slavery, and Emilio Wilson, her descendant, a prominent Sint Maarten preservationist (www.rainforestadventure.com; opening times fit in with cruise schedules).

THE FRENCH SIDE OF THE ISLAND

Unless your time here is very short, try to get over to **St-Martin**, the French side of the island since it was divided between Holland and France in 1648. This is the prettier part, and the big cruise ships will usually offer tours to Marigot, the French capital, from Philipsburg – a 3-hour excursion will take you past the Great Salt Pond at the rear of town to Mount William's Hill, where there is a good view of the port. From there you'll travel to the Dutch–French border (open; there's no need to show a passport) and drive on to Marigot, via some traditional French villages, for some free time.

Other excursion options include catamaran trips from Philipsburg, lasting about 3.5 hours, with opportunities to swim or snorkel, with lunch and drinks included in the price; or a drive to the lovely Baie Orientale for a swim, sunbathing (chairs provided) and lunch, which is also included.

THE BEST BEACHES

The most convenient beaches from Philipsburg are **Great Bay** and **Little Bay**, slightly further west, but they may be crowded. For more privacy, take a taxi to Simpson Bay Beach (good for watersports); Dawn Beach (great for snorkeling); or for a party vibe and a sense of the unreal, check out Maho Bay Beach, where you can sunbathe at the end of the airport runway and watch plane spotters gathering in the sea to cheer and duck as the vast aircraft roar into land.

On the French side, **Baie Orientale** is gorgeous, with good beachside cafés and a classic French Riviera atmosphere, but the sea can be rough. Baie Rouge is best for snorkelers, while Baie Longue is the longest beach on the island and is less crowded.

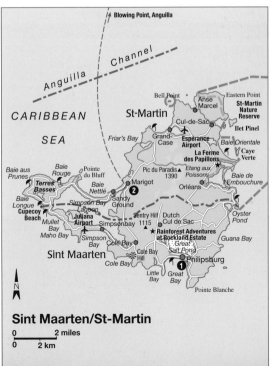

L'Escargot café.

Hula babies.

Les Anses d'Arlet, Martinique.

SOUTHERN SAILING

It was when the cruise lines started basing some of their ships in Caribbean ports that they were able to respond to demand and make more of the southern region available to passengers.

When modern Caribbean cruising began in earnest in the late 1960s, most ships started in Miami and went no further than the Bahamas, the US Virgin Islands and maybe San Juan, on itineraries that lasted a week – the favorite duration for most passengers, then as now. But, once hooked, cruise passengers tend to come back for more, and the lines realized that they needed to come up with new ports and new islands on their itineraries.

First, they sent their ships west to Mexico's Yucatán Peninsula, to Cozumel and Playa del Carmen (within reach of the Maya ruins), and then they turned south. But to get down south and see more than just one or two islands would take longer than a week if a ship started in Miami or another Florida port, so the cruise lines started to base some of their ships deep in the Caribbean, in San Juan and Barbados, an easy hop to the islands of the Lesser Antilles and beyond.

SOUTHERN VARIETY

Southern Caribbean cruises now encompass an ever-expanding range of port and island combinations.

The lines with the biggest ships and largest fleets are in the Caribbean year-round and their ships tend to follow each other around to the best-known islands. Lines with smaller ships, which are more luxurious and more expensive, including sail-assisted or even authentic sailing ships, are able to offer more innovative itineraries. They go where the real yachties go, to the smaller islands – or the smaller ports of the larger ones – in the Windwards, Leewards and Grenadines.

One of the bonuses of starting and ending a cruise in a Caribbean port is that a holiday can be extended by

Creative use of palm leaves.

Fact

If you want a more unusual itinerary, pick a cruise that goes from point to point rather than round-trip; there are small ships, like those of Noble Caledonia, for example, that roam the region, focusing on more out-of-the-way ports.

staying an extra week on the island. It is also possible to combine one cruise with another (on the same ship or two different ones) for two weeks' cruising.

If passengers find it more convenient to cruise from Florida, it is still possible to reach the southern islands in a week, although these cruises inevitably feature calls in other parts of the Caribbean and include fewer ports than those which start and finish in the Caribbean itself.

EUROPEAN PREFERENCES

As the European cruise market is so strong now, Europe-based lines offer a wide variety of Caribbean cruises to appeal to the tastes and travel habits of British, German, French, Spanish and Italian cruisers among others. There are now ships based on the Dutch side of Sint Maarten, served by regular flights direct from Paris and Amsterdam, for the winter months, with passengers from Europe flying directly to the island to join them. The same applies to Barbados and San Juan, both popular departure ports.

Whichever combination of ports and islands makes up your southern Caribbean itinerary, there will always be a cosmopolitan flavor to the cruise. A visit to a number of different islands in this region delivers a heady cultural mix of European and indigenous influences.

NEW EXPERIENCES

With an increase in world voyages every year, and variations on these, like extended round-South America cruises, many lines are heading back through the Caribbean to end these winter getaways in Miami. This broadens out the scope of Caribbean cruising. You could, for example, combine a journey along the Amazon with a few days chilling in the islands afterwards, or even, in theory, sail most of the way round South America, taking in the glaciers of Chile and the Caribbean sunshine on the same vacation.

Panama, too, has evolved as a cruise destination in recent years. Over the last decade, billions of dollars have been spent on developing cruise ports at Colón (and Balboa) on the Pacific side of the Panama Canal, and cruise lines have been given financial incentives to call there. Frequent Caribbean cruise passengers needed no incentive to pay Panama a first visit, especially since, from Colón, a historic railway link to Panama City has been reactivated. Now, with the opening of the new locks, much bigger ships are able to transit, meaning the biggest ships on long world voyages may now build in the Panama Canal and Caribbean into their itineraries.

Although the investment has not been as large, the Central American countries of Belize, Costa Rica, Honduras and Guatemala (see page 141) have also been sprucing up to encourage cruise calls. Usually found on western Caribbean cruise

Motorized boats off Playa Valdez, Isla Margarita.

itineraries, the attractions here include the rainforests and the Maya ruins, and – like Panama– they provide a fascinating contrast in lifestyles to the Caribbean islands.

Meanwhile, 'new' islands are coming into fashion: the relatively unknown Saba and nearby Anguilla; the tiny island of Montserrat, all but destroyed in the mid-1990s by its active volcano, but now welcoming cruise ships once more; and the gorgeous Iles des Saintes, a yachting hideaway off the coast of Guadeloupe, visited by the smallest and most exclusive ships.

CONTRASTING ISLANDS

There is also a contrast within the southern Caribbean itself, between the larger, more developed islands, which have become major tourist destinations in their own right, and the smaller islands, which are still largely off the main tourist track and have a pleasantly undiscovered feel.

The larger islands include the almost genteel Barbados, with its English-style parishes; cosmopolitan Trinidad and Tobago; the volcanic island of St Lucia, with its dramatic Pitons and lush interior contrasting with the well-developed resort areas; the sophisticated French islands of Martinique and Guadeloupe; the distinctly Dutch-flavored ABC islands of Aruba, Bonaire and Curaçao just off the South American coast; and the double-value Sint Maarten/St-Martin (see page 209), which is half Dutch and half French, divided by the least secure and most nondescript border crossing in the world.

MAGICAL BEACHES

It is also down in the south that the classic Caribbean islands of everybody's dreams are to be found. The white sandy beaches, the fishing boats in hidden coves, the safe and scenic harbors sought out by the private yachts of the rich and famous, all combine with each other and with the larger islands to ensure cruises with genuinely romantic appeal. Whichever you visit, there are superb beaches and

The fleshy petals of the ginger lily (Alpina purpurata).

Crayfish to be proud of.

Lunch laid out in the British Virgin Islands.

Mind those wandering iguanas.

great underwater sites for snorkeling and scuba diving.

Nowhere in the world – including the South Pacific – is there such a wide collection of exotic islands to which ships, even some of the largest ones, can cruise. For a real escape from the 21st century, it's hard to beat the British Virgin Islands. These are 40 tiny islands, few large enough for the smallest cruise ships. Tortola and Virgin Gorda are the largest and even these are minuscule. And now it's possible, on a small ship, to cruise to even smaller islands, like Jost Van Dyke and Norman Island.

The US Virgin Islands, St Thomas and St John, with wonderful beaches and some of the cheapest and best duty-free goods, usually appear on eastern Caribbean itineraries (see page 201), but there is some crossover. Best of all, it is a short boat ride from St Thomas to St John – a delightful island which, courtesy of the Rockefellers, is almost entirely a national park. Some ships call at St John instead of St Thomas, but regular cruise visitors to the latter know that they should do their shopping in the morning in Charlotte Amalie, then take a short water-taxi ride to St John for an afternoon on one of its glorious beaches.

THE LEEWARDS AND THE GRENADINES

The gems in the next cluster of islands (the Leewards) include St-Barths (or St-Barthélemy, to give its full name), which is a smaller version of Martinique or Guadeloupe, very French (although originally Swedish), with glitzy boutiques and fine – if expensive – restaurants, and glamorous people eating in them; St Kitts and its smaller sister island, Nevis, both lush and verdant islands which prospered through their sugar plantations (Nevis, with its exclusive plantation-house hotels, is particularly tranquil); and beautiful, unspoilt Dominica, which is right on the whale migration route, making for some exciting boat trips.

Further south, it is mainly the smaller cruise and sailing ships that call at the 30-odd coral islands known collectively as the Grenadines. This is the most popular part of the Caribbean for private and chartered yacht sailing since there are scores of beautiful bays, beaches and good sites for swimming, snorkeling and diving. Also, at the handful of islands in the Grenadines which are inhabited, such as St Vincent and Bequia, an infrastructure has been built up to serve the visiting yachties' needs – stores, boat-taxis, restaurants etc – useful for cruise passengers too.

Finally, cruising further south, lies Grenada, one of the larger islands in the region and one of the most beautiful. Known rightly as the Spice Island, Grenada has one of the most beautiful harbors in the area – St George's – which is also the island's capital.

Soper's Hole, Tortola.

THE BRITISH VIRGIN ISLANDS: TORTOLA

Tortola and Virgin Gorda are laid-back islands where some gentle swimming, snorkeling and shopping will be quite enough activity to fill a day ashore.

More than 50 volcanic rocky outcrops set in the Caribbean Sea, a stone's throw from the much snazzier US Virgin Islands, the British Virgin Islands might – at first sight – seem less than impressive. Indeed, Christopher Columbus found them so when he first clapped eyes on them in 1493. Two centuries later, however, the British took a different view; they took possession of them in 1664 and have hung on to them ever since, although nowadays they are a British Overseas Territory, in which the islanders govern themselves.

The majority of the British Virgin Islands are lightly inhabited, the 18,000-strong population being concentrated on the three biggest – **Tortola**, **Virgin Gorda** and **Jost Van Dyke**. The topography of Tortola and Virgin Gorda – both of which rise sharply from the sea to volcanic heights – is rugged: Tortola's Mount Sage is 1,709ft (536 meters) and VG's Gorda Peak 1,369ft (414 meters). This has made the islands hard to get around and difficult to develop, but it has also been the key to the islands' success as a tourist destination. Hurricanes Irma and Maria in 2017 destroyed 70 percent of homes in the BVI. Tourism was quick to spring back but it has taken longer for islanders to rebuild their lives.

These islands are the place to visit if you prefer quiet beaches and a

Sea cave, Virgin Gorda.

calm, frozen-in-time atmosphere to skyscraper hotels, casinos and glitzy shopping malls. Their main visitors are yachties who know more than most about the pleasures of the simple life. The islands are more likely to feature on the itineraries of small-ship cruise companies than on the big-ship schedules.

TRIPS TO THE BEST BEACHES

Visiting ships can go alongside at Tortola's pretty capital, **Road Town ❶**, where the pier accommodates two large ships at a time. Road Town lies on the island's

Main attractions
Cane Garden Bay beach, Tortola
Mount Sage National Park, Tortola
The Baths, Virgin Gorda
Spring Bay beach, Virgin Gorda

Map on page 222

⊙ Tip

Although these are the British Virgin Islands, remember that the local currency is the US dollar, so don't go ashore laden with sterling.

south coast, while the best beaches – Robinson Crusoe-style havens rich in banana trees, palms and mangoes – are on the north coast, overlooked by dramatic mountain peaks. Fortunately, a road around the island was completed in the early 1980s and, with taxis lined up to greet every visiting cruise ship, it's relatively easy to get about.

As on many Caribbean islands, round-trip taxi tours are available; fares are set by law, but pick-up times for the return journey should be negotiated in advance (around US$24 each way for one to three people to Cane Garden Bay beach).

The best beach for an all-around good time is **Cane Garden Bay**, where Myett's restaurant, on the beach, serves tasty snacks, salads and cocktails. The beach gets packed when a big ship is in so snorkelers or those in search of peace might want to try **Brewer's Bay**, which has vivid underwater life.

TO THE CAPITAL

Road Town has very little to offer in its own right, but Main Street – five minutes'

walk from the tender pier at Wickhams Cay – is worth a stroll. Until the 1960s it was on the waterfront, but landfill has been used to create Wickhams Cay and Waterfront Drive. Many of its traditional Caribbean wooden houses are being restored, there is a variety of shops and a lively crafts market to explore.

Local ceramics, glassware from Mexico, Cuban cigars and English chinaware are the best buys in the shops – alongside the ubiquitous spices. In the crafts market, look out for brightly colored mobiles, driftwood napkin rings and other wacky-but-fun items.

For lunch, try Pusser's Pub on the waterfront for conch fritters and their famous Painkiller rum cocktails. Otherwise, there are pizza parlours, or plenty of places selling local dishes if you are feeling more adventurous.

CHECKING THE POSSIBILITIES

Some ships offer excursions on open-air safari buses, including a stop for a swim at Cane Garden Bay. There are also companies that organize boat and snorkeling tours from the pier, so before

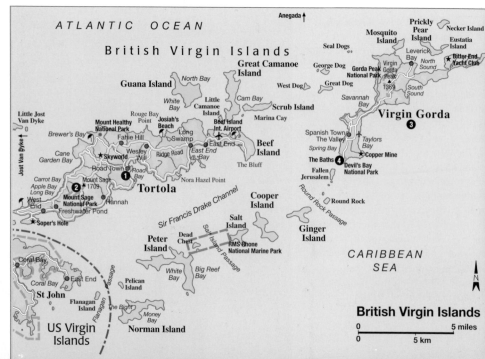

you leave Road Town take stock of what local tours are available. You can get a 2- or 3-hour island tour for about US$55 per hour (for one to two people) and – if you've got time and confidence – local buses will get you round the island very cheaply. Just hail them and they'll stop – in theory, at least.

For a good walk, the best bet is to head by taxi to the **Mount Sage National Park ❷**, where you can hike along a rainforest trail and enjoy a picnic.

If you happen to be staying in the BVI when the full moon falls, don't miss one of the legendary full moon parties. Various beach shacks throw them, with barbecues, flowing rum punch and dancing on the sand.

VIRGIN GORDA

Most ships will offer tenders to **Virgin Gorda ❸**, 12 miles (20km) from Tortola (if yours doesn't you can easily find a boat to ferry you out from the pier). Try to visit this little place if you can – it's a real fantasy island with silvery beaches and the most enticing turquoise waters you'll see outside the South Pacific.

Many cruise ships run shore excursions to **The Baths ❹**, a beautiful beach where gigantic boulders have toppled together to form myriad cave-like structures and saltwater pools. Alternatively, you could negotiate a round-trip fare to The Baths or the island's best beach, **Spring Bay** (excellent for snorkeling), with one of the taxi drivers plying for trade at **Spanish Town**, where the small boats to Virgin Gorda disgorge their passengers.

If you go to the Baths, leave time to make the 15-minute walk through the boulder-strewn coastal scenery to **Devil's Bay National Park**.

Spanish Town itself offers limited shopping at a waterfront plaza. Walk past this to the Virgin Gorda yacht harbor and you'll find a pretty view and a great place to eat, **The Bath and Turtle Pub**, which serves everything from freshly caught seafood to pizzas, nachos and chili.

However you choose to spend your day ashore in the British Virgin Islands, don't rush about and try to do too much. The secret here is to relax and let the islands' laid-back atmosphere wash your cares away.

Don't miss local specialties.

An aerial view of the Baths and Devil's Bay, Virgin Gorda.

Spinnakers catching the wind.

ST-BARTHÉLEMY, SABA AND MONTSERRAT

These tiny islands offer bite-size servings of French, Dutch and British colonial heritage: St-Barths with its chic Riviera attitude; Saba with its love of the outdoors; and Montserrat, forever defined by its active volcano.

Although these three small islands lie within striking distance of each other in the northern Lesser Antilles, they have very little in common, both geographically and culturally speaking. St-Barths, at 10 sq miles (25 sq km), possesses craggy hills, cliffs and gorgeous white-sand beaches in its numerous bays. Saba has no beaches and rises almost sheer out of the sea; with very little flat land on its 5 sq miles (13 sq km) of rocky slopes, its Mount Scenery matches the highest point in the Netherlands with a summit of 2,885ft (870 meters). Montserrat offered an easier farming life with its rich volcanic soil and gentle hills in the north, while the south of the pear-shaped, 39-sq-mile (102-sq-km) island was home to the capital, Plymouth, under the Soufrière Hills. All that changed, however, with the reawakening of the volcano in 1995, and the south now lies abandoned, with development focused in the north.

ST-BARTHÉLEMY

St-Barths is rocky and arid; there are no streams to provide fresh water, making it unattractive as a plantation economy, and not even the Caribs chose to set up home here. The first French settlement thrived on piracy, plundering passing ships. In 1784

Louis XVI gave the island to King Gustaf III of Sweden in exchange for trading rights in the port of Gothenburg, and from that point onward it enjoyed growing prosperity. The capital was named Gustavia, the port was declared duty free, cobbled streets were laid out around the harbor and warehouses were built. Three forts were built to protect it: Oscar, Karl and Gustav, which can still be seen today. However, after a series of natural and economic disasters, Sweden sold its colony back to France in 1878. Its citizens have

Main attractions

Gustavia
Anse de la Grande Saline
Windwardside
Mount Scenery
Montserrat Volcano
  Observatory

**Maps on pages
226, 228**

Yacht Harbor, Gustavia, St-Barths.

⊙ Tip

If you are hiring a car on St-Barths, make sure it is a very small one. Smart Cars are the vehicle of choice as parking space is at a premium and they can easily negotiate the twisting, narrow roads.

remained under the French umbrella and the majority have no wish to seek independence. Tourism supports the economy and the island has become a magnet for the rich and famous: film stars, musicians, supermodels, royalty and billionaires hide out here in luxury villas, while scores of day-trippers come over from Sint Maarten to try and spot them.

Visiting cruise ships tender passengers ashore at St-Barths' pretty capital, **Gustavia ❶**. Set around a yacht-filled harbor and careenage too small for cruise ships, the picturesque buildings of the capital climb up the steep hillside. High fashion, from Versace to Vilebrequin is available right here in the exclusive boutiques, along with Gucci leathers, Vuitton suitcases and Charles Jourdan footwear. Boat loads of shoppers arrive from Sint Maarten, and cafés spill out onto the streets Parisian style, buzzing with a young, chic crowd.

There are no beggars or hucksters here, no ramshackle shops; and no

colorful, aromatic market clogs the waterfront. You will, however, smell baguettes and croissants baking in the *boulangeries* and coffee wafting from the cafés, while lunchtime is a veritable feast for the senses with the delights of French and Créole cooking. St-Barths is not cheap and you should expect to pay French prices, in euros. From Gustavia waterfront, a 5-minute walk past the ruins of Fort Karl brings you to **Anse de Grand Galets**, also called **Shell Beach**, which is a pretty, sheltered beach covered with shells.

Corossol is a fishing village west of the capital, with a brown-sand beach and many traditional old wooden houses. Further along the coast, **Colombier** beach is totally unspoiled. Reached by boat or by a 30-minute walk from the road with great views of all the little islands offshore, this is a place to swim and relax. In contrast, the most popular beach at **St Jean**, on the north coast, is backed by shops, hotels and bistros. Further east, **Lorient**, where the first French settlers lived, offers good surfing or snorkeling, depending on the mood of the sea. Windsurfers head for **Grand Cul de Sac** at the eastern end, which has a sandy bay protected by a coral reef and is backed by a large salt pond.

Anse de la Grande Saline, in the south, is a long white beach also next

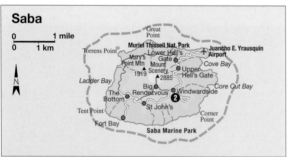

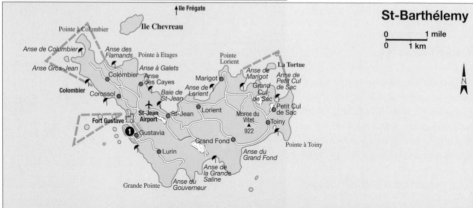

to a salt pond. Surfers gather here for the waves while waterfowl enjoy the pond. There are no beach bars, sun-beds or umbrellas for shade to spoil the natural aspect, although there is a good restaurant by the pond. Taxis will bring you here and collect you after a few hours, but it is easy to hire a car and explore the whole of the island, allowing yourself to reach any beach, eat where you fancy and do a spot of shopping along the way.

SABA

Four villages of pretty, pristinely kept, white houses with red roofs, once linked only by hundreds of steps, are dotted around the green mountain-ous terrain of this tiny volcanic island. Around 2,000 inhabitants call Saba home, half of Dutch origin and half of African origin, descended from the first settlers and their slaves. It was never suitable for a plantation economy and the island changed hands many times after Columbus spotted it in 1493, finally becoming Dutch in 1812 and staying that way. Although other islands in the Netherlands Antilles have taken the road to independence, Saba has chosen to become a Dutch municipality, remaining part of the Kingdom of the Netherlands.

A single road links the villages, run-ning 6.5 miles (10.5km) the length of the island from the pier to the airport. **Fort Bay** is the only inlet in the tow-ering cliffs where boats can dock and it is here that the ferry comes in from Sint Maarten bringing day-trippers and cruise passengers on excursions. Dive boats depart for exploration of the marine park around the island, the underwater scenery being as spectac-ular as that on land. Saba is renowned for having some of the best diving in the Caribbean. Most of the dive sites are on the west coast and, as there is little fishing in these waters and no anchoring allowed, there is a wide variety of fish, and coral of all sizes and colors.

Until the mid-20th century when the road was built, people had to walk up hundreds of steps to reach **The Bot-tom**, 820ft (250 meters) above sea

The idyllic setting of Windwardside.

Saba is renowned for the variety of fish in its waters, red hind included.

⊘ THE IRISH CONNECTION

On arrival in Montserrat, expect your pass-port to be stamped with a green shamrock, a legacy of the Irish who first settled the island. By the mid-17th century there were 1,000 Irish families here, the first being Catholics finding sanctuary from Protestant persecution on St Kitts. Later, Oliver Cromwell deported some of his Irish politi-cal prisoners to the island.

Although the vast majority of Montserrat's population is descended from African slaves, the Irish heritage is still felt today and the island is often called the 'second Emerald Isle.' The island's flag and crest show Erin, a figure from Irish mythology, with her harp. You can also hear the occasional Irish expression in use, detect Irish step dances in the local folk dancing, hear the fife and drum similar to the Irish bodhran and celebrate St Patrick's Day in March.

Playing cricket at the foot of the volcano, Montserrat.

level. This village serves as the island's capital with its government building, school, hospital, medical school, church and small museum.

The road continues through **St John's** village, where there are schools, and on to the picturesque village of **Windwardside ②**. Despite the souvenir shops selling Saba lace, a bank, a museum, dive shops and a few small hotels and restaurants, it is still very much a Dutch Caribbean idyll in its peaceful setting between Mount Scenery and Booby Hill. If you are fit and have 3 hours to spare, the hike up the 1,064 irregular steps through tropical montane cloud forest to the elfin forest at the windswept top of **Mount Scenery** is well worthwhile. This is one of many hilly trails around the island. Before you set off, register at the Saba Trail Shop (Windwardside, tel: 599-416 3295, www.sabapark.org; Mon–Fri 10am–4pm, Sat–Sun 10am–2pm) to pay a small maintenance fee.

Finally the road winds its way north to Hell's Gate and down through a series of hairpin bends to the airport, which, because of the tiny amount of flat land available on the island, has the shortest commercial runway in the world at 1,312ft (400 meters).

MONTSERRAT

Where once Montserrat was a sleepy backwater, valued by people who loved the 'old-fashioned' lifestyle, the volcano has put the island on the map, making it a tourist attraction like no other. The people of Montserrat are still rebuilding following the volcanic eruptions in the Soufrière Hills that started in July 1995, eventually destroying all the infrastructure in the south of the island. Pyroclastic flows of rock, ash and gases devastated the capital, Plymouth, and in 1997, 19 people were killed when they failed to evacuate their farms in time. More than half the population of 11,000 left the island, most of them never to return. Government headquarters were moved to Brades, and **Little Bay**, in the north, is now being developed as the new capital. The volcano continues to be active and is constantly monitored.

Visitors are usually taken to the **Montserrat Volcano Observatory ③** (visitor's center; tel: 664-491 5647; www.mvo.ms; Mon–Fri 8.30am–4.30pm), where you can get a spectacular view of the volcano, Belham Valley and ash-covered Plymouth from the viewing deck. Visits are self-guided and there is an interesting documentary describing the history and impact of the eruption (hourly 10.15am–3.15pm).

An unexpected benefit of the volcanic eruptions has been that the exclusion zone around the south of the island has created a marine reserve untouched by human activity. As a result, the waters around Montserrat are now teeming with fish, coral and sponges, while their larvae have drifted north to where the best dive sites are. The area is now an extremely rewarding one for divers.

Map: Montserrat

North West Bluff
Hell's Gate
1322
Rendezvous Bay
Silver Hills
Drummond's
Yellow Hole
ATLANTIC
CARIBBEAN Little Bay
Davy
Marguerita Bay
Carr's Bay
Hill
Gerald's
SEA
Sweeney's
Brades
Blake's Estate
OCEAN
St Peter
St John's
Cudjoe Head
Baker
St Peter's
Hill
Woodlands Bay
Montserrat
Safe Zone
National Trust
Olveston
Trant's Bay
Lime Kiln Bay
2429
Jack Boy
Salem
Centre
Hill
Old Road
Hills
Farm Bay
Bluff
③ Montserrat
Spanish Point
Old Road Bay
Old
Volcano Observatory
Towne
Frith
Fleming
Iles Bay
St Georges
Daytime
Foxes Bay
Entry
Exclusion
Bransby
Zone
Zone
Bluff
(subject to change)
Richmond
Hill
Soufrière
Hills
Plymouth
Volcano
St Anthony
Sugar Bay
Roche's
Bluff
Germans Bay
South
Soufrière
Landing Bay
Hills
Montserrat
0   2 miles
0   2 km
Old Fort
Point
subject to change

In Antigua the beach is never far away.

ANTIGUA

A stroll around St John's will give you a flavor of a small Caribbean town, while excursions further afield take you to a renovated 18th-century dockyard and some stunning beaches.

Numerous gleaming, multi-decked vessels have glided into port since the intrepid Lady Liston penned her travel journal in 1800: 'The bay of St John's is extremely pretty, and although a bar prevents the entrance to large ships, it is filled with smaller ones.' Today, St John's, the capital of Antigua, still gently tumbles to the sea along narrow, trenched streets and canopied terraces, while the wooden jetties continue to harbor fishing boats and small craft. The sandbar, however, has long since been dredged, allowing modern nautical colossi to muscle into the sheltered waters. Once dependent on slave and merchant vessels to fill its wharves, the present economy relies on cruise ships. In addition to the busy itineraries that can be pre-booked before landing, Antigua offers much for the visitor beyond beach, boat or boutique trips.

ON THE QUAYSIDE

In **St John's ❶**, **Redcliffe** and **Heritage** quays are the first points of call. The former is the more picturesque, offering a range of shops and restaurants in a pleasantly shaded setting of restored wooden buildings, with latticework balconies. The latter is a breezy, pastel-colored mall, with an air-conditioned casino, and duty-free shops to lure visitors. Between them, local traders selling bright sarongs, sunhats and

St John's vibrant waterfront

T-shirts are gathered under the roof of the Vendors' Mall.

A third quay, **Nevis Street Pier**, has opened up the waters to even larger ships and their holiday cargoes. With full moorings, up to 10,000 visitors may arrive in the capital of Antigua; some ships moor in the deep water harbor, too. The center of town can get very crowded at peak hours, but a quieter, calmer Caribbean lies just a 5-minute roam up the sloping streets. A short walk north along Popeshead Street, east up St Mary's Street or south via

Main attractions
St John's
Museum of Antigua and Barbuda
Nelson's Dockyard
Betty's Hope
Boggy Peak

Map on page 232

One of the beautiful stained-glass windows in the Cathedral of St John the Divine.

Market Street reveals the full range of city life.

URBAN WALKABOUT

The portside area provides the entire selection of shopping, eating, banking and telecommunication facilities. The last two are located on High and Long streets, while the rest are sandwiched between the sea and Thames Street. Island cash tills readily swallow US dollars, although paying with local currency normally means slightly lower prices, once you calculate the exchange rates.

A walk through town might not be the usual agenda for a cruise holiday, but St John's, with its single-story wooden houses flanking the narrow lanes, offers the perfect chance to see something of the urban Caribbean.

ISLAND HISTORY

An early morning start, grabbing a coffee and cake from one of the excellent local bakeries or cafés in lower St Mary's Street or Redcliffe Quay, accompanied by a copy of the *Outlet* or *Daily Observer* newspaper, will give an insight into the often intriguing events of a small Caribbean island. A few minutes from the quayside, the former courthouse on Long Street, solidly built in 1747 from local stone, is now the **Museum of Antigua and Barbuda** (tel: 268-462 1469; Mon–Sat 8.30am–4.30pm, donation). The renovated building is packed with local heritage. An airy main hall highlights island life and history, while next door houses a database of monument inscriptions from around Antigua and the associated isle of Barbuda.

The Anglican **Cathedral of St John the Divine**, further up Long Street, originally dates from 1683 but it was damaged and restored after an earthquake in 1834. The towers of this striking Baroque edifice have long proclaimed St John's presence to new arrivals.

Across the road, the **Antigua Recreation Ground** is the hallowed home of Antiguan cricket, and the spot where local hero Sir Vivian Richards, the 'Master Blaster,' knocked off the fastest century in cricket. However, a new ground with higher specifications, named after Sir Vivian, was built for the

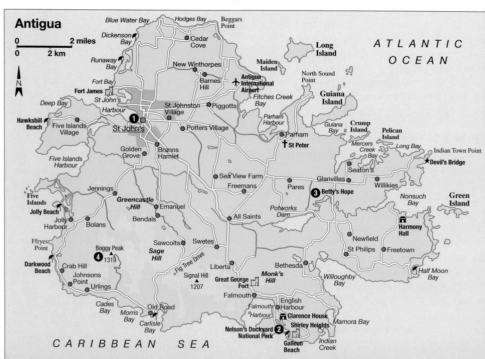

2007 World Cup further out towards the airport, and Test matches are now held there. Returning down Redcliffe and St Mary's streets, the Ebenezer Methodist Church was completed in 1839, but twice restored after earthquakes rattled its foundations. On Market Street, opposite the West Bus Station, you can buy tropical fruits in the covered **Heritage Market**, and craftwork in the building next door.

THE SITES BEYOND THE TOWN

Nowhere is far away in Antigua, but the full range of stunning beaches and historic sites lies out of walking distance. Cycling will get you a bit further, and the best biking destination is **Fort Bay**, a leisurely 20-minute ride northwest of the town center. Continue along Popeshead Street and turn left at the sign for Miller's-by-the-Sea to reach this popular locals' beach. At the southern end of the promontory, **Fort James** dates from 1739 and guards perfect views out to sea.

Further afield, **English Harbour** to the southeast receives small cruise ships and yachts, many of which have done the transatlantic crossing. The Antigua Yacht Club is here and organizes regattas and other sailing festivals. One of Antigua's most popular attractions, **Nelson's Dockyard ❷** (daily 8am–5pm), is also here. It's about 30 minutes away from St John's by regular bus service from the West Bus Station or by taxi. A series of beautifully restored mid-18th-century buildings give this harbor a historic feel. It was once a key command post for the British Navy, and home to Admiral Horatio Nelson while he commanded HMS *Boreas*. The bay is overlooked by the impressive fortifications of **Shirley Heights** (daily; combined ticket with the dockyard), which livens up with reggae, steel bands and barbecues on Sunday afternoon and evening.

Taxi drivers offer a tour of the whole island, but if time is limited, it's worth slowing down to savor one or two sites. **Betty's Hope ❸** (Pares Village,

Mon–Sat 9am–4pm), on the loop back from English Harbour, was built in the 1650s as the first sugar plantation on the island. The husks of former sugar mills are scattered across the island, but here the sugar mill has been restored and occasionally grinds in full sail. Other plantation buildings remain in ruins due to lack of finance, but there is a small visitor's center.

To the east, **Devil's Bridge** and art gallery of **Harmony Hall**, a former plantation house, offer relaxing excursions, en route to **Half Moon Bay**. Every Antiguan promotes a favorite beach: Darkwood Beach, Hawksbill Bay, Dickenson Bay and Ffryes Bay on the west coast are all strong contenders.

Boggy Peak ❹ (1,319ft/402 meters), at Antigua's highest point, is a rewarding 2-hour hike in the southwest of the island. Ask to be dropped at the start of the track just beyond Urlings. After the quiet town of Old Road, the return route to St John's climbs **Fig Tree Drive**, lined with remnants of rainforest that once covered the isle, protected as the Wallings Forest Reserve.

Boat pillars, Nelson's Dockyard.

📷 THE SPLENDORS OF THE DEEP

The dramatic seascape of the Caribbean is still a widely unexplored realm of beauty, even though generations of settlers have changed the landscape.

Tourism has set off the spirits of invention: More and more tiny submarines seating about 20 or so passengers are being launched throughout the region to give the ordinary visitor a chance of sharing the kind of underwater experience previously only available to the rapidly growing crowd of scuba divers.

THE POOL IS OPEN

With its warm and shallow waters, 75°F (24°C) being the average temperature, the Caribbean Sea is an ideal spot to learn to scuba dive. Hundreds of dive shops certify beginners after 4 or 5 days of theory and practice in shallow waters (PADI, NAUI courses). More advanced divers and budding marine biologists will also meet instructors to help them find the best sites and produce exquisite underwater photography.

Some of the most beautiful dive sites are located in protected marine areas. The boom in tourism – more fish to be caught, more sewage to be disposed of, more beach pollution and reef damage from ships' anchors and tender boats – has severely endangered the fragile and highly complex reef ecosystem. The tiny island of Bonaire was the first to protect the coastal waters around the island as a marine park; others such as Saba and the British Virgin Islands followed suit. Jacques-Yves Cousteau initiated a marine park on the western shore of Guadeloupe, St Eustatius now protects its historic treasures below the water line, and most islands have some sort of reef protection.

A fisherman from Belize shows off a conch shell and star fish. Remember that many sea creatures are protected by international legislation and should not be bought as souvenirs.

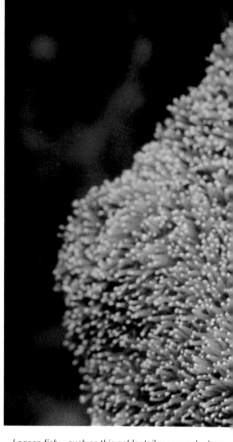

Lagoon fish – such as this goldentail moray eel – have developed clever tactics for hiding from enemies and catching their prey unawares.

Gorgonians, known as sea fans, move with the current as though blown by the breeze. These soft corals come in many colors, such as purple, yellow or red and are often home to seahorses and flamingo tongue snails.

Wreck diving at Curaçao.

Recaptured by the sea

Many islands have wrecks old and new for divers and snorkelers to explore. One of the most recent ships to be scuttled, in 2011, is the USS *Kittiwake* off Seven Mile Beach in Grand Cayman, which rests 64ft (20 meters) deep although its top is only 10ft (3 meters) from the surface. Within weeks it had become home to grouper, barracuda, blue tangs, sergeant majors and squirrelfish (www.dive365cayman.com). Aruba also offers an assortment of about a dozen underwater wrecks of ships and planes. Off its western shores, around 33ft (10 meters) under water is the *Pedernales*, the remnants of a tanker torpedoed during World War II.

At 460ft (140 meters) long, the *Antilla* is one of the biggest wrecks in the Caribbean and it is living proof of nature's rapid move to integrate: corals, sponges, anemones and other invertebrates have attached themselves to the huge hull and transformed it into a multicolored patchwork. Bigger still is the 1,000ft (200m) container ship *Anina*, scuttled in 100ft (30 meters) of clear water off Grenada in 2018 as a dive attraction and artificial reef. There are plenty of books on each island documenting their shipwrecks and other dive sites, including the *Proselyte* in Great Bay (Sint Maarten), RMS *Rhone* in the Rhone Marine Park, off Tortola, and a load of old cars which tumbled from a barge off Vaersenbaai, Curaçao.

naire has a pristine underwater world and is known for superb snorkeling, as well as being a prime scuba ing destination.

arning to dive requires skills training best done in the ety of a swimming pool, like here in Aruba, where you n get familiar with your scuba equipment.

It's essential to carry out the routine safety checks with one's diving buddy before taking to the water.

ST KITTS AND NEVIS

St Kitts is going through a tourist boom in the south, but retains its old-world atmosphere in the north. If you get your timing right, you can also sample the charms of nearby Nevis.

Travelers in search of the 'real' West Indies will get a feel for it on this small island, which crams an astonishing range of terrain – from salt ponds and dry scrub to rainforest and mountains – into its 65 sq miles (170 sq km).

Arriving at the capital, **Basseterre ❶**, you can start exploring almost immediately since the Port Zante cruise terminal, with its duty-free shops, restaurants and a casino, lies only a few minutes' walk from the heart of town.

Palm-filled Basseterre has old-world charm by the bucketload, and restoration of many of Basseterre's gingerbread-trimmed public buildings and homes has made it a big hit with cruise passengers. **Independence Square**, a former slave market and now an attractive park surrounded by 18th-century houses, is particularly worth a look, as is **The Circus** traffic intersection on Fort Street, with a clock tower of elaborately worked cast iron.

For local color, wander through the back streets off Bay Road, where you'll find goats and chickens wandering free, and roadside stalls selling fish, fruit and flowers. The town has a few galleries stocked with good-quality art, crafts and antiques. The best local buys are leather and cotton goods, spices, pottery and sea opal jewelry.

An eye for mischief, Basseterre.

EXPLORING FURTHER AFIELD

If you plan to explore further afield by taxi, check the rates listed in the cruise terminal, as they are not displayed in cabs. You should also establish the fare before boarding – although the East Caribbean Dollar is the local currency, US dollars are widely accepted, so make sure you know which currency the quoted price is in.

A taxi will charge US$50 for a round trip to **Brimstone Hill Fortress National Park ❷** (tel: 869-465 2609; www.brimstonehillfortress.org; 9.30am–5.30pm), a huge fortress and Unesco World Heritage

⊙ Main attractions
Basseterre
Brimstone Hill Fortress National Park
Romney Manor
Wingfield Estate
Turtle Beach
St Kitts Scenic Railway

Map on page 238

⊙ Tip

Taxi drivers offer guided tours of St Kitts from around $35 per person for a couple of hours to $300 per taxi (four passengers) for a day. If you fancy seeing the island this way, spend some time making arrangements as soon as you disembark.

Site set atop an 800ft (245-meter) volcanic mound, with breathtaking views. The British called this 'the Gibraltar of the West Indies' until, embarrassingly, it was captured by the French in 1782 (although they were thrown out a few months later). As one of the best-preserved historical fortifications in the Americas, this is one not to miss.

After touring the fortress you can follow nature trails and spot green vervet monkeys larking about – a good way to stretch your legs after being on a ship. The views are tremendous and you should be able to see several neighboring islands from the top. Take your credit card since the gift shop sells some very tempting prints of old Caribbean maps.

Romney Manor ❸ (Old Road Town; tel: 869-465 6253; www.caribellebatik stkitts.com; Mon–Fri 8.30am–4pm, Sat 9am–1pm) possesses six acres (2.4 hectares) of glorious gardens containing a saman tree believed to be more than 400 years old. At 24ft (7.3 meters) in diameter, its canopy covers half an acre. Romney Manor is known primarily for being the home of Caribelle Batik,

and you can watch the traditional hand-dyeing process on Sea Island cotton and purchase garments in their shop.

A 3-minute walk from Romney Manor is **Wingfield Estate**, with the ruins of a mighty sugar mill and rum distillery. Knowledgeable guides will explain the processes to you. Wingfield is also the place to come for the **Sky Safari** zip line tour (tel: 869-466 4259; www.skysafarist kitts.com), where cables allow you to fly over Wingfield River..

A DAY AT THE BEACH

If a day at the beach is more to your liking, the closest one to head for is **Frigate Bay ❹**, a stretch of soft white sand a few miles to the southeast of Basseterre. From Frigate Bay a 6-mile (10km) road runs down the narrow peninsula to Major's Bay. From the top you can see **South Friar's Bay**, with a wild beach on the Atlantic Ocean on one side and a calm beach on the Caribbean Sea on the other and Nevis in the distance.

Turtle Beach is heaven for bird-watchers, nature lovers and watersports enthusiasts. Here, you can

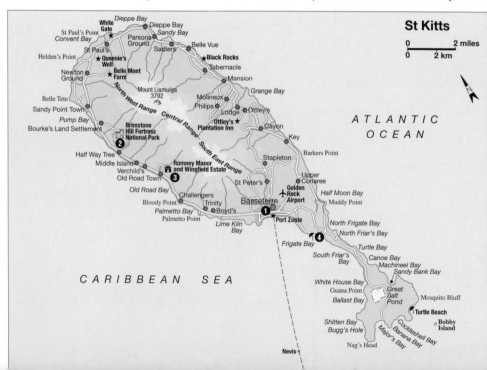

snorkel, see monkeys, spot rare birds, hire a kayak or windsurf. This southern peninsula is, however, a target for tourism development and there is considerable hotel construction under way.

You may decide that the easiest way to get around is to book a shore excursion from your ship. One of the tours offered, unique to St Kitts, is the **St Kitts Scenic Railway** (tel: 869-465 7263; www.stkittsscenicrailway.com). When sugar was king, a narrow-gauge railway was built in 1912–26 to take the cane from the fields to the sugar mill in Basseterre. This track has been renovated and a tourist route (dubbed the 'last railway of the West Indies') offers a 3-hour circular tour of the island, partly by train, partly by coach, passing ruined sugar estate buildings and offering a better view of the countryside than you get from the road.

VISITING NEVIS

If you have enough time, you could cross the 12 miles (20km) to **Nevis** in 30 to 45 minutes by ferry, which is an experience in itself. You can either travel in style or choose the cargo boat and find yourself sharing the ride with livestock and sacks of vegetables. The round trip (which costs US$8–15) will take you to the capital, **Charlestown**, an attractive place of leafy gardens and pastel-tinted, gingerbread-trimmed houses.

Here, street vendors will ply you with fruit wines made from gooseberry, sorrel and pawpaw (papaya) – and you may need them if you sample the island's specialty, hot pepper sauce. You can also buy batik and handicrafts from artisans at the Cotton Ginnery on the waterfront. For a good lunch, grab a cab to **Pinney's Beach**, which is just a short hop from Charlestown.

Some cruise lines offer excursions from St Kitts to Nevis, which may include a visit to Charlestown and the Botanical Gardens, or a tour to Nevis Peak and a rainforest hike. They are quite expensive, but at least everything is organized for you in advance and saves you time. If you decide to go it alone, *do* check ferry schedules and allow plenty of time – you don't want to miss your ship, as it won't wait unless you're on a ship's excursion.

The Celebrity Eclipse, docked in St Kitts.

Downtown Charlestown.

A dazzling – and somewhat terrifying – view from Dominica's Rainforest Aerial Tram in Morne Trois Pitons National Park.

DOMINICA

Untamed and beautiful, this lush volcanic island has jungle trails, sulfurous pools and coral reefs. Above and below sea level it is a mecca for nature lovers, from birdwatchers to whale watchers.

As the most lush mountainous island in the eastern Caribbean, Dominica is a place of lofty peaks and precipices, tropical forests and steep-sided valleys, 365 rivers, 12 major waterfalls and sulfurous springs. Wild and untamed, with nearly two-thirds of its territory still under natural vegetation, Dominica is conceivably the only island that Christopher Columbus would recognize some 500 years later. Yet Dominica is defined as much by what it is not as by what it is. It is not a Caribbean Eden of palm-fringed, white sandy beaches and boisterous rum-punch parties. It has no casinos, no golf courses, no marinas lined with sleek yachts, nor significant shopping opportunities. Instead, Dominica offers nature in the raw. Indicative of this emphasis is the latest tourist attraction to be completed: the **Waitukubuli National Trail**, which runs 115 miles (184km) from the far north to the far south, touching both east and west coasts, up and down mountains, across rivers and through forest reserves – a hiker's dream.

COLONIAL PAST

Set in the Windward Islands, between French Guadeloupe and Martinique, Dominica bears the imprint of both Britain and France. English is the official language, but a French-influenced Creole patois is equally prevalent. In the 1750s,

Munching on sugar cane.

the French settled on the island, virtually wiping out the Carib race, before the territory was declared British in 1763 and colonized as a plantation economy. Yet, despite persecution, Dominica remains the last outpost of the Carib Indians (or Kalinago, as they call themselves).

Cocoa and coffee-growing under the French gave way to the cultivation of sugar and limes under the British. Dominica was the world's foremost lime producer before bananas became the byword for economic success in the 1930s. The inability of small islands

Main attractions
Waitukubuli National Trail
Cabrits National Park and
  Fort Shirley
Indian River
Kalinago Barana Auté
Roseau
Trafalgar Falls
Titou Gorge
Morne Trois Pitons
  National Park
Whale watching

Map on page 245

Jean Rhys, the Dominica-born writer, evoked her childhood in her novel, *Wide Sargasso Sea*: 'Too much purple, too much green. The flowers too red, the mountains too high, the hills too near.' The island has dramatic weather to match – on the same day that torrid sun bakes the Caribbean side, storms break on the Atlantic coast, and the interior dissolves into rolling clouds, mists and rainbows.

Village hut on Carib Territory.

to compete with cheaper, mass-produced Latin American bananas has led Dominica to diversify into eco-tourism. Nevertheless, the toil of subsistence farming and the reality of unemployment has driven a lot of Dominicans to start a new life in Antigua, St Thomas or Guadeloupe. The island was badly damaged by Hurricane Maria in 2017 but largely recovered within 18 months.

NORTHERN SHORE EXCURSIONS

Since Dominica has two cruise ship terminals, certain excursions are more convenient from one or the other. **Portsmouth ❶**, the northern port, has access to a range of natural and historical attractions. The town itself is of little tourist interest, but it is busy with hundreds of students from the Ross University Medical School campus. To the north is the **Cabrits National Park,** and the lovingly restored buildings of **Fort Shirley**. It is a moving sight to see small cruise ships under sail come into Prince Rupert Bay and anchor just under the fortress, much as ships must have done since the 18th century when it was built.

The Waitukubuli National Trail starts from here, heading north along the coast to Capuchin before winding its way to the east coast and eventually to Soufrière.

South of the town, a popular trip is to travel by colorful wooden boat along the Indian River, which is festooned with foliage – the boatman will point out herons in the reeds and iguanas in the trees. The trip pauses at a rustic bar for a rum punch and loud music before returning to the sea. Booking is not necessary – enterprising (licensed) boatmen will be keen to take you.

The northeast coast has some lovely, wild, sandy beaches, particularly around Calibishie. A taxi tour around the north could allow you some time here (and no doubt your driver would point out locations used in the filming of *Pirates of the Caribbean*) on your way to the Carib Territory.

THE KALINAGO

Dominica is home to the last surviving pocket of the Kalinago/Carib people. The island's 3,000 Kalinago are descendants of the Amerindian people who once

dominated the region. Waves of colonial persecution forced the Kalinago to retreat to Dominica, the last major island to be settled by the European powers. The most popular shore excursion from Portsmouth sets off in search of their culture, skirting their lands in the northeast. As well as growing coconuts and bananas, the Kalinago survive on fishing, carving, weaving and basket-making. In the Carib Territory there is a model village, **Kalinago Barana Auté** (tel: 767-445 7979; www.kalinagobaranaaute.com), where guides explain the culture and history of the people and you can watch women weaving their intricate and beautiful baskets, before a singing and dancing folklore troupe bids visitors a traditional farewell.

ROSEAU

Roseau ❷, the capital in the south, offers an even wider range of options. The little town is squeezed between the sea and the mountains, with outlying villages running up the valleys and along the coastal road. Slightly ramshackle, with its French colonial houses with hanging verandas, tin roofs and narrow streets, it is worth a stroll. A T-shaped cruise ship pier allows you to disembark in the middle of town for a bit of sightseeing followed by a meal at the historic Fort Young, now a waterfront hotel. The small **Dominica Museum** (Bayfront; Mon–Fri 9am–4pm, Sat 9am–noon), is housed in the old post office, and covers everything from island geology and economy to the history of the slave trade. Behind it is the Old Market Plaza, still used by vendors of crafts and souvenirs, and containing the old, red, market cross. A walk up King George V Street will lead you to the **Botanical Gardens**, the main recreational park, used for cultural events.

For an unusual sensation, take a taxi to Champagne Beach, just north of Roseau, and swim in the water amid millions of fine bubbles, which originate from fissures in the ocean floor.

SOUTHERN SHORE EXCURSIONS

There are many tours offered, with varying levels of activity, from a Jeep safari into the tropical interior to a trek to the

Fort Shirley.

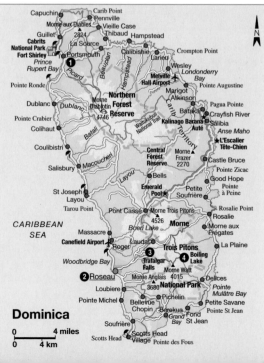

Dominica

⊙ Tip

Ken's Hinterland Adventure Tours (tel: 866-880 0508; www.khattstours.com), based at the Fort Young Hotel in Roseau, can organize virtually any kind of excursion, from whale-watching to extreme sports. Trips to rivers, falls and pools are available at relatively short notice. For diving and snorkeling, call Dive Dominica (tel: 767-414 7626; www.divedominica.com).

Valley of Desolation and Boiling Lake or canyoning in one of the gorges. Most cruise lines focus on trips (by minibus or Jeep) to the Emerald Pool, Titou Gorge or Trafalgar Falls, with maybe a canopy tour in the cloud forest, but these are also accessible by taxi. Canyoning along the rivers is an exhilarating activity, suitable for most able-bodied visitors. There are also kayaking, river tubing, snorkeling and scuba-diving trips, as well as whale-watching safaris on the west coast.

For those who want soft adventure, the best land-based excursion is a half-day Jeep safari into the forest. The tour takes you from Roseau up the slopes of Morne Bruce, where you get a good view of the capital, port and cruise ship, then sets off into rainforest towards **Trafalgar Falls ❸**, crossing a wild valley that was once a productive lime and cocoa plantation. All around are calabash trees, bananas, avocados and mangoes, orchids, heliconia and ginger lily, as well as the cinnamon tree. The short trail to the waterfalls is signaled by a handy bar and restaurant, with craft vendors round the parking lot.

Sulfur springs on the Boiling Lake Trail.

An invigorating but comfortable climb through dense vegetation ends at a viewing platform overlooking two waterfalls. Keen swimmers can clamber over slippery rocks to bathe in the pool, but swimming is better at the **Titou Gorge**, where hot and cold streams intermingle in a natural plunge pool. The gorge looks distinctly unprepossessing, but it is an outlet of Freshwater Lake, one of the most significant mountain crater lakes in the Caribbean. After clambering into the invigorating waters of the pool, the group swims in Indian file towards a luminous cavern. Wacky Rollers Adventure Park (tel: 767-440 4386; www.wackyrollers.com) offers high ropes courses, ziplining, tubing, kayaking and off-road jeep tours, and will pick cruise passengers up at the dock.

BOILING LAKE TRAIL

The Boiling Lake trail is a spectacular trek, one of the toughest in the Caribbean, used as a fitness test by the Dominican army, and offered only by cruise lines with a fair proportion of active passengers. This full-day hike

⊙ WHALE-WATCHING TRIPS

One of the features of Dominica's underwater landscape is the steep drop-off very close to shore, which provides very deep water and feeding grounds for whales. Dominica is the ideal place to spot pilot whales, false killer whales, mixed pods of sperm whales and spotted whales, as well as bottle-nosed dolphins. Between November and March, a classic whale and dolphin safari offers a 90 percent success rate in spotting both creatures.

The skippers have boats equipped with sonar, backed up by a lookout scanning the surface for telltale signs, including the distinctive musky, oily scent of a sperm whale. The boats head along the west coast, stopping regularly to take soundings and listen for each creature's signature tune, from the singing of humpbacks and the clicking of sperm whales to the pinging of pilot whales and the whistling of dolphins. The humpback whale is more often heard than seen, but the flipping of any great black tailfin creates a frisson of excitement, particularly as a whale can dive as deep as 6,000ft (2,000 meters). The pilot whale prefers to travel in pods of up to 60, while the sperm whale might be accompanied by 20ft (6-meter) calves. As for dolphins, apart from the bottle-nosed variety, acrobatic spotted and spinner dolphins love to surf the wake of the boat and provide ample consolation for any missed whale sightings.

from the Titou Gorge up into the **Morne Trois Pitons National Park**, a Unesco World Heritage Site, takes up to 4 hours in each direction. Rewards include the pleasures of passing under canopies of greenery formed by giant tree ferns, fording mineral-rich streams, relishing rare vistas of Martinique and Guadeloupe, and climbing knife-edged ridges into a primeval landscape. The **Valley of Desolation** is a long, jagged volcanic fissure with fumaroles venting stinking clouds of sulfurous gases. The rocks are cast in metallic colors and bisected by a scalding river rich in mineral deposits.

Beyond lies the **Boiling Lake 4**, often concealed behind clouds of steam. When the seething mists clear, the magma-heated cauldron reveals a surface ruffled by bubbles. As the second-largest cauldron of boiling water in the world, this flooded fumarole is the highlight of the exhilarating trek.

BENEATH THE WAVES

Most shore excursions include the option of scuba diving or snorkeling, exploring the majestic underwater seascapes, from submerged pinnacles to corals and sponges populated by reef fish. It is best near Soufrière Bay and Scotts Head, where hot and cold springs bubble under the surface, but diving is also feasible in the north, around the Cabrits peninsula. Part of Dominica's appeal is the sharpness with which the ocean floor drops off from the shore, reaching depths of several hundred meters just a stone's throw from the coast. Sediment swiftly falls away, leaving the water crystal-clear. Kayaking and snorkeling are also best in the calm waters on the leeward side, including around Scotts Head, where leaping dolphins or frigate birds and pelicans diving for fish draw your eyes upwards.

INDEPENDENT EXCURSIONS

Taxi tours can get you off the beaten track as well, to explore more of the island. Note, though, that Dominica's rainforest and cloud forest is green and lush for a reason. It rains frequently and short, sharp showers are common, so dress appropriately (most tour operators provide waterproofs).

Diving aficionados opt for the diving afforded either to the south or to the north of the island.

Trafalgar Falls.

Drummer in Carnival parade.

MARTINIQUE

This far-flung *département* of France has some stunning and original buildings as well as fascinating botanical gardens, rum distilleries and the poignant ruins left by a volcanic eruption.

Caribbean **Martinique** Sea

Welcome to France! Strange as it may seem, setting foot on the island of Martinique means that you are entering the French Republic and visiting a far-flung corner of the European Union, where the local currency is the euro. It may not look much like it, but this Caribbean island is politically and constitutionally a part of France. Since 1946, when its people voted to become an overseas *département*, Martinique, like Guadeloupe, has been a little tropical piece of Europe. Its people are French citizens, enjoying the same rights as any other *citoyens*, and in many ways act just like their European compatriots, but with one major exception – they are also Caribbean.

Although all Martinicans speak Créole, the local French-based dialect, the official language is French. Many people don't speak English and they appreciate attempts to communicate, however clumsily; so have a go, if you speak any French at all. However, most people you'll come into contact with as a tourist, such as taxi-drivers and guides, will do their best to speak English.

FORT-DE-FRANCE

Cruise ships arrive in **Fort-de-France ❶**, the island's main port and capital, a city of more than 170,000 inhabitants. Some dock at Quai des

Tourelles, to the east of the old city, by the naval dockyard. From here it is a US$10 taxi ride into the center of Fort-de-France, or a long, hot walk. If you are luckier, your ship will berth at the purpose-built Pointe Simon terminal, close to the heart of the city; the biggest ships can now dock here and a small market appears every time a large ship calls, selling local trinkets. In a matter of minutes you are in the bustling and unmistakably French-flavored shopping streets of the center of Fort-de-France. There is

⊙ Main attractions
St-Louis Cathedral
Bibliothèque Schoelcher
Fort-de-France markets
Jardin de Balata
St-Pierre and the
    Volcanological Museum

Map on page 251

A map of Martinique first published in 1755.

little to keep you at the cruise terminal and it is better to head straight out onto the Boulevard Alfassa, the road running parallel to the waterfront. Take any of the major streets to your left and you will quickly find yourself right in the middle of things.

Like most Caribbean ports, Fort-de-France has had its fair share of fires, earthquakes and other natural disasters, so there are many modern structures among the more interesting 19th-century (and earlier) buildings. What hasn't changed, however, is the grid of narrow streets, which makes driving a nightmare and walking a pleasure. In these busy thoroughfares there are countless small boutiques selling high fashion as well as local crafts and clothes. Heading away from the sea up rue de la République or rue Victor Schoelcher (named after an anti-slavery campaigner), you reach rue Victor Hugo, where a couple of small shopping malls offer an impressive array of designer perfumes and clothing. Further up rue de la République the

The Fort St-Louis market.

street is pedestrianized until you reach a square and a much larger shopping mall, Cour Perrinon, with a parking lot.

FRENCH IMPRESSIONS

Occasional buildings stand out as a reminder of Martinique's long French history. Some houses have ornate gingerbread fretwork, a style imported from Louisiana in the 19th century, intricate wrought-ironwork and pretty pastel colors. Most eye-catching, perhaps, are two buildings credited to the architect Henri Picq, a contemporary of Gustave Eiffel and, some claim, the true designer of the Eiffel Tower. The Romanesque-style **St Louis Cathedral**, on rue Schoelcher, hints at the architect's love affair with metal girders and joists, its steel-reinforced spire rising 200ft (60 meters) into the sky. Built in 1895 to withstand any earthquake, this blend of tradition and innovation, known as the 'iron cathedral,' has a cool interior and fine stained-glass windows.

A few streets away stands Picq's other lasting contribution to Fort-de-France's exotic architectural heritage. The imposing library, the **Bibliothèque Schoelcher** (tel: 596-702 667; Mon 1–5.30pm, Tue–Thu 8.30am–5.30pm, Fri 8.30am–5pm, Sat 8.30am–noon; free), is a spectacular blend of Romanesque, Byzantine and Egyptian influences, again dominated by prefabricated cast-iron and steel features. With ornate gables, a large glass dome and colored metal panels, this is a truly unique building, illuminated at night and decorated with clusters of French flags and exotic tropical trees. The library contains the abolitionist Schoelcher's private collection of books, and often stages exhibitions.

This eccentric structure looks over Fort-de-France's 'green lung,' the large expanse of grass, palms and tamarind trees known as **La Savane**.

Traditionally the place to sit and while the hours away, the park retains its relaxed atmosphere. You can sit on one of the benches and watch the local ferries that set off from the nearby pier. Alternatively, have a drink or meal at one of the hotels or restaurants that line the rue de la Liberté, next to La Savane.

Two statues on La Savane recall Martinique's Frenchness. A bronze image of Pierre Belain d'Esnambuc, the Norman nobleman who led the first French settlers in 1635, gazes out over the tranquil bay. Further inland stands a statue to the Empress Joséphine, Napoléon Bonaparte's first wife, who was born in Martinique. Modern-day Martinicans do not remember Joséphine with much affection as she is reputed to have told her husband to reintroduce slavery after it was first abolished in 1791. As a result, the white marble statue has lost its head (to local vandals), red paint splashed over it in a symbolic local version of the guillotine.

Across the bay is the impressive bulk of **Fort St-Louis**. The citadel has been occupied by the French military since the mid-17th century and is still an active naval base. One interesting feature is its unusually low ceilings, reputedly designed to deter attacks from taller British troops in the era of inter-European rivalry.

RESTAURANTS AND MARKETS

The center of Fort-de-France can be explored comfortably on foot in 3 or 4 hours, and there will still be time for a leisurely meal at one of the city's many excellent restaurants (try the delicious *accras*, deep-fried fritters stuffed with prawns or salted cod). More adventurous visitors might like to round off the tour by taking a look at the busy markets, which operate all day every day, but are most colorful on Friday and Saturday. The fish market takes place from early in the morning until dusk on the banks of the Rivière Madame, a 15-minute walk north of the Pointe Simon terminal. There, and in the adjacent fruit and flower market, you will

The Bibliothèque Schoelcher.

Just one brand of Martinique's famous sugar cane-derived white rum.

be dazzled by the sounds, smells and colors. Amid the high-decibel Créole conversations and piles of exotic vegetables, you will realize that this is no ordinary *département* of France.

OUTSIDE FORT-DE-FRANCE

Martinique is not a large island, but it is clearly impossible to see everything in the space of a few hours. Most cruise ships organize excursions to one or more of the chief attractions, and these normally involve a trip to a rum distillery, to the beautiful Balata Botanical Gardens or to the historic town of St-Pierre, victim of the 20th century's worst volcanic disaster. All these are worth doing, although the expedition to St-Pierre takes the longest (you should allow an hour each way).

Martinique is dotted with sugar plantations and rum distilleries, producing the world-famous *rhum agricole*, a white rum made from sugar cane juice rather than molasses. Most are open for free visits, but you will be encouraged to taste (and buy) some of the potent rum at the gift shop. One of

Haunting St-Pierre.

the most interesting tours is on offer at the Depaz plantation (9am–5pm), north of St-Pierre, where a signposted trail leads visitors through the stages of rum manufacturing.

Those more interested in tropical flora than rum cocktails should take a tour to the **Jardin de Balata** ❷ (Balata Botanical Garden; tel: 596-596-644 873; www.jardindebalata.fr; daily 9am–6pm, last entry 4.30pm), just north of Fort-de-France. At their best, after the rainy season at the end of the year, these gardens have a stunning collection of anthuriums, exotic trees and shrubs. Jewel-like hummingbirds flit among the flowers, while lizards scuttle along the paths. Nearby, the Sacré Coeur church, a smaller but almost exact replica of the Parisian original, stands among tropical foliage and spectacular mountain views.

Perhaps the most evocative place in Martinique is the town of **St-Pierre** ❸, situated on the northwest coast under the brooding Montagne Pelée volcano. In May 1902 this volcano erupted, killing all but one of the town's 30,000 inhabitants and devastating what was known as the 'Paris of the Antilles.' Many of the ruins of this sophisticated and fun-loving place, such as its grand theatre and main church, lie just as they have for more than a century.

A new town has grown among the rubble of the old, and there are cafés and restaurants to refresh the curious visitor. While the memory of the eruption is poignant, St-Pierre is not a gloomy place, and the local tourist office organizes fascinating tours of the historic ruins. The **Musée Franck Perret** (tel: 596-596-781 516; daily 9am–5pm), created by an American volcanologist, has graphic images and artifacts from both before and after the cataclysm, showing the ferocity of Montagne Pelée's 1902 eruption, and explaining how modern science has made a repetition of the disaster impossible.

Spices at Saint Antoine Market.

GUADELOUPE

Its cuisine and cultural scene might be reminiscent of France, but the lush tropical vegetation, white beaches and an active volcano will remind you that Europe is far away.

Guadeloupe is shaped like a butterfly, but that's not the only beautiful thing about this volcanic island in the French West Indies. Its terrain is varied and stunning. The eastern region, called Grande-Terre, is a lush land rich in banana plantations, cane fields and gentle hills but with a stormy, wind-hewn Atlantic coastline. It is also reasonably well developed as a tourist playground, with hotels and beach resorts.

Basse-Terre to the west, divided from Grande-Terre by the slender Rivière Salée strait, has more attractions for hikers and nature lovers. A dramatically mountainous region, it has a live volcano, La Soufrière, and dense forests, but the seas are calm and the beaches are white and glorious. You get from one region to the other via a drawbridge across the strait.

None of these gorgeous attributes will be apparent, however, when you first emerge from the cruise terminal in the capital, **Pointe-à-Pitre** **❶**. Although you'll find some nice facilities at the recently upgraded port – including landscaped gardens and duty-free shops, with more shops and small markets close by, as well as the dazzling new ACTe Memorial – you will need to negotiate heavy traffic to explore the main town. With the Musée des Beaux-Art, these two impressive new museums make it worth the effort, though. Speaking French is

Young woman in Antillean creole dress.

very useful if you want directions; while the tourist office staff at the port speak English, locals tend not to.

POINTE-À-PITRE

A short stroll along the waterfront to **Place de la Victoire** **Ⓐ** (where French troops defeated British invaders in 1794) will show you some wonderfully elaborate French colonial houses, complete with balconies and shutters, and the pretty harbor of **La Darse**, which lies off the square. Here you will find the main tourist information office, which is

Ⓞ Main attractions
Markets and museums in Pointe-à-Pitre
Parc Naturel de la Guadeloupe
La Soufrière
Chutes du Carbet
Fort Napoléon, Terre-de-Haut
Beaches of Les Saintes

Map on pages 256

⊙ Tip

You can hire a car in Guadeloupe, but it's a time-consuming process, and you'll have to negotiate steep mountain roads and drive on the right-hand side.

worth popping into, since Guadeloupe is not the easiest island to explore on your own. There is also a small but helpful information bureau in the cruise terminal, where you can pick up local maps, hook up with a scrupulous taxi guide, perhaps, and get useful advice on getting about. For example, you can hop on a cheap bus to the beaches of Gosier, if you know where to look.

If your ship gets in early, go to the rue St-John Perse to find **Marché Couvert** **ⓑ**, the town's covered market, which is bordered by rues St-John Perse, Schoelcher, Frébault and Peynier. It is at its bustling, colorful best in the morning. Here you can pick up stylish cotton clothing, straw bags and local crafts and feast your senses at stalls piled high with

fragrant spices and exotic fruits and vegetables, then head off for a decent coffee and a pastry from a pavement café.

For more serious shopping, the rues Schoelcher, Nozières and Frébault have the best boutiques, while the Distillerie Bellevue on rue Bellevue Damoiseau is the best place to sample and buy Rhum Agricole, the island's distinctive falling-down water, which locals claim will not give you a hangover because it's made from pure cane sugar juice – but don't take that too seriously. As a French territory, Guadeloupe offers the best bargains for perfume, crystal-ware, cosmetics and fashion accessories from French designer houses; prepare to stock up on Lalique, Hermès, Dior, Chanel and French lingerie.

MUSEUMS AND SIGHTSEEING

There are several museums worth a visit. The impressive **ACTe Memorial** (www.memorial-acte.fr; Tue–Thu 9am–7pm, Fri–Sat 9am–8pm, Sun 10am–6pm) is a starkly modernist, silver latticework structure perched on the waterfront on the site of an old sugar factory. It tells the story of the slave trade in graphic detail and is deeply moving. If you do one cultural activity, make it this. The **Musée de St-John Perse** (9 rue Nozières and rue A R Boisneuf; tel: 590-590-900 192; Mon–Fri 9am–5pm, Sat 8.30–12.30pm) is a beautifully restored colonial building commemorating the work of the island's Nobel Prize-winning poet, while the **Musée Schoelcher** (24 rue Peynier; tel: 590-590-820 804; Mon–Fri 9am–5.30pm, closed refurbishment so call for details) celebrates the life and anti-slavery campaigns of Victor Schoelcher, a leading 19th-century abolitionist. Pointe-a-Pitre also has a new art museum, the **Musée des Beaux-Arts de Saint-François**, housing a collection from the 16th century to the present day

Afterwards, head northeast to the Place de l'Eglise to see the exquisite stained-glass (and apparently hurricane-proof) windows of the **Cathédrale de St-Pierre et St-Paul**, which has a fragrant flower market near its entrance.

FRANCE IN THE CARIBBEAN

Like Martinique, Guadeloupe is a little bit of France dropped into the Caribbean Sea. You will have to pay for everything in euros, not US dollars, so either take a good supply with you or get some from an ATM ashore. Also be prepared to trawl your memory for basic French; the local people can be chilly about speaking English, but will be more cooperative if you smile a lot and make a bit of an effort.

You'll also have to negotiate hard over taxi fares if you want to explore further afield. Fares are theoretically regulated by the government and should be listed at taxi stands, but some local drivers will get more out of you. Always agree a firm price before you start or, ideally, ask the tourist bureau at the port to find you a cooperative driver.

> ⊙ **Tip**
>
> Hikes in the Parc National are graded by levels of difficulty, but it's advisable to hire a guide if you are planning anything really adventurous.

Marina du Gosier, Grande-Terre.

⊙ TOP HATS

Around the islands of Les Saintes you will sometimes see people wearing a strange round hat made of bamboo and madras cotton, called a salako. There are only three or four people on the islands who make these distinctive hats nowadays, but they are still the traditional headgear of choice for the islanders to keep the sun off their heads. Legend has it that in the 19th century, a sailor from Les Saintes returned from Indo-China with a souvenir hat. French naval officers were stationed in Tonkin in 1873 and they wore a 'salacco' similar to the Santoise hats. The sailor's friends and family were so taken with it that they all started wearing them. Fishermen found it particularly useful while they were out in their 'santoises,' or boats.

ⓘ Fact

The popular British-French TV comedy-drama series *Death in Paradise*, starring Kris Marshall and Joséphine Jobert (following the departure of original leads Ben Miller and Sara Martins), has been filmed on Guadeloupe since 2011. In 2015, the show's creator Robert Thorogood published a novel, *A Meditation on Murder (A Death in Paradise novel)*, featuring characters from the series.

GRANDE-TERRE

The advantage of landing at Pointe-à-Pitre is that it lies on the 'body' of the butterfly-shaped island near the bridge over the Rivière Salée, and so is well placed for exploring both Grande-Terre and Basse-Terre. But if you didn't find the main port to your taste, you may prefer **La Marina** at **Bas-du-Fort**, a 10-minute taxi ride from the cruise terminal. Here, you'll find an attractive, boat-filled marina surrounded by shops, restaurants and cafés. You can hire a motorboat or join an excursion vessel to tour Guadeloupe's mangrove swamps, or visit a giant aquarium which houses more than 900 Caribbean sea species (tel: 590-590-909 238; daily 9am–7pm).

Further east from Pointe-à-Pitre, on Grande-Terre's south coast, lies **Le Gosier**, which has 5 miles (8km) of beach bordered by some of the region's best resorts. A spectacular 18th-century fortress, **Fort Fleur-d'Epée ❷**, is also situated here and commands fine views. Head even further along, to the east coast of Grande-Terre, and you'll discover breathtaking maritime scenery, somewhat reminiscent of Ireland's west coast. This coast borders the Atlantic, and the ferocity of its waves has carved elaborate patterns into the cliffs – a sight worth seeing if you enjoy high drama and natural beauty. Almost at the southeastern tip of the island, at Saint-François, there's a new art gallery, Musée des Beaux-Arts (tel: 590 590 284 318; Wed–Sun 11am–7pm) worth dropping in on if you're touring the island; there are 150 works dating from the 16th century, some by local artists.

BASSE-TERRE

Nature lovers will also be enthralled by Basse-Terre's huge **Parc National de la Guadeloupe ❸**, a latter-day Eden where you can freely enjoy a picnic, a hike and a swim beneath a clear-as-crystal waterfall. Just driving along the coast road which borders the park is a delight – the road winds up through lavish vegetation, passing lovely little bays and picturesque waterfront villages.

The best beach in Basse-Terre – and, indeed, on the whole island – is **Grande Anse** on the northwest coast, though **Deshaies** (slightly to the south) is more popular with snorkelers.

The biggest attraction on Basse-Terre has to be **La Grande Soufrière ❹** volcano, which soars 4,812ft (1,467 meters) above sea level. To reach its peak (if you dare) you'll have to drive up twisting roads past banana trees and tropical vegetation, stopping en route to view the lovely tropical gardens 1,900ft (580 meters) up at St-Claude. The road ends at 3,300ft (1,000 meters), but hikers can walk the rest and experience the ground beneath their feet growing hotter, and the rotten-egg reek of sulfur growing more intense, as they ascend.

The scenery on Basse-Terre's eastern coast is, by contrast, less dramatic. On your way back to the port from Soufrière, ask your driver to show you the **Parc Archéologique des Roches Gravées** – ancient rocks etched with images of men and animals, which

Suspended forest walkway on the Chutes du Carbet trail.

were carved by the Amerindians who originally inhabited Guadeloupe – at Trois Rivières on the southeast coast.

If going it alone sounds like too much hassle, you will find that cruise ship excursions cover most of the main sights outside Pointe-à-Pitre. Most cruise lines offer 3- to 4-hour tours around one or both parts of the island, and to Soufrière; the price sometimes includes lunch.

Also available are trips to the beach and tours to plantations. For the more adventurous, hikes through the rainforests of Basse-Terre are available from some cruise companies. They include transport to Basse-Terre and a guided 30-minute walk through dense tropical vegetation, followed by a swim beneath the three **Chutes du Carbet**.

ILES DES SAINTES

Of the string of small islands, named Los Santos by Columbus, only Terre-de-Haut and Terre-de-Bas are inhabited. **Terre-de-Haut** is the main island visited by tourists, with a good natural harbor suitable for small cruise ships. Easily reached by ferry from Guadeloupe, it can get busy with day-trippers during public holidays. About 3.5 miles (6km) long and 1 mile (1.6km) at its widest point, covering 1,290 acres (522 hectares), it supports a population of some 1,700 people, most of whom are descended from Breton colonists. There was never a plantation economy here, so African slaves were not imported.

Fort Napoléon (9am–12.30pm) is one of the few historical sites, built in the 1840s high up on Pointe à l'Eau and today, inhabited by the large green iguanas that populate the islands. The fort contains a museum giving the French view of the Battle of Les Saintes, which took place offshore in 1782. The French fleet, commanded by the Comte de Grasse, were on their way to attack Jamaica but were routed by the English Admiral Rodney, who came from St Lucia to intercept them.

There are some good trails to hike, some easy, such as the 2½-mile (4km) **Trace des Crêtes**, which starts in town and heads to the east coast, some involving more climbing, such as the steep hike up Le Chameau. There are also some lovely beaches, including **Pompierre**, a horseshoe-shaped bay with the Roches Percées guarding its entrance. Scuba diving can be arranged at the pier and snorkeling is good, but the beach gets busy, despite being a half-hour walk from the ship. **Grand Anse** is a long stretch of white sand on the east coast looking out to Dominica and Marie Galante, but swimming is not allowed owing to the rough seas. One of the prettiest beaches is **Plage du Pain de Sucre**, a 45-minute walk west of town with some tricky parts, so wear good shoes. There is a beach either side of the headland; one gets the wind and the other is protected, so choose carefully where the path divides. Alternatively, just sit in a bar on the waterfront in the tiny town and watch local life; the charm of the Iles des Saintes is their sleepiness.

Terre-de-Bas, one of the two inhabited islands in the Iles des Saintes grouping.

The third of the Chutes du Carbet.

Marigot Bay.

The magnificent Pitons and Soufrière.

ST LUCIA

Volcanic peaks, tropical vegetation, whale-watching opportunities and vibrant local culture make this delightful island a popular port of call on cruise itineraries.

Caribbean Sea

St Lucia

St Lucia is a favorite port of call for all the right reasons: the island is among the loveliest in the Caribbean, and the people are arguably the friendliest. Sandwiched between Martinique and St Vincent, St Lucia is the largest of the Windward Islands, with its calm Caribbean coast acting as a counterpoint to the wind-buffeted Atlantic shore. The mango-shaped island is lush and has preserved its green heart, with banana plantations giving way to botanical gardens and vibrant forests. The south is dominated by the Pitons, the jungle-clad twin peaks that symbolize St Lucia.

Yet these sailors' landmarks are only part of the island's sensory overload. The interior is a Gauguin-esque palette of tropical scenery: primary colors and parrots; hummingbirds and hibiscus; bougainvillea and bananas; volcanic waterfalls and sulfurous springs; Creole cuisine, calypso and secluded coves; coral reefs, and the best botanical gardens in the West Indies. St Lucia is both the quintessential Caribbean island and a patch of paradise.

Ships anchor in Castries either at Pointe Seraphine, where there are duty-free shops and plenty of souvenir stalls, or at La Place Carenage on the south side of the harbor, close to the main Castries market and the adjacent craft market (Mon–Sat 6am–5pm).

Mountain biking in the forest.

A DELIGHTFUL MIX

The island is an engaging mix of cultures, with Caribbean flair, Creole artlessness and French finesse underscored by traditional British values. The island has changed hands 14 times, with the French flag and the Union Jack alternating from 1650, when French settlers first landed. From the 1760s, the island operated a plantation economy, based on African slave labor. St Lucia became British for good in 1814; it gained independence in 1979 but remains part of the Commonwealth.

◎ Main attractions
The Pitons
Soufrière
Diamond Botanical
  Gardens
Pigeon Island National
  Landmark
Fond Latisab Creole Park

Map on page 265

⊘ Tip

When deciding whether to take an organized excursion or go it alone, bear in mind that while the ships always wait for delayed official excursions, independent travelers have much less leeway.

English is the official language but Creole patois – known as *kwéyòl* – is commonplace: French vocabulary imposed on African grammar, with a smattering of Spanish thrown in. St Lucia feels safe but wild, forthright yet not as in-your-face as Jamaica, as friendly as Barbados but less primly British.

Until recently, agriculture, chiefly bananas, was the mainstay of the economy, so tourism has not erased cultural traditions. As in most islands, the tourism dollar is yet to filter down to everybody, but the government is working on education and training to improve the skills of its citizens. St Lucia has luxurious hotels and low-key inns for those who wish to extend their stay. As a port of call, **Castries ❶** is perfectly suited to the largest cruise ships and offers an unparalleled variety of excursions.

EXCURSION TO PARADISE

While St Lucia is safe for independent visitors following well-trodden tracks to the beaches, or to the peaks and the volcano, first-time visitors would do well to book the classic 1-day excursion

The harbor at Castries.

through their cruise ship. Generally known as 'Land and Sea to Soufrière,' this full-day trip is arguably the best excursion in the Caribbean – a voyage through the island's history, culture, geology and geography. The day begins with a visit to the panoramic heights above Castries, followed by a leisurely drive through the lush interior to Soufrière, a walk round a quaint fishing village and a visit to the 'drive-in' volcano cowering under cone-shaped peaks. The volcano acquired its name because cars were allowed to park between two sets of bubbling, belching springs before tourism made this unfeasible. After a stroll around impressive botanical gardens, there's a lively Creole lunch on a former plantation estate. From the tiny port nearby, a catamaran sweeps visitors back to Castries, making stops for swimming, generally just before the chic marina of Marigot Bay.

There is usually time for an independent stroll around the cruise terminal, which is packed with jewelry and craft shops, or around the market alongside for fruit, vegetables, cocoa and spices,

hot sauce or a hot T-shirt. While elements of this trip could easily be done independently, this tried and tested formula is best left to professional guides, who handle it with humor and panache, as well as ensuring a return to the cruise ship in good time. And as all tour operators use comfortable minibuses, it will not feel impersonal.

LUCKY FOR SOME

From the cruise terminal, the trip ascends the slopes of Castries to **Morne Fortune**, the 'hill of luck,' yet equally unlucky to French and British forces. The main square in Castries was renamed Derek Walcott Square in 1993, in honor of the St Lucian poet who won the Nobel Prize for literature. The square is shaded by a huge, 400-year-old Saman tree known locally as a *massair*; the story runs that a foreigner once asked the name of the tree and was told *massair*, which simply means 'I don't know' in Creole, but the 'I-don't-know' tree it has been ever since. The undistinguished look of the town is the result of the devastating fire of 1948. Even

so, the hill is redeemed by panoramic views of the bay and by pink, weather-boarded colonial-style houses on the hill, which survived the fire. The classic photo opportunity is the view over the bay, usually dominated by cruise ships.

BAGS OF BANANAS

The tour continues into the lush interior, beginning with the banana plantations of **Cul de Sac Valley**. Until lack of international competitiveness led to the collapse of the local cash crop, bananas were the backbone of the St Lucian economy, but now the few surviving plantations depend entirely on exports to the British market. High in potassium and oil, the precious fruit finds its way into countless local recipes, from sweet banana ketchup and banana bread to banana wine, daiquiri and fruit punch. St Lucians claim that the volcanic soil makes these the sweetest, juiciest bananas on earth.

A foray to the coast reveals the lovely fishing village of **Anse la Raye ❷**, where trinket-sellers and fishermen cluster around the beachfront; beyond lie jaunty

A farmer holds up a cocoa pod at Fondoux Plantation.

Steam clouds the sulfur springs.

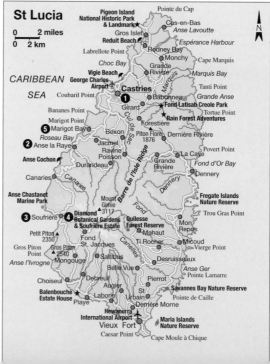

St Lucia

The trumpet-shaped red tropical hibiscus.

Exploring St Lucia's underwater world.

canoes bobbing beside a battered jetty. Traditionally, the fishermen used to make boats out of gum trees, and sails from sacks. From here, the excursion skirts the lush rainforest, with sightings of the dramatic **Pitons**, the twin cones which tower over the trees. **Gros Piton** rises over 2,540ft (798 meters) above the sea, while **Petit Piton** stands 2,350ft (743 meters) high. Thought to be the sides of an eroded volcanic crater, the peaks have always had a certain mystique: The Amerindians left sacred carvings on the rock, believing that the Petit Piton, the 'small' peak that dwarfs Soufrière, was giving birth to a baby.

SOUFRIÈRE

The quaintly ramshackle town of **Soufrière** ❸ nestles under the twin peaks and marks the gateway to a 7-acre (3-hectare) volcanic crater. The volcano's fans stress the rejuvenating properties of the sulfurous vapors, the positive effect on the sinuses and the therapeutic value of the volcanic springs. However, most visitors are overwhelmed by the familiar, sickly-sweet rotten-eggs smell

of the sulfur springs, the result of a volcanic eruption. The collapsed crater has pools of lava that steam away like an inferno. The seething mass slowly reveals its mineral-rich colors: greenish-yellow spells sulfur deposits; dark-green means copper oxide; white is lime and chalk; and purple is magnesium.

Since a vaporous explosion occurred in 1766, little of significance has disturbed the scene of these hissing grey fumaroles and local people believe the dormant volcano is safe. Even so, one guide nearly died trying to show German cruise ship visitors how unstable the volcanic crust was – it proved his point by collapsing and taking him down to his armpits. Hurricane Tomas changed the look of the sulfur springs in 2010, by felling surrounding vegetation and burying the access road. Unable to remove the trees from the hot ground, staff have had to leave them where they fell. In the meantime, transport comes in alongside Hotel Chocolat's Rabot Estate cocoa plantation.

LUSH VEGETATION

Nearby are the beautifully maintained **Diamond Botanical Gardens** ❹ (tel: 758-459 7155; www.diamondstlucia.com; Mon–Sat 10am–5pm, Sun 10am–3pm) and **Diamond Falls**, complete with a waterfall and the remains of a 3-mile (5km) 18th-century aqueduct linked to the Soufrière Estate. The gardens were created in 1785, just before the French Revolution, with funds provided by Louis XVI. While it is unsafe to swim in the volcanic falls, bathing in the rejuvenating mineral baths, fed by hot springs, is permissible. Given time constraints, visitors often have to choose between a dip in the baths or a stroll around the grounds, including the Japanese water gardens.

The exotic plants usually win, even if the lack of botanical labeling makes a good guide invaluable. Among the foliage are bold red and yellow crab's claw, ginger lily, rare orchids, trailing red heliconia, mimosa, poinsettia and over 140 types of fern. Beyond are coconut palms, Honduras mahogany, red cedars, sandalwood and the gri-gri palm, distinguished by its hairy trunk.

Also on display is an array of local crops, from coconuts to cassava and cinnamon, from pawpaw (papaya) to pumpkin, plantain, yams, breadfruit and dasheen, a root vegetable. Every crop has its own place in Caribbean history: Slaves were fed on breadfruit by their colonial masters, while coconut palms are known as the trees of life because every part of the palm and nut serves a useful purpose, from food to medicine, baskets to toothpicks.

LUNCHING AND SWIMMING

Lunch is often on the neighboring **Soufrière Estate**, which incorporates a former sugar mill and a restored water wheel, first used to crush limes and later to generate power. The property represents part of a 2,000-acre (810-hectare) estate that Louis XIV presented to his loyal subjects, the Devaux family, in 1713. Savoring the Creole buffet offers a chance to taste some of the crops presented in the botanical gardens. Tour groups also use the **Fond Doux Estate** (tel: 758-459 7545; www.fonddouxestate.com; daily 8am–4pm for tours), which serves a buffet lunch in the restaurant beside the estate house. A working plantation, you can see cocoa, coffee, banana, mango, citrus fruits, coconut, spices and vegetables being grown, and be shown the cocoa-drying racks and the chocolate-making process. Cocoa sticks, jams, jellies and other local products are sold in the little shop.

Afterwards, the excursion meets a catamaran at **Anse Chastanet**, the best place on the island for snorkeling and sailing. The catamaran cruise back to Castries conjures up a carnival atmosphere, with Caribbean music, tropical fruit and unlimited rum punch on board. Views of the Piton peaks give way to a series of sheltered coves, of which **Anse Cochon** is the most beguiling. This is a regular swimming and snorkeling stop, marred only by the myriad conch-shell vendors and banana- and bead-sellers, whose frantically paddled canoes surround the catamaran. Stray

Fond Doux Estate.

⊘ INDEPENDENT TRIPS

If you want to visit the island under your own steam rather than on a cruise ship tour, to visit the beaches on the north coast or to go snorkeling, a taxi from Castries is the obvious option. An official 'minder' at the head of the taxi rank establishes routes, states prices and helps form small groups to visit places together. Prices are standardized for set routes, but to double-check, call in at the tourist office booth close by.

The most popular beach is Reduit Beach on Rodney Bay, which has plenty of facilities, from sun-beds and parasols to watersports and restaurants. Official cabs are generally reliable in respecting the agreed pick-up time, but it is easy to call a taxi should the original one fail to turn up.

Snorkeling in the marine park off Anse Chastanet.

Zip-line through the forest for an adrenaline rush.

swimmers are rounded up and the cat-amaran sails north to **Marigot Bay** ❺, a magnificent steep-sided cove that is used as an exclusive marina for glitzy yachts, with some upmarket hotels and restaurants. The excursion ends with rum-sozzled passengers deposited at the cruise terminal, delighted to be addressed by their guide as *dou-dou*, Creole for 'darling' or 'sweetie.'

DOLPHINS, WHALES AND DEEP-SEA FISHING

While the above trip is probably the best way to spend your day ashore, there are other activities on offer, and for reasons of cost, numbers, reliable timing and tight organization, most of them are best organized through the ship's cruise excursion manager. On the water, these include whale- and dolphin-watching, deep-sea fishing, kayaking around Pigeon Island or in the mangroves on the east coast, or scuba diving at Anse Chastenet or near Marigot Bay.

The whale- and dolphin-watching trips off the west coast offer a 75 per-cent chance of seeing humpback whales and dolphins. A hydrophone-equipped boat enables the skipper to trace pass-ing whale pods while on-board sonar equipment allows everyone to tune in to the strange sounds made by these extraordinary and exciting mammals.

If you are more interested in catching marine life, the deep-sea fishing trip sets out in search of blue marlin and big-game fish, from barracuda to tuna and dorado. Depending on the partici-pants' wishes, the fish can be given to the captain or put back in the sea on a conservation-minded 'tag and release' basis. Alternatively, for a memorable island overview, a short but dramatic helicopter trip sweeps along the Carib-bean coast south towards Soufrière and the Pitons, revealing the majesty of the peaks, rainforest and volcanic springs.

NORTHERN ATTRACTIONS

There are many other tours on offer in other areas of the island, including plantation tours, hiking and zip-lining. The coastal region to the north of Cas-tries is the island's foremost resort area, with sheltered bays and upmarket

hotels, a marina, shopping malls and historic landmarks. **Rodney Bay** is the main town, offering the best shopping on the island and a great range of services and entertainment. The main street, lined with restaurants and bars, leads to **Reduit Beach**, one of the best on the island. The crescent-shaped beach extends as far as Pigeon Island further north, interrupted only by the mouth of the yacht harbor and marina.

Pigeon Island National Historic Park and Landmark (daily 9am–5pm) was once a separate island, accessible only by boat, but was joined to the mainland by a man-made causeway, completed in 1972. Operated by the St Lucia National Trust, Pigeon Island is of significant archaeological and historical importance. It is also the venue for events, including the annual St Lucia Jazz Festival. The hilly land that spans 18 hectares (45 acres) is thought to have been inhabited by Amerindians, who used the island's caves for shelter and grew staple crops such as sweet potatoes and cassava (manioc). Later it became a base for French pirates in the 1550s and a British naval outpost in the 1780s. Admiral Rodney sailed from here to defeat French forces at the Battle of Les Saintes in 1782. The ruins of the military buildings can be explored and you can climb to the vantage point of Fort Rodney or the lookout point on Signal Peak for a spectacular view. There's a restaurant and a beach in the park to rest in.

NORTHERN EXCURSIONS

To understand something of the local people's cultural heritage, visit the **Fond Latisab Creole Park** (tel: 758-450 5461; Sun–Fri, tours by appointment), a few miles south east of Babonneau via narrow country lanes in the small farming community of Fond Assau. The 4-hectare (11-acre) working farm cultivates nutmeg, cocoa and cinnamon and produces its own honey. Fond Latisab maintains many aspects of traditional St Lucian culture, some of which stem back to when Amerindians inhabited the land, and practices farm techniques passed down from father to son. Local guides are summoned by drumbeat and visitors can watch log-sawing done to the beating of drums accompanied by a *chak chak* band; the men sing *kwéyòl* folk songs, accompanied by the band and the drumbeats, which help to maintain rhythm and momentum. You can also see local people crayfishing, using traditional bamboo pots. Homemade cassava bread is sold when there is a tour, and home-grown nutmeg and cinnamon can also be purchased.

Down the road from Fond Latisab is the popular **Rain Forest Adventures** (tel: 758-458 5151; www.rainforestadventure.com; year-round, Wed–Fri and Sun–Mon). During a 2-hour tour, visitors are transported above the forest in a tram, which provides a bird's-eye view of the landscape. Each gondola carries eight seated people and a guide as you glide through the forest canopy. Afterwards, buckle up to zip-line and glide through the forest: an enjoyable adrenaline rush and only a basic level of fitness is required.

One of the professional naturalist guides on the combined aerial tram and canopy zipline experience.

Kayaking, another of the activities on offer.

Parliament Buildings,
Bridgetown.

BARBADOS

One of the most popular Caribbean cruise stops, this island has a colorful heritage, a fascinating capital, some great hiking trails and an excellent reputation for nightlife and cuisine.

The most easterly of the Windward Islands, Barbados is not blessed with dramatic mountains and lush rainforest like some of its neighbors. Instead, it has open, rolling countryside with fields of sugar cane rippling in the breezes coming in off the Atlantic, which crashes in huge rollers along the sweeping beaches of the exposed east coast.

Outside Bridgetown, the capital, the island is dotted with sleepy villages and some beautiful botanical gardens and plantation houses. The pretty chattel houses, wooden shacks that were once home to plantation workers, have become an architectural feature. Painted in primary colors and pastel shades, with intricate fretwork around the windows, they often double as craft shops.

The sheltered west coast is lined with some of the Caribbean's most glamorous and expensive hotels, whose patrons return year after year. The island has gained a reputation as a millionaire's playground, particularly thanks to US$1,500-a-night establishments like Sandy Lane, and several very smart restaurants, as fashionable London venues spread to the tropics.

Barbados has a distinctly British feel, with village cricket, polo matches and red post boxes. The island was settled by the British in the 17th century and is still a member of the Commonwealth.

It is clean, friendly and regarded as safe, although the usual issues of extreme wealth flaunted in the face of relative poverty exist. Despite years of colonialism, Barbados has its own colorful heritage; its annual Cropover festival in July, celebrating the end of the sugar cane harvest, is rated as one of the best events in the Caribbean. The jazz festival in January attracts big names like Patti LaBelle and the late Ray Charles, while the Barbados Reggae Festival in April encompasses a beach party, a reggae cruise, vintage

⊙ Main attractions

Garrison Historical Area
Barbados Museum
Bathsheba
Andromeda Botanic
  Garden
Harrison's Cave
Gun Hill

Map on page 272

Steel-drum (or steel-pan) musicians are known as pannists.

Tip

Buses charge a flat fare of B$2 anywhere on the island, but if you change buses you have to pay again. Almost all buses start in Bridgetown and bus stops simply say 'To city' or 'Out of city.'

reggae and a Reggae on the Hill concert at Farley Hill.

A POPULAR CHOICE

Barbados is one of the Caribbean islands most visited by cruise passengers, with a ship a day calling during the high-season winter months. Apart from a gleam in the eyes of the shopkeepers, a cruise ship in town does not make a vast difference to daily life, as the island has a well-developed infrastructure and the visitor attractions are spread out.

A lot of cruises start and finish here, particularly those carrying a high proportion of passengers from Europe, as the island is well served by non-stop flights. It is one of the easiest destinations in which to extend a cruise, which is well

worth doing, if only to sample the nightlife, which varies from fine cuisine under the stars at Sandy Lane to scruffy rum shops in Bridgetown's Baxters Road.

The cruise terminal is about 1 mile (1.6km) from the center of town, at Deep Water Harbor. There's a duty-free shopping center for jewelry, cameras and electrical goods, as well as souvenir stands selling T-shirts and pretty chattel houses displaying local crafts. You need a passport, airline ticket or cruise line ID to qualify for duty-free prices. You can hire bikes, arrange tours and book horse-riding here.

Other facilities include an internet café, a sports bar and a restaurant. Brighton Beach is right in front of the Deep Water Harbor and perfectly fine

for an afternoon if you don't want to travel; there's a popular bar here, Weisers, where you can watch or join in a game of beach volleyball.

The island is sports mad. From January to March and again in October and November, there is high-class cricket to watch. Golf is popular and, if you want to play on a prestigious course like Sandy Lane or Royal Westmoreland, advance booking is recommended. The best horse riding is across the central highlands and, as you would expect, there's a wide array of watersports to enjoy.

FINDING YOUR WAY AROUND

Barbados is a relatively easy island to explore independently and is only 21 miles (34km) long, although twisting country roads make distances seem further, especially when the sugar cane is high and views are obscured; they are not always clearly marked, either. Shore excursions involve many permutations of the island tour and are usually comprehensive, but the fun of exploring is lost if you travel by coach.

An open-sided mini-moke is a better way to get around, and in a day trip from Bridgetown you should be able to reach the northernmost point and return via the wild coastal scenery of the east coast around Bathsheba.

Driving is on the left, and all visitors must have a visitor's driving permit, which will be arranged by the car-rental company. Rush hour starts at 4pm and, while all roads lead to Bridgetown, progress may be painfully slow around this time (nobody is in much of a hurry anyway), so do allow for this.

Taxis are plentiful and are lined up outside the cruise terminal. Drivers are more than willing to do day-trips. Fares are fixed but there is no meter system, so always agree a price in advance. The island has a comprehensive bus network and the single flat fare is a bargain, but buses are crowded and journeys take time. They are, however, a good way to meet local people.

BRIDGETOWN

If you have only a few hours to spare, there is plenty to see and do without

☉ Drink

'Corn and oil' is a cocktail of rum and falernum, a sweet, usually slightly alcoholic mixer with a hint of almond, lime, ginger and/or cloves, and vanilla or allspice.

Bridge House Bar in The Careenage, Bridgetown.

St Michael's Cathedral was built from coral limestone in Greek Classical style. It is believed to have the oldest manual organ in the Caribbean.

The Animal Flower Cave.

leaving **Bridgetown ①**. It is perfectly pleasant just to wander along the careenage, which is lined with yachts and fishing boats, and have a lazy lunch at the famous **Waterfront Café** and a browse around the shops. Broad Street is the main shopping area. Cave Shepherd is the principal Bajan department stores; if you don't have time to leave town, look out for the beautifully crafted pottery from Earthworks, made in the parish of St Thomas, which is on sale in Cave Shepherd and also at the cruise terminal.

The Best of Barbados gift shops are a good bet for locally made souvenirs, crafts, foods and prints – everything on sale is produced on the island.

Likrish Food Tours will take you on a walking food tour through the streets of Bridgetown, offering a chance to sample local treats while learning about the island's history and culture (www.lickrishfoodtours.com; Mon–Fri 11am–2pm).

HISTORY AND RUM

Bridgetown has several interesting sights. **National Heroes Square ②** (formerly Trafalgar Square) is dedicated to 10 national heroes. The Gothic-style Parliament building dates back to 1872, while nearby **St Michael's Cathedral ③** stands on the grounds of the first church in Barbados, built in 1665.

Sugar cane means rum, and close to the port, on Spring Garden Highway, is the **Mount Gay ②** rum blending and bottling plant (tel: 246-227 8800; Mon–Fri, tours every half-hour 9.30am–2.30pm), which does comprehensive 45-minute tours, including a tasting.

A short taxi ride around Carlisle Bay is the **Garrison Historical Area ③**, dating from the mid-17th century and once the most important military location on the island. The area is packed with historic interest, with forts, monuments, military buildings and the world's largest collection of 17th-century cannons.

The Garrison Savannah Parade Ground is now a 6-furlong horse-race course, the scene of much excitement on race days. The **Barbados Museum** (tel: 246-427 0201; www.barbmuse.org.bb; Mon–Sat 9am–5pm, Sun 2–6pm) is also here, covering everything from historic maps to colonial furniture.

OUT OF TOWN

The west coast, dubbed the Platinum Coast, is lined with smart hotels and exclusive villas. Narrow side roads lead to emerald polo fields and the undulating fairways of the Sandy Lane golf course on the right opposite white soft-sand beaches on the left. The first settlers landed at **Holetown** ❹ in 1627, an event that is commemorated every February with street fairs and a music festival.

Lone Star is unquestionably the place to hang out here – an ultra-trendy restaurant, bar and hotel, in a beautiful location on the beach, selling everything from Sevruga caviar to Jamaican jerk chicken. Nearby **Folkestone Park and Marine Reserve** (Mon–Fri 9am–5pm) has an underwater snorkel trail over a coral reef, as well as a small aquarium and changing facilities.

Continuing up the coast, stop at the John Moore bar on the beach at Weston. This is the place for flying fish and chips and a cold Banks (the excellent local beer), or the more adventurous 'pudding and souse,' a local specialty containing the ears and snout of a pig.

If you're anxious to feel terra firma after days at sea, the Barbados National Trust organizes free guided hikes every Sunday at either 6am (varying abilities) or 3.30pm (medium ability). On the Sunday closest to a full moon, the afternoon hike starts at 5.30pm, all hikes last approximately 3 hours. See www.barbados.org for details including starting location of the hikes.

❺, the main town on the west coast. There are two routes, 3.5 miles (5.5km) and 4.5 miles (7.5km), one leading through the town and one along the coast and through limestone gullies.

Cutting through the parish of St Lucy, you'll come to **North Point**, at the tip of the island, with sheltered but remote beaches, sheer cliffs and pounding waves crashing onto jagged rocks. A lot of the cruise excursions don't get this far.

The **Animal Flower Cave** (daily 9am–4.30pm unless the sea is rough; charge) is a network of slippery caves supposedly inhabited by sea anemones. It's not worth the trip in itself, only if you are in the area. A rather more

Vibrant red flora at Andromeda Gardens.

All aboard for an island safari.

interesting detour is to **Morgan Lewis Mill** (Mon–Sat) in St Andrew. This is the island's only functioning windmill and you can climb to the top. Call at neighboring Cherry Tree Hill, too, for yet more spectacular views.

BATHSHEBA AND THE ANDROMEDA GARDENS

The real reason to come here, though, is the beautifully desolate coastal scenery; you can see miles of Atlantic rollers and dazzling white cliffs all the way to **Bathsheba ⑥**, and there is little building or development of any kind – just the occasional craft stall by the road. Although you'll see surfers on the beaches, it is not safe to swim, but on a hot and humid day there will always be a cooling breeze and it's a nice place for a picnic.

At Bathsheba itself, the **Andromeda Botanic Gardens** (www.andromedabarbados.com; daily 9am–4.30pm) are a wonderful place for a rest from driving. The calming waterfalls splash gently through the gardens, which are dazzling with tropical blooms from all over

Stalactites at Harrison's Cave.

the Caribbean, including a wide variety of orchids.

FORESTS, CAVES AND POTTERY

From here, there are three fascinating examples of natural Barbados just inland. The **Flower Forest** in St Joseph (www.flowerforestbarbados.com; daily 8am–4pm) is a pretty walking trail through lush tropical gardens. The trail covers 50 acres (20 hectares) and is a good walk affording lovely views downhill to the east coast. **Welchman Hall Gully ⑦** (www.welchmanhallgullybarbados.com; daily 9am–4pm) is a deep ravine just off the main road, Highway 2, maintained by the National Trust, with a 0.75-mile (1.2km) trail leading through rainforest, bamboo, palms, giant overhanging ferns, mango trees and mahogany forest. For an added treat, keep a lookout for monkeys and colorful birds in the trees.

Just south of here is **Harrison's Cave** (tel: 246-417 3700; daily 9am–4.30pm), a limestone cave complete with underground lakes, cascading water, stalactites and stalagmites, all of which can be experienced by means of a small electric train.

A little further south on Highway 2 is the **Earthworks Pottery** (www.earthworks-pottery.com, Mon–Fri 9am–5pm, Sat 9am–1pm; free), which produces unique ceramics and tableware decorated in bright Caribbean colors. If you have the luxury of an evening departure, wait until 'magic hour,' late in the afternoon, to end up at **Gun Hill ⑧** (Mon–Sat), a restored signal tower in St George parish, a few miles outside Bridgetown. The signal station served a dual purpose: to watch for approaching ships and to survey the island for slave uprisings after a rebellion in 1816. The views over the south of the island are breathtaking, especially at this time of day, just before sunset, when the light is soft and luminous.

📷 GINGERBREAD AND BALLAST BRICK

Caribbean architecture reveals influences from Amerindians, Africa and the European colonizers, from simple Kunuku cottages to Great Houses.

When Columbus hit upon the West Indies at the end of the 15th century, the dwellings he found there were nothing compared to what he was used to in Europe, and he wrote to a friend that the '[Indians] live in rocks and mountains, without fixed settlements, and not like ourselves.' In fact, Amerindians slept in round or oval-shaped huts built of timber and covered with a conical roof made of palms or grass from swamps.

The first Europeans left on islands to set up trading posts, and then the settlers, copied these Indian shelters, but soon introduced wall construction with wooden beams and shingles for the roofs. However, even after Emancipation the slaves rarely built with stone, and single-roomed thatched houses with walls of clay and straw were still in use in the 20th century.

Plaza Vieja, Cuba, was built in the 1500s as a space for fiestas and bullfights. The square is now a flagship for the city's renovation, beautifully restored with museums, cafés and even a micro-brewery.

A MEDLEY OF STYLES

When the sugar trade to Europe started, many ships brought huge amounts of red brick and stone in their hulls as ballast. Wealthy planters and merchants on islands like Barbados and Antigua built their Great Houses with it. In Statia's heyday ballast was used for the warehouses on the waterfront. Several styles developed, the Spanish adopting Moorish traditions, while the French introduced cast iron. Later, the American invention of mechanical saws gave rise to the intricate wooden lacework – gingerbread – on many façades.

Cathédrale St-Louis, Fort-de-France, Martinique, is known as the 'iron cathedral.' Built in 1895 to withstand hurricanes and earthquakes, its steel-reinforced spire soars above the city.

Planters modeled their homes on European styles, adapting them to suit the climate with shutters, etc. Elegant Rose Hall in Jamaica is a calendar house – with 365 windows, 52 doors and 12 bedrooms.

Small and sweet chattel house in Barbados.

Chattel Houses Mobile Homes

For the black population of Barbados, mobility was once essential to survival. After Emancipation the planters had to employ labor and, still wanting to control the freed slaves, allowed them to establish small settlements on their land. This made the workers dependent on their employer's goodwill, and they were rapidly chased off the land if there were any problems. So the chattel house was developed: a small wooden 'sleeping box' easy to dismantle and take along on a cart to another plantation.

Supported by big rocks or concrete blocks so that rainwater can pass underneath, the one-room house with an optional partition inside is made up of wooden planks fixed to a framework. Makeshift steps lead up to the only door, opening on to the family's living space. Here parents and children, and often grandparents as well, used to sleep in one room. The cooking was done outside, as was any entertaining of neighbors and friends.

This nucleus of a family home – with one or two extensions – is still a common sight in Barbados, especially in the more remote country districts, and only a few years ago a whole village moved from a hilltop to a valley, where running water was available.

...ollmeyer's Castle, or Killarney, inspired by Scottish and ...erman castles, is one of the Magnificent Seven colonial ...ansions built between 1904 and 1910 along the west ...de of Queen's Park Savannah, Port of Spain, Trinidad.

...utch colonial architecture in Willemstad, Curaçao, is ...plicated by new hotels and other buildings with fanciful ...bles and colorful walls.

Shady verandahs keep rooms cool even when there is no air conditioning, as well as encouraging sociable outdoor living.

Trekking to Soufrière Volcano.

ST VINCENT AND THE GRENADINES

Volcanic and lush, St Vincent is a nature lover's paradise. Strong walkers climb Soufrière volcano, others take gentle walks, while Bequia and Mayreau are for those who just want to chill out.

Caribbean Sea

St Vincent and The Grenadines

St Vincent, at 18 by 11 miles (30 by 18km), is the largest and most developed of the cluster of the 32 islands collectively known as the Grenadines, between St Lucia and Grenada.

At **Kingstown** , the island port and capital, there are berths for two ships. The terminal has telephones, a tourist information desk, exchange facilities (EC dollars is the local currency although US dollars, as ever in the Caribbean, serve just as well), a selection of duty-free and souvenir shops and a number of cafés, bars and fast-food outlets. The shops of downtown Kingstown exist mainly to serve local needs. The indoor fruit and vegetable market in the center (Upper Bay) and an indoor fish market, known as Little Tokyo, by the dock, add some color and interest.

Kingstown has a Catholic **Cathedral of the Assumption**, a bizarre mixture of Moorish, Romanesque, Byzantine, Venetian and Flemish architectural styles, despite being built in the 1930s. And there is an 18th-century fortress, **Fort Charlotte**, above the town, overlooking Kingstown and the Caribbean.

MAKING THE MOST OF THE DAY

Most visitors head out of town fairly quickly. There are plenty of taxis waiting outside the terminal, all keen to offer guided tours around the island.

Admiralty Bay, St Vincent.

Alternatively, minibuses heading to specific places leave regularly from the fish market.

Outside Kingstown, St Vincent is a lush, forested island, and this is reflected in one of its main points of interest, the **Botanical Gardens** ❷ in Montrose, a 5- to 10-minute drive from the port (6am–6pm). Dating back to 1765, these gardens are reputedly the oldest in the Western Hemisphere and have a breadfruit tree that dates back to the original plant brought to the island by Captain Bligh of *Mutiny on the Bounty* fame (or infamy).

⊙ **Main attractions**
Botanic Gardens
Falls of Baleine
Vermont Nature Trail
Belmont Lookout
Owia Salt Pond
Bequia
Mayreau

⊙ Map on page 282

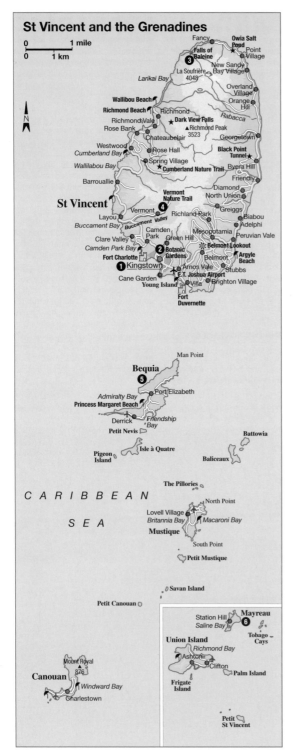

St Vincent and the Grenadines

The gardens, the cathedral and the fort are always included on the basic island tours (lasting between 2 and 4 hours) offered on the ships' excursion programs, but if there are two or more of you travelling together, all these places can be visited more cheaply on an independent guided taxi tour.

A popular excursion is by boat (usually a catamaran) from Kingstown along the Leeward (Caribbean) coast, past sugar and banana plantations, a former whaling village – Barrouallie – rocky coves, black-sand beaches and mountains, including the Soufrière volcano which erupted as recently as 1979. This tour, lasting 3 to 5 hours, will include a beach stop for swimming and snorkeling, and possibly a visit to the **Falls of Baleine ❸**, where you take a boat upriver between dark, looming cliffs and can swim in the rocky pool below the 60ft (18-meter) waterfall.

If you're touring the west by road, **Dark View Falls** are in the foothills of Richmond Peak, twin falls created by lava and pyroclastic flows. A bamboo suspension bridge leads to the falls; the upper one is a steep climb, hidden in the forest, but the lower one is easy, with the natural rock pool extended by concrete for swimming.

WALKING TOURS

The great advantage of visiting St Vincent is the scope for walking tours – from gentle nature hikes right up to a strenuous ascent of the 4,048ft (1,234-meter) **La Soufrière**.

The latter, however, will take a full day, including getting from Kingstown in the southwest to the volcano's location in the northeast corner; and whether this is a feasible option will depend on your fitness and walking experience, the weather and the departure time of your ship. Check with the tourist office in the terminal, where it is also possible to hire a guide for the hike.

Easier hikes, include the **Vermont Nature Trail ❹**, a winding 2-mile trail on the edge of the Buccament Valley in the reserve for the protection of the national bird, the St Vincent Parrot. This is a good birdwatching site and you should spot many species. The **Cumberland Nature Trail** (charge) on the west coast is a manageable 2-hour hike through some scenic countryside. The **Mesapotamia Valley** near the east (Atlantic) coast offers more challenging walking through forests and plantations. From the 900ft (275-meter) viewing platform of the **Belmont Lookout** you get a good view over the valley, the remnant of an extinct volcano and a major agricultural zone, while still home to agouti, manicou and other wildlife.

At the northern tip of the island is **Owia Salt Pond**, a natural swimming pool protected from the crashing Atlantic surf by volcanic rocks. Facilities have been built here with parking, a craft center, bar, washrooms and showers.

St Vincent is largely unspoiled, mostly cultivated for farming. The only major tourist resort is self-contained on **Young Island**, just off the south coast, where some of the very small, upscale ships call.

BEQUIA AND MAYREAU

Port Elizabeth is the entry point for **Bequia ❺**, but although only the smallest cruise ships – often sailing vessels – call here, they all have to anchor in Admiralty Bay. Once on the jetty (where the ferries from St Vincent also disembark), it is only a short walk to a group of smart shops and restaurants, with a tourist information office in the middle. There are more places to shop and eat along the front (Belmont Walkway), or you could head inland for a few minutes along Front Street, where you will find an open-air market.

There is not much more to Port Elizabeth, but Bequia is really about the water. Swimming, snorkeling and scuba diving are the reasons people come here – more come by air than by sea, although it is only an hour by ferry – and you can move around parts of the island as easily by water-taxi as by more conventional road taxis.

It costs only a few dollars to go by boat from the main jetty to the nearest beach. And – unlike on volcanic St Vincent – the beaches are all white sand, not black. The best diving sites are within the 7-mile (12km) coral reef, which has been designated a national marine park. Your cruise ship will organize dive trips on its own or local boats, and this is a better option than trying to sort this out independently.

Mayreau ❻ is surrounded by soft, sandy beaches and reefs and is used for landing by small ships.. You will probably be taken directly to **Saline Bay Beach** for a relaxing day just chilling out.

Other Grenadine islands at which some ships call (apart from Carriacou, which is part of Grenada, see page 285) include Tobago Cays, which offers some of the best snorkeling in the Caribbean; Palm Island; Canouan; Union Island; and Mustique. On the latter there is only limited access for cruise ship passengers because so many celebrities have homes or take holidays on the island and they guard their privacy very fiercely.

Yachting in the blue waters of Tobago Cays.

GRENADA AND CARRIACOU

With a pretty harbor, expanses of rainforest, waterfalls, a bird sanctuary and white beaches protected from development, the Spice Island of Grenada is worth exploring.

Grenada is the island you can almost smell before you can see it – in the nicest possible way, of course. Known as the Spice Island, it is not only the world's second-largest exporter of nutmeg, growing 20 percent of the world's total crop, but also produces more spices per square mile than anywhere else on the planet. Cocoa is another staple and you'll see island-made chocolate on sale everywhere.

Sailors down the centuries have rated St George's ❶, the island capital, as one of the world's prettiest harbors, and it's hard to disagree. Horseshoe-shaped and set in a long-dormant volcanic crater, it is a natural harbor flanked by two forts (Fort George and Fort Frederick) and has colorful French colonial-style buildings ranged along the front.

The cruise ship terminal is north, on the other side of the Fort George promontory, on the Esplanade, which runs north at Melville Street. Small ships sometimes dock at the Carenage, on the waterfront. At the main terminal, two mega-ships can berth at the pier, while up to four more can anchor in the outer harbor and tender in, making Grenada very busy on popular days. This is reclaimed land and has been developed to hold the cruise ship terminal, bus terminal, a parking lot and the fish market. Turn left outside the terminal, walk a block along the

Esplanade, then turn right up Granby Street to get to the **market**, where you can find local produce, herbs, spices, crafts, nutmeg oil, nutmeg soap and cocoa balls. The streets of St George's are very steep, but the Sendall Tunnel connects the Esplanade with the Carenage round the inner harbor, making an easier connection for vehicles.

THE CARENAGE AND BAYTOWN

The inner harbor is known as the **Carenage**, and this name is also used

◯ Main attractions
St George's
Gouyave Nutmeg
  Processing Station
Levera National Park
Belmont Estate
Grand Etang National
  Park
Grand Anse
Carriacou

Map on page 287

Grand Anse Beach, Grenada.

Bumping along on a Grenada forest tour.

locally for the promenade around the harborfront. It is a pleasant walk past the jetties, the old warehouses, small shops and offices and a selection of bars and restaurants. Many of these are upstairs above shops, where the open windows look out over the harbor and let in the cooling sea breezes. There is still plenty of maritime activity to watch here with trading vessels loading and unloading – the ferry from Carriacou also comes in here. The Grenada Yacht Club and Port Louis Marina in the Lagoon attract yachts of all sizes to berth and take part in regattas.

You will see plenty of seafood – including conch – on the menus, and some traditional Grenadian dishes. The food and the cheek-by-jowl seating in the Carenage cafés are – like the rest of St George's – refreshingly unpretentious and very enjoyable. So is a visit to the ice-cream parlors on the harborfront; nutmeg ice cream is something that simply has to be tried while visiting the Spice Island. While the Carenage is brash and

bustling almost round the clock, the rest of St George's seems a tranquil, sleepy town. On Young Street, off the Carenage near the cafés, is the small **National Museum** (tel: 473-440 3725; Mon–Fri 9am–4.30pm, Sat 10am–1.30pm). It used to be part of the French barracks, built in 1704, but the British later used parts of it as a prison, then a warehouse with a hotel upstairs. The exhibits cover a wide range of subjects. Also of note is the **public library**, in a renovated brick building on the Carenage. The bricks, stones and roof tiles of the old buildings in this area would have come over as ballast from Europe in sailing ships.

GRAND ANSE BEACH

The first unmissable place out of town is **Grand Anse ❷**, just around the bay to the south of the harbor, which is Grenada's main resort area. The 2-mile (3km) stretch of white sand is one of the Caribbean's finest, and worth a visit even if you do not usually spend time on the beach. There

are three ways to get there – by taxi, shared mini-van or water-taxi. Of these, the water-taxi is easily the best option, cheaper than land taxis and much more fun. It's a short, breezy journey and the boats depart almost non-stop from the jetty by the cruise ship terminal when there's a cruise ship in port.

There are strict rules about any kind of development on Grenada, which apply particularly to beaches. Effectively, this comes down to nothing taller than a palm tree and nothing close to the water's edge being allowed.

FINDING YOUR WAY AROUND

Grenada is just 12 miles (20km) wide by 21 miles (32km) long, but it seems larger because the interior is so densely forested in parts and journey times are longer than they might appear from the map. A drive through the interior takes in some dramatic sights – waterfalls, mountain valleys, rainforests, lakes and volcanic craters. Driving can be hot and tiring on roads that are

sometimes barely adequate, so don't be too ambitious.

Driving is on the left, and you need a special local license (about US$12) that can be acquired either from one of the car-rental firms in St George's or from the Traffic Department offices at the fire station building. But, as you only have a day, you may prefer to take a tour, hire a taxi for a guided tour (negotiate the price before setting off) or, possibly, self-drive but hire a guide. There are old-fashioned and overcrowded buses which run (slowly) to most parts of the island from St George's Market Square. Minivans are more comfortable, although they operate on a shared basis and only on short routes with flat fares.

GRENADA'S BEST

The following are the best places to visit in Grenada. All have nominal entrance charges and there's no need to book beforehand. But you will have to choose which you want to see, as it is not possible to visit them all in a single day.

The Carenage.

Finding tranquility beside a waterfall – of which Grenada has a particularly high number.

Grand Etang National Park and Forest Reserve ❸ is a rainforest with a volcanic crater-turned-lake at its center. There are hiking and nature trails, and fishing and boating in the shadow of **Mount Qua Qua**, a 2,300ft (700-meter) peak. The reserve is in the center of the island, northeast of St George's.

Belmont Estate (tel: 473-442 9524; www.belmontestate.net; Sun–Fri, 8am–4pm) is a working plantation offering tours of the organic farm, gardens, heritage museum and cocoa-processing facilities. Just above here is the Grenada Chocolate Company's cooperative (www.grenadachocolate.com; Mon–Fri 9am–4pm), producing fine, dark organic chocolate that's exported worldwide.

River Antoine Rum Distillery ❹ is further along the same road on the northeast coast. There are guided tours of this working distillery, which uses exactly the same methods as it did in the 18th century (Mon–Sat 9am–5pm).

Levera National Park and Bird Sanctuary ❺ was designated a national park in 1994. It is about 5 miles (8km) further north, the furthest point on the northeast coast. The park stretches inland from coral-reef-protected white sandy beaches to a lake and mangrove swamp full of exotic plants and birdlife.

Gouyave Nutmeg Processing Cooperative is northwest of Grand Etang. The cooperative offers a chance to see how the island's most famous export is handled. It's fascinating, but the heat inside the factory is almost unbearable Within a couple of miles of Gouyave, there is the chance to tour a working spice plantation, **Dougaldston Estate**.

Grenada also has what it claims to be the world's first underwater sculpture park, an incredible underwater gallery in the Moliniere Beauséjour Marine Protected Area, just north of St George. The sculptures, produced by local artists in eco-friendly media, blend into the reef and are colonised by marine life. There are some intriguing pieces, not least a man sitting at a desk, on the sea bed, with his typewriter.

An old hut near the Caribbean Lagoon.

SHIPS' EXCURSIONS

All these attractions appear on most ships' excursion lists. There is a 3- to 4-hour island coach tour that takes in Grand Etang, the Grenville Nutmeg plant, the 50ft (15-meter) Annandale waterfall and some picturesque east coast villages. Similar tours by Jeep are also offered. They are more expensive, but you do have the advantage of traveling in a much smaller group.

Other tours include the Rhum Runner beach party cruise; whale- and dolphin-watching trips – the company reckons that there is a 90 percent chance of seeing dolphins and a 70 percent chance of seeing pilot or humpback whales; as well as snorkeling and scuba-diving trips.

Sailing and diving are highly recommended for enthusiasts. Most of the dive sites – around coral reefs and shipwrecks – are within easy reach of the shore. Snorkelers can reach them from the beach or, occasionally, by a short boat trip. The wreck diving is particularly good; the Bianca C, an Italian ocean liner, sank off the southwest coast in the 1960s. Sport fishing is also a popular option; and there is a nine-hole golf course and tennis center near Grand Anse.

CARRIACOU

If you admire the way Grenada has remained largely unspoiled, the neighboring island of **Carriacou** ⑥ (23 miles/38km away) should appeal to you even more, as it has just a handful of hotels to go with some great beaches and sites for snorkeling and diving. **Sandy Island**, off the west coast and reached by a local motorboat, is the best. There is even a decent museum in the main town, Hillsborough. However, Carriacou is a 3-hour boat trip or a 20-minute flight, so cruise ship passengers only have time to reach it by air, and ships rarely include it among their excursions. There are a few small cruise ships that anchor off Carriacou, as part of their itinerary, but the majority don't.

The pristine stretches of Sandy Island, Carriacou.

Staff at the Grenada Chocolate Company.

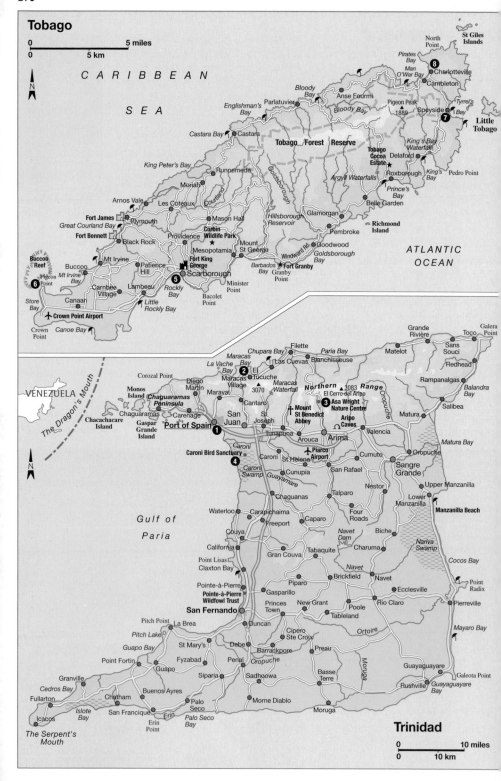

Tobago

0 _____ 5 miles
0 _____ 5 km

N

CARIBBEAN

SEA

St Giles Islands

North Point

Pirates Bay
Man O'War Bay
⑧ Charlotteville
Cambleton

Bloody Bay
Anse Fourmi

Englishman's Bay
Parlatuvier
Bloody Bay

Pigeon Peak 1889
Speyside
Tyrrel's Bay
⑦
Little Tobago

Castara Bay
Castara

Tobago Forest Reserve

King's Bay Waterfall
Tobago Cocoa Estate
Delaford

King Peter's Bay
Runnemede

Goldsborough
Argyll Waterfalls
Roxborough
King's Bay
Pedro Point

Moriah

Courland

Arnos Vale
Les Coteaux

Prince's Bay
Belle Garden

Fort James
Great Courland Bay
Fort Bennett
Plymouth
Mason Hall
Providence
Glamorgan
Pembroke

Hillsborough Reservoir

Richmond Island

Black Rock
Corbin Wildlife Park
Mesopotamia
Mount St George
Goodwood
Goldsborough Bay

ATLANTIC OCEAN

Buccoo Reef
Buccoo
Mt Irvine
Patience Hill
Fort King George
★ **Scarborough**
Barbados Bay
Fort Granby
Granby Point
Windward Rd

Pigeon Point
⑥
Mt Irvine Bay
Carnbee Village
Lambeau
Rockly Bay
⑤
Minister Point

Store Bay
Canaan
Little Rockly Bay
Bacolet Point

Crown Point
Canoe Bay
✈ **Crown Point Airport**

Grande Rivière
Toco
Galera Point

Chupara Bay
Filette
Paria Bay
Matelot
Sans Souci

VENEZUELA

The Dragon's Mouth

Corozal Point

Maracas Bay
La Vache Bay
② El
Las Cuevas
Blanchisseuse
Redhead

Diego Martin
Maracas Village
Tucuche
Maracas Waterfall
Northern Range
3083
El Cerro del Aripo
Oropouche
Rampanalgas

Monos Island
Chaguaramas Peninsula
Maraval
3070
Cantaro
③ **Asa Wright Nature Centre**

Balandra Bay

Chacachacare Island
Chaguaramas
Gaspar Grande Island
Carenage
San Juan
St Joseph
✝ **Mount St Benedict Abbey**
Aripo Caves

Matura

Port of Spain ①
Tunapuna
Arouca
Arima
Valencia

Matura Bay

N

Caroni
Caroni Bird Sanctuary
④
Caroni
St Helena
✈ Piarco Airport

Cumuto
Oropuche

Sangre Grande

Caroni Swamp
Guayamare
Cunupia
San Rafael

Upper Manzanilla

Chaguanas
Talparo
Nestor

Lower Manzanilla
Manzanilla Beach

Gulf of

Paria

Waterloo
Carapichaima
Freeport
Caparo
Four Roads
Biche

Nariva Swamp

Couva
Navet Dam
Charuma

Cocos Bay

California
Gran Couva
Tabaquite

Point Lisas
Claxton Bay
Piparo
Brickfield
Navet

Point Radix

Pointe-à-Pierre
Pointe-à-Pierre Wildfowl Trust
Gasparillo
New Grant
Poole
Rio Claro
Ecclesville

Pierreville

San Fernando
Princes Town
Tableland

Mayaro Bay

Pitch Point
La Brea
Duncan
Cipero
Ste Croix
Preau

Pitch Lake
St Mary's
Debe
Barrackpore
Ortoire
Guayaguayare

Guapo Bay
Fyzabad
Penal
Oropuche
Basse Terre
Galeota Point

Point Fortin
Guapo
Siparia
Sadhoowa
Moruga
Rushville
Guayaguayare Bay

Granville
Buenos Ayres
Palo Seco
Morne Diablo

Cedros Bay
Chatham
San Francique
Erin
Palo Seco Bay
Moruga

Fullarton
Icacos
Islote Bay
Erin Point

The Serpent's Mouth

Trinidad

0 _____ 10 miles
0 _____ 10 km

TRINIDAD AND TOBAGO

Trinidad is famous for its annual Carnival in Port of Spain, but the color, music and rich cultural diversity of these two islands are entrancing throughout the year.

Across the road from the buzzing center of Port of Spain lies the modern cruise ship complex, so it is very easy to get to the heart of the cosmopolitan capital of Trinidad, the British Caribbean's most vibrant city and the southernmost port of call in the island chain.

In complete contrast to the sleepy charm of Windward Island capitals or that of its own sister isle, Tobago, fast-paced **Port of Spain** ❶ (also known as PoS) is unique for its ethnic diversity and cultural richness, and mixes styles with a Latin flair born from its proximity to Venezuela. Elegant French-Creole townhouses with distinctive gingerbread fretwork and ornate wrought-iron balconies nestle beneath 21st-century smoked-glass corporate blocks. Rastafari craftsmen display their leatherwork on the streets right next to country women selling fresh herbs, while air-conditioned malls offer local designer clothes and the latest in Miami consumer retail therapy.

Port of Spain is also home base for the mother of all carnivals, the pre-Lenten festival which climaxes on the two days before Ash Wednesday, when the streets explode with the colors of thousands of local and visiting masqueraders driven by turbo-charged soca music or the sweet sound of steelpans.

The Carnival in Port of Spain is unrivaled in the Caribbean.

GETTING TO KNOW THE CITY

Port of Spain and its suburbs sprawl across a plain that slopes gently from the foothills of the Northern Range down to the Gulf of Paria. On the waterfront, the cruise ship complex, where passengers disembark directly, is located between the container ship docks to the west and Queen's Wharf, the mooring for inter-island traders and the Tobago ferry, to the east.

The complex has the usual facilities, including gift shops. For those who prefer not to stray far from the ship, there

◉ Main attractions

Queen's Park Savannah
Royal Botanic Gardens
Maracas Bay
Asa Wright Nature Center
Caroni Bird Sanctuary

Map on page 290

are craft stalls outside; and, to the left, on Wrightson Road, is the Breakfast Shed, famous for cheap and authentic Creole and East Indian cuisine: fresh fish, fried, stewed or served in a peppery-hot broth laced with ground provisions such as dasheen, eddoes, cassava or green figs and heavy with dumplings.

Across the road stretches the Brian Lara promenade (named after the record-breaking Trinidadian cricketer) on **Independence Square**, centerpiece of the modern city center. Here chess-players congregate around concrete tables with built-in boards, Trinis practise the national pastime of liming (doing nothing in particular, but with style) and free soca, steelpan, jazz or gospel concerts are held. Besides the fast-food outlets, there are vendors selling coconuts full of milk for drinking, and doubles – the cheapest East Indian snack: curried chickpeas in batter, garnished with mango or coconut chutney and fiery pepper sauce.

Most cruise lines offer guided taxi tours of the city and half- or whole-day excursions outside. Unfortunately it can be unsafe to walk around the city due to the high risk of tourists being mugged, so take a taxi to attractions. For moving further afield there are fixed-rate taxis at the rank opposite Frederick Street on Independence Square and much cheaper shared-route taxis at Woodford Square.

Founded by the Spanish in 1757, PoS began to take shape only after the British seized the island in 1797. The square grid plan is the legacy of Governor Sir Ralph Woodford. Many colonial buildings disappeared after independence in 1962 and during the oil boom of the 1970s to early 1980s, but both the Roman Catholic cathedral on Independence Square and the Anglican cathedral on Woodford Square are 19th-century survivors.

The modern skyline, however, is dominated by the Twin Towers financial complex and the National Library at the corner of Hart and Abercromby streets. The library is located next to a historic landmark – the Old Fire Brigade Station – which has been restored and incorporated into the new complex.

The Presidential Palace, Port of Spain.

CULTURE, SPORT AND MUSIC

The old Spanish **Fort San Andres** on South Quay is now a museum (tel: 868-623 5941,Tue–Fri 9am–5pm; free) hosting exhibitions by young local artists. British-built **Fort George** in the hills above the western suburb of St James offers both a breathtaking panorama of the city and views of the islands off the Chaguaramas peninsula.

Frederick Street is the main artery, leading north to **Queen's Park Savannah**, via Woodford Square where the imposing Red House parliament building is situated. At the top of Frederick Street opposite Memorial Park is the **National Museum and Art Gallery** (tel: 868-623 5941 Tue–Sat 10am–6pm, free). The Savannah plays an integral part in Trinidadian sporting and cultural life. The grandstand is the major venue for Carnival competitions and cultural shows. On Maraval Road, on the western flank of the Savannah, are the **Magnificent Seven**, a row of early 20th-century colonial mansions, superb examples of idiosyncratic Trini-Creole architecture. To the north are the beautiful **Royal Botanic**

Maracas Bay, a hit with Trinidadians.

Gardens (daily 6am–6pm; free), where the plants are all well labeled, and the President's House.

A good introduction to the national instrument, the steelpan, is a visit to a **panyard**, where steel bands rehearse: Amoco Renegades at the top of Charlotte Street, Witco Desperadoes up Laventille Hill or Phase II on Hamilton Street, in the western suburb of Woodbrook, where there are excellent restaurants on Ariapita Avenue. Also in Woodbrook is the **Queen's Park Oval** cricket ground, the oldest ground in the Caribbean, where international Test matches are played. West of Woodbrook is St James, lively with bars and clubs.

AROUND THE ISLAND

There is a variety of half- and whole-day excursions available outside PoS. West of town are the **Blue Basin Waterfall**, north of Diego Martin; Maqueripe beach at the end of the beautiful **Tucker Valley**; the **Chaguaramas Military History and Aviation Museum** (tel: 868-634 4391; Tue–Sun 9am–6pm), and the **Gasparee Caves** (tel: 868-634 4364) on Gaspar

The steel drum often has a part to play in Carnival celebrations.

⊘ GLORIOUS FESTIVALS

The many and varied immigrants to Trinidad and Tobago have brought and adapted their own celebrations in addition to Carnival, a pre-Lenten festival with Christian origins. The Hindu festival of Phagwa, or Holi, involves color and everyone gets squirted with brightly colored dyes. Divali, the festival of light, involves the consumption of a lot of good food while pretty lamps and candles burn outside. Muslims have the Hosay Festival, celebrated during Muharram, the first month of the Islamic lunar calendar, a 3-day event with lively processions accompanied by dancing, singing and the sound of *tassa* drums. Not to be forgotten, descendants of the original Amerindians celebrate the Feast of St Rose of Lima in Arima, when they walk in solemn procession around the church.

A hummingbird feeding.

A flock of scarlet ibis, the national bird.

Grande island, a 20-minute round-trip boat ride from the Crews Inn marina (call the Chaguaramas Development Authority, tel: 868-225 4323, to book tours).

Maracas Bay ❷, Trinidad's most popular beach, is a spectacular 40-minute drive north of the capital, while to the east there is the **Maracas Waterfall**, up the valley from the original Spanish capital, St Joseph; **El Tucuche**, the second-highest peak (a whole-day strenuous hike) and **Mount St Benedict** monastery, with panoramic views of the central plain. The **Asa Wright Nature Center ❸** (tel: 868-667 4655; www.asawright.org; daily 9am–5pm) is internationally famous for birdwatching, and a fascinating excursion with a good buffet lunch. Southeast of PoS is the **Caroni Bird Sanctuary ❹** (tel: 868-681 8274, where the national bird, the scarlet ibis, roosts at dusk in the swamp. Boats take visitors to watch this spectacular sight every evening.

The Corbin Local Wildlife Park shows native animals and flora in their natural habitat (68 Belmont Farm Road; tel: 868-327 4182).

SCARBOROUGH, TOBAGO'S CAPITAL

While PoS is very much a city, **Scarborough ❺**, the capital of Trinidad's sister isle, **Tobago**, has both the look and the feel of a small provincial town, and most of it can be covered on foot (with a few steep climbs) in a morning. After the multi-cultural mix of Trinidad, Tobago's predominantly Afro-Creole culture and lifestyle is immediately noticeable, as is the much slower pace.

Cruise passengers disembark at the modern terminal opposite a busy market, a good spot for sampling hearty Tobagonian cooking, especially curried crab and dumplings. The terminal has basic amenities, and taxis for around-town or out-of-town tours can be hired outside).

In town, the main attractions are the Botanic Gardens, the House of Assembly on James Park and the Fort King George complex, which houses the excellent **Tobago Museum** (tel: 868-639 3970, Mon–Fri 9am–5pm) and has fantastic views over the town and up the coast.

As the island is only 26 miles (40km) long and 9 miles (15km) wide, it is

possible to reach virtually anywhere within a couple of hours by car and sample Tobago's treasures: idyllic white-sand beaches and coral reefs; superb scuba diving, snorkeling and watersports; waterfalls, volcanic hills and the Western Hemisphere's oldest protected rainforest; abundant bird and wildlife and authentic Afro-Creole culture. The latter can be found at its vibrant best in the hilltop villages of Les Coteaux, Whim and Moriah, which are major venues for July's lively Heritage Festival.

THE DEVELOPED SOUTHWEST

Close to Scarborough is the developed southwest end of the island, where most tourist activity is centered around the luxury resorts and hotels at Crown Point and Store Bay. Glass-bottomed boats can be hired at Store Bay for trips out to Buccoo Reef and the Nylon Pool, while the beach at **Pigeon Point** ❻ has become a familiar Caribbean icon.

On the Windward (southern) coast turn inland to the Hillsborough Reservoir,

a favorite birdwatching spot. Further down the coast, the Argyll waterfalls are a 10-minute walk from the road. Nearby, in the Roxborough area, you can tour a cocoa plantation, **Tobago Cocoa Estate** (tel: 868-788 3971, www.tobagococoa. com, tours Fri at 11am), learn about the chocolate-making process, buy its single-estate fine chocolate and try other local culinary delights. Longer tours, with meals, are available.

Divers and nature lovers head for **Speyside** ❼ and **Charlotteville** ❽, at the eastern tip. These two fishing villages are spectacularly located at the foot of plunging forested hills and are the jumping-off points for some of the best diving in the eastern Caribbean, where the rare underwater life includes giant manta rays and huge brain coral. Little Tobago, off Speyside, is a bird sanctuary.

The best beaches (both for bathing and for turtle watching) are on the Leeward (northern) coast: Castara, Englishman's Bay, Parlatuvier, Bloody Bay and Man O'War Bay are all excellent options.

Perfect beaches are in reliable supply.

The beach at Pigeon Point.

📷 THE GREATEST STREET PARTY ON EARTH

Carnival in the Caribbean gets bigger and more extravagant every year as the islands fill up with revelers from all over the world.

Not age, nor profession, nor money nor skin color matter when, every February, thousands of Trinidadians and visitors seem to drown in a sea of colors, feathers, rhythm and rum. From J'ouvert, the wild street party from dawn on the Monday before Ash Wednesday, until King Momo's fire death in the last hours of Tuesday, Port of Spain is one big anarchic Carnival party. The heroes are *soca* stars and ingenious costume designers highly revered by a hip-swinging crowd dizzy with the beat and pulsating rhythm of the steel pans.

CARNIVAL TRADITIONS

Trinidad hosts the biggest Caribbean Carnival, which originated out of the Christian tradition of having a last big feast before fasting during Lent. The oldest carnival is in La Vega, the Dominican Republic, which has been celebrating since 1510 and participants wear elaborate masks. In Guadeloupe and Martinique people dress in black and white on Ash Wednesday and bury King Vaval, while on St-Barthélemy, King Moui Moui is burnt. Other carnivals in the summer months have developed from the harvest festivals after the sugar cane had been cut, such as Crop Over in Barbados, which includes the ceremonial delivery of the last canes. In Cuba, Fidel Castro timed the 1953 Moncada rebellion to coincide with Santiago's Carnival in July so that gunfire would be mistaken for fireworks. Some islands have only recently established carnivals for tourism's sake – any excuse for an extended street party.

When the slaves started creating their costumes, the mythology of their African ancestors inspired them to figures of good and evil – even nasty devils get clad in robes and jewels.

Carnival is the most lavish party on earth, with spectacular costumes and extravagant jewelry to create riot of color.

Junkanoo in the Bahamas is held on December 26 and January 1 from 2am to 8am, with colorful street parade and wild dancing to the beat of goat skin drums and cow bells.

Outrageously flamboyant Carnival float.

Playing Mas in Trinidad

As soon as one Carnival ends the designers' imaginations are hard at work on the next one. Great Carnival designers such as Trinidadian Peter Minshall – whose renowned costumes led him to design the costumes for the opening of the Olympic Games in 1992 and 1996 – set up Mas Camps (workshops) in which vast numbers of costumes are made on a theme for their bands. Each band has a Carnival King and Queen who wear the masterpieces which are judged on Dimanche Gras, the night before Carnival officially begins.

The Mas tradition started in the late 18th century with French plantation owners organizing masquerades (mas) and balls before they had to endure the fasting of Lent. Slaves copied and lampooned their masters, and once set free from forced labor, their frustrations found a platform in clever calypso lyrics mocking their former masters. Anybody can join the Trinidad carnival, for a fee; see www.destinationtnt.com for all you need to know.

the effigy of Vaval – a papier-mâché figure embodying Carnival – is consumed by flames, dancing in Martinique's Carnival celebrations reaches its climax on Ash Wednesday.

Many of the island carnivals have a special day set aside for the children just before the official start. Their costumes are often made in the Mas camps of Trinidad.

All the fun of the fair – a thrilling display of pyrotechnics adds to the sheer energy of the carnival party in Trinidad.

Baby bridge, Aruba.

Aruba's windblown divi-divi tree.

ARUBA AND CURAÇAO

These two small islands in the Dutch Antilles make interesting cruise stops: desert landscapes, international cuisine and protected architecture are among the discoveries to be made.

Caribbean
Sea

Aruba
Curaçao

The move by cruise lines to base some of their ships in ports beyond Florida for easy access to the 'deep Caribbean' has brought a boom in prosperity to the islands of Aruba and Curaçao. Both can be visited as part of a weeklong cruise from San Juan, Puerto Rico, although they are also included on some longer trips from Fort Lauderdale, Florida. These small islands in the Lesser Antilles, off the coast of Venezuela, have a lot to offer cruise ship passengers on short stopovers.

One reason for the success of **Aruba** is that it crams a lot into a little: excellent beaches and watersports, world-class shopping, giant casinos, stunning sea views and wild tracts of desert landscape scattered with giant boulders and exotic cacti are all yours to enjoy, without traveling very far.

ARUBA: ORANJESTAD

The only downside of this success is that you have to share the pleasures of the capital, **Oranjestad ❶**, with thousands of other visitors, particularly when a number of big ships are in at the Aruba Port Authority Terminal.

Well-developed Oranjestad has enough facilities to absorb the throng of visitors, however. Turn right outside the cruise terminal and within a few minutes' walk you will find the shop-lined L.G. Smith Boulevard, home to

Renaissance Marketplace – which has hundreds of shops, many restaurants and two casinos – and the equally extensive Royal Plaza, which is crammed with posh shops.

If, instead of turning right, you cross the road straight ahead, you can explore Oranjestad's prime shopping area, Caya G.F. Betico Coes, where pretty Dutch and Spanish-style buildings house stores selling top-quality cameras, jewelry and alcohol. You can pick up Delft china, Dutch cheese, Danish silverware and embroidery from Madeira at low

◉ Main attractions
Oranjestad
San Nicolas
Aruba's Northern
  Landscape
Natural Bridge
Willemstad
Christoffel National Park
Curaçao Seaquarium
Hato Caves

◉ Map on page 302

The Insulinde, Belgian-built in 1931, Curaçao.

Costa Linda, on Aruba's west coast.

levels of duty and without a sales tax. US dollars are accepted, although the local currency is the Aruba florin. Dutch is the official language but you will hear quite a lot of Spanish, and almost everybody speaks some English, too.

For local color, head along the waterfront to **Paardenbaai** (Schooner Harbor), which is crammed with brightly painted little boats and craft stalls selling the boat-owners' wares. This is a great setting for a photo, and you will also be entertained by flamboyant exchanges in Papiamento, the local patois.

There is more than a touch of Old Europe to be found here. Oranjestad has some magnificent examples of 16th and 17th-century Dutch architecture. You should head for Wilheminastraad,

a few streets up from the harbor, to see the best examples. Also worth a visit is **Wilhemina Park**, a lovely tropical garden set on the waterfront.

MAKE A BREAK FOR THE BEACH

If you are more keen to get to a beach than to admire architecture and gardens, you will find some of the world's best on Aruba. **Eagle Beach** ❷ and **Palm Beach** are long stretches of snowy-white sand bordered by casinos and hotels, which will (for a fee) provide all the facilities you need to swim, sunbathe and lunch in style. Use of the beaches is free, however, if you don't want any of the extras. Up to four people can share a one-way cab to these beaches for around US$12.

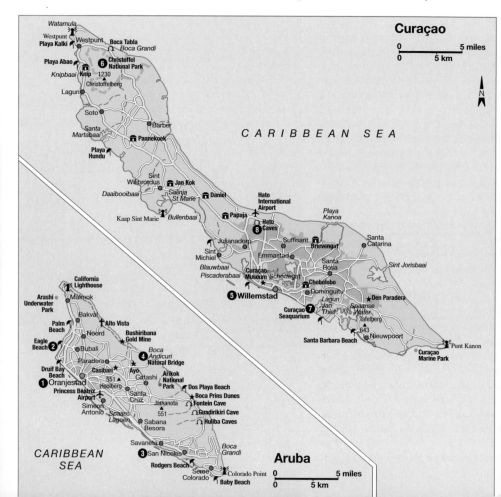

If you have a young family, the aptly-named **Baby Beach** to the southeast of Oranjestad is the best one to head for since it is shallow-watered, sheltered and very safe. En route to Baby Beach lies Aruba's oldest village, **San Nicolas ❸**, a former oil refinery and port which is now a tourist haven of unusual shops and al fresco cafés. San Nicolas is also famous for its dazzling street art, so make a stop here to admire it. Also to the east – but not as far from the port – is Spaan Lagoen (Spanish Lagoon), which was once the haunt of pirates and is now a scenic spot popular for picnics and country walks.

The beaches on the east coast have some lovely sand dunes, popular with nesting turtles. The sea is rougher here, which isn't good for swimming, but the surf is good for bodysurfing, particularly at **Dos Playa**.

EXCURSIONS

With plenty of taxis serving the cruise terminal and good tourist information available, it is easy to explore Aruba under your own steam (a 1-hour taxi tour for up to four people costs from US$30), but some of the cruise-line excursions are worth considering.

Diving 100ft (30 meters) beneath the waves in the Atlantis submarine (www.depalmtours.com) is a great introduction to the sea life of the **Barcadera Reef**. Cheaper, and more appropriate for anyone who is claustrophobic, are trips in a glass-bottomed boat. Among other organized tour options are trips to the beach, with snorkel gear provided, and trimaran trips, which also have snorkeling included in the price. Scuba diving is good, and Aruba is well known for its wreck diving, with a couple of ships dating from World War II and others more recently sunk, including a plane. North of Palm Beach is an area known as **Fisherman's Huts**, where there is world-class windsurfing and kitesurfing off Malmok and Arashi beaches, although they take place at

different times so as not to interfere with each other.

If you're keen to explore Aruba's arid landscape, a 3-hour coach tour of the island will show you the dramatic rock formations of the north, which includes the famous **Natural Bridge ❹**, hewn by nature from limestone (now collapsed, but a baby bridge also exists), fantastical boulders, gigantic cacti and caves full of weirdly shaped stalactites and stalagmites.

Some cruise lines also offer self-drive safari tours in four-wheel-drive vehicles, where you travel in convoy, or even on bicycles. This is a good compromise for travelers who are concerned about getting lost on their own, but hate to be treated like sheep. Tours last from 5 to 6 hours, with a swimming stop, and lunch is included in the price.

CURAÇAO: A TROPICAL AMSTERDAM

Curaçao, 38 miles long by just over 7 miles wide (60 by 11km), is the largest island of the former Dutch Antilles and home to more than 50 nationalities,

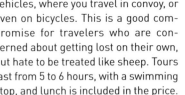

Kids will love Aruba's sandy beaches.

The gabled roofs of Wilheminastraat, Oranjestad.

The Floating Market in Willemstad.

Dutch influence in the tropics – Handelskade, Willemstadt.

who give it a liberal, cosmopolitan and welcoming atmosphere.

If you love the architecture and waterways of Amsterdam but find the weather too dreary, pick a cruise which has Curaçao's capital, **Willemstad** ❺, on the itinerary. Sadly, if you travel on a mega-ship, you might miss the best way of arriving in this pretty port: through the swing-aside **Queen Emma pontoon bridge** and up **Santa Anna Bay** to the old terminal. The bay, which divides the town in two, is a narrow channel flanked by pastel-tinted, traditionally gabled Dutch houses. Instead, mega-ship passengers will disembark at the port's US$9million big-ship terminal, the Curacao Megapier, on the coast just outside the bay. But at least the newer terminal has good shops and a nearby golf course, and lies only a short walk from town.

EXPLORING WILLEMSTAD

Be prepared to devote 2 to 3 hours to exploring Willemstad, as you'll find plenty to see and do here. Maps are available at the cruise terminal to help

you find your way around. First colonized by the Dutch in the 1630s, it is a beautiful town, resplendent with fine examples of 17th-, 18th- and 19th-century Dutch and Spanish colonial architecture, some of the best examples of which are to be found on the bay front. Willemstad has been placed on the Unesco World Cultural Heritage List, with 765 protected monuments and sites.

Smaller ships able to sail past the Queen Emma Bridge will bring you alongside at **Otrobanda**, which means 'the other side.' It is worth exploring in its own right if you enjoy architecture, as its maze of winding streets are flanked by fine Dutch colonial houses. If you want to get straight to where the action is, a short walk across the distinctly wobbly Queen Emma bridge (or a hop on the free ferry which runs when the bridge is open to let ships pass) will get you to **Punda**. This is where you will find the colorful **Floating Market**, lined with boats from Colombia, Venezuela and other islands, selling fresh fish, produce, spices and handicrafts, as well as a variety of duty-free shops.

Just as you come off the bridge, you will see **Fort Amsterdam**, a sandstone waterfront fortress which dates from 1700 and now houses the Governor's Palace. Fortkerk, a mid18th-century Protestant church, stands, nearby, with a British cannonball still embedded in its walls.

At one corner of the fort is **Breederstraat**, one of Willemstad's best shopping streets and gateway to the main shopping district, where you can buy everything from Delft pottery and clogs to Italian silk scarves and ties, Swiss watches, Portuguese embroidery, Japanese electrical goods, Indonesian clothing and, of course, deep-blue Curaçao liqueur.

MUSEUMS AND SITES

Not far from the market, on van den Brandhofstraat 7, Scharloo Abou, is the **Maritime Museum** (tel: 5999-465 2327; www.curacaomaritime.com; Mon–Sat 9am–4pm). The museum has some fascinating exhibits, including 16th-century maps, 17th-century ship models and multimedia displays, plus a café and gift shop. Staff at the museum can arrange harbor tours by water-taxi.

The best museum, however, is the **Kurá Holanda Museum** (Klipstraat 9; tel: 5999-434 7700; www.kurahulanda.com/en/museumx; Mon-Sat 9.30am-4.30pm), on the site of a former slave yard. As an anthropological museum, it focuses on the predominant cultures of Curacao, the origin of man, the African slave trade, west African empires, pre-Colombian gold, Mesopotamian relics and Antillean art. There is a shop on site that sells shirts, caps, posters, postcards and African art.

Also within walking distance of the Queen Emma bridge (on van Leeuwenhoekstraat) is the **Curaçao Museum** (tel: 5999-462 3873; www.thecuracaomuseum.com; Tue–Fri 8.30am–4.30pm, Sat 10am–4pm), a 19th-century former military hospital set in pleasant shady grounds, which now holds colonial antiques and artifacts of the region's Caiquetio tribes, not to mention a collection of paintings.

To explore further afield, hire a taxi and take a look at Curaçao's cactus-rich, spaghetti-western-style countryside (approximately US$30 an hour for a party of four). Top attractions within

> **⊘ Fact**
>
> If you didn't reach the town by sailing up the channel, you can do the next best thing – stand in the main street and watch ships sail serenely past the shops and houses at the end, creating the illusion that they are plunging up a street at the crossroads.

Hitting the shops in Curaçao.

an hour's drive include the 4,500-acre (1,820-hectare) **Christoffel National Park** ❻ (tel: 5999-864 0363; www.christ offelpark.org; Mon–Sat 7.30am–4pm), where nature lovers can hike and glory in rare orchids and cacti, abundant bird-life and the sight of wild goats, donkeys and iguanas.

Its underwater equivalent is the **Curaçao Seaquarium** ❼ (Bapor Kibra z/n; tel: 5999-461 6666; www.curacao-sea-aquarium.com; daily 8am–5pm), which features more than 350 species of sea life, including giant turtles, 20ft (6-meter) sharks and moray eels, some of them in touch tanks. Four times a day there is a guided tour and a feeding display. There is also an underwater observatory, a semi-submarine and an Animal Encounters facility where experienced swimmers can mix with stingrays, angelfish and parrotfish. In the Shark Encounter enclosure, visitors can swim on one side of a clear plexiglass screen in close proximity to the sharks swimming on the other side. For these encounters, however, reservations must be made 24 hours in advance.

Iguana in Christoffel National Park.

Curaçao is one port of call where you really don't need to take a ship's excursion, as you will easily find most places on your own or in a cab. If you like organized exploration, however, you could take a 3.5-hour tour that includes the Seaquarium and a trip on the submarine, as well as a visit to the **Curaçao Liqueur Factory** (tel: 5999-352 6461; www.curacaoliqueur.com; Mon–Fri 8am–5pm; free). The liqueur was discovered by accident. The Spaniards planted orange trees on the island in the 16th century, then found the climate was unsuitable. The oranges were bitter and inedible, but the peel, when dried, exuded an aromatic oil. Combined with exotic spices, this produced the liqueur, which went into commercial production in the late 19th century.

There are also tours to the **Hato Caves** archeological site, ❽ (Rooseveltweg; tel: 5999-868 0379; www.curacaohatocaves.com; daily 9am–4pm, guided tours every hour), which has a mirror-smooth underground lake, stalagmites, stalactites, bats and Caquetio rock drawings.

⊘ ISLA DE MARGARITA

Just 25 miles (40km) off Venezuela's Caribbean coast, Margarita Island was famous first as a base for pearl diving, but became a favorite holiday destination for Venezuelans from the 1980s. It developed as a popular cruise port, with ships anchoring just outside Puerto de la Mar and ferrying passenger ashore to beautiful sandy beaches and the duty-free shopping in the Spanish colonial-style main town, Porlamar.

Venezuela has, however, suffered from growing unrest, high crime levels, hyperinflation, mass protests and then, a mass exodus; 2.4 million people have fled since 2004. While Margarita is separate from the mainland, at the time of writing, only a couple of ships call here as the situation in Venezuela remains unpredictable.

You'll find French angelfish at the Seaquarium.

Another magnificent sunrise over the Caribbean Sea.

CARIBBEAN CRUISES

TRAVEL TIPS

PLANNING THE TRIP

KNOW THE AREA

The Caribbean embraces several groups of islands. The Lesser Antilles include the Windward Islands (Barbados and St Lucia, for example) and the Leeward Islands (the Virgin Islands and Antigua). The Netherlands Antilles, off the coast of Venezuela, include Aruba, Curaçao and Bonaire.

The Greater Antilles is an archipelago of larger islands, including Cuba, Hispaniola, the Cayman Islands and Jamaica. To the north of this area, the Bahamas archipelago spans 500 miles (900km) from the eastern, Atlantic coast of Florida to the edge of the Caribbean Sea, although cruise itineraries widely include the Bahamas in 'Caribbean' itineraries.

PASSPORTS AND VISAS

Cruise passengers should not be surprised when they part with their passport at check-in and only see it again when the cruise is over. This is common practice. Ships are cleared by customs and immigration in every port before passengers may disembark and they will be allowed ashore

⊘ Visiting Cuba

All visitors entering Cuba must show a passport that is valid for at least six months beyond the date of arrival in the country. In addition, most visitors must show a tourist card (tarjeta de turista), issued by the Cuban consulate directly or, more commonly, through a travel agent or cruise line. US citizens are only allowed to travel to Cuba if they meet certain criteria, which are listed at www.travel.state.gov.

without their passports, but must have a copy of the document or other photo id. Anyone wishing to visit a casino ashore may, however, need to temporarily retrieve their passport from the purser's desk.

Instead of passports, passengers carry a cruise ship ID card. This is swiped and checked every time the cardholder leaves the ship. Usually, the card doubles as a room key and a charge card. Most importantly, it tells the crew whether or not the passenger is on board when the ship is about to depart.

All luggage is X-rayed by cruise lines before boarding and passengers are required to walk through a security gate every time they return to the ship. Visitors are rarely allowed on board nowadays due to tight security.

Passport rules for US citizens changed in 2009 and everybody must now present a passport book, passport card, or WHTI-compliant document when entering the United States, regardless of whether their cruise began and ended in a US port (for 'closed-loop' voyages such as these, a passport wasn't required prior to 2009).

Citizens from outside North America also need to carry a passport. All travelers going to – or even passing through – Trinidad and Tobago, or Cuba, must have passports.

Visas are usually required only of visitors from Eastern Europe and Cuba. In addition all travelers must have, upon entering the islands, a return or onward ticket and adequate funds to support themselves for the duration of their stay.

Cruise passengers arriving via a US gateway city such as Miami or Puerto Rico have to obtain Electronic System for Travel Authorisation (ESTA) before flying or sailing. This includes citizens from all of the 37

countries that previously participated in the US Visa Waiver Scheme. The ESTA requires that you have more than six months remaining on your passport before its expiry date and that you have a machine-readable passport to enter the United States. The fee for ESTA is US$14 per person. If unsure, check with the passport issuing authority in your home country that your passport is still valid.

US TRAVELERS

For US travelers returning to the United States from the USVI, there are a number of importation options. Each individual can bring back up to US$1,600 worth of purchases duty-free. Travelers may also ship goods home from the USVI to the value of US$1,000, at a flat duty of 1.5 percent. Keep track of where you bought duty-free goods and have the receipts handy to show customs officials on re-entering the USA.

JEWELRY AND ART

US law allows the importation, duty-free, of original works of art. Because of concessions made to developing countries, jewelry made in the Caribbean may qualify as original art and thus be duty-free. If you purchase jewelry, be sure to obtain a certificate from the place of purchase stating that the jewelry was made in the islands. To make sure that the articles you want to bring back fall into this category, contact the US Customs Service for further details.

PETS

Cruise ships do not allow pets, with the exception of Queen Mary 2, which has a kennel on board, and animals are even then only allowed on board for transatlantic crossings. Companion or service dogs are sometimes permitted on ships, but arrangements must always be made in advance with the cruise line. Owners are allowed to exercise their dogs on certain areas of the deck and a sandbox is provided as a dog toilet.

FIREARMS

The importation of firearms, including air pistols and rifles, is prohibited.

HEALTH

Health hazards

All cruise ships have a doctor and nurse on board (the exception being cargo ships or private yachts carrying fewer than 12 people, which are not required to have a doctor). Facilities vary from ship to ship but a doctor should be able to treat most ailments, including heart attacks and appendicitis. Seriously ill passengers may be stabilized until the ship arrives in port, or airlifted off. There will always be a fee for consulting the ship's doctor, although many ships hand out sea-sickness tablets free of charge. Passengers should, however, bring their own supplies of any medication they use, as the ship's doctor will not be able to provide it.

The main (though small) health risk to travelers on land in the Caribbean is infectious hepatitis

⊘ Duty-free allowances

Travelers arriving in the Caribbean are generally allowed to bring in the following duty-free items:
personal effects.
200 cigarettes or 50 cigars, or 250g of tobacco.
1 litre of wine or spirits.
170ml or 6oz perfume.

or Hepatitis A. Although it is not a requirement, an injection of gamma globulin, administered as close as possible before departure, gives good protection against Hepatitis A. There are also growing incidences of the chikungunya virus which, although not fatal, is very unpleasant. It is transmitted by mosquitoes, so be vigilant in protecting yourself against bites. If you are pregnant, or trying to get pregnant, check the current advice on countries where the Zika virus is present.

In addition, make sure you observe scrupulous personal hygiene, wash and peel fruit and avoid contaminated water (drink bottled water if you are unsure).

Sun protection

To those unaccustomed to the tropical sun, 80–90°F (27–32°C) may sound 'just like summer temperatures back home', but don't be fooled. The sun in the tropics is much more direct than in temperate regions and is even stronger at sea as it reflects off the water.

Bring a high-factor sunscreen and wear it whenever you go out. For starters, expose yourself for only brief periods, preferably in the

morning or late afternoon when the sun's rays are less intense. You can increase your sunning time each day, but avoid sitting in the sun for long periods because of the danger of sunburn and skin cancer. Always use high-factor protection on small children and be sure to reapply sunscreen after a dip in the pool or sea. Try to keep babies cool and always in the shade. Bring a brimmed hat and a pair of good quality sunglasses, especially if you plan to do any extended hiking, walking or playing in the midday sun.

Drinking water

In undeveloped areas away from resorts, it is best to avoid drinking tap water, especially after hurricanes, when water supplies can become contaminated. In these areas, stick to bottled water and avoid ice in your drinks.

Drinking water on cruise ships is heavily chlorinated and while safe, does not taste good to most people and also explains why cruise ship tea and coffee is so strange tasting. All ships provide bottled water, although many charge for it. Buy supplies in port to save money.

Insects

Mosquitoes are generally only a nuisance in port in the evening. To combat mosquitoes, pack a plentiful supply of insect repellent. Dengue-carrying mosquitoes bite during the day and present a small risk. The only area that usually carries a malaria risk is Hispaniola, more in Haiti than the Dominican Republic. Caribbean islands occasionally report cases of the viruses

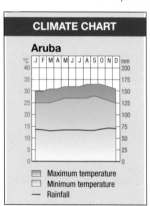

CLIMATE CHART

Aruba

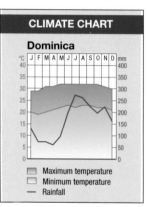

CLIMATE CHART

Dominica

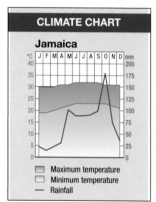

CLIMATE CHART

Jamaica

chikungunya and Zika, both transmitted by mosquitoes. For more information, see wwwnc.cdc.gov.

Immunization

No immunizations are required for travelers to the Caribbean, unless the traveler is coming from an infected or endemic area. However, it is a good idea to have a tetanus shot if you are not already covered and possibly gamma globulin (see Health Hazards). Check with a Public Health Department or other source before traveling, just to make sure there are no precautionary steps to take.

AIDS

AIDS presents a serious risk in the Caribbean among all sectors of the population. The Caribbean has the second-highest prevalence of living with HIV in the world after Sub-Saharan Africa, with the infection rate standing at 1.5 percent in Jamaica and highest in the Bahamas, where it is 2 percent. Heterosexual sex is the principal route of transmission. Using condoms and practicing safe sex is highly advised.

In medical situations, while the risk of catching HIV from an unsterilized needle is negligible, if you are at all concerned that this is not the case, ask before you are injected. Passengers wishing to travel with their own set of needles should pack them in the hold baggage or they may be confiscated.

Insurance

Though you are unlikely to have to claim, you should always arrange comprehensive travel insurance to cover both yourself and your belongings. Your own insurance company or travel agent can advise you on policies, but shop around since rates vary. Make sure you are covered for baggage or document loss, trip cancellation, emergency medical care and repatriation and accidental death.

CLIMATE

The principal characteristic of the Caribbean's climate is the relative lack of temperature change from

⊙ Carnival

Carnival, or Mardi Gras, is celebrated at different times on different islands, with the dates falling roughly into three main groups:

On Trinidad and Tobago, Dominica, Dominican Republic, St Thomas, Aruba, Bonaire, Curaçao, St Lucia, Martinique, Guadeloupe, Haiti, St-Martin (French side) and St-Barthélemy, Carnival preserves an association with Easter, being celebrated (on all of these islands except St Thomas) in the period leading up to and sometimes including Ash Wednesday. On St Thomas, the Cayman Islands, Jamaica and Puerto Rico, the celebration occurs after Easter.

On Curaçao, Bonaire, Puerto Rico, St Vincent, Anguilla, St John, Barbados, Grenada, the British

Virgin Islands, Antigua, Saba, St Eustatius, Cuba and Nevis, Carnival takes place in June, July or early August. On these islands, Carnival is often held in association with the 'August Monday' holiday, which marks the end of the sugar cane harvest and the freeing of slaves in the British islands in 1834.

On St Kitts, Montserrat, the Bahamas and St Croix (in the USVI), Carnival takes place in December and early January, in conjunction with the Christmas season.

On Sint Maarten (Dutch side), Carnival takes place in late April, coinciding with the Dutch Queen's birthday celebrations on April 30.

Cruises can be timed to coincide with the big festivals.

season to season. The islands' proximity to the equator means that seasonal temperature changes are limited to less than 10°F (6°C). An added bonus is the trade winds, which bring regular, cooling breezes to most of the islands.

Year-round, temperatures average around 80°F (27°C) throughout the region. During the winter (December to March) – which is peak season for tourists – night-time lows can drop to about 60°F (16°C), with daytime highs reaching as much as 90°F (32°C).

Rainfall varies, ranging from around 20ins (50cm) a year in Curaçao up to 75ins (190cm) a year in Grenada. Rainfall is generally heaviest during October and November, though June is wettest in Trinidad and Tobago. Hurricanes can strike from June to October. The 'dry' period coincides with the peak tourist season: December to April or May.

Hurricanes

Hurricanes are one of the most damaging and dangerous phenomena affecting the Caribbean. Devastating hurricanes have included, most recently, Irma and Maria in 2017, which destroyed Barbuda and caused devastating damage to Puerto Rico and the US and British Virgin Islands. Katrina pounded New Orleans in 2005, and

Tomas in 2010 caused terrible damage to the island of St Lucia and St Vincent. Sandy in 2012 caused widespread damage in Cuba and along the east coast of the US. Prior to Sandy, in 2008, Cuba was pounded by three hurricanes in quick succession: Gustav, Ike and Paloma. Ivan in 2004 caused damage to 90 percent of buildings in Grenada and left more than 30 people dead. The storm also hit Grand Cayman, Jamaica and St Vincent. Hugo in 1989 affected the Leeward Islands; Luis in September 1995 pounded Antigua, St Martin and nearby islands; and Marilyn a month later caused flooding in Antigua but most damage to the US Virgin Islands. In 1998 Hurricane Georges caused devastation throughout the Caribbean, although Puerto Rico was most severely affected.

Hurricanes usually occur between July and October, although visitations have been known in June and November and the 'hurricane season' stretches from the beginning of June to the beginning of November, when some islands celebrate with a Hurricane Deliverance Day. The average lifespan of a hurricane is 8 to 10 days.

In summer months, weather-pattern disturbances are common all over the tropics. It is from these that tropical depressions and then tropical storms develop, which can bring gales of up to 73mph (117kph) and heavy rains. A hurricane warning is issued when the storm reaches winds of at least 74mph (119kph) and high water and storm surges are expected in a specific area within 24 hours. Warnings will identify specific coastal areas where these conditions may occur.

Would-be cruisers should not be deterred by the thought of hurricanes. Cruise itineraries are designed to avoid bad weather and a ship's captain will always put passenger safety first. Cruise ships are built to withstand bad weather and all modern vessels are fitted with stabilizers (fins under the water level) to reduce the pitch and roll of the ship.

It is better to cruise outside hurricane season if the thought is off-putting. There are, however, ships in the Caribbean year-round, with bargains to be had in the months that are less dependable for weather.

MONEY MATTERS

A range of currencies is used in the islands. Whatever the official currency, the US dollar and sometimes the British pound or the euro are readily accepted throughout and are the most practical to bring, although you will usually lose out on the exchange rate if paying in sterling. In addition, major credit cards are welcome when settling on-board bills and at most major hotels, restaurants and shops. On some of the French and Dutch islands, the euro is the local currency, although the US dollar is accepted on many. Travelers' checks are becoming less and less common.

Cuba has two currencies: foreigners are expected to use the *peso convertible* (CUC), You can change foreign currency into CUC at CADECA exchange bureaus and some banks. In Old Havana they can be found on Calle Obispo and Calle Oficios, and elsewhere. Bring sterling or euros if possible as a 10 percent tax is charged on US dollars. Euros can be used in the large resorts: Varadero, Cayo Largo, Caya Coco and Santa Lucía. Credit cards and travelers' checks from US banks are not accepted.

If you are bringing US dollars or pounds sterling, it is a good idea to check around before converting your currency, especially if you are on a limited budget. Try to get price quotes in both the local currency and the currency you are carrying. Then check the applicable exchange rate. You may find you can save some money by making purchases in whichever currency gives you greater value.

Currency on board most ships is the US dollar, although P&O, Fred. Olsen and Saga Cruises use sterling. Exchange rates on ships are not competitive; use a bank in port instead.

These are the currencies in the Caribbean area:

Aruban Florin/Guilder (Awg/Afl): Aruba.
Bahamian Dollar (B$): Bahamas.
Barbados Dollar (BDS$): Barbados.
Cayman Dollar (CI$): Cayman Islands.
Cuban Convertible Peso ($): Cuba.
Dominican Peso (RD$): Dominican Republic.
Eastern Caribbean Dollar (EC$): Dominica, Grenada, Montserrat, St Kitts and Nevis, St Lucia, St Vincent and the Grenadines, Anguilla, Antigua and Barbuda.
Euro (€): Martinique, Guadeloupe, St-Martin, St-Barthélemy, Saba, St Eustatius, Bonaire, Curaçao and Sint Maarten.
Jamaican Dollar (J$): Jamaica.
US Dollar (US$): The US and British Virgin Islands, the Turks and Caicos Islands, Aruba.
Trinidad and Tobago Dollar (TT$): Trinidad and Tobago.

BUSINESS HOURS

The siesta is alive and well in the Caribbean and throughout the region small shops close for a couple of hours in the early afternoon, when the sun is at its hottest. As a result, business hours of some small shops generally follow this pattern. Shops open early, usually by 8am, certainly by 9am. They begin closing for siesta at noon or a little before, though in some areas, shops may stay open until 1pm. This can be inconvenient if the ship only has a brief stay in port, so time shopping expeditions accordingly. Business resumes about 2 hours later – 2pm in most places – with shops remaining open until 6pm. Again, there is some variation; on a few islands, closing time may be as early as 4pm. On Saturday, most shops are open in the morning and many have full afternoon hours as well. Sunday is generally a day of rest. Duty-free complexes whose *raison d'être* is to serve cruise passengers do not tend to take a siesta at all.

On the larger islands, such as Barbados, Trinidad and Tobago, shops generally do not close for extended periods in the afternoon.

Banking hours

Banks are normally open from Monday until Friday from 8 or 8.30am to noon. Many banks also have afternoon opening hours, especially on a Friday. A few banks open on Saturday mornings. As US dollars, credit cards and to a lesser extent, travelers' checks are widely accepted in the islands, visitors need not worry about finding a money exchange facility immediately upon arrival. You can also use your credit and debit cards to withdraw cash from ATMs. Before you leave home, make sure you know your PIN number and find out which ATM system will accept your card. See under individual islands for variations in bank opening hours and for locations of ATM machines. Some ships now have ATMs on board but read the small print very carefully as charges for using them are almost always punitive.

GETTING THERE

Once you have decided on the cruise that you want, talk to a travel agent, tourist board or airline company to determine the most efficient way to get to the starting point of your cruise. Many cruises are sold as fly-cruises, with the flight included, as well as transfers from the airport to the ship.

Cruise lines

Azamara Club Cruises, US: 1050 Caribbean Way, Miami, Fl 33132, tel: 877-999 9553; UK: tel: 0844 493 4016, www.azamaraclubcruises.com
Carnival Cruise Lines, US: 3655 NW 87th Avenue, Miami, FL 33178, tel: 1-800 CARNIVAL; UK: 100 Harbour Parade, Southampton, Hampshire SO15 1st; tel: 0808-234 0680, www.carnival.com
Large, modern fleet offering value-for-money cruises in a lively

☉ Taxes

There are several taxes that may come as a surprise during your travels in the Caribbean:

The **government room tax** is charged on all hotel room bills and generally averages 5–10 percent of the total bill. It varies from country to country and obviously only applies to hotel stays, not cruises.

The **departure tax** is normally around US$20, but can be as high as US$30 in certain islands. It is payable upon departure from each of the islands. Remember to keep enough cash to pay the departure tax, usually required in the local currency.

A cruise price may not always include **port taxes**, so double check before buying as these can amount to well over US$140 for a week's cruise. Port taxes are paid to the cruise line before the cruise, not in individual ports.

environment. Passengers are mainly Americans and are of all ages.

Celebrity Cruises, US: 1050 Caribbean Way, Miami, FL 33132, tel: 800-647 2251; UK: The Heights, Brooklands, Weybridge, Surrey KT13 0NY, tel: 0844 493 2043, www.celebritycruises.com or www.celebritycruises.co.uk
Sister line of Royal Caribbean, with contemporary fleet of large ships.

Costa Cruises, US: 200 South Park Road, Suite 200, Hollywood, FL 33021, tel: 1-800-GO COSTA, www.costacruise.com; UK: tel: 0800 389 0622, www.costacruises.co.uk
Italian-run subsidiary of Carnival Corporation. Fleet of mixed-age (including some large) modern ships ideally suited to Caribbean cruising. Passengers are mainly Italian and American and are of all ages.

Cruise & Maritime Voyages, UK: Gateway House, Stonehouse Lane, Purfleet, Essex RM19 1NS, tel: 0844-998 3943, www.cruiseandmaritime.com
British line using older ships on long, seasonal voyages from the UK to the Caribbean and South America.

Cunard Line, US: 24305 Town Center Drive, Santa Clarita, CA 91355, tel: 661-753 1000, www.cunard.com; UK: Carnival House, 100 Harbour Parade, Southampton, SO15 1ST, tel: 0344-338 8650, www.cunard.co.uk
Subsidiary of Carnival Corporation with three ships, *Queen Victoria*,

Queen Elizabeth and the *Queen Mary 2*, which carry an international mix of passengers, particularly on transatlantic runs.

Disney Cruise Line, US: Disney Cruise Vacations, Guest Communications, PO Box 10299, Lake Buena Vista, FL 32830-0238, tel: 0800-951 3532; UK: tel: 0800 171 2317
Four ships operating short cruises around the Caribbean. Attracting all ages and nationalities; superb for families, but also appealing to adults.

Fred. Olsen Cruise Lines, UK: Fred Olsen House, Whitehouse Road, Ipswich, Suffolk IP1 5LL, tel: 0800-860 6143, www.fredolsencruises.com
Four ships appealing to a mainly British market. Comfortable rather than the height of luxury, with a loyal following.

Hapag-Lloyd Cruises, Germany: Hapag-Lloyd Kreuzfahrten GmbH, Cruises-Club, Ballindamm 25, 20095 Hamburg, tel: 0049 40 3070 30 555, www.hl-cruises.com
German-owned line operating ultra-luxury cruises attracting both German and international guests.

Holland America Line, US: 450 Third Avenue West, Seattle, WA 98119, tel: 1 877-932 4259; UK: 100 Harbour Parade, Southampton, Hampshire SO15 1st, tel: 0344-338 8605, www.hollandamerica.com
Subsidiary of Carnival Corporation. Large fleet of elegant ships appealing mainly to Americans in the older age bracket, although the Caribbean generally attracts younger people.

MSC Cruises, US: 6750 North Andrews Avenue, Fort Lauderdale, FL 33309, tel: 877-665 4655, www.msccruises.com; UK: 5 Roundwood Avenue, Stockley Park, Uxbridge, UB11 1AF, tel: 020-3856 3087, www.msccruises.co.uk
Italian-owned cruise line. Lively, value-for-money ships appealing to all ages and nationalities.

Norwegian Cruise Line, US: 7665 Corporate Center Drive, Miami, FL 33126, tel: 305-436 4000, www.ncl.com; UK: 4th Floor, Mountbatten House, Grosvenor Square, Southampton SO15 2JU, tel: 0333-241 2319, www.ncl.co.uk
Large, pioneer of Freestyle Cruising; all ships offer an informal setting and there's a wide choice of dining options. Wide international appeal, attracting a good mix of ages, including families.

Oceania Cruises, US: 8300 NW 33rd Street, Suite 308, Miami, FL 33122,

tel: 305-514 2300; UK: 2nd Floor, Mountbatten House, Grosvenor Square, Southampton, SO15 2JU, tel: 0345-505 1920, www.oceania cruises.com
Luxury line with elegant ships and unstructured lifestyle on board.

P&O Cruises, Carnival House, 100 Harbour Parade, Southampton, SO15 1st, tel0344-338 8003, www.pocruises.com
British sister company of Princess Cruises. Large, modern ships appealing to a mainly British market. Particularly suited to families.

Princess Cruises, US: 24844 Avenue Rockefeller, Santa Clarita, CA 91355 California, tel: 661-753 0000; UK: Carnival House, 100 Harbour Parade, Southampton, SO15 1st, tel: 0344-338 8663, www.princess.com
Large, luxurious, modern ships with broad appeal across all ages.

Regent Seven Seas Cruises, US: 8300 NW 33rd St # 100, Doral, FL 33122, tel: 305-514 2300, FL 33122, tel: 800-285 1835; UK: Mountbatten House, Grosvenor Square, Southampton, SO15 2JU, tel: 02380 682 280, www.rssc.com
Upscale, mid-sized ships in which all cabins are suites.

Royal Caribbean International, US: 1050 Caribbean Way, Miami, FL 33132, tel: 305-539 6000; UK: Royal Caribbean Cruise Line, The Heights, Brooklands, Weybridge, Surrey KT13 0NY, tel: 0844 493 4005, www.royalcaribbean.com or www.royalcaribbean.co.uk
Large, resort-style ships, based in the Caribbean year-round.

Saga Cruises, UK: Middelburg Square, Folkestone, CT20 1AZ, tel: 0800 096 0079, http://travel.saga.com
Comfortable ships for the over-50s.

Seabourn, US: 450 Third Avenue West, Seattle, WA 98119, tel: 800-442 4448; UK: Carnival House, 100 Harbour Parade, Southampton, SO15 1st, tel: 0344 338 8615, www.seabourn.com
Elegant yacht-ships cruising the smaller Caribbean islands. All-inclusive and very upmarket.

SeaDream Yacht Club, US: 601 Brickell Key Drive, Suite 1050, Miami, FL 33131, tel: 800-707 4911; UK: tel: 0800 783 1373, www.seadream.com
Twin, 110-passenger yachts, all-inclusive, operating Caribbean cruises during the winter to smaller islands.

Silversea Cruises, US: 333 Avenue of the Americas, Suite 2600 (333

Southeast 2nd Avenue) Miami, FL 33131, tel: 800-722 9955; UK: Level 3, 21 Palmer Street, London, SW1H 0AD, tel: 0844-251-0837, www.silversea.com Elegant, luxurious ships cruising the smaller Caribbean islands. Excellent European-style service and cuisine; appeals to mainly North Americans, but there is a good mix of nationalities.

Star Clippers, US: 760 NW 107th Ave, Miami, FL 33172, tel: 305-442 0550; UK: c/o Fred. Olsen, Fred Olsen House, Whitehouse Road, Ipswich, Suffolk, IP1 5LL, tel: 0845 200 1645, www.starclippers.com or www.starclippers.co.uk Romantic sailing cruises on elegant clipper ships. International appeal.

Windstar Cruises, US: 2101 Fourth Avenue, Suite 210, Seattle WA 98121, tel: 800-216 9373, UK: c/o Mundy Cruising, 50-51 Wells Street, London, W1T 3PP, tel: 020 7399 7670, www.windstarcruises.com Luxurious yachts with a glamorous appeal, two of which travel partly under sail.

Cargo ships

For the traveler in search of something out of the ordinary, a cargo ship offers a different type of cruise: comfortable cabins for only a handful of passengers (evening meals are generally taken with the officers) on a working cargo ship.

Geest 'banana boats', for example, leave Portsmouth on a round trip lasting approximately 25 days, calling in at some of the following ports: Antigua, Barbados, Dominica, Grenada, Guadeloupe, Martinique, St Kitts, St Lucia, St Vincent and Trinidad. Note that, although ships depart weekly, not all vessels allow passengers on board.

Horn Linie 'banana boats' taking 12 passengers depart weekly from Dover and sail to Martinique, Guadeloupe, Cartagena in Venezuela and Costa Rica. Enquiries should be made to the following travel agents:

UK

The Cruise People (tel: 020 7723 2450, www.cruisepeople.co.uk) is the UK's main agency selling cargo ship voyages.

US

Freighter Cruises, 84-1320 State Route 9, Champlain, NY 12919, tel: 203-936 7447, www.freightercruises.com

Staying on

If you plan to spend a few pre- or post-cruise days in the Caribbean you can book a hotel directly.

When writing to a hotel, be sure to complete all mailing addresses, unless otherwise noted, with: (name of island), WI. For full details and reservations (which are recommended), contact the hotel directly by phone, email or through a travel agent. Alternatively, try the island's tourist office in your home country, or book online.

Restaurant reservations are recommended, especially in the winter season; essential at some restaurants.

Tourist information

Addresses of on-island tourist offices and representative offices in other countries can be found in the listings for individual islands. In addition, you can visit www.caribbeantravel.com, the website of the Caribbean Tourism Organization, or contact the following offices for any enquiry about the islands within the region:

Caribbean Tourism Organization
UK: Suites 52A & 53, 5th Floor AMP House, Dingwall Road, Croydon CR0 2LX, tel: 020 8948 0057, email: ctolon@caribtourism.com, www.caribbean.co.uk
USA: 80 Broad Street, Suite 3200, New York, NY 10004, tel: 212-635 9530, email: ctony@caribtourism.com, www.onecaribbean.org

What to wear

Cruising in the Caribbean can mean bringing two different wardrobes, one for the cruise and one for any overland travel afterwards.

Some cruise lines, inspired by Norwegian Cruise Line's informal 'Freestyle' cruising, have done away with compulsory formal nights, although Cunard, Fred. Olsen, P&O, Seabourn, and Holland America Line are just a few that do have gala nights. Dress code for evenings on board is usually:

Casual: smart casual wear but no shorts or vests.

Informal: pants and smart shirt/jacket for men; cocktail dress for women.

Formal: tuxedos or dark suits for men; evening dress for women.

A week's cruise will generally have one or two formal nights and a mixture of casual and informal on other nights. Some lines, like Cunard, just have casual or formal nowadays, with no in between, while others, such as Oceania Cruises, have every night as 'resort casual', meaning you can leave the ball gown at home.

For shore excursions and extended holidays, 'casual' is the word in the Caribbean. Light cotton dresses, trousers, skirts, shorts and blouses for women and informal pants, shorts and comfortable open-necked shirts for men should make up the majority of your wardrobe. The breezes are cooler at night during the winter, so visitors are advised to bring a light jacket or cotton jumper, just in case. Men should bring a jacket and tie, especially if they plan to visit any casinos – most of them (and some of the fancier restaurants and hotels) require at least a jacket for the evening. For the feet, light sandals are appropriate and comfortable on the beach and around town. A light raincoat, or an umbrella, is useful in case of sudden showers. For those planning walks or hikes in the mountains and rainforests, a pair of sturdy walking shoes is essential. Swimsuits and other beach attire are definitely not appropriate around town. When you venture from the beach or poolside into town, cover up – a simple T-shirt and a pair of shorts will do the trick. This simply shows respect for the standards of many island residents.

Nude or topless (for women) bathing is prohibited everywhere except for Guadeloupe, Martinique, St-Martin, St-Barthélemy and Bonaire. Guadeloupe, St-Martin and Bonaire have at least one designated nudist beach.

Getting married

There are several ways to get married on a cruise. Most unusual is the old-fashioned notion of being married at sea by the captain. This can be done and is increasingly popular nowadays as more cruise lines are changing the countries of registration of their ships; certain 'flags', like Bermuda and Malta, permit the captain to marry a couple on board. The captain can be held legally liable for marrying a couple not actually entitled to wed and not all are willing to perform the ceremony. Several cruise lines offer same-sex wedding ceremonies but this depends on where the cruise ship is flagged; Bermuda, for example, does not recognize same-sex marriage.

At sea

Princess Cruises' ships are registered so that their captains can legally perform weddings at sea, although even the basic package starts at around US$1,500. Weddings are only carried out on sea days and must be booked well in advance. P&O Cruises' captains can also conduct weddings at sea but weddings must always be planned ahead with the cruise line; spontaneous ceremonies, romantic though they may sound, cannot be accommodated as paperwork is required. Celebrity Cruises and Azamara Club Cruises also allow weddings on sea days officiated by the captain. An increasingly popular option (and a money-spinner for the cruise lines) is renewal of vows ceremonies, which, as they have no legal status, can be performed on the bridge by the captain. There is a charge for this.

In port

More common is being married on the ship while it is in port, with couples bringing their own priest or rabbi on board. Many ships have wedding chapels, although these tend to veer towards the kitsch, or appear to be dismal, unromantic afterthoughts in ship design, in which case a prettier spot on deck can be used. Princess, Carnival and Holland America will all arrange weddings on board.

Another option is to get married in one of the ports of call and have either a honeymoon, or a reception, or both at sea. Cruise lines are always happy to arrange private functions and usually do them very well. There are endless options for getting married ashore if you arrange it independently but Carnival, Princess and Disney Cruise Line will all organize a shore-side wedding with a cruise, often using their private islands for the ceremony.

Dispersal of ashes at sea

Some cruise lines will allow guests to scatter a loved one's ashes at sea. Various rules apply, including the distance from port and the type of container in which the ashes are housed (it should be biodegradable). Not all cruise lines will permit this ceremony but those that do, such as Carnival, Holland America Line and P&O Cruises, handle it with great sensitivity, usually appointing an officer to take the family to a quiet spot and say a prayer and sometimes supplying a wreath and a commemorative certificate with the coordinates of the ship at the time. Do not try to scatter ashes from a balcony or from the deck; for a start, it's forbidden to throw anything overboard and second, there are many stories of ashes being blown back onto the ship. Cruise lines that will help you do not charge for the service.

For a detailed description of every aspect of the cruising experience, plus money-saving tips and exhaustive reviews of around 275 cruise ships, we recommend the *Berlitz Complete Guide to Cruising and Cruise Ships* by Douglas Ward, published annually. Online, visit www.cruisecritic.com, or in the UK, www.cruisecritic.co.uk, for impartial advice and thousands of cruise reviews by members.

LIFE ON BOARD

TELECOMMUNICATIONS

Telephoning from a ship's satellite system is extremely expensive, at up to US$12 per minute. It is much cheaper to make calls from a mobile phone with a roaming agreement.

Payphones are disappearing fast as mobile telephony is ubiquitous now, as much so in the Caribbean as anywhere else. All visitors with a roaming-enabled cellphone will receive a signal in the Caribbean. Many ships also now have their own network, when the vessel is at sea and out of range, but be warned – calls on these are extremely expensive and when the vessel is sailing, it is prudent to switch off data on phones.

All islands in the Caribbean and many of the cruise terminals have internet cafés. All ships, too, offer internet access although charges vary enormously; think about how much you are likely to want to be online and buy a package, which is cheaper than paying per minute. Ship internet is notoriously slow, too, with the exception of Royal Caribbean, which has invested heavily in technology and now offers super-fast WiFi, powerful enough to stream movies in your cabin if you so wish.

Most travelers, though, wait until they are in port to find a WiFi signal and enable data on their device to send and receive emails.

ELECTRICITY

Different islands run on different electrical currents: 110–120V/60 cycle (US current): Bahamas, US Virgin Islands, British Virgin Islands, Aruba, St-Martin (Dutch side), Trinidad and Tobago. Also Belize, Honduras and Mexico.

110V/60 cycle: Cuba, Dominican Republic.

110–130V/50 cycle: Anguilla, Bonaire, Barbados, Curaçao, Jamaica.

220–230V/60 cycle: St Kitts and Nevis, Montserrat, Antigua and Barbuda.

220–240V/50 cycle: Bonaire, Curaçao, Dominica, Grenada, St-Barthélémy, Saba, St Eustatius, St-Martin (French side), Guadeloupe, Martinique, St Lucia and St Vincent and the Grenadines.

In the US it is 110-115V/60 cycle.

TRAVELING WITH CHILDREN

Despite its one-time image as an old people's vacation, cruising can be a perfect family holiday. In the Caribbean, the average age of passengers is younger than elsewhere and multi-generation groups can be seen on all ships, with plenty of distractions for toddlers, teenagers, parents and grandparents.

Some ships are more suitable than others for families. The facilities on *Disney Wonder, Disney Dream, Disney Fantasy* and *Disney Magic* are superb (with special adult-only areas for those who need a break from children), while Princess, Royal Caribbean and Norwegian Cruise Line all have good children's

> ⊘ **US area codes**
>
> Fort Lauderdale **954**
> Galveston **409**
> Houston **713**
> Miami **305** and **786**
> New Orleans **504**
> Key West **305**
> Port Canaveral **321**
> Tampa **813**
> code+area code+local number.
> When in the US, make use of toll-free (no-charge) numbers. They start with 800, 888 or 877.

facilities and entertainment. Among the British cruise lines, P&O is excellent and Cunard's *three Queens* also have good children's clubs. Parents of toddlers love P&O and Princess ships because they offer a night nursery, providing free care for sleeping infants while the parents relax.

Typical facilities on a modern ship should include air-conditioned children's clubs divided into different age groups, with qualified carers and a suitable ratio of staff to children. Be warned that these clubs may not operate on port days and that parents cannot both go ashore and leave their children in a club.

Some ships will have children's menus and almost all offer alternative casual dining, so small children do not have to join their parents in the evening in the main dining room. High chairs should be provided. In-cabin babysitting can sometimes (but not always) be arranged through the purser's desk and the babysitter is normally paid cash. Baby food is usually available but check first. Some ships allow you to pre-order other supplies, like nappies, too.

The larger the ship, the more there will be to do for children. More than one pool is good, as there will generally be a deck area and pool to which families are steered.

Anyone who does not like the idea of spending their holiday with children would be advised to avoid a big ship in the school holidays and anybody who has a horror of hundreds of noisy teens should avoid the US Spring Break holiday, when huge groups take to the seas from the US homeports.

For staying on, the islands are a perfect holiday destination for a family. Many resorts now offer children's programs including babysitting facilities; some of the best include Windjammer Landing on

St Lucia; Carlisle Bay on Antigua; Almond Beach on Barbados; and Beaches Negril on Jamaica. Do check, however, as some hotels may not allow children under 12 during the winter high season.

FACILITIES FOR DISABLED TRAVELERS

Generally speaking, cruising can be an ideal holiday for someone in a wheelchair as most ships provide a relaxing, sociable setting while visiting numerous destinations with minimal hassle. Take the advice of a specialist cruise travel agent before booking and make sure they provide specific information about the facilities on board and the cabin itself. All new ships by law must provide accessible cabins and generally speaking, the newer the ship, the better the facilities. Older ships may have a couple of adapted cabins, but wheelchair users need to be aware of hazards like doorways with a lip, or a lack of ramps, or small elevators. Sailing ships like those of Star Clippers are not suitable for wheelchair users or those with limited mobility as getting on and off the tenders can be challenging.

The quality of cabins for the disabled, however, varies, with passengers complaining of such oversights as lack of low-down mirrors, no panic buttons, a cabin with a wide door but a narrow bathroom door, and lack of storage space with low rails.

If specially fitted cabins are not available but you have mobility issues, choose as large a cabin as possible, close to the elevator. When arranging mealtimes, make sure the maitre d' allocates you a table with space for a wheelchair.

Questions to ask when booking:

Are there any areas of the ship that will be inaccessible?

How easy will it be to board the tenders? For example, do you board from a platform or down a steep gangway?

Do I need to bring a traveling companion (the answer is, yes, if you are in a wheelchair)?

Will there be facilities on shore excursions for disabled passengers?

When choosing a cruise, pick an itinerary with as few tender ports (where passengers are ferried ashore in small boats) as possible. Wheelchair passengers can use tenders but may be restricted if the sea is choppy.

When it comes to shore excursions, a person's ability to participate depends entirely on their mobility and determination. The Caribbean is not generally geared up to wheelchair users; a common complaint is that the wheels of the chair get stuck in the sand. There are few special facilities such as ramps in public places. However you will find them in modern shopping centers, restaurants and many resorts and most excursions can be adapted to accommodate a wheelchair.

The same applies to staying on. Resort hotels may well have a few specially adapted bedrooms or, failing that, ground-floor rooms and minimal steps to public rooms. Booking through a good travel agent is advised.

Cruising can be ideal for the less able bodied, but make enquiries.

RELIGIOUS SERVICES

All the mainstream church denominations can be found on the islands, as well as little-known cults. Attending a local service, perhaps Baptist or Seventh Day Adventist, is a wonderful way to experience an important aspect of Caribbean life and you will be assured of a warm welcome, as long as you dress smartly and act with decorum and respect. Local tourist offices and free tourist publications should be able to advise times of services.

Interdenominational services are held on most cruise ships, conducted either by the captain or staff captain. Special Jewish charters will usually have a rabbi on board and some offer kosher food.

TIPPING

Tipping is a big bone of contention on cruise ships, particularly for Europeans. American passengers live in a tipping culture and tend to be more generous. Tips on a cruise can make a big difference to the cost of the holiday.

What's confusing about tipping is that it is different on every ship, whether it's a matter of stuffing cash in an envelope and posting it into a box, or adding gratuities automatically to each passenger's on-board

⊘ Hot tips for cruisers

Don't feel you have to tip people like the maître d' or the head waiter unless they have performed a special service for you – ordering a birthday cake or arranging a special menu, for example.

If the service is poor, don't pay the tip – but at the same time do raise the issue with the hotel manager on board.

It is good practice to tip your cabin steward extra if you leave your cabin in disarray.

On some ships, it is forbidden for staff to accept cash tips.

If you really want to reward someone, the cruise lines suggest you buy them a small gift instead (although the reality is that most of the staff would prefer the cash). If you do give them cash, don't hand it over conspicuously.

If tips are automatically added to your on-board account, you are perfectly entitled to adjust the amount.

If you want to do more than give a tip, a genuine 'Thank you' and a letter to the employee's boss is a thoughtful gesture.

account, which is most common nowadays.

The recommended amount to tip varies, as do the people who will receive the money. Ships provide guidelines for basic tips (usually to the room stewards and dining room waiters) but are vague about the remainder of the staff, including the maître d', the wine waiter and the bartender. The important thing is to keep it in perspective. Many cruise lines pay particularly low wages to cabin stewards and dining room waiters, on the assumption that their salaries will be made up with tips, while behind-the-scenes employees like chefs get paid more.

There is a move towards including tips in the cruise price. On Silversea, Seabourn, SeaDream, Regent Seven Seas, Marella Cruises and Saga Cruises, some or all of the tips are included in the price. Many lines, including Carnival, Disney and Royal Caribbean, allow or even insist that tips be pre-paid.

Regardless of tipping policy, ships carrying a lot of Americans usually add a 15 or 18 percent gratuity to the bar bill 'for your convenience,' a practice many passengers resent. This is also common practice in the ships' spas.

ETIQUETTE

On board, there are only a few etiquette rules to observe. Cruise lines are getting much stricter about smoking and smokers may well find themselves huddled outside or confined to one cigar lounge. Never throw a lit cigarette overboard as it can blow back onto the ship and start a fire.

Remember, too, that it is forbidden to film or record any of the ship's entertainers, for copyright reasons. If you take a drone on vacation, you'll find that most cruise lines have been quick to ban their use on board, for safety reasons.

On land, common politeness is as desirable on the islands as it is anywhere else. 'Please', 'Thank you' and a respectful and friendly demeanor will go a long way towards returning the warm welcome you are likely to receive. 'Hello', 'Goodbye', 'Good Morning' and 'Goodnight' are always used to friends, family or just to people you might pass on the road.

⊘ Getting around on shore

By car

Hiring a car for a day in port is more practical on some islands than others. The US Virgin Islands, for example, are compact, reasonably well signposted and easy to get around. Jamaica is deceptively large, with potholed roads and hectic driving, so not recommended for a self-drive car rental. In the Dominican Republic, you'll need a good map and a command of Spanish to stand a chance.

If you want to rent a car, the purser can arrange this in advance so the car is waiting on the dock when the ship comes in, saving valuable time. Otherwise, on islands like Barbados, Mini-Mokes can be rented at or close to the port for short excursions. You will need a visitor's permit on most islands, which the rental company can arrange for a fee.

For longer stays, the islands are well stocked with auto-rental agencies. Travel by car allows great freedom and flexibility to explore the nooks and crannies of the islands, but there are a few things the driver should be aware of. Many of the islands are mountainous and on all of them roads are narrower than most US and European drivers will be familiar with. Driving may be a little more harrowing than at home; it is not for the faint-hearted. Also, in some areas yearly rainfall is quite light and this allows a film of oil to build up on road surfaces.

If you need to ask directions or advice always greet the person *before* asking a question.

Slow down: life operates on a different timescale in the sleepy Caribbean. Loss of temper, impatience and aggression will not produce results.

Two more points: don't take anyone's picture without first asking permission – it is often seen as invasive – and don't drag up shades of colonialism and old B-grade Hollywood movies by referring to island residents as 'natives.'

When it does rain on these roads, they become especially slick, requiring extra caution. All in all, drivers should prepare to drive defensively and with caution, perhaps following the advice of one of the islands' tourist agencies to 'sound the horn frequently,' especially when approaching bends. Regulations on driving licenses vary from island to island – see under the listings for individual islands.

Hiring a motorbike is often an option but apply the same rules as you would at home. Far too many tourists are killed or injured on holiday by riding in swimwear with no crash helmet.

A car is by far the best way to get around if you are extending a cruise in the United States. Most rental agencies require that you are at least 21 years old (sometimes 25), have a valid driving license and a major credit card. Some will take a cash deposit in lieu of a credit card, but this might be as high as $500. Travelers from some foreign countries may need to produce an international driving license from their own country. Rental vehicles range from modest economy cars to vans and luxury convertibles.

Be sure to check insurance provisions before signing anything. Cover is usually around US$25 per day. You may already be covered by your own car insurance or credit card company, however, so check first.

And lastly: do check which side of the road you should drive on!

PRIMARY LANGUAGES

The multiplicity of languages in the Caribbean reflects the region's checkered colonial past. All of the islands use their own patois as well as a whole array of primary languages that include:

English: Anguilla, Antigua and Barbuda, British Virgin Islands, Cayman Islands, Dominica, Grenada, Jamaica, Montserrat, St Kitts and Nevis, St Lucia, St Vincent and the Grenadines, Sint Maarten, Barbados, Trinidad and Tobago and the US Virgin Islands.

⊘ Getting around on shore ctd

By Taxi

Perhaps the most common means of transport for cruise passengers exploring independently is the taxi. Not only are taxis convenient and, by US or European standards, often quite inexpensive, but taking a taxi also gives you access to the resources of the driver. Where else could you chat with an island expert for the price of a cab ride? Most taxi drivers will gladly help you find things you are looking for, or that you aren't looking for, but may be delighted to find. It is usually possible to find a taxi driver who is willing to give you a tour of his or her island and, in some places, drivers are specially trained to do this.

Another positive feature of taxi travel for island visitors is that rates are generally fixed and published. Often, printed sheets with detailed rates are available from points of entry, drivers and tourist offices. Make sure you agree a rate with the driver before departing and only pay the full fare when you have returned to the ship. Remember that it is your responsibility to get back on time and the ship will not wait for latecomers.

In the US taxis are available in all the main tourism centers and wait for passengers at dedicated ranks at some of the ports. Elsewhere do not hail a passing cab; your hotel should call for you, but otherwise numbers are listed in the Yellow Pages. Fares are metered and drivers, like anyone providing a service in the USA, expect a tip – around 10–15 percent is usual.

By Bus

Local buses are not really practical for cruise passengers with only a few hours to 'do' a destination, but for an extended stay, buses are quite inexpensive and have the advantage of allowing travelers to get a small taste of how local residents live. Your hotel, a tourist office, or a police station should be able to supply information on schedules and fellow riders and drivers are usually friendly and helpful in making sure that bewildered visitors get off at the right stop.

Tour buses (mini and full-sized), vans, jeeps and 'communal taxis' are available on all the islands, for taking groups sightseeing.

In the US the national bus line, Greyhound, as well as a number of smaller charter companies, provide an impressive network of ground travel throughout the country. While some inter-city services include many stops en route, there are also 'express' buses that take in fewer stops.

Reservations and local bus station details are available on 800-231 2222, or at www.greyhound.com.

Inter-Island Links

Many cruise passengers choose to stay on in the Caribbean after their week or two at sea to island-hop. As you might expect in this region of small-to-tiny islands cut off from one another by the sea, the options for getting around between islands are legion. For the traveler desiring quick transfers (and perhaps the novelty of a ride in a seaplane), there are at least 20 airline companies operating inter-island routes. For example, LIAT (www.liat.com) is probably the largest and best-known of these, while Caribbean Airlines (www.caribbean-airlines.com) offers inter-island flights as well as longer haul services to the US and the UK.

On the sea, an armada of ferries operates regularly between islands. Some of these ferries are the familiar steel-and-smokestack variety, while the inquisitive and adventurous traveler will find hydrofoils, schooners and other types of sailing vessel plying the waters between islands. Services include Great Bay Express, which sails between St-Barths and St Maarten (www.greatbayferry.com), or travel on one of the six ferries that connect St Kitts and Nevis, considered one of the most beautiful journeys in the Caribbean. It is often possible for travelers to bargain with fishermen and other small boat owners to arrange rides out to the many small islands that lie off the shores of the major islands.

However, although there are ferries between groups of islands (BVI/USVI, Windwards) and islands of the same nationality, there are no real long-distance ferries and it is impossible to island-hop the whole chain by sea.

French: Guadeloupe, Haiti, Martinique, St-Barthélemy and St-Martin.
Dutch: Aruba, Bonaire, Curaçao, Saba, Sint Eustatius and Sint Maarten.
Spanish: Cuba and Dominican Republic.
Papiamento is the local language of Aruba, Bonaire, Curaçao, Saba, Sint Eustatius and Sint Maarten. It has evolved from Spanish, Dutch, Portuguese, English and African and Caribbean languages.

In addition to the languages listed above, Chinese is among the languages spoken on Aruba. English (and, to a lesser extent, other European languages) is spoken in several areas throughout the islands that have a high concentration of foreign travelers, but don't expect everyone to understand you – especially in rural areas and smaller towns. Efforts to communicate with island residents in their own languages are always appreciated.

English is the main language of almost all cruise lines, although some carry a lot of international guests, for example, Germans on Hapag Lloyd, or French travelers on Ponant.

SPORT

The climate and geography of the Caribbean make the islands perfect for sports enthusiasts and tourism has helped spark the development of a variety of sports facilities. Following is a list of some of the more popular sporting activities; see listings under individual islands for more information.

Watersports

Some smaller ships, namely those of Star Clippers, SeaDream Yacht Club, Seabourn and Windstar, have a watersports platform which can be lowered from the back of the ship. All of these carry their own equipment. The big cruise lines, namely Royal Caribbean, Norwegian Cruise Line, Princess and Carnival, have private islands where most Caribbean cruises will spend one day. In reality, these 'islands' are usually a remote beach where the cruise line has installed watersports equipment and other facilities.

On land, everything from mini Sunfish to stand-up paddleboards,

⊘ Postcards

Postcards mailed from the US are likely to arrive home quicker than those mailed from the islands.

two-masted yachts and large motor-boats can be hired, either from hotels or from independent beach operators.

Waterskiing is available on most islands and all the necessary equipment may be rented. If you are interested in chartering a yacht, either crewed or bareboat, for a day or a considerable period of time, see Getting There, page 313.

Fishing is a popular sport throughout the Caribbean. Most fishing boats can be chartered by the day or half-day and can usually accommodate several passengers. Many will quote rates which are all-inclusive of lunch, drinks, snacks, bait, equipment and any other essential items you might need on your fishing trip.

Golf

In the Antilles, there are golf courses on Antigua, Aruba, Barbados, British Virgin Islands, Cuba, Curaçao, Grenada, St Kitts and Nevis, St Lucia, Sint Maarten, the US Virgin Islands, St Vincent and the Grenadines, Guadeloupe and Martinique. Barbados, Jamaica, Dominican Republic and the Bahamas have some of the most prestigious courses, often world-class. Tee times on many courses can be booked in advance through the ship's shore excursion desk – or choose a cruise line with its own golf program, such as Norwegian or Fred. Olsen Cruises.

Tennis

Tennis is played on all islands, to varying degrees. Courts are found primarily within the premises of hotels and arrangements can be made to use these courts even if you are not a hotel guest. Some islands also have private clubs, which are open to visitors and public courts that operate on a 'first come, first served' basis. Most of the big, contemporary ships have paddle-tennis courts, which are slightly smaller than a normal court and use softer balls.

Hiking

Rainforests, mountains, waterfalls and gorgeous views await you. Many of the islands have good-sized national parks with prime hiking opportunities (Dominica, Guadeloupe, Grenada, St Kitts and St John in the US Virgin Islands). In St Lucia, anyone fit can climb up the Pitons without the need for specialist mountain equipment.

Guides often lead excursions. If you plan to hike alone, plan the route carefully and allow enough time to get back to the ship, or it could sail without you. Do check local regulations however, as some islands will not allow you to hike on your own in a national park.

NIGHTLIFE

Nightlife on cruise ships varies from high-tech nightclubs and Broadway-standard shows to a solitary has-been with an electric piano. Bigger, more modern ships tend to have better nightlife and entertainment will be geared to the nationality that predominates on board.

Evening entertainment on the islands ranges from relaxing over a leisurely dinner in a restaurant with a veranda facing onto the beach, to frittering your money away in a casino. In between these options are nightclubs, bars, discos and live music. The larger hotels provide much of the evening entertainment on the islands, including music and dancing both during and after dinner, flashy floor shows usually featuring a limbo dancer and 'folkloric evenings' composed of elements of the music and dance. Travelers with an interest in culture may wish to venture beyond hotel walls in search of steel band, calypso and reggae music and of bars and clubs frequented by local people.

Casinos

The casino is an integral part of any modern cruise ship, with only a tiny minority not offering tables and one-armed bandits.

Ships' casinos are closed in port, but open as soon as the ship sails and are often the focal point of activity late at night. Newcomers will often be offered free gambling

⊘ Birdwatching

Several islands in the Lesser Antilles are noted for their birds. In the US, birdwatching tours are organized by:
Field Guides Incorporated, tel: 800-728 4953, www.fieldguides.com
In the UK, try:
MotMot Travel, tel: 01327 359 622, www.motmottravel.com

lessons; cruise lines make a lot of money from casinos.

A number of the islands have casinos and even some of the region's more relaxed islands have a casino or two. If you do plan to gamble, be sure to bring along appropriate clothes. Dress codes in the casinos tend to be a little more formal than those prevailing elsewhere.

The legal gambling age is 18 on most islands, but on Guadeloupe and Martinique you must be 21. Photo ID will sometimes be required for admittance and some casinos charge an admission.

TIME ZONES

All of the islands except Trinidad and Tobago are in the Atlantic Time Zone, which is 1 hour later than Eastern Standard Time and 4 hours earlier than Greenwich Mean Time. When the United States goes onto Daylight Saving Time, the islands do not change, so during this time of year, time in the eastern part of the US is identical to Island time. Trinidad and Tobago are both in the Eastern Time Zone which is the same as the eastern US during Standard Time.

⊘ Responsible cruising

Visitors can take some initiatives to protect the Caribbean way of life and the environment:
Disembark in every port.
Check out tours available at the quaysides.
Use local restaurants or cafés.
Buy locally made souvenirs.
Dispose of litter responsibly.
Hire a guide to show you around.
Use reef-friendly sunblock if you go snorkeling.
Only take photos of people with their permission.

ACCOMMODATIONS

Types of accommodations

In **Florida**, the accommodations on offer range from luxury resorts to basic motels, as well as pretty bed & breakfast inns.

Many cruise lines offer special rates at selected hotels as part of a cruise-and-stay package. If you find yourself in Miami, the most popular areas to stay in are South Beach (the location of the Art Deco hotels), Bal Harbor and Key Biscayne. In contrast to the big, glitzy resorts found along the coast in mainland Florida, hotels in Key West tend to be small and quaint.

Whatever your budget, you should find something to suit in Texas. In addition to independently owned hotels and motels in every price range, there are also chains and historic inns.

Cozumel, **Playa del Carmen** and **Puerto Costa Maya**: in Mexico, there's a huge choice of hotels, from big resorts and tower blocks (in Cancún) to smaller, friendlier inns.

Belize: Hotels vary from eco-lodges in the rainforest to simple resorts on the Cayes; business properties and guesthouses in the cities too.

Head for **Roatán** in Honduras, and accommodations are in attractive villas and beach huts. There are no high-rises on Roatán for the moment.

Accommodations on **Isla Margarita** (Venezuela) tend to comprise low-grade hotels, some with all-inclusive packages.

On **Grand Cayman**, condos and villas are very popular with people vacationing here, but there is actually a wide range of accommodations available – from locally-owned guest houses offering bed and breakfast to luxury resorts slap bang on the beach.

In **Jamaica**, hotels range from small inns to some of the finest resorts in the Caribbean. Jamaica is the home of all-inclusive resorts, with many Sandals, SuperClubs, Couples and other brand names offering package holidays; and yet independent travelers can find plenty of alternative accommodations. The Jamaican-owned Island Outpost chain of boutique hotels offers the most interesting and appealing places to stay, but there are many family-owned guest houses and small hotels both close to the beach and inland in the mountains.

ARRIVING BY SEA

Florida

Fort Lauderdale

The cruise pier is at Port Everglades, the largest cruise port in the world after Miami and home base to several luxury lines. You'll find that there is very little to do in the vicinity of the port so a taxi or hire car is essential. The downtown area is 10 minutes' drive away.

Key West

Ships dock at Mallory Square, in the heart of Old Town, or there is also a dock at The Mole, linked to Old Town by a five-minute train ride. Some ships tender, with drop-offs at Mallory Square.

Miami

The Port of Miami is the largest cruise port in the world and is the home base for giants such as Royal Caribbean and Norwegian Cruise Line. The port is just a five-minute ride from downtown and Miami Beach. For general information on the port, call 305-347 4800.

Port Canaveral

Ships dock at Port Canaveral, north of Cocoa Beach and close to the Kennedy Space Center. The best way to get around is by car, although there are taxis at the port.

Tampa

Cruise ships dock at the Port of Tampa in the Channel District downtown, just in front of the Florida Aquarium and the Channelside entertainment center. There are shops in the immediate vicinity.

Louisiana

New Orleans

Cruise ships dock at the port, next to the Ernest N. Morial Convention Center. The Julia Street Cruise Terminal complex includes a huge shopping mall and next door is the Erato Street Terminal. Both cruise terminals are on the streetcar Riverfront Line. Taxis wait at the port, or you can walk into town.

Texas

Galveston

Ships dock at the Port on Pier 25, which is adjacent to the historic Strand District.

Mexico and Central America

Cozumel, Playa del Carmen and Puerto Costa Maya

Cozumel: Cruise ships dock at the Cozumel International Pier, a 10-minute drive from downtown. A ferry makes the journey to Playa del Carmen throughout the day, taking around 45 minutes. Some ships dock at Punta Langosta, closer to downtown area. Puerto Costa Maya, a 15-minute cab ride, is also used and finally, large ships may anchor offshore on a busy day.

Playa del Carmen: Usually a tender port.

Puerto Costa Maya: Cruise ships dock at the pier. Most onward transport from here is with organized shore excursions. Good access but 175-mile (280-km) journey to Playa del Carmen and Cozumel and further to Cancún.

Belize

Only small ships can moor up in Belize City, the main port of call. Others use tenders. The main points of interest are outside Belize City but the Belize Tourism Village, which has over 50 shops, restaurants and tour desks, is a short hop by water-taxi from where the tenders drop off.

Roatán (Honduras)

Ships dock at Coxen Hole, close to the shops and bars of the West End.

Costa Rica

Cruise ships dock at Puerto Limón on the Caribbean coast and the majority of passengers are ferried off immediately on excursions.

On the west coast, ships dock at Puntarenas or Caldera opening up the Pacific coastline for exploring.

Isla Margarita (Venezuela)

Cruise ships arrive in Guamache (near Margarita's ferry dock), 30 minutes away from the shops of Porlamar, the main town, by taxi or bus.

Caribbean arc

Grand Cayman

Cruise ships dock in downtown George Town, within easy walking distance of the shops and the beginning of Seven Mile Beach.

Jamaica

Cruise ships dock at Ocho Rios, Falmouth, Antonio and Montego Bay, all on the north coast.

Montego Bay: Cruise ships dock at the Freeport complex, on a spit of reclaimed land to the west of the bay. Most ships run a shuttle service for the 20-minute journey into town; failing this, there will be a long line of willing taxi drivers outside the terminal.

Falmouth: Falmouth's cruise ship dock can receive the biggest ships. The pier is triangular and has been developed as an 18th-century concept town with cobbled streets, shops, boutiques, restaurants, bars and shady parks. Tram cars and horse-drawn buggies are available for tours of the town.

Ocho Rios: The cruise terminal is located on the edge of town and has telephones, toilets, an information desk and outside, a taxi rank.

Port Antonio: The cruise ship pier is a low-key affair and shopping is mainly in the town. However, plans have been drawn up for phased redevelopment to provide berthing for medium-sized cruise ships, mega yachts and smaller craft, together with hotels and shops.

CALENDAR OF EVENTS

Florida

Fort Lauderdale

January: Orange Bowl
March: Museum of Art/Las Olas Arts Festival
April: Fort Lauderdale Seafood Festival
May: Pompano Beach Fishing Rodeo; Cajun/Zydeco Crawfish Festival
June/July: Philharmonic 'Beethoven by the Beach' Summer Fest
July: Hollywood 4th of July Celebration
September: Las Olas Art Fair
October: Fort Lauderdale International Film Festival
November: Hollywood Jazz Festival

Key West

March: Historic Seaport Music Festival
June: Florida Keys Tropical Fruit Fiesta
July: Hemingway Days Festival
October: 10-day Annual Fantasy Fest
November: Pirates in Paradise, Historic Seaport

Miami

February: South Miami Arts Festival; Miami Film Festival; Chinese New Year
February/March: Carnaval Miami (Caribbean-style carnival celebrations)
March: St Patrick's Day celebrations, Calle Ocho street party

October: Halloween celebrations
November: Veterans' Day celebrations
December: Annual King Mango Strut (street parades, carnival in the Coconut Grove area)

Port Canaveral

March: Florida Marlins' Spring Training; TICO Warbird Air Show (next best thing to a shuttle launch); Port Canaveral SeaFest (food festival).
April: Melbourne Art Festival.
November: Space Coast State Fair; Space Coast Birding and Wildlife Festival

Tampa

January: Black Heritage Festival
February: Gasparilla Pirate Festival
March: Gasparilla Festival of the Arts; Apollo Beach Manatee Arts Festival
4 July: Freedom Festival
October: Halloween celebrations
November: Cigar Heritage Festival

Louisiana

New Orleans

February/March: Mardi Gras – several days of exuberant celebration.
Spring: International Jazz and Heritage Festival
4 July: Go 4th on the River – Independence Day Celebrations.
October: Halloween celebrations are becoming a major event with mask-wearing and eye-popping costumes
Year-round: Jazz and blues events throughout the city

Texas

Galveston

February: Mardi Gras; Houston Livestock Show & Rodeo
April: Houston International Festival; WorldFest: Houston International Film Festival
May: Cinco De Mayo Celebration; Galveston Historic Homes Tours
June: Juneteenth Celebration (blues, gospel and jazz)
September: Fiestas Patrias Mexican festival
December: Dickens on the Strand

Mexico and Central America

Cozumel, Playa del Carmen and Puerto Costa Maya

Equinox Seasonal Event: On **March 21** and **September 21** – the Spring and Summer Equinoxes – an illusion

created by the ancient Maya causes a snake-shaped shadow to fall on the El Castillo pyramid and rise up the steps at Chichén-Itzá.
February/March: Carnival of Cozumel
September: San Miguel Arcangel Fiesta (Cozumel). Huge festivities in homage to San Miguel, Cozumel's patron saint
2 November: All Souls' Day – Day of the Dead
12 December: Feast Day of the Virgin of Guadalupe

Belize

February: Carnival, held one week before Lent
March: Baron Bliss Day celebrations held nationwide to honor this great benefactor of Belize.
May: Cashew Festival, Crooked Tree Village; Coconut Festival, Caye Caulker
June: Día de San Pedro – boats and fishermen are blessed, a special Mass is held and a fiesta/jump-up follows.
August: International Sea and Air Festival, San Pedro. A festival of music, dance and foods from Belize, Mexico and neighboring countries.

Costa Rica

March: National Craft Fair, San José
15 September: Independence Day
12 October: Carnival, Puerto Limón
31 December: New Year's Eve

Isla Margarita (Venezuela)

February: Carnival – before Ash Wednesday
March/April: Easter – parades and solemn ceremonies
24 June: St John the Baptist day
14 August: Feast of the Assumption
31 December: New Year's Eve – traditional festivities

Caribbean Arc

Grand Cayman

January: Culinary Month
March: Carnival Batabano
November: Pirates' week; Underwater Film Festival

Jamaica

February: Bob Marley Birthday celebrations
March/April: Carnival
May: Calabash International Literary Festival
June: Jamaica International Ocho Rios Jazz Festival

July: Reggae Sumfest
October: Port Antonio International Marlin Tournament

EATING OUT

Western Shores Cuisine

The cuisine of Florida is not all luminously fresh shellfish, conch chowder, alligator tail steak and Key lime pie –there's no single Florida cuisine, but rather a panoply of Southern, Anglo, European, Caribbean and Latin American trends that enliven an ever-changing food culture, one of the most exciting in the US. By far the biggest news on the Florida food scene over the past few decades has been the impact made by the variegated cuisines of Latin America – from the hot Cuban sandwich traditionally stuffed with ham, roast pork, Swiss cheese and pickles, served hot from a press; to the Haitian fish boiled with lime juice, onion and garlic and hot pepper; to the South American ceviches of raw fish pickled in piquant citrus and chillis. Different areas have their variations of course – take Cape Canaveral, famous for seafood: lobster, scallops, crayfish, shrimp, fish and crab, as well as specialties including octopus, fried frog legs, alligator and shark. Local desserts include Key lime pie and 'astronaut ice cream' (a replica of the freeze-dried dessert that went to the moon).

The extraordinary range of food in **New Orleans** includes everything from haute cuisine and Bananas Foster to blackened catfish and Creole sole. Other local favorites are: red beans and rice, kidney beans stewed with salt pork, ham hocks, onions and garlic; jambalaya, a version of the Spanish paella, with either seafood or meat; gumbo (spicy soup, originally with okra); crayfish; King Cake (multicolored pastries); beignet doughnuts; café au lait with chicory.

Don't plan on dieting while in **Texas**. Texans love food and a visit wouldn't be complete without sampling a good portion of it. State favorites include barbecue, chicken-fried steak (an inexpensive steak covered with batter, fried and served with gravy), pecan pie and, of course, Tex-Mex food.

In **Mexico** – more particularly Cozumel, Playa del Carmen and

Puerto Costa Maya – and alongside the usual Mexican specialties you'll find some tasty local dishes such as poc-huc (marinated pork), pollo pibil (chicken baked in a pit) and red snapper stuffed with vegetables.

The national dish of **Belize** may be rice and beans, but that doesn't mean that local cuisine stops there. Tropical reef fish, lobster and conch (available in season on the cayes and transported across Belize) are luxurious ingredients for a national cuisine. Conch should not be eaten during the out-of-season months of July, August and September, since it will have been illegally caught. Belize also offers an exotic range of tropical fruits, especially in the interior. Sample a 'soursap; milkshake and ask for whatever other unusual produce is the local favorite. Try to experience some of the smaller Belizean restaurants, which is a good way to meet Belizeans and appreciate their friendliness.

Roatán, Honduras: beans and rice is the staple diet, although mango-glazed chicken and conch soup are worth a try. Restaurants tend to be basic beach shacks, mainly in fabulous settings, or small establishments in town.

Isla Margarita, Venezuela: local specialties have a Caribbean flavor and include casado (rice, beans, stewed beef, plantains and cabbage); Olla de Came (beef and plantain soup); and sopa negra, a rich black bean soup. Agua de sapo (toad water) is nicer than it sounds – a refreshing beverage prepared with lemon juice, molasses, ginger and rum.

In **Jamaica**, restaurants have a huge array of unusual fruits and vegetables for you to try. The traditional breakfast is saltfish and ackee, while curried goat is a staple lunch. Jamaica is famous for its jerk pork or chicken, highly spiced and cooked in the earth covered with wood and coals, guaranteed to bring you out in a sweat. Some of the best can be found on roadside stalls.

GETTING AROUND

Florida

Fort Lauderdale

By car
Car-rental firms at Port Everglades include Avis, tel: 954-359 2500;

Alamo, tel: 888-826 6893; Continental Rent-A-Car, tel: 954-332 1125. Fun Rentals, tel: 877-983 9826, rents out scooters, two-person scootcars, bicycles and skates.

By taxi
Taxis line up at the cruise pier.

By bus
Public buses service over 410 sq miles (1,062 sq km), with 250 buses plus 30 community buses on 40 routes. A free trolley service operates throughout downtown Fort Lauderdale, connecting Broward Performing Arts Center with Las Olas Boulevard boutiques and restaurants (www.suntrolley.com).

Intra/Interstate Service is provided by Greyhound Lines. The main bus station is located at 515 NE 3rd Street, Fort Lauderdale. Transportation between Port Everglades and the station is available by taxi.

By rail
Rail Passenger Service is provided by Amtrak and Tri-Rail Commuter Line. The nearest passenger station is at 200 SW 21st Terrace, Fort Lauderdale and is accessible from either Broward Boulevard or the interstate I-95.

Tri-rail, a 67-mile (108km) commuter railway, connects Palm Beach, Broward and Dade counties with modern double-decker cars. There are six stations in Greater Fort Lauderdale and free shuttle buses connect to the airport and major business and shopping centers. Tel: 800-TRI-RAIL. Scheduled water taxis also operate on the canals between hotels, restaurants, nightclubs, theatres, shops, beaches, marinas and more. Tel: 954-467 6677 (www.watertaxi.com).

Links to the Caribbean
Fort Lauderdale-Hollywood Airport has comprehensive links to several Caribbean islands. Tel: 866-435 9355.
Otherwise, Miami is a short drive down the coast.

Key West

By car
It is not worth hiring a car in Key West as everything is within walking distance. Scooters and bicycles are can be hired at shops on Duval Street.

Further afield, the drive along the Overseas Highway is famous; first built atop the remains of tycoon Henry Flagler's Overseas Railroad, 193 miles (310km) of bridges string the low-lying Keys together.

By bus and trolley
The Old Town Trolley operates from Mallory Square. For journeys out of Key West, Greyhound Lines makes numerous scheduled stops between Miami International Airport and the Keys, including Key Largo. Tel: 305-296 9072. The Keys Shuttle offers a door-to-door service from Fort Lauderdale and Miami International airports to Key Largo and other points in the Keys. Call 24 hours ahead to book. Tel: 888-765 9997/305-289 9997.

Links to the Caribbean
Key West has its own airport for mainly domestic services. The nearest big international airports are Miami and Fort Lauderdale-Hollywood, with regular services to the Caribbean.

Miami

By car
Car hire firms at the Port of Miami include Hertz, tel: 786-425 2515; and Alamo, tel: 888-826 6893.

By taxi
Taxis in Miami tend to be expensive and you usually have to telephone in advance for pick-up.

Public transport
There are three forms of short-distance public transport. Metrorail is a 21-mile (34km) elevated railway, with stops roughly once every mile; Metromover is a series of little cars on an elevated track extending from the downtown area and is free to ride; Metrobus has 60 routes throughout the metropolis.

Links to the Caribbean
Miami International Airport is the state's largest in total passenger numbers and airlines. It is also a major jumping-off point for direct flights to the Caribbean and South America.

As well as various US airlines operating services to the main gateway airports in the Caribbean, there are many smaller regional carriers such as Cayman Airways and LIAT linking the islands to Miami, as well as the main Caribbean airlines like Caribbean Airlines and Bahamasair.

Port Canaveral

By car
Hire companies at or near the port include Avis, tel: 321-783 3643; and Alamo, tel: 321-866 0324.
Taxis wait at the port.

By bus/rail
A beach trolley service runs from Port Canaveral to 13th Street in Cocoa Beach, Mon–Sat 7am–9pm and Sun 8am–5pm. More information at www.cocoabeach.com/trolley.html.

Links to the Caribbean
Orlando, a 50-minute drive away, is the nearest large international airport, served by all the main US carriers and offering links to the Caribbean islands and the Bahamas. There are various small and charter-only airfields along the Space Coast.

Tampa

By car
Car rental agencies in Tampa include: Enterprise Rent-A-Car, , tel: 813-254 4221; U-Save Car & Truck Rental, tel: 800-282 8619.

By taxi
Taxis cannot be hailed on the street – you have to pick one up at a rank or call in advance. Bay Shuttle, tel: 813-259 9998, or Yellow Cab of Tampa, tel: 813-666 6666.

By trolley
A streetcar system connects the uptown and downtown areas. Tel: 813-254 4278, www.tecolinestreetcar.org.

By rail
Amtrak offers leisurely services from America's Midwest, Northeast and South – and connecting services from points west – to certain Florida cities. There are daily services from New York City to Tampa on the Silver Star.

Links to the Caribbean
Tampa International Airport (tel: 813-870 8700) links to many US cities and has international flights to Europe and the Caribbean.

Louisiana

New Orleans

By car
Don't hire a car for a day stop – walk or use the streetcar instead. For

longer stays, try: Alamo Rent-A-Car, New Orleans International Airport, tel: 888-826 6893; or Avis Car Rental, 2024 Canal St, tel: 504-523-4318. Note that driving and especially parking, in the French Quarter is not easy. Streets are narrow and often congested; cars parked illegally are towed away swiftly and it is expensive to retrieve them.

By taxi
Taxis can be hailed on the street and operate on a meter system.

By bus
Public buses run 6am–6.30pm. For schedules, visit www.norta.com.

By streetcar
The streetcar is by far the best way to get around. The sightseeing excursion from Canal Street to Carrollton and back is just over 13 miles (21km), takes about 1.5 hours, and is a bargain at $1.25. The Riverfront Line is also good for sightseeing. Timetables are available at the Regional Transit Authority (RTA) office: 2817 Canal Street, tel: 504-248 3900. A VisiTour pass, available for one or three days, allows unlimited on-and-off privileges for the streetcars and buses.

Links to the Caribbean
All the main American airlines serve New Orleans, including Delta, United and American, with regular links to gateways such as Fort Lauderdale, Miami and Orlando.

Texas

Galveston

By car
For a day visit, Galveston is easily walkable.

Hitting the road in the Yucatán.

By taxi
Taxis need to be called in advance; you can't just hail one on the street. All cabs are metered;, Busy Bee, tel: 409-762 8429 or Yellow Cab 409-763 3333.

Links to the Caribbean
Hobby Airport or George Bush Intercontinental Airport in Houston, the closest gateway to Galveston, both have regular connections to the Caribbean and to many USA destinations, served by the major airlines such as American, Continental and Delta.

Mexico and Central America

Cozumel, Playa del Carmen and Puerto Costa Maya

By car
Most people hire a four-wheel-drive or a jeep to explore the antiquities of the Yucatán independently. If you've only got a day, it's better to go on a guided tour. Car hire agencies in Cozumel include: Smart Rent a Car, tel: 987-105 4650 or Hertz, tel: 800-709 5000.

By taxi
Cozumel: from Punta Langosta, walk downtown. Otherwise, taxis line up at the International Pier.
Playa del Carmen: taxis line up at the ferry dock.
Puerto Costa Maya: taxis line up at the pier if you want to strike out on your own. But as most places of interest are not close by, it's probably better to opt for a shore excursion on a day visit.

By ferry
Ferries run between Cozumel and Isla Mujeres and the Yucatán

Peninsula. The latter are mainly passenger ferries, traveling short distances.

By bus
There is an extensive public transport network with first-class air-conditioned buses and local buses throughout the Yucatán.

Links to the Caribbean
Aeromexico operates a comprehensive network of domestic and international flights. Short hops around the Caribbean, however, are usually via Miami or Fort Lauderdale.

Belize

By car
There are plenty of car rental companies but driving outside Belize City is not recommended. It's easy to get lost, there are a lot of remote areas and roads can be bad. On a day trip, a guided tour is recommended. Car rental agencies in Belize City include: Budget Rent A Car, tel: 501-223 2435 or Safari/Hertz, tel: 501-223 5395.

By taxi
Taxis are available in towns and resort areas and have green license plates. There are no meters, so always negotiate the fare before you set off.

By bus
The least expensive way to get around Belize on a day-to-day basis is by bus. Buses run regular schedules and by Central American standards, Belizean buses are clean, roomy and efficient, although they do get very full. You can view bus timetables online at www.travelbelize.org.

Links to the Caribbean
The following charter/local scheduled airlines have links domestically and to the Cayes:
Caribee Air Service, tel: 501-224 4253, www.caribeeair.com;
Maya Island Air, tel: 501-223 1140; www.mayaislandair.com;
Javier's Flying Service, tel: 501-824 0460, www.javiersflyingservice.com;
Tropic Air, tel: 501-226 2626, www.tropicair.com;
Flights to Belize go through Miami, Dallas, Houston and Los Angeles. The major airlines servicing Belize are American Airlines, Continental, Tropic Air and Maya Island Air.

Roatán (Honduras)

By car

The island is only about 30 miles (48km) long and exploring is easy. Consider a moped or bicycle, available in Coxen Hole. Car hire firms: Caribbean Rent a Car, tel: 504-2455 7351; Avis, tel: 504-9977 6950.

By taxi and bus

Taxis can be hailed in towns – they will sound their horns if they are free. The first place you are likely to find one is a short distance from the ship on the paved road to Coxen Hole. Agree the rate before setting off. The vehicles can be dilapidated.

Dark blue minibuses serve the West End – simply wave to stop one. They are cheaper than taxis around town but for a trip further afield, take a private taxi.

There's also a water taxi service between West End and West Bay. You can take a water-taxi elsewhere, but negotiate the fare first.

Links to the Caribbean

Continental and Delta offer flights to Roatán, flying from Houston and Atlanta. All other flights are via the Honduras mainland.

The ferry Galaxy Wave travels between the Bay Islands and La Ceiba on the mainland of Honduras, a 1 hour 20 min trip. Tel: 504-2445 1775, www.roatanferry.com.

Costa Rica

By car

By far the best way to get around on a brief visit is to take a shore excursion. For touring the country, a four-wheel-drive is recommended. Roads are good, but can be rough in places. Visitors can drive with an international driving license. All hire companies have their head office in San José; call first for details of rentals in Puerto Limón. In San José: Adobe Rent-a-Car, tel: 506-2542 4800; Europcar, tel: 506-2440 0990.

By taxi

Taxis wait at the port when ships call. Always agree the price of a trip beforehand. Taxis can represent good value for sightseeing.

By bus

Buses are operated by private companies which link San José with the principal provincial towns and cities,

seaports and tourist areas. With good-quality vehicles and frequent buses, travel around the country is relatively easy.

Links to the Caribbean

Most Latin American carriers fly regularly to San José. The Costa Rican Airline, Avianca connects with many points in the US and codeshares with several partners in the Star Alliance. International airlines serving San José include American, British Airways, Continental, Iberia and KLM. American carriers fly from Miami, Atlanta, New York, Dallas, Houston and Mexico City.

Isla Margarita (Venezuela)

By Car

Self-drive is not recommended as security in Venezuela is unpredictable.

By taxi

Taxis can be hailed in towns, but are unmetered so negotiate fares before you set off.

By bus

Buses are cheap, crowded and serve most of the island. Bus stops can vary from driver to driver – this is not a quick way to get around.

Caribbean Arc

Grand Cayman

By car

Driving is on the left. Drivers must be at least 21. The island is easy to get around by car, scooter or bicycle. Car-rental firms include Dollar Rent-a-Car, tel: 345-949 4790; www.dollar.com, or Economy Car Rental, tel: 345 936-9105; www.economycarrental.com.ky.

By taxi

Taxis are available in the cruise dock and there's a sign showing rates.

By bus

The bus terminal is located adjacent to the public library on Edward Street in downtown George Town and serves as the dispatch point for buses to all districts. There are 38 minibuses operated by 24 licensed operators, serving nine routes. Daily service starts at 6am from the depot.

The system uses color-coded logos displayed on the front and rear of buses to identify routes. Licensed

buses are identified by blue license plates. Tel: 349-946 1323.

Inter-island links

By air: Cayman Airways (in Miami), the Cayman Islands' national flag carrier, operates jet services (on 737-300 aircraft) between Grand Cayman and Miami, Tampa, Chicago, Washington DC, New York, Havana, Montego Bay, Honduras and Kingston (Jamaica). It also operates jet services (Twin Otter) from Grand Cayman to Cayman Brac. Tel: 345-949 2311; www.caymanairways.com. Cayman Airways Express operates several daily scheduled flights between Grand Cayman, Cayman Brac and Little Cayman. Day trips and private charters are also available.

Jamaica

By car

Driving is on the left. To hire any vehicle, visitors may use a driving license (valid for at least 12 months) for up to a 3-month period if American, or up to 12 months if a UK citizen. Drivers must be at least 25 years of age to hire a car and must post a bond to meet insurance regulations with cash, major credit card, or travelers' checks. Service stations are open daily and will only accept cash. Distances are long between the main attractions and minor roads are potholed. It is not worth hiring a car for a day visit. Take an excursion or a taxi instead. Many visitors do, however, hire cars for an extended stay. Hire companies include Island Car Rentals, tel: 876-929 5875, www.islandcarrentals.com; Rainbow Car Rental & Tours, Ocho Rios, tel: 876-974 7114.

By taxi

Taxis wait at the cruise terminals and have predetermined rates between one location and another. All cabs have red PPV plates (Public Passenger Vehicle) along with ordinary license plates.

By bus

Limousines, air-conditioned coaches and local bus services connect all villages, cities and towns. The buses are a colorful, if time-consuming way of exploring the island.

By Air

Caribbean Airlines (tel: 1-800-920 4225, www.caribbean-airlines.com) has a wide network of flights across the Caribbean. Airlink Express operates domestic flights in Jamaica between all the main airports, tel: 876-940 6660, www.intlairlink.net.

Inter-island links

By Air: Cayman Airways (tel: 345-949 2311; www.caymanairways.com) serves the Cayman Islands and flies to Cuba and many other islands; Copa Airlines (tel: 1-800-234 2672; www.copaair.com) flies to Aruba, Havana, Port-au-Prince, Punta Cana, San Juan, Santiago de los Caballeros, Santo Domingo and a range of Latin American destinations; Caribbean Airlines (tel: 1-800-920 4225; www.caribbean-airlines.com) flies from Kingston to Antigua, Barbados, Caracas, Georgetown, Paramaribo, Port of Spain, Sint Maarten and Tobago.

MONEY MATTERS

Mexico and Central America

Cozumel, Playa del Carmen and Puerto Costa Maya

The unit of currency is the Mexican peso. Banks are open Mon–Fri 9am–4.30pm. The safest and easiest way to bring money to Mexico is as dollar travelers' checks from a well-known issuer, in fairly large denominations. They can be cashed in banks. If you are bringing cash, the best place to change your money is a bank or a *casa de cambio*

Hats for keeping out that midday sun, Mexico.

(money exchange). You can also change money at hotels. American Express will cash personal checks for card holders. Avoid carrying large amounts of cash; Mexican pickpockets are efficient. Major credit cards are widely accepted in tourist areas, but for public markets and many smaller, less expensive hotels, restaurants and shops, you will have to pay cash.

Belize

The Belize Dollar (BZ$) has a fixed rate of exchange of BZ$2 to US$1. Most hotels, resorts, restaurants and tour operators will accept US currency, travelers' checks or credit cards. Always check which dollar rate is being quoted. Banking hours are Mon–Thu 8am–1pm, Fri 8am–4.30pm.

Roatán (Honduras)

The local currency is the lempira. The US dollar is widely accepted in tourist areas and easy to exchange.

Costa Rica

The currency unit is the colón. The current rate of exchange can be found in the English-language *Tico Times* business pages or the same section of the daily *La Nación*. Cash machines are available in the biggest shopping centers and credit cards are widely accepted. Banking hours are Mon–Fri 9am–3pm.

Isla Margarita (Venezuela)

The unit of currency is the bolivar. ATMs may have been tampered

with, so beware. Change money using a Visa or MasterCard and keep exchange receipts for conversion of bolivars back into dollars. Credit cards are accepted in most tourist destinations.

Caribbean Arc

Grand Cayman

The unit of currency is the Cayman Islands dollar. US dollars are widely accepted, as are credit cards.

Jamaica

The currency is the Jamaican dollar (J$). US dollars are widely accepted, with change given in Jamaican dollars. Credit cards are widely accepted, too and there are exchange facilities in all the main tourist areas.

POSTAL SERVICES

Mexico and Central America

Cozumel, Playa del Carmen and Puerto Costa Maya

Post offices usually stay open all day (only mornings on Saturdays) but mail deliveries are slow and when receiving mail it is safest to have it sent to your hotel. Mail sent to post offices to be picked up (within 10 days) should be addressed to Lista de Correos.

Belize

Belize has a reasonable postal service. The country's stamps are amongst the most beautiful in the world, with their depictions of native flora and fauna, but they are becoming difficult to obtain. There are postal facilities in the Belize Tourism Village, Belize City. The office is open 8am–noon and 1–5pm (until 4.30pm on Fridays).

Roatán (Honduras)

There are postal facilities in Coxen Hole.

Costa Rica

There are postal and telegraph offices in cities and villages throughout the country, Mon–Fri.

Isla Margarita (Venezuela)

You can send postcards from Margarita – there is a post office in Porlamar.

Caribbean Arc

Grand Cayman

Branches of the Philatelic Bureau are located in the main post office in George Town and the Westshore branch on West Bay Road. There's also a tiny post office in Hell, which means you can postmark your cards 'from Hell'.

Jamaica

There are postal facilities in Ocho Rios and Montego Bay center.

PUBLIC HOLIDAYS

Florida

1 January: New Year's Day
16 January: M.L. King Jr Day
20 February: Presidents' Day
March/April: Good Friday
28 May: Memorial Day
4 July: Independence Day
3 September: Labor Day
October: (2nd Monday) Columbus Day
11 November: Veterans' Day
22 November: Thanksgiving Day
25 December: Christmas Day

Mexico and Central America

Cozumel, Playa del Carmen and Puerto Costa Maya
6 January: Día de Los Reyes (Day of the Kings)
17 January: Día de San Antonio Abad
5 February: Constitution Day
24 February: Flag Day
21 March: Birthday of Benito Juarez
April: Santa Samana (pre-Easter Holy Week)
1 May: Labor Day
3 May: Día de la Cruz (Day of the Cross)
5 May: Cinco de Mayo
16 September: Independence Day
12 October: Día de la Raza (Columbus Day)
20 November: Revolution Day (Anniversary: Revolution of 1910–17)
1 December: Inauguration Day
25 December: Christmas Day

Belize

1 January: New Year's Day
9 March: Baron Bliss Day
March/April: Good Friday; Holy Saturday; Easter Sunday; Easter Monday
1 May: Labor Day

24 May: Commonwealth Day
1 September: St George's Caye Day
21 September: National Independence Day
12 October: Columbus Day
19 November: Garífuna Day
25 December: Christmas Day
26 December: Boxing Day

Roatán (Honduras)

1 January: New Year's Day
March/April: Easter
14 April: America's Day
1 May: Labor Day
15 September: Independence Day
3 October: Morazan or Soldiers' Day
12 October: Columbus Day
21 October: Armed Forces Day
25 December: Christmas Day

Costa Rica

1 January: New Year's Day
March/April: Easter
11 April: Anniversary of the Battle of Rivas (banks remain open)
1 May: Labor Day
29 June: St Peter and St Paul
25 July: Anniversary of the Annexation of Guanacaste Province
2 August: Our Lady of the Angels (banks remain open)
15 August: Assumption/Mother's Day
15 September: Independence Day
8 December: Immaculate Conception (banks remain open)
24 December: Christmas Eve (banks remain open)
25 December: Christmas Day
28–31 December: Christmas Holiday

Isla Margarita (Venezuela)

1 January: New Year's Day
February/March: Carnival (Monday and Tuesday before Ash Wednesday)
March/April: Thursday and Friday of Holy Week (Easter week)
19 April: National Declaration of Independence
1 May: Labor Day
24 June: St John the Baptist day
5 and 24 July: Signing of National Independence Act; Birth of Simon Bolívar (24th)
12 October: Columbus Day
25 December: Christmas Day

Caribbean arc

Grand Cayman
1 January: New Year's Day
February/March: Ash Wednesday
March/April: Good Friday, Easter Monday
May: (3rd Monday) Discovery Day

May/June: Whit Monday
June: (Monday following second Saturday) Queen's Birthday
July: (1st Monday): Constitution Day
11 November: Remembrance Day
25 December: Christmas Day

Jamaica

1 January: New Year's Day
February/March: Ash Wednesday
March/April: Good Friday, Easter Monday
23 May: Labor Day
1 August: Emancipation Day
6 August: Independence Day
October (3rd Monday): National Heroes' Day
25 December: Christmas Day
26 December: Boxing Day

SHOPPING

Florida

If you are into kitsch – plastic flamingo ashtrays, canned sunshine, orange perfume and the like – you will find Florida a veritable treasure house. From roadside shacks to massive, futuristic malls, stores carry plenty of traditional souvenirs. And then, of course there are the homegrown souvenirs like citrus fruit that can be shipped home for a small fee. But if you look a little harder, Florida also has an array of quality goods to take home from a trip. There are shops worth seeking that sell designer clothing at factory prices, Haitian art, Art Deco and Florida antiques, Native Indian crafts and shells that forever smell of the sea. Good buys for European visitors are designer-label jeans, sneakers and sportswear at a fraction of the price paid at home.

Fort Lauderdale

Fort Lauderdale is home to Sawgrass Mills Factory Outlet Mall, 12801 W. Sunrise Boulevard, tel: 954-846 2350, Mon–Sat 10am–9.30pm, Sun 11am–8pm. This is one of the largest factory outlet malls in the US, with about 300 stores. Also try Swap Shop of Fort Lauderdale, 3291 West Sunrise Boulevard, tel: 954-791 7927, Mon–Fri 9am–6pm, Sat–Sun 7.30am–6.30pm. Not far from Sawgrass Mills, this is a bargain-hunter's paradise, with rows and rows of stalls selling jewelry, sunglasses and more at rock-bottom prices. The carnival, drive-in movie theater and free circus are added attractions. Las Olas Boulevard in town has several good art galleries and restaurants as well as shops.

Key West

The souvenir, fashion, art and general kitsch shops located all along Duval Street sell lots of Hemingway and fishing memorabilia; also some great art, surf gear and clothing.

Miami

Best areas include Bal Harbor Shops, 9700 Collins Avenue, Bal Harbor, tel: 305-866 0311, Mon–Sat 10am–9pm, Sun noon–6pm. Bayside Marketplace, 401 Biscayne Boulevard, tel: 305-577 3344 is a specialty shopping and entertainment complex in downtown Miami. Mon–Thu 10am–10pm, Fri–Sat 10am–11pm, Sun 11am–9pm. Loehmann's Fashion Island, 18711 Biscayne Boulevard, tel: 305-931 3761 is great for discounted designer wear. Mon–Fri 10am–9pm, Sun noon–6pm. Also try Coconut Grove for fashion and the shops of South Beach for fashions and sportswear.

Port Canaveral

Main Street Titusville, Olde Cocoa Village and downtown Melbourne offer the best souvenir and knick-knack shops, while the best beach and surf shop is the Ron Jon Surf Shop, claiming to sell 'everything under the sun.'

Tampa

Among the best buys are designer clothes and cigars. Old Hyde Park Village is an outdoor-style shopping mall and there are plenty of shops in the Channelside complex and in Centro Ybor. University Mall combines well with a visit to Busch Gardens.

Louisiana

New Orleans

Things to buy include antiques, voodoo dolls, vintage clothing, Mardi Gras souvenirs, jazz and blues music, packaged spices and cookbooks. Royal Street in the French Quarter is the place for local color; the Riverwalk Shopping Center is near the port. Magazine Street is great for antiques, crafts and second-hand books.

Texas

Galveston

Browse the boutiques and shops in the Strand, which is also good for antiques.

Houston

The Galleria, Houston's largest and best-known retail mall, has 375 stores and is visited by more than 16 million people annually. The oldest shopping district is the River Oaks Shopping Center. Also try Rice Village for a huge mixture of stores, from funky fashions and crafts to big names.

Mexico and Central America

Cozumel, Playa del Carmen and Puerto Costa Maya

It doesn't get much better than Mexico. Look for beautiful ceramics, woodwork, masks, gourd bowls, wooden trays and fine lacquerware; hand-made bird cages; mahogany and cedar furniture; wooden musical instruments; basketware; palm-leaf mats; Panama-style hats; hammocks; rugs; wool and cotton clothing; embroidery; jewelry. Remember to bargain in markets.

Cozumel's San Miguel and Playa del Carmen have decent shopping. Many cruise lines offer excursions to the huge resort of Cancún specifically for shoppers. In Calica and along the Costa Maya, opportunities are more limited although vendors are everywhere.

In Playa del Carmen, Avenida 5 and Puerto Antigua are the main shopping areas for handicrafts. Cozumel has a great flea market. Plaza del Sol is just a few minutes' walk from the pier. Duty-free shopping is available in Cancún – look for silver, gold, Kahlua liqueur, traditional Mexican arts and crafts and hand-rolled cigars.

Belize

Shopping is not spectacular and many goods are imported. Look for Maya-style pottery and slate carving; native Guatemalan handicrafts; Belizean art and music; Maria Sharps Habanero Salsa, a chili sauce that comes in three different strengths; Belizean rum or cane spirit. Don't buy black-coral or turtle-shell souvenirs – it is illegal, and encourages its depletion. Most products can be found in the Belize

⊘ Diving

At almost 300km (185 miles) long, the coral reef off Belize is second only to Australia's Great Barrier Reef and is a favorite location for scuba divers. Three of the four major atolls in the Western Hemisphere are located here, including Lighthouse Reef with its nearly perfectly circular and highly photographed, Blue Hole. The Hole itself is over 450ft (135 meters) deep. **Sea Sports Belize** (tel: 501-223 5505, www.seasportsbelize.com) offers trips to nearby spots as well as charter services to outer cayes and atolls.

Shopping Village, a local-style mall in Belize City, built with cruise passengers in mind.

Roatán (Honduras)

Hammocks, arts and crafts, wood-carvings and quilts are good buys. Shopping areas include Coxen Hole, the West End, French Harbor and Punta Gorda.

Costa Rica

There are street vendors everywhere, particularly in the tourist areas. Look for wooden items, including bowls, plates, cutting boards and boxes; leather bags, wallets and briefcases; woven bags; jewelry and handmade paper. Coffee and coffee liqueurs also make good souvenirs. Do not buy coral, tortoiseshell items, furs or alligator or lizard skins.

Isla Margarita (Venezuela)

Margarita is duty-free, so electronics, jewelry, cosmetics, perfumes, designer clothes and spirits are cheap. Bargain for jewelry and make sure it comes with a guarantee. The main shopping district is Porlamar, which is packed with duty-free outlets.

Caribbean arc

Grand Cayman

Good things to buy in Grand Cayman include jewelry, antiques, old maps, perfumes, cosmetics, gemstones, local paintings, rugs, sculpture and rum cakes. You'll find everything you need in George Town and volcanic gifts and gimmicks at Hell.

Jamaica

Local crafts include 'Annabella' boxes made of wood and painted or otherwise adorned by hand; pimento-filled Spanish jars; beautiful hand-embroidered linens with motifs of birds and flora; silk and cotton hand-painted or batiked in daring colors; wood carvings; paintings and excellent pottery/ceramics. Lignum vitae, an extremely hard and heavy wood, with a dark-to-black center and light-to-yellow edge, is used in a lot of the carvings, some excellent and it makes very useful and unusual chopping boards. Also look for Reggae to Wear clothing, Jamaican fragrances (White Witch, Pirate's Gold, Khus Khus, Jamaica Island Lyme and Jamaica Island Bay Rum) and handmade soaps in unusual fragrances (cerasee and mint, mint and bay, ortanique). A special favorite is Starfish Aromatic Oils' Blue Mountain coffee candle, which can permeate your kitchen with the aroma of freshly brewed coffee. Rums and liqueurs, reggae music, Blue Mountain coffee and cigars also make good souvenirs.

In Ocho Rios, visit the craft market on Main Street and shops on Pineapple Place. Harmony Hall has a good selection of the best island crafts. In Montego Bay, there are shops all along Gloucester Avenue.

SHORE ACTIVITIES

Florida

Fort Lauderdale

Excursions
Everglades swamp safaris by buggy, airboat and kayak; Butterfly World in Coconut Creek; dolphin 'encounters'; riverboat dinner cruises; a scenic Riverwalk, linking downtown attractions; shopping at Sawgrass Mills; day trips to the Bahamas; Stranahan House (museum); Delray Beach for historic buildings and cool restaurants; Morikami Museum (Japanese museum with tranquil gardens).

Best beaches
Hollywood, Dania Beach, Fort Lauderdale, Pompano Beach and Deerfield Beach all offer excellent facilities.

Watersports
For a look at the coral reefs contact **Sea Experience**, who have glass-bottomed boats and offer scuba diving and snorkeling, tel: 954-770 3483, www.seaxp.com.
Best Boat Club lets you dive, snorkel or waterski with powerboats, tel: 954-779 3866, www.fortlauderdaleboatrentals.com.
Action Sportfishing, tel: 954-423 8700, arranges fishing charters for all standards, www.actionsportfishing.com.

Key West

Excursions
Art galleries on Duval Street; street entertainment at sunset in Mallory Square; tall ships in the Historic Seaport; Ernest Hemingway's home & museum; golf; dolphin 'encounters'; day sailing trips.

Best beaches
The Fort Zachary Taylor State Historic Site beach is clean and shaded by pines. Smathers Beach is good for watersports.

Watersports
Dolphin encounters can be arranged with **Captain Seaweed Charters**, tel: 954-423 8700, www.actionsportfishing.com. The *Yankee Freedom II* provides daily ferry service from Key West to the Dry Tortugas National Park and Fort Jefferson, including lunch and snorkel gear, tel: 305-294 7009 or 800-634 0939. There are also many day sails and deep-sea fishing charters. For windsurfing and sailing, try **Sunset Watersports**, tel: 855-378 6386, www.sunsetwatersportskeywest.com.

Miami

Excursions
Miami Seaquarium; architecture in Coral Gables; shops and restaurants in Coconut Grove; Little Havana (Eighth Street) for the Cuban Museum and the El Credito cigar factory; watersports; fishing; beaches; walking tours of the Art Deco buildings in South Beach; the newly redesigned Zoo Miami; the animal park at Jungle Island.

Best beaches
South Beach is huge, with every facility under the sun from watersports to volleyball and rollerblading; there is a gay beach area at 12th Street. Haulover Beach Park has a nudist area. Hobie Beach and Windsurfer Beach are good for watersports. Homestead Bayfront Park is a more off-the-beaten-path option.

Watersports
For fishing trips try:
SailAway Yacht Charter Consultants, 9771 Wayne Avenue, Miami, FL 33157, tel: 800-724 5292, www.1800sailaway.com.
Day and week yacht charters.
Sailboards Miami, along beach, about 1 mile past the toll plaza at 2601 Brickell Avenue, Miami, tel: 305-892 8992, www.sailboardsmiami.com.
Windsurfing, kayaking, paddleboarding and kiteboarding.

Port Canaveral

Excursions
Merritt Island, home of Kennedy Space Center, a huge exhibit of the history of space travel with spectacular IMAX films and astronaut encounters. To see an actual launch, get a Launch Viewing Ticket through the KSC Visitor Complex, tel: 855-433 4210 or www.kennedyspacecenter.com. Walt Disney World at Orlando is an hour's drive, 0800 028 0778 in UK or 407-939-5277, https://disneyworld.disney.go.com from Florida. Merritt Island National Wildlife Refuge, tel: 321-861-5601, www.fws.gov, has numerous hiking trails. Shops and restaurants at Cocoa Village; also try deep-sea fishing.

Best beaches
Cocoa Beach is one of the most popular tourist areas, known for its clean beaches and seafood restaurants. Canaveral National Seashore is more remote, with 24 miles (29km) of wetlands offering good bird- and wildlife-watching.

Watersports
Watersports gear is available to hire from all the main beaches. Surfing, snorkeling, sailing and deep-sea fishing are all popular and there are several surf festivals during the year.

Tampa

Excursions
The waterfront, with its spectacular aquarium and Channelside

entertainment district, including an IMAX cinema and Pop City; historic Ybor City, once a Cuban settlement, with handsome architecture and great atmosphere; Salvador Dali Museum in nearby St Petersburg; Duck Tours (amphibious sightseeing vehicles seating around 28); Busch Gardens, one of Florida's main attractions; the Manatee and Aquatic Center at the zoo; Museum of Science and Technology, including the Gulf Coast Hurricane Chamber; canoeing on the Hillsborough River, alligators and all.

Best beaches
Clearwater Beach, famous for its soft sand and lined by smart hotels. Indian Rocks beach if you haven't got much time. St Pete's Beach for watersports.

Louisiana

New Orleans

Excursions
French Quarter for cafés, bars, galleries and markets; Jackson Square for historic buildings, museums, antiques, art galleries, perfume shops, sidewalk cafés and tearooms; French Market; Bourbon Street; New Orleans City Park; elegant homes in the Garden District; D-Day Museum; swamp adventures in the Bayou; steamboat cruises. If you're overnighting, don't miss the jazz and blues clubs.
Haunted History Tours, for voodoo, cemetery, vampire, Halloween and ghost tours. Tel: 504-861 2727; www.hauntedhistorytours.com.

Sports
Lake Pontchartrain is ideal for fishing, hiking and canoeing. The wider area of Pontchartrain Basin is known for its rivers, bayous, swamps and hardwood forests. There are several golf courses around the city.

Texas

Galveston and Houston

Excursions
Houston: Six Flags AstroWorld and WaterWorld theme parks; Splashtown water park; Space Center Houston; Houston Zoo; Museum District; shopping at The Galleria mall.
Galveston: day trips include the newly restored beach at 10th Street;

Victorian mansions, shops, restaurants and bars of the Strand district; Moody Gardens, a fabulous interactive natural history exhibition with designs by NASA; Haak vineyard; Big Reef Nature Park; local history at the Texas Seaport Museum.

Best beach
In Galveston, at 10th Street, there are sun-loungers, umbrellas, watersports and food vendors on the beach.

Mexico and Central America

Cozumel, Playa del Carmen and Puerto Costa Maya

Excursions
From All Three Ports: Coach or flightseeing excursions to Chichén Itzá, 100 miles (161km) west of Cancún, including a walking tour of the temples and pyramids; Tulum ruins (beautiful coastal location) and Xel-Ha Lagoon; Sian Kaían Biosphere Reserve, just south of Tulum; the Cobá Mayan ruins excursion includes a short hike; shopping trips to Cancún.
From Cozumel: Day trip around the island, including San Gervasio ruins deep in the jungle; Chankanab Nature Park with jungle trails, a botanical garden with more than 300 plant species; Archaeological Park; Cozumel Island Museum; El Cedral, the oldest Maya structure on Cozumel; Punta Celarain, a lighthouse with amazing views; Punta Sur ecological park with lagoon, mangrove jungles, white sand beaches and reefs and electric bikes for hire.
From Puerto Costa Maya: World class snorkeling and diving; off-road dune buggy jungle and beach safaris; Kohunlich and Chacchoben Maya ruins and museum.
From Playa del Carmen: Xcaret environmental/adventure park, built along caverns, tunnels and underground rivers for tubing, snorkeling, hiking, diving and more.

Best beaches
Cozumel: Playa San Francisco has a wide variety of watersports and restaurants. Also try Playa Mac, Playa del Sol, Playa Azul, Playa Palancar. Playa Chen Rio is quieter.
Puerto Costa Maya: There's a beach club right by the port, with facilities for everyone including the disabled.

Watersports
The Costa Maya is one of the Caribbean's best-known areas for snorkeling and scuba diving. Nearby is the beautiful white Jungle Beach Break.
From Cozumel: Spend the day exploring Chankanaab National Park on Cozumel Island or take the ferry over to Xel-Ha. Snorkeling trips at both destinations are widely available. Dive tours are offered to San Francisco and Palancar – two of the most popular dive sights on the island.
From Playa del Carmen: Reef snorkeling or boat trip to Akumal where there's a sunken Spanish ship.

Belize

Excursions
Belize City: Fort George, St John's Cathedral, Bliss Institute, Government House. Main attractions are outside the city: Altún Ha Maya site; Lamanai Maya site by boat up the New River, Community Baboon Sanctuary; Río Frio caves; Crooked Tree Wildlife Sanctuary; Belize River; manatee-spotting trips; swimming with sharks and rays; diving on the reef. Action Belize offers pre-bookable excursions and adventure on cruise ship days for independent travelers. Tel: 701-544 0214, www.actionbelize.com.

Belize World Heritage sites, such as the Blue Hole and the Barrier Reef, are easily accessible.

Ideal starting point for high adventure jungle and caving expeditions, especially cave tubing through 6 miles (10km) of river caves and abseiling over 300ft (91 meters) into the abyss.

Best beaches
Take a fast boat from Belize City to the Cayes. Ambergris Caye has facilities but is still unspoilt; Laughing Bird Caye is pretty and remote; Glover's Reef Atoll is a great picnic spot. If you are sailing with NCL, you will dock at Harvest Caye, the line's new private beach, with snorkeling, all other watersports, bars and restaurants.

Roatán (Honduras)

Excursions
A tour of unspoiled Roatán can include a visit to Garífuna fishing villages, the Tropical Treasure Bird Park, with its large colorful parrot

collection, Carambola Gardens, or Jonesville, a stilt village. Snorkeling and diving around the spectacular coral reef is popular, so is lazing on the beach. The Institute of Marine Sciences runs dolphin shows and encounters. Visitors can also see the Museum of Roatán, or hike the island's interior.

Best beaches
Tabyana Beach, a short drive from Coxen Hole, has beautiful white sand and easy access to the barrier reef.

Watersports
Barefoot Divers is a five-star PADI accredited dive company offering everything from snorkel rental and paddleboards to fully fledged dives, scheduled to fit in with cruise ship visits, Tel: 504-9967 3642, www.barefootdiversroatan.com.

Costa Rica

Excursions
Coastal tour with jungle scenery, handicraft shopping and lunch; rainforest aerial tramway; hiking in the Río Dante rainforest with a guide; canoe excursion along the Tortuguero Canal to spot wildlife; overnight tours to spot turtles (at the right time of year); white-water rafting; banana plantation visits; south to Cahuita National Park.

On the Pacific Coast, trips to Nicoya Peninsula; crocodile spotting near Jacó; visit to Manuel Antonio National Park.

Best beaches
Cahuita National Park borders the beaches that give access to the coastline's only coral reefs. Puerto Viejo, close to the town, is also a good bet for a day trip. Tortuguero, to the north, is only accessible by boat or plane; turtles, caimans and manatees can be spotted here. Barra del Colorado is best for fishing and has several luxurious fishing lodges.

Sports
Hiking, horse riding, white-water rafting, canoeing and golf can all be arranged. Hire scuba and snorkeling equipment on Cahuita beach.

Isla Margarita (Venezuela)

Excursions
Island tours, day trips to Canaima/ Angel Falls, longer trips to the Orinoco Delta, Parque del Agua water park for kids; Los Roques National Park; boats to Isla de Coche; Los Frailes islands; horse riding; boat trips.

Best beaches
Playa del Agua for facilities and a long, clean strip of sand; Coche Island; Moreno and El Yaque for windsurfing.

Watersports
For diving trips try **Scubadiving Margarita**, part of Scuba Schools International, tel: 412 1964 47, www.scubadivingmargarita.com. Windsurfing equipment for hire on Playa del Agua beach and at Moreno.

Horse-riding
For countryside hacks and beach rides, contact Macanao Ranch, tel: 0295 416 3584, email: margarita.island@gmail.com.

Other sports
Paragliding and ultralight aircraft are popular for sightseeing. There are bungee jumps at Playa del Agua and Parguito beaches.

Caribbean arc

Grand Cayman

Excursions
Relax on Seven Mile Beach, or see the volcanic rocks at Hell. Less than a mile away is the Cayman Turtle Farm. An island tour can also include a trip to Queen Elizabeth II Botanic Park or the Pedro St James historic monument. A boat trip that always gets booked up is to Stingray City to feed the stingrays.

Best beaches
Seven Mile Beach has everything – space, restaurants, watersports, snorkeling and clean sand.

Watersports
There are dozens of long-established dive operators; see www.divecayman.ky for a listing. The Cayman Islands has superb wall dives and wrecks. The newest wreck dive and snorkeling site, the USS *Kittiwake*, is a private reserve with a charge. Equipment for other sports can be rented by the day on Seven Mile Beach. Red Sail Sports can arrange any water sport you fancy and can be found at all major resorts on Grand

Cayman, tel: 877-506 6368, www.redsailcayman.com.

Golf
There are three golf courses: North Sound, Britannia and the 9-hole Blue Tip course for the exclusive use of Ritz Carlton guests.

Jamaica

Excursions
From Montego Bay: There are historic walking tours of the town, better known for duty-free shopping. There are also guided tours of the great houses: Rose Hall and Greenwood. **From Falmouth:** Take a relaxing river rafting trip along the Martha Brae and tour the Good Hope Great House. **From Ocho Rios**: One of the islands most visited attractions is Dunn's River Falls; you can tour the working Prospect Plantation or lunch at Harmony Hall, formerly a great house and now an art gallery and restaurant. Nature lovers can drive through lush Fern Gully or see the pretty Shaw Park Gardens, Coyaba River Garden and Museum, or take a rural cycling tour. East of Ocho Rios is Firefly, Noël Coward's beautiful house, open to the public. **From Port Antonio**: Take a tour of the town and spend half a day rafting down the Rio Grande.

Best beaches
Montego Bay Area: Doctor's Cave Beach, with its white sand and clear water, believed to be fed by mineral springs. Daily, 8.30am–6.30pm (charge), tel: 876-952 2566, www.doctorscavebathingclub.com. Rose Hall Beach Club: with volleyball, other games and watersports, two bars and restaurant, (charge), tel: 876-953 9982.
Falmouth Area: Half Moon Beach offers a perfectly shaped crescent of white sand and calm, clear water for a relaxing day on the beach.
Ocho Rios Area: James Bond Beach, Oracabessa. Tel: 876-975 3665, 9am–6pm, closed for clean-up on Mondays except public holidays (charge). Three magnificent white-sand beaches ring this private peninsula, 20 minutes from Ocho Rios, and on offer are watersports; jet ski safari, a restaurant/bar and marina facilities.
Port Antonio Area: Portland's beaches are incomparable; those at

is Firefly, Noël Coward's beautiful house, open to the public.

From Port Antonio: Take a tour of the town and spend half a day rafting down the Rio Grande.

Best beaches

Montego Bay Area: Doctor's Cave Beach, with its white sand and clear water, believed to be fed by mineral springs. Daily, 8.30am–6.30pm (charge), tel: 876-952 2566, www.doctorscavebathingclub.com. Rose Hall Beach Club: with volleyball, other games and watersports, two bars and restaurant, (charge), tel: 876-953 9982.

Falmouth Area: Half Moon Beach offers a perfectly shaped crescent of white sand and calm, clear water for a relaxing day on the beach.

Ocho Rios Area: James Bond Beach, Oracabessa. Tel: 876-975 3665, 9am–6pm, closed for clean-up on Mondays except public holidays (charge). Three magnificent white-sand beaches ring this private peninsula, 20 minutes from Ocho Rios, and on offer are watersports; jet ski safari, a restaurant/bar and marina facilities.

Port Antonio Area: Portland's beaches are incomparable; those at Frenchman's Cove and Dragons Bay are considered among the finest in the world. Boston Beach is popular for bathing and the waves are high enough for surfing.

Watersports

There are hire facilities at all the main beaches, including Doctor's Cave and James Bond Beach.

Horse-riding

Chukka Caribbean Adventures, based in Ocho Rios (tel: 876-619 1441, www.chukkacaribbean.com), has extensive polo facilities and also organizes tubing, rafting, ziplining and other adventures. Riding on the beach and in the sea is available for day visitors, but it is worth considering the environmental damage done to the reef by the horses' excrement, which increases nitrogen levels in the water causing algae to smother the coral.

Golf

Jamaica is home to many excellent courses, including: Cinnamon Hill at Rose Hall, Half Moon at Rose Hall, Sandals Golf and Country Club at Ocho Rios, SuperClubs Golf Club at Runaway Bay, SuperClubs Ironshore

Golf and Country Club at Montego Bay, The Tryall Club at Montego Bay and the White Witch Golf Course at Rose Hall. For details of all clubs and courses, see www.jamaicagolf.com. Book tee times well in advance, either through the ship's purser or directly.

TELECOMMUNICATIONS

Mexico and Central America

Cozumel, Playa del Carmen and Puerto Costa Maya

The country code is 52. The area code for Cozumel is 987; Playa del Carmen's is 984. Mexico's telephone company, Telmex, has installed Ladatel phones in all but the remotest spots in the country. To use one you'll need a phone card, available at newsstands and convenience stores for 30, 50 or 100 pesos. You can make both local and long-distance calls with these cards, if you have enough credit (shown automatically when you insert the card in the phone). Occasionally you'll even find a coin-operated machine that takes a peso or 50 centavos, but these are exclusively for local and reverse-charge calls.

There are numerous internet cafés in both Playa del Carmen and Cozumel.

Belize

The country code is **501**. Belize Telecommunications Limited (BTL) provides service between Belize and the United States and Canada. The BTL main offices are located at the corner of Albert and Church streets in Belize City and the corner of Princess Margaret Drive and St Thomas Street. Phone cards are available at numerous locations. There is an internet center in the Belize Tourism Village.

Roatán (Honduras)

The dialing code for Honduras is **504**. You can dial direct from some of the larger hotels and from payphones in Coxen Hole.

Café Costa Rica

The dialing code is **506**. Some payphones support IDD. Dial 001 and then the country code. Public phones require a coin or card deposit before dialing a direct access number. Calls from hotels are very expensive.

Long-distance access numbers include: **BT**: 167; **Canada Telecom**:

161; **AT&T Direct**: 0-800 0 114 114; **US AT&T**: 114; US **MCI**: 162; **US Sprint**: 163.

There are cafés with WiFi hotspots in most major resorts.

Isla Margarita (Venezuela)

The international dialing code is **58** and the area code for Margarita is **295**. Most phones can be used to dial direct internationally; buy a CANTV *tarjeta* (phone card) to use a public phone. There are cafés with WiFi in Porlamar and Playa del Agua.

Caribbean arc

Grand Cayman

Modern telephone service is available 24 hours a day, with international direct dialing. Flow (www.discoverflow.co)and Digicel (www.digicelgroup.com).

The area code for the Cayman Islands is **345**. CardPhone service is now available at select locations on all three islands. Pre-paid phone cards come in values of CI$10 upwards. WiFi internet access is widely available in hotels, cafés and many bars.

Jamaica

Jamaica's dialing code is **876**. Direct international telephone service operates 24 hours a day. There are internet cafés and calling offices in Montego Bay, Ocho Rios and all major towns. Phone cards are available for calling overseas or locally. Cell phone service is available through Digicel (www.digiceljamaica.com) and Flow (www.discoverflow.co).

TOURIST OFFICES

Florida

Information is available from various outlets in Florida and from:

In the US

Visit Florida, 2540 W. Executive Center Circle, Suite 200, Tallahassee, FL 32301

Tel: 888-735 2872

www.visitflorida.com

Fort Lauderdale

In the UK

Greater Fort Lauderdale Convention & Visitors Bureau, c/o Hills Balfour, 58 Southwark Bridge Road, London, SE1 0AS

Tel: 020-7593 1700

In Fort Lauderdale

Tel: 813-223 2752
www.visittampabay.com

Louisiana

New Orleans
New Orleans Convention and Visitors Bureau, 2020 St Charles Avenue, New Orleans, LA 70130
Tel: 800-672 6124
The New Orleans Welcome Center 701 Canal St, New Orleans, LA 70130
www.neworleans.com

Texas

Galveston
In the US
Texas State Board of Tourism, PO Box 141009, Austin, TX 78714-1009
Tel: 512-463 2000
In Galveston
Galveston Island Visitor Information Center, 2328 Broadway, Galveston, TX 77550
Tel: 888-425 4753
www.traveltex.com

Mexico and Central America

Cozumel, Playa del Carmen and Puerto Costa Maya
Mexican Government Tourist Offices (MGTO) are located:
In the UK
4th Floor Westpoint, 33–34 Warple Way, London W3 0RG
Tel: 020 7488 9392
Email: uk@visitmexico.com
In the US
152 Madison Avenue, Suite 1800, New York, NY 10016
Tel: 212-308 2110
2401 West 6th St 4th floor, Los Angeles, California 90057
Tel: 213-739 3663
1399 SW 1st. Ave. 3rd. Floor Miami, FL. 33130
Tel: 786-621 2909
In Canada
Suite 658-409 De Granville Street, Vancouver, B.C. V6C 1T2
Tel: 604-669 2845
1 Place Ville Marie, Suite 1931, Montreal, Quebec H3B 2C3
Tel: 514-871 1052
In the Yucatán
The State of Yucatán has a tourist office at Mérida airport (tel: 994 61300) and another in downtown Mérida (corner of calles 60 and 57, tel: 999-925 5186). In Campeche, the office is on Avenida Ruis Cortinex in the Plaza Moch Cuoch (tel: 981-127 3300, www.campeche.travel). For

A novel way to predict the weather (Tina's Hostel, Belize).

Chetumal tourist office, tel: 983 20855.
Websites
www.visitmexico.com
www.divecozumel.com

Belize
Belize Tourism Board, PO Box 325, 64 Regent Street, Belize City
Tel: 800-624 0686/501-227 2420
www.travelbelize.org

Roatán (Honduras)
The best information is provided online by independent websites. Try:
www.roatanonline.com
www.roatanet.com
www.travel-roatan.com

Costa Rica
Costa Rican Tourism Board (ICT: Instituto Costarricense de Turismo), East side of the Juan Pablo II Bridge, over General Canas Highway, 7771000 San José
Tel: 506-2299 5800
www.visitcostarica.com

Isla Margarita (Venezuela)
www.venezuela.embassyhomepage.com has some tourist information, as does https://insel-margarita-venezuela. de but be fully informed about the security situation before considering travel in mainland Venezuela.

Caribbean arc

Grand Cayman

In Canada
1200 Bay Street, Suite 1101, Toronto, ON M5R 2A5
Tel: 800-263 5805/416-485 1550
In the UK

Cayman Islands Department of Tourism, 4th Floor, Dover House, 34 Dover Street, London W1S 4NG
Tel: 020-7491 7771
In the US
Empire State Building, 350 Fifth Ave, Suite 2720, New York, NY 10018
Tel: 212-889 9009
In Grand Cayman
Cayman Islands Department of Tourism, PO Box 134, Grand Cayman, Cayman Islands, KY1-9000
Tel: 345-949 0623
There is a tourist information office at Royal Watler Port, just north of North Terminal in George Town Harbor.
Websites
www.caymanislands.ky
www.caymanislands.co.uk

Jamaica

In Canada
303 Eglinton Avenue E, Suite 200, Toronto, Ontario, M4P 1L3
Tel: 416-482 7850
Toll-free: 800-465 2624
In the UK
1–2 Prince Consort Road, London, SW7 2BZ
Tel: 020 7225 9090
In the US
5201 Blue Lagoon Drive, Suite 670, Miami, FL 33126
Tel: 305-665 0557
In Jamaica
Tourism Centre, Montego Bay Convention Centre, Rose Hall, St. James
Tel: 876-952 4425
64 Knutsford Boulevard, Kingston 5
Tel: 876-929 9200
Website
www.visitjamaica.com

A-Z EASTERN CARIBBEAN

ACCOMMODATIONS

To begin with **The Bahamas**, accommodations in that destination range from intimate inns and cottages to huge resort and casino complexes.

Cuba-way, the hotels in Old Havana are mostly renovated colonial palaces and mansions and are delightful, atmospheric places to stay. Further afield in the city there are many modern four- to five-star international hotels popular with a business clientele; while at the other end of the scale, licensed Cuban families rent out their spare bedrooms, offering bed and breakfast and often an evening meal – a good budget option allowing you to see another side of Cuba.

There are some delightful places to stay in the Zona Colonial – aka the historic center – of Santo Domingo, **Dominican Republic**, in converted old mansions. Hotels in the rest of the city are mainly designed for business travelers, although they also offer casinos, nightclubs and discos. The main beach resort area of Punta Cana specializes in all-inclusive hotels, huge, sprawling affairs, many with their own golf courses or marinas; but these are isolated from the rest of the country. The Samaná peninsula still has a range of small boutique hotels and guest houses on the beach, although larger, all-inclusive hotels have now been built as well. The Puerto Plata region of the north coast was where the first all-inclusive resorts sprang up, but there are also many independent hotels, particularly in Cabarete, the windsurfing capital. Up in the mountains, there are a few charming, rural hotels and guest houses which specialize in adventure tourism and provide a break from the beach.

In **Puerto Rico**, within the San Juan metro area, the major hotel resorts generally have casinos, live entertainment, discotheques, restaurants, bars and sports facilities. For a lot less you can stay in one of a number of guest houses and smaller places throughout Condado or Ocean Park.

The **US Virgin Islands** carry a wide choice of lodgings, from small, family-run guest houses to large hotels which are part of international chains. The cheaper places to stay are situated in town or in the countryside, while the expensive hotels are to be found on the beach. There are also plenty of villas and apartments for self-catering.

Hotels on **St-Martin/Sint Maarten** are not cheap, especially during the peak winter season. There are several large resort hotels, mostly on the Dutch side, and many of them have casinos. Both the French and Dutch sides have small guest houses, apartments and villas, which can be rented at weekly or monthly rates, but be aware that many properties on the French side were destroyed by Hurricane Irma in 2017.

ARRIVING BY SEA

The Bahamas

Nassau: Ships line up at the huge dock in Nassau's center, a short walk to the shops and the Straw Market. Festival Place on Prince George Wharf has information on tours and transportation, as well as shops and places to eat and drink. **Grand Bahama Island**: Ships dock at the Lucayan Harbour Cruise Facility, which lies west of Freeport. There are taxis but no public buses at the port.

Cuba

Cruise ships dock at the waterfront terminal in the heart of Old Havana, a short walk from the city center. Some cruise lines are now offering other stops around the island, including Cienfuegos, jumping off points for Trinidad (a Unesco World Heritage Site), Isla de la Juventud (a former prison island), Santiago de Cuba (the island's second city and musical capital of the east) and Cayo Saetía (a small island with beaches and a wildlife reserve).

Dominican Republic

Cruise ships dock either side of the river by the colonial zone in Santo Domingo, in the port at La Romana, at the marina at Casa de Campo and at the dock in Santa Bárbara de Samaná. Carnival Corporation's ships also dock at the new Amber Cove facility on the north coast, near Puerto Plata.

Puerto Rico

Ships dock at the port in Old San Juan, near the historic center.

US Virgin Islands

St Thomas: Cruise ships dock at Havensight, where there are plenty of shops, or Crown Bay. On busy days some cruise ships operate tenders straight into Charlotte Amalie. **St John**: Passengers arrive by tender into National Park Dock. **St Croix**: Big ships moor in Frederiksted, smaller vessels in Christiansted.

St-Martin/Sint Maarten

On the French side, ships tender passengers to the center of Marigot's seafront. On the Dutch side, the cruise pier is at Pointe Blanche, about 1 mile (2km) from the center of Philipsburg. On busy days, some ships tender passengers to the Little Pier in the town center.

CALENDAR OF EVENTS

The Bahamas

April: Bahamas Heritage Festival
May: Eight Mile Rock International Cultural Festival, Grand Bahama
June: Eleuthera Pineapple Festival
September: Bahamas Atlantis Superboat Challenge (international powerboating)
November: One Bahamas Music and Heritage Festival
December/January: Junkanoo; Bahamas International Film Festival

Cuba

January: New Year's Day and Anniversary of the Revolution
July: Carnival in Santiago
August: Carnival in Havana
October: International Ballet Festival
December: Havana International Jazz Festival and New Latin American Cinema

Dominican Republic

January: New Year and Day of the Vírgen de la Altagracia
February: Carnival
April: Holy Week
July: Merengue Festival in Santo Domingo with gastronomy festival
September: Merengue Festival in Sosúa
November: Merengue Festival in Puerto Plata

Puerto Rico

Each town has its patron saint's day, which is a celebration not to be missed. See http://seepuertorico.com for a list of saints' days. The biggest celebrations are on 24 April during the St John the Baptist patron saint festival in San Juan. Also worth a look:
6 January: Three Kings' Day
January: Fiestas de la Calle San Sebastián, San Juan
February: Coffee harvest festival
March: Rum Festival
May: Heineken Jazz festival

US Virgin Islands

6 December–January: St Croix Festival
March: International Rolex Regatta, St Thomas
17 March: St Patrick's Day Festival, St Croix
April: St Croix Food and Wine Experience
April/May: St Thomas Carnival
July: (week of the 4th) St John's Carnival
October: St Croix Jazz and Caribbean Music and Arts Festival

St-Martin/Sint Maarten

February: Lent Carnival St-Martin
April: Carnival Sint Maarten
May: Black Heritage Week and Abolition Day, St-Martin
14 July: Bastille Day
July: Victor Schoelcher Grand Case Festival
11 November: St-Martin Day/ Discovery Day

EATING OUT

In **The Bahamas**, you'll discover that fish turns up for dinner, lunch and even breakfast, with snapper and grouper being the most common. Seafood specialties include turtle steaks, crayfish, grouper, conch (pronounced 'conk') and the delicious clawless Bahamian lobster. Among the top favorites are cracked conch, for which the conch is pounded until tender, battered and deep-fried; and steamed conch (cooked with sautéed onions, peppers, thyme, tomatoes and maybe okra or carrots). Conch chowder is a rich, spicy soup with vegetables; conch salad contains minced raw conch, marinated in lime juice, and mixed with chopped onions and peppers.

Most of **Cuba**'s state-run restaurants tend to serve bland, international fare rather than Cuban Creole cuisine, although they are improving. Menus can seem monotonous and some ingredients can become unavailable due to harvest or transport difficulties. Fried chicken (*pollo frito*) turns up all the time, while the most common lunch snack in cafés is the ham and cheese sandwich (*sandwich de jamón y queso*).

For an authentic Cuban meal, try the private restaurants or *paladares*, which traditionally consist of a few tables in somebody's home (legally, they can have a maximum of just 12 covers), and have a more congenial atmosphere than state-run restaurants.

The local cuisine of the **Dominican Republic** (*comida criolla*) has its roots in the Spanish colonizers, the Taíno original inhabitants and the African slaves brought in to work the plantations, but there are also influences from later immigrants: traders from the Middle East, businessmen from China and, of course, modern tourists.

The national dish is *bandera dominicana* (Dominican flag), consisting of meat, beans and rice, accompanied by *tostones or fritos verdes* (fried green banana) and salad. There is a huge variety of delicious tropical fruit, much of which you will find on the breakfast table or in fresh fruit juices. Dominicans have a very sweet tooth, having become accustomed to an unlimited supply of sugar, so you may want to treat their desserts and sweets with care.

The local specialties of **Puerto Rico** include *frijoles negros* (black bean soup), *arroz con pollo* (chicken with rice), *asopao* (a gumbo soup) and *lechón* (roast suckling pig). The local rum is excellent.

In the **USVI**, locally produced fruit and veggies, and fresh seafood provide the raw materials for island cooks who create anything from bullfoot soup (what it sounds like) and *fungi* (cornmeal pudding), to French food.

On both sides of **St-Martin**, traditional French cooking and spicy Caribbean cuisine are available with excellent seafood; but the French side tends to have more gourmet restaurants, and offers the option of a short hop across to Anguilla for lunch. On the Dutch side, options include Dutch favorites such as pea soup and sausages and Indonesian *rijstaffel*, a banquet of up to 40 dishes.

GETTING AROUND

The Bahamas

By car

Driving is on the left and an international license is required. Most car-rental firms are based at the airport but the following have other offices: KSR Rent-a-Car, on Queen's Highway near the harbor, Freeport, tel: 242-351 5737, http://ksrrentacar. biz; Avis, downtown Nassau and Paradise Island, www.avis.com.bs. Alternatively, hire a scooter.

By taxi

You can call a cab or hail one on the street. Cab stands are also located at most large hotels. Cabs are metered and surcharges often apply for more than two persons and extra luggage.

By bus

Buses are also called 'jitneys' and run daily until around 8pm. They are reliable, but can be crowded.

By air

Internal flights are operated by Bahamasair (tel: 242-300 8359 https://bahamasair.com, which links islands in the chain using a 'hub and spoke' system via Nassau, which means all flights start and finish in Nassau. Current domestic routes out of Nassau include Grand Bahama, Abaco, Eleuthera, Exuma, Crooked Island, Acklins, Mayaguana, Inagua, San Salvador, Long Island and Cat Island. For a group of people, private charter can be cost effective and there are plenty of light aircraft charter companies; try Sky Bahamas, tel: 242-702 2600, www.skybahamas.net or Golden Wings Charter, tel: 242-377 0039, www.goldenwingscharter. com.

By ferry

Inter-island ferries are operated by Bahamas Ferries (tel: 242-323 2166, www.bahamasferries.com) from Potter's Cay ferry terminal in Nassau to Spanish Wells and Harbour Island; Governor's Harbour, Eleuthera; Fresh Creek, Andros; Current, Eleuthera; George Town, Exuma. Mail boats carry passengers from Nassau to Freeport.

Cuba

By car

Cuban highways and secondary roads are fairly well maintained, but look out for the potholes and animals. Cubans are ever helpful with directions – even though they are often vague when it comes to

distances. Road signs are scarce. Rental cars are expensive and visitors should take out maximum insurance cover to allow for scams on the part of the hire-company staff.

Be sure to check the car carefully for damage, including scratches. Draw attention to anything you find, and insist any damages are noted on the paperwork. Cars can be hired through major hotels in Havana and other towns. The main rental companies include: Havanautos, www. havanautos.com; Rex, www.rexcarrental. com.

It is not worthwhile renting a car if you've only got a day – distances are great and there is plenty to see in Havana itself.

By taxi

Private taxis are a good way to see Havana. Set a price before you go and remember that an old American gas-guzzler will cost more. Taxis all over the island (which includes some very long distances) are available from www.taxincuba.com. You can tour Havana and other cities in vintage cars (with driver) via Old Car Tours, www.oldcartours.com. There are also coco-taxis, little round, yellow, two-seater motorbike taxis, and bici-taxis, rickshaw-type vehicles, drawn by bicycles.

By bus

City buses, known as *guaguas*, are often crowded and uncomfortable. In some towns, buses are horse-drawn and foreigners are not encouraged to take them. Long-distance bus services are provided by Víazul with a fleet of comfortable and efficient air-conditioned buses (www.viazul. com).

By train

Trains cover the whole island, but they are slow, crowded, uncomfortable and break down frequently. Tickets have to be bought in advance and there is a complicated queuing process. Train travel is not recommended.

By air

If short of time, this is the best way of getting from one end of the island to the other or to remote beach resorts. Cubana (www.cubana. cu) has regular scheduled flights from Havana to 13 Cuban cities. Aerogaviota (www.aerogaviota.com)

operates charter flights to Cayo Largo, Cayo Coco, Cayo Santa María and other popular destinations. Tickets can be bought in hotels.

Inter-island links

Bahamasair flies from Nassau to Havana on most days. Other scheduled flights operate from Kingston, Montego Bay, Nassau and Pointe-a-Pitre. There are dozens of flights between Miami and Cuba.

Dominican Republic

By car

A car can be useful if you are staying on and have time to get used to the vagaries of Dominican driving, but organized tours are better for short visits. Car-rental companies are available at all the airports. You must have a valid license from your country of residence or an international license.

By taxi

Taxis are available at the port and at hotels. Radio taxis are reliable. For long distances negotiate a fare first. Motorcyclists (motoconchos) also offer a taxi service, but safety standards are very low. In Samaná there are rickshaws drawn by cyclists.

By bus

In Santo Domingo there are buses for commuters covering the main arterial routes. There are also several long-distance bus companies operating on routes to different parts of the country, which are efficient and good value. In rural areas you can find guaguas, usually minibuses or pick-ups, or carros, also known as públicos, which are cars operating on set routes.

By rail

A 16-stop Metro line crosses Santo Domingo, running for 15km (10 miles) north-south until it nears the coast, then turning west. A second line runs east-west and is currently being extended.

By air

There are 11 airports around the country, of which the main four used for international flights are Santo Domingo, Punta Cana, Samaná and Puerto Plata. There are plans afoot to make Punta Cana a point of entry to the US, with immigration carried out at the airport to avoid waiting in line when arriving in the USA. Charter services are available from Colonial Tours, www.colonialtours.com.do.

Inter-island links

A regular ferry service operates between Santo Domingo and Puerto Rico, sailing three times a week (ferriesdelcaribe.com).

PUERTO RICO

By car

A car is a good idea if you are staying on, but not necessary for a day visit. Most car rental companies are based at Condado, a 10-minute taxi ride from the port. Try Charlie Car Rental, tel: 787-728 2418 or 800-289 1227 (US), www.charliecars.com.

By taxi

Taxis wait at the port and can be found all over the city and hailed on the street. They are metered and charge extra for things like suitcases. Cruise passengers are often seen as gullible targets for an increased fare.

By bus

Local city buses are called *guaguas*; all small yellow trolleys run around the old town and are free.

By rail

The Tren Urbano works with the public bus system and covers most of the Metro area, running daily 5.30am–11.30pm.

Inter-island links

San Juan airport is a major international hub. International flights are operated by American Eagle, British Airways, Continental, Copa, Delta, Iberia, JetBlue, LIAT, Spirit Airlines, United, US Airways and Virgin Atlantic.

Local airlines include American Eagle, Air Flamenco and Vieques Air Link, and they have offices either at the Luis Muñoz Marin International Airport or the Isla Grande Airport. There are daily American Eagle flights between San Juan and Ponce. Air Flamenco flies to Culebra and St Thomas from Fajardo and San Juan. Some charter or inter-island flights leave from the Isla Grande Airport.

US Virgin Islands

By car

Driving is on the left. A US driver's license is valid in the USVI. Vehicles to rent range from a saloon to a jeep.
St Thomas: Budget, tel: 340-776 5774, 800-626 4516, www.budgetstt.com; Dependable Car Rental, tel: 340-774 2253, toll-free: 800-522 3076, www.dependablecar.com
St Croix: Avis, tel: 340-778 9355; Olympic Rent-a-Car, tel: 340-718 3000.
St John: St John Car Rental, tel: 340-776 6103.

By taxi

Taxis can be picked up at the cruise terminals in St Croix and St John. In St Thomas, taxis tend to be shared minibuses or jeeps with fixed fares. Fares are published by the Virgin Islands Taxi Association, but you should verify rates before boarding.

Taxi companies include:
St Thomas: VI Taxi Association, tel: 340-693 7530, www.vitaxi.com.
St Croix: St Croix Taxi Association, tel: 340-778 1088 at the airport, www.stcroixtaxi.com.

By bus

There are regular bus services on St Thomas, St John and St Croix; look for the Vitran bus stop signs. On St Croix buses run every half-hour between Christiansted and Frederiksted (17 miles/27km).

By ferry

From St Thomas (Charlotte Amalie) to St Croix, contact Smith's Ferry (tel: 340-775 7292, www.smithsferryservices.com). From St Thomas (Red Hook or Charlotte Amalie) to St John (Cruz Bay) contact Transportation Services and Varlack Ventures (tel: 340-776 6412, www.varlack-ventures.com). Other ferry schedules can be found on www.vinow.com.

By air

There are airports on St Thomas and St Croix. You can fly between the USVI on Cape Air (tel: 340-227 3247, www.flycapeair.com).

Inter-island links

There are regular ferry services from St Thomas and St John to Tortola in the BVI with Road Town Fast Ferry, tel: 340-777 2800, www.roadtownfastferry.com; and Inter Island Boat Services, tel: 340-776

6597, www.interislandboatservices.com). Local airlines link the USVI with nearby islands: Puerto Rico, the BVI, Anguilla and St-Martin. Airlines: Seaborne Airlines (www.seaborneairlines.com), Cape Air (www.capeair.com), LIAT (www.liat.com), American Eagle (www.aa.com).

St-Martin/Sint Maarten

By car

Driving is on the right. Foreign licenses are accepted. Car-rental companies operating on the island include:
Paradise Car Rental, Airport Boulevard 38, Simpson Bay, tel: 599-545 3737, www.paradisecarrental-sxm.com.

By taxi

Taxis are available in the centers of both towns. Wait either at the pier or where the tenders drop off. There are no meters, but there are fixed charges so check the price before you start.

By bus

Buses travel regularly from 6am to midnight between Philipsburg and Marigot, as well as on other principal routes. Ask at the tourist office about island tours by minibus.

Inter-island links

Juliana airport is one of the busiest in the region and, in addition to a large number of long-haul flights, there are good connections with all the other Caribbean islands from the Dominican Republic down the chain to Trinidad and Tobago. Inter-island airlines include: Winair, tel: 866 466 0410, www.fly-winair.com; and LIAT, tel: 888-844 5428, www.liat.com. There is a small airport on the French side too: L'Espérance, at Grand Case, although this is closed at the time of writing following hurricane damage in 2017.There are frequent ferries linking the island with its immediate neighbors: Anguilla, St-Barthélemy and Saba. A ferry from Blowing Point, Anguilla, crosses to Marigot about every 30 minutes (7am–7pm, 20-minute journey time, passport required, departure tax payable in addition to fare). There is also a less frequent ferry from Anguilla to Philipsburg (tel: 264-497 6665). Numerous boat owners offer charters and ferry services, almost like hiring a taxi; try Link, www.link.ai. The Edge connects St Maarten with Saba on Wednesdays, Fridays and Sundays (tel: 599-416 2246, www.seasaba.com). Great Bay Express operates from Bobby's Marina, Philipsburg, to Gustavia, tel: 599-520 5015, www.greatbayferry.com.

MONEY MATTERS

The Bahamas

The unit of currency is the Bahamian dollar at par with the US dollar. These currencies are used interchangeably. Credit cards are widely accepted.

Cuba

Cuba has two currencies: the peso Cubano (Cuban peso, CUP), divided into 100 centavos, and the peso convertible (CUC) at par with the US dollar. US dollars are not legal tender but are widely accepted, with change given in CUC. Foreigners are expected to use CUC most of the time, though, and will be charged in CUC for all accommodations, most food, and transport.

You can change US dollars into CUC at Government licensed Cadeca booths or banks. Credit cards issued outside the US are accepted in some, but not many tourist outlets. Most bank branches open Mon–Fri 8.30am–3pm. You can expect long queues at the bank; if you are arriving in Havana by ship, it is far better to use the exchange booths at the cruise terminal.

Dominican Republic

The currency is the Dominican peso (RD$), divided into 100 cents. Banks will give you a better exchange rate than hotels. Credit cards are widely accepted. Most banks have ATMs.

Puerto Rico

The currency is the US dollar. Credit cards are widely accepted and there are ATMs at banks in Old San Juan.

US Virgin Islands

The currency is the US dollar. There are ATMs at the dock in Frederiksted

on St Croix and in Charlotte Amalie, St Thomas. All major credit cards are accepted on the main islands.

St-Martin/Sint Maarten

The official currency is the euro on the French side and the Antillean guilder or florin on the Dutch side, but US dollars are also universally accepted. Normal banking hours are Mon–Fri 8.30am–3pm. Several banks have ATMs.

POSTAL SERVICES

The Bahamas

Post offices on Nassau/Paradise Island are located at Cable Beach, Carmichael Road, Clarence A. Bain, Elizabeth Estates, Fox Hill, Grants Town, Nassau International Airport and Shirley Street. In Freeport the post office is downtown, on Explorer's Way. Main post offices usually open Mon–Fri 8.30am–5.30pm and Sat 8.30am–12.30pm.

Cuba

Every rural town has a post office, and major cities have a central post office with municipal branches.

Mail to Europe and the Americas arrives a month or more after posting, even when sent via airmail.

Dominican Republic

The postal service is very slow and the mailboxes are unreliable. It is better to pay a little extra for *entrega especial* (special delivery), for which post offices have a separate window.

Puerto Rico

There are post offices in Old San Juan and in Hato Rey. Hotels also sell stamps. Two-day Priority Mail service is available and overnight documents can be sent via Federal Express. United Parcel Service and DHL also have offices here.

US Virgin Islands

Post offices can be found in the main towns of the three islands as well as in smaller towns such as Frederiksted.

St-Martin/Sint Maarten

In Marigot, the main post office is on Rue de la Liberté, with branches at Baie Nettlé, Howell Center, Grand Case and Quartier d'Orléans.

The Philipsburg post office is behind the Landsradio building, in the Pondfill section of town, between Loodsteeg and Market Street, with another branch at Juliana airport.

PUBLIC HOLIDAYS

The Bahamas

1 January: New Year's Day
March/April: Good Friday; Easter Monday
May/June: Whit Monday
June: (1st Friday) Labour Day
10 July: Independence Day
August: (1st Monday) Emancipation Day
12 October: National Heroes Day
1 November: Bahamas Day
25 December: Christmas Day

Cuba

1 January: Liberation day
1 May: Labour Day
25–27 July: Revolution Day celebrations
8 October: Death of Che Guevara
10 October: Beginning of the War of Independence
25 December: Christmas Day
In addition to these official public holidays, there are innumerable other important dates which are commemorated, including:
28 January: Death of José Martí (1895)

Dominican Republic

1 January: New Year's Day
6 January: Three Kings' Day
21 January: Our Lady of Altagracia
26 January: Birthday of Juan Pablo Duarte, founding father
27 February: Independence Day
March/April: Good Friday
1 May: International Labor Day
May: Corpus Christi
16 August: Restoration Day
24 September: Our Lady of Las Mercedes
12 October: Columbus Day
6 November: Constitution Day
25 December: Christmas Day

Puerto Rico

1 January: New Year's Day
6 January: Three Kings' Day
11 January: Eugenio María de Hostos' Birthday
January (3rd Monday): Martin Luther King Jr Day
February (3rd Monday): Washington's birthday
22 March: Emancipation Day
March/April: Good Friday
16 April: Jose de Diego's birthday
May (last Monday): Memorial Day
4 July: US Independence Day
July (3rd Monday): Luis Muñoz Rivera Day
25 July: Commonwealth Constitution Day
27 July: Dr José Celso Barbosa Day
September (1st Monday): Labor Day
October (2nd Monday): Columbus Day
11 November: Veterans' Day
19 November: Discovery of Puerto Rico Day
November: (4th Thursday) Thanksgiving Day
24 December: Christmas Eve
25 December: Christmas Day

US Virgin Islands

1 January: New Year's Day/Three Kings' Day
6 January: Martin Luther King Day
February: (3rd Monday) Presidents' Day
31 March: Transfer Day
March/April: Good Friday; Easter Monday
20 June: Organic Act Day
3 July: Emancipation Day
4 July: Independence Day
23 July: Supplication Day
1 November: Liberty Day
November: (third Thursday) Thanksgiving Day
25 December: Christmas Day
26 December: Boxing Day

St-Martin/Sint Maarten

Sint Maarten

1 January: New Year's Day
March/April: Good Friday/Easter Sunday/Easter Monday
29 April: Jouvert Jump-up
30 April: Queen's Birthday
1 May: Labour Day
June: Ascension Day
June: Whit Sunday (Pentecost)
11 November: St Maarten Day
15 December: Kingdom Day
25 December: Christmas Day
26 December: second day of Christmas

St-Martin

1 January: New Year's Day
March/April: Good Friday/Easter Sunday/Easter Monday
1 May: Labour Day
8 May: VE Day
June: Ascension Day
June: Whit Monday
14 July: Bastille Day/Fête Nationale
21 July: Schoelcher Day
15 August: Feast of the Assumption
1 November: All Saints' Day
11 November: St-Martin Day/Armistice Day
25 December: Christmas Day
26 December: second day of Christmas

SHOPPING

The Bahamas

With no sales tax and low tariffs, the Bahamas can be a bargain-hunter's delight. Some merchants sell imported goods at prices 30 to 50 percent lower than in the US, but compare the prices of goods at home before you go.

Bay Street in Nassau offers the biggest and best selection of shops. For fine china, crystal and figurines, visit Little Switzerland and John Bull. Several stores, like Colombian Emeralds, sell fine gems. For guaranteed Bahamian-made goods, try Bahamian Tings (cards, artwork and pottery) and The Plait Lady (strawwork). Balmain Antiques sells fabulous old maps of the Caribbean.

Finally, there is the open-air straw market selling hand-woven goods. Bargain here, but not at other Bay Street establishments.

Cuba

Cigars and rum are two of the best gifts to take home from a trip to Cuba – Cohiba is one of the more famous cigar brands. Note that cigars cannot be taken into the US. Cuban coffee is also excellent; Cubita, Turquina and Hola are the best brands. Also look for Cuban music CDs and pre-Revolution books and magazines.

Dominican Republic

The Zona Colonial in Santo Domingo has plenty of shopping opportunities for handicrafts made from leather, wood or horn, as well as baskets, pottery, embroidery and cotton clothing. Amber and larimar jewelry are local specialties and there is a wide variety of artwork – although much of it is heavily influenced by Haitian naïf art and you need to go to a gallery to find the best Dominican painters. Dominican cigars and rum are of high quality, valued internationally, while local coffee and cocoa is also good. CDs of the local merengue or other Latin music styles are widely available, from the latest hits to old classics. There are plenty of shops at the new Amber Cove port, too, selling local handicrafts as well as duty free items.

Puerto Rico

The more upmarket shopping areas tend to be concentrated in the Old City and the Condado. Old San Juan has more of a boutique atmosphere of the two. Plaza de Las Américas is the Caribbean's largest shopping mall, in Hato Rey. Puerto Rico is a good place to find interesting jewelry, arts and crafts, cigars, music, leather goods, wooden masks and designer clothes.

US Virgin Islands

The USVI enjoy a duty and sales tax-free status so that most things are 20–50 percent cheaper than on the mainland. Expect big crowds when there are a lot of ships in port. **St Thomas** has the widest choice of duty-free shopping with a large proportion in Charlotte Amalie; Havensight Mall by the cruise terminal and Red Hook on the east coast are shopping malls packed with outlets selling jewelry, watches, cameras, spirits and other duty-free goods. St Thomas also has a selection of handicraft outlets.

St Croix's King's Alley Walk is a shopping area in Christiansted. In St Croix Leap in the west, there are some excellent wood carvers. **St John** has a variety of local arts and crafts. The most popular areas are Mongoose Junction and Wharfside Village in Cruz Bay.

St-Martin/Sint Maarten

The French side is best for designer clothes, perfumes, chocolate, cigars and wine; good bargains on the Dutch side include duty-frees, electronics and spirits. For duty-free goods head for Front Street, Philipsburg, and rue de la République and Marina Porte la Royale, Marigot.

SHORE ACTIVITIES

The Bahamas

Excursions

Some of Nassau's and Paradise Island's attractions include: Government House; Parliament Square and Fort Charlotte; Pirates Museum; Atlantis Resort (special day rates for cruise passengers); Botanical Gardens; and dolphin encounters. In Grand Bahama: Garden of the Groves; snorkeling and diving off Deadman's Reef.

Best beaches

Arawak Cay for peace and quiet; Paradise Island for watersports and the big hotels.

Watersports

Everything is available here, from Hartley's Underwater Walk (wearing a dive helmet) to snorkeling, sailing, powerboating and windsurfing. For an adventurous day-trip to one of the out islands, try Powerboat Adventures, tel: 242-363-2265; www. powerboatadventures.com. For a day of sailing, call Barefoot Sailing Cruises, tel: 242-393 0820, www.barefootsailingcruises.com.

Horse-riding

Windsor Equestrian Centre (aka Happy Trails Stables) offers beach and countryside rides, and riding lessons, tel: 242-362 1820; www.windsorequestriancentre.com.

Cuba

Excursions

Walking and driving tours of Havana, including the convents of San Francisco and Santa Clara, the cigar factories, Museo de la Revolución; excursions to Cojímar and the Hemingway Museum (gardens only); beach visits.

Best beaches

The Playas del Este (eastern beaches) are the best within easy reach of the capital – a string of beaches starting some 10 miles (16km) from the city. All along the north coast and northern cays are spectacular beaches, many now with resort hotels on them.

Sports

The Marina Hemingway (at Santa Fe, 20 minutes by taxi) offers sport fishing and scuba diving.

If you are staying on, the beach resorts further afield have good facilities, and will often have qualified instructors for a whole range of sports including waterskiing, sailing, snorkeling, diving, fishing and yachting, as well as volleyball, tennis and horse riding. Some hotels also have bicycles and mopeds for rent. Birdwatching is good all over Cuba, but tours tend to concentrate on the

Zapata peninsula where thousands of migratory birds nest each winter.

Dominican Republic

Excursions

Walk around Santo Domingo's colonial zone visiting museums, mansions, churches and fortifications or take a trip to the Botanical Gardens. From La Romana, ATV or truck safari tours into the countryside are offered. From Samaná in January-March, whale watching is the 'must do' activity.

Best beaches

Boca Chica and Juan Dolio are within easy reach of the capital. The former is protected by an island and a reef, and the water is clean, shallow and calm. Beach bars and vendors provide refreshment. Catalina Island has beautiful sand and turquoise water, as do Bayahibe and Isla Saona further along the coast. These are pristine beaches and the snorkeling and diving are good too. On the Samaná peninsula, Las Galeras and Las Terrenas face north and the sand is darker, but along this coast there are some spectacular bays backed by forested hills and palm trees. Cayo Levantado, at the mouth of the Samaná Bay, is protected and its west end has a huge sweep of golden sand interspersed with palm trees for shade. If you are staying longer, or sailing into Amber Cove, the prettiest beaches are on the north coast from Puerto Plata to Río San Juan, while most of the beach resorts have been built around Punta Cana and Bávaro on the eastern tip, where the sand and coconut palms stretch for miles.

Watersports

Diving is always good at Bayahibe, particularly in the Parque Nacional del Este, which includes Isla Saona. There is also good diving closer to Santo Domingo in the Parque Submarino La Caleta, where a wreck has created an artificial reef full of coral, sponges and lots of colorful fish. Deep-sea fishing is popular and there are fishing tournaments for marlin, bonito and dorado held during the year; contact the Club Náutico de Santo Domingo, tel: 809-683 2582, www.clubnautico.com.do. The north coast is windy and the best

---

⊘ Diving

Some of the finest diving in the Caribbean is to be found in the USVI.

On **St Thomas**, a particularly lively spot is Coki Beach, which specializes in beginners. Coki Beach Dive Club, tel: 340-998 4196; www.cokidive.com. Also try Red Hook Dive Center, Red Hook, tel: 340-777 3483; http://redhookdivecenter.com. Magen's Bay, Sapphire and Coki Beach all have watersports equipment for hire.

On **St John**, located in Wharfside Village, Cruz Bay, is Low Key Watersports, a PADI facility offering daily diving from beginners to advanced, and

kayaking (tel: 340-693 8999; www.divelowkey.com). There is an underwater snorkeling trail off Trunk Bay; Cinnamon Bay and Salt Pond Bay also have good snorkeling. Windsurfing equipment can be hired at Cinnamon and Maho Bay.

St Croix has amazing underwater scenery at Cane Bay, where a dramatic wall drops off thousands of feet very close to the shore. Try Dive Experience, tel: 340-773 3307, www.divexp.com, or Cane Bay Dive Shop, tel: 340-718 9913, www.canebayscuba.com. Sailing equipment is available at Hotel on the Cay.

windsurfing and kitesurfing are at Cabarete, where international competitions are held.

Golf

There are dozens of golf courses on the island, particularly in the eastern half of the country. At Casa de Campo there are three championship courses designed by Pete Dye. Other designers include Robert Trent Jones, with a course in Playa Dorada in the north, and Jack Nicklaus and Tom Fazio, with courses around Punta Cana.

Puerto Rico

Excursions

Walking around Old San Juan – see Casa Blanca, Museo de las Américas, the Dominican Convent, San Cristóbal Fortress, the tourist board office, La Princesa, El Morro fort, cellist Pablo Casal's house, La Fortaleza, and walk along the city walls. Shore excursions include the Bacardi rum distillery, hiking in El Yunque rainforest, golf, kayaking, snorkeling and horse riding.

Best beaches

San Juan as a port is not really a beach destination, although there are beaches at Condado and Isla Verde, a 10-minute taxi ride from the port. Luquillo beach, near the El Yunque National Park, is a lovely long stretch of sand with watersports.

Watersports

Pine Beach Grove in Isla Verde is good for surfing, and novice windsurfers will enjoy the usually flat water of the Condado lagoon. The eastern end of the island and on the Puerto Rico Wall to the south are good scuba diving areas. Try Caribe Aquatic Adventures, tel: 787-281 8858.www.caribeaquaticadventures. com.

For fishing, call Castillo Fishing Charters, based at Punta Las Marías, tel: 787-726 5752; http://fishinpuertorico.com.

Golf

There are 24 golf courses on the island, many of them world-class. Try the Dorado Beach Resort & Club, tel: 787-796-1234, or Bahía Beach Resort & Golf Club, tel: 787-809 8920, both of which accept non-members.

US Virgin Islands

Excursions

St John: Annaberg Sugar Plantation; hiking trails; beaches and watersports.

St Thomas: Paradise Point Tramway for great views (opposite the Havensight Mall); St Peter Great House; Coral World Ocean Park (underwater observatory); sea plane excursions; day-trips to St John; duty-free shopping in Charlotte Amalie.

St Croix: historic Christiansted; Estate Whim Plantation Museum; Buck Island National Park (for snorkeling); cycling and watersports.

Best beaches

St John: Trunk Bay (snorkeling trail), and Hawksnest.

St Thomas: Magen's Bay, Sapphire, Coki for watersports.

St Croix: Sandy Point; Cane Bay for snorkeling; Hotel on the Cay for soft sand and watersports.

Golf

St Thomas has a championship course with beautiful views – Mahogany Run, although it is currently closed due to hurricane damage, so check for details (tel: 340-777 6250; www.mahoganyrun-golf.com). **St Croix** has two 18-hole courses – Carambola (tel: 340-778 5638; www.golfcarambola.com) and Buccaneer (tel: 340-712 2100 www.thebuccaneer.com).

Hiking

Two-thirds of **St John** is a US National Park so there are many trails to choose from. The National Park visitors' center in Cruz Bay is open daily 8am–4.30pm, tel: 340-776 6201. Reef Bay Trail (tel: 340-776 6201 ext 238) is a lovely downhill hike passing a ruined sugar mill and a spectacular beach (www.nps.gov). Book in advance.

St-Martin/Sint Maarten

Excursions

Sint Maarten: snorkeling and diving (book in advance for the wreck dive) at Proselyte Reef; duty-free shopping; regatta in the America's Cup yachts (often organized as a shore excursion); art galleries in St Philipsburg; ziplining at Rockland Estate; day-trips to Marigot and Anguilla.

St-Martin: Beach at Grand Case, 20 minutes from Marigot; fruit, spice and fish market in Marigot on Wednesday and Sunday; trip to Philipsburg for duty-free shopping; day-trip to Anguilla.

Best beaches

Sint Maarten: Orient Beach for watersports; Baie Rouge for nude/topless sunbathing

St-Martin: Mullet Bay; Cupecoy Beach for privacy in shelter of caves and cliffs. For the sheer novelty of sunbathing as enormous jets fly right overhead, visit Maho Beach at the end of the airport runway; there's an all-day party vibe, and flight arrivals and departures are displayed on a surfboard.

Watersports

Diving, snorkeling, windsurfing and sailing can be arranged from all the main beaches.

TELECOMMUNICATIONS

The Bahamas

The dialing code is **242**. The telephone system is sophisticated, with high-speed internet access, roaming agreements with many US cellular networks, and international direct-dialing all over the world. You can buy pre-paid SIM cards that will work on any unlocked phone.

Nassau has a communications center in Festival Place at the cruise ship dock and several cafes offer free WiFi.

Cuba

The dialing code is **53**. Each province has a separate dialing code; for example, the code for Havana is **7**.

The local telephone service is somewhat unreliable. If you must make a call, go to a hotel or a telephone office (signed Telecorreos or Etecsa). You can rent (rather than buy) a local SIM card at the ETECSA booth at the airport. It is not practical to expect to check email on a day visit to Havana; the best facilities are in hotel business centers.

Dominican Republic

The dialing code is **809**. There are call centers you can use for international calls and phone cards for local calls from public pay phones. Cellphones are commonly used and phone rental is available for visitors, or local SIM cards for purchase. Internet access is available at the ports and there are cybercafes in Santo Domingo. Many hotels, eateries and malls offer WiFi.

Puerto Rico

The dialing code is **787**. There are internet cafes and WiFi hotspots in San Juan, or you can buy a local SIM card.

US Virgin Islands

The dialing code is **340**. AT&T has good reception, with rates the same as at home for US customers. Verizon is not covered but ATT and Sprint are.

St-Martin/Sint Maarten

The dialing code for the Dutch side is **599**, for the French side **590**. To call the French side from the Dutch, use the international code 00-590-590 followed by a 6-digit number. To call the Dutch side from the French use the international code 00-599 followed by a 7-digit number. To call Sint Maarten from the US dial 599-54 and the 7-digit number. To call St-Martin from the US dial 590-590 and the 6-digit number. Local SIM cards are sold at the airport and there are numerous hotels, bars and restaurants offering WiFi.

TOURIST OFFICES

The Bahamas

In Canada
212-2150 Islington Ave Etobicoke, ON M9P3V4
Tel: 416-241 6183
In the UK
Bahamas Tourist Office, 10 Chesterfield Street, London, W1J 5JL
Tel: 020 7355 0800
Email: info@bahamas.co.uk
In the US
1200 South Pine Island Road, Suite 750, Plantation, FL 33324
Tel: 954-236 9292
In the Bahamas

The Bahamas Ministry of Tourism, George Street, PO Box N-3701, Nassau
Tel: 242-302 2000
Email: tourism@bahamas.com
Nassau/Paradise Island Promotion Board, West Bay Street, Nassau
Tel: 242-322 8381
www.nassauparadiseisland.com
Grand Bahama Island Tourism Board, PO Box F-40251, Grand Bahama
Tel: 242-352 8356
www.grandbahamavacations.com
Websites
www.bahamas.com
www.bahamas.co.uk

Cuba

In Canada
Cuba Tourist Board, 1200 Bay Street. Suite 305. Toronto. Ontario M5R 2A5
Tel: 416-362 0700
www.gocuba.ca
In the UK
Cuba Tourist Office, Embassy of Cuba, 167 High Holborn, London, WC1V 6PA
Tel: 020 7240 6655
www.travel2cuba.co.uk
In Cuba
Ministerio de Turismo de Cuba, Calle Tercera, # 6 entre G Y F, El Vedado Ciudad de La Habana
Tel: 011-537-832-7535-39
www.cubatravel.cu/en
General tourist information offices do not really exist outside Havana. In the capital, Infotur has kiosks at the airport and on Calle Obispo. Instead, there is a whole range of tourism enterprises, whose services sometimes overlap but which concentrate on offering packages or other specific services rather than telling visitors the opening hours of a museum and so on. Useful websites include: www.cubasi.cu; www.cubanacan.cu and www.infotur.cu, the website of Infotur – a company offering a network of tourist information bureaus.

Dominican Republic

In Canada
26 Wellington St East Suite 201, Toronto M5E 1S2
Tel: 416-361 2126
2055 Peel Street, Suite 550, Montreal, H3A 1V4
Tel: 514-499 1918

In the UK
85 Uxbridge Road, London W5 5TH
Tel: 020 3794 0661
In the US
136 E 57 Street, Suite 805, New York, NY 10020
Tel: 212-588 1012
848 Brickell Avenue, Suite 747, Miami, FL 33131
Tel: 305-358 2899
In the Dominican Republic
Ministry of Tourism, Calle Cayetano Germosen, corner Avenida Gregorio Luperón, Santo Domingo
Tel: 809-221 4660
Website
www.godominicanrepublic.com

Puerto Rico

In Canada
6-295 Queen Street East, Suite 465, Brampton, Ontario L6W 4S6
Tel: 416-368 2680
In Europe
2nd floor, 67A High Street, Walton on Thames, Surrey KT12 1DJ
Tel: 01932 253302
In the US
135 West, 50th Street, 22nd floor, New York, NY 10020
Tel: 212-586 6262
Toll-free: 800-223 6530
In Puerto Rico
Puerto Rico Tourism Company, Paseo La Princesa, #2, P.O. Box 902-3960, San Juan, Puerto Rico 00902-3960
Tel: 787-721 2400
There is also a tourist office near Pier One at the port.
Website
www.seepuertorico.com

US Virgin Islands

In Canada
3300 Bloor Street West, Suite 3120, Centre Tower, Toronto, Ontario M8X 2X3
Tel: 416-622 7600
In the US
3460 Wilshire Boulevard, Suite 412, Los Angeles, CA 90010
Tel: 213-739 0138
2655 Le Jeune Road, Suite 907, Miami, FL 33134
Tel: 305-442 7200
1270 Avenue of the Americas, Suite 2108, New York, NY 10020
Tel: 212-332 2222
In USVI
U.S. Virgin Islands Department of Tourism, P.O. Box 6400, Charlotte Amalie St. Thomas, USVI 00804

Tel: 340-774-8784
Website
www.visitusvi.com
St Thomas: there are two visitor bureaus; one at Tolbod Gade, Charlotte Amalie, another at the Welcome Center, Havensight Dock.
St Croix: 53A Company Street, Christiansted.
St John: located next to the post office in Cruz Bay.
Websites
www.usvi.net
www.usvi-on-line.com
www.gotostcroix.com

St-Martin/Sint Maarten

In France
Office de Tourisme de Saint Martin, 54, rue de Varenne, 75007 Paris
Tel: +33 1 53 29 99 99
In the US
St-Martin promotional office, 825 Third Avenue, 29th floor, New York, NY 10022-7519
Sint Maarten, 77 North Centre Avenue, Suite 215, Rockville Centre, NY 11570
www.vinow.com
Tel: 516-594 4100
In St-Martin
Route de Sandy Ground, Marigot 97150, St-Martin
Tel: 590-875 721
In Sint Maarten
St. Maarten Tourist Bureau, Krippa Commercial Building, Juancho Yrausquin Blvd. #6, Philipsburg, St. Maarten, Netherlands Antilles
Tel: 721-549 0200
Websites
www.stmartinisland.org
www.vacationstmaarten.com

A-Z SOUTHERN CARIBBEAN

ACCOMMODATIONS

It is easier to find a four- or five-star deluxe hotel on the **British Virgin Islands** than a budget guest house. However, there are five campgrounds: three on Anegada, one at White Bay on Jost Van Dyke, and one at Brewer's Bay on Tortola. There are also villas for rent (on a weekly or monthly basis). Some of the smartest hotels are on the outer islands.

Saba, **St-Barths**, **Montserrat**: hotels on all three islands are small and intimate with no large, all-inclusive resorts. Those on St-Barths are top of the range, expensive and luxurious, although there are a few guest houses and a couple of simple hotels in Gustavia. Most visitors, however, stay in one of the many stylish villas on the beach or up in the hills with fabulous views and sea breezes. The hotels of Saba are small, friendly and unpretentious, usually designed with the needs of divers and hikers in mind. Cottages can be rented on a weekly or monthly basis if you want to stay longer. Montserrat has only one hotel and some guest houses, but traditionally visitors have rented villas and this still continues.

Antigua, quite straightforwardly, has luxury resort hotels, villas, guest houses and apartments.

Hotels in **St Kitts** and **Nevis** are generally small, although on St Kitts there is the large Marriott hotel on Frigate Bay and on Nevis there is the Four Seasons hotel, both of which have golf courses. The nicest and most romantic places to stay are converted plantation houses and sugar mills. St Kitts and Nevis also have cottages, apartments and condominiums.

Hotels on **Dominica** are small and intimate, ranging from rustic guest houses to luxury boutique hotels. Many have been used by film crews and have stories to tell. There are a

few beach hotels and some dedicated dive resorts, while others are in the lush interior on forested hillsides with glorious views. Local people also take in hikers on the Waitukubuli National Trail, where a network of guest houses is being established for the 14 segments of the trail.

Martinique has a wide selection of accommodations, including attractive, smaller places which form the Relais Créoles group of hotels.

Accommodations on **Guadeloupe** vary from large luxury resorts to small family-run guest houses and campgrounds. Hotels are concentrated around Gosier, Grande-Terre.

On **St Lucia** you'll find a wide choice of places to stay, from vast all-inclusive resorts and luxury hotels to intimate inns and guest houses.

Barbados is a natural place in which to extend a cruise holiday as so many cruises start and finish here. Most of Barbados' expensive hotels line the west coast – also known as the Platinum Coast – with less expensive ones located along the southeast coast. Renting a villa or an apartment is a good alternative to a hotel.

St Vincent and **The Grenadines**: apart from St Vincent and Bequia, three islands are given over entirely to upscale holiday resorts – Young Island, just 200yd off St Vincent's shore, Palm Island and Petit St Vincent in the Grenadines.

Many of the expensive hotels on **Grenada** are dotted around the southern tip of the island, especially along the Grande Anse beach. Guest houses tend to be rudimentary and there are also plenty of self-catering apartments.

Stay-over visitors come to **Trinidad** for business, birdwatching and sport, mainly cricket. There are accommodations for all budgets, from cheap and cheerful bed and breakfast inns to hotels of

international standard, such as the Hilton. On **Tobago**, hotels are more geared to beach tourism, but in addition to beach resorts you can find out-of-the-way guest houses offering personal attention.

High season in **Aruba** and **Curaçao** is generally from mid-December to mid-April. Prices are usually lower in summer.

ARRIVING BY SEA

British Virgin Islands

The pier at Road Town on Tortola can accommodate two large ships and is currently being extended further. Smaller ships anchor off the islands of Virgin Gorda and Jost van Dyke and tender passengers ashore.

St-Barthélemy, Saba and Montserrat

St-Barths: Cruise ships stay offshore and tender passengers into Gustavia harbor.
Saba: Passengers arrive by tender to the pier at Fort Bay.
Montserrat: Ships come in to Little Bay, where new port facilities are under construction for cruise ships.

Antigua

Cruise ships dock at Heritage Quay, in the center of St Johns, or Deepwater Harbour, a 3-minute taxi ride away. Some small ships anchor in English Harbour.

St Kitts and Nevis

Cruise ships dock at Port Zante terminal in Basseterre, St Kitts, a short walk from the center of town. There are shops and restaurants at the terminal.

Dominica

The main cruise terminal is in the capital, Roseau, in the center of the town's waterfront. An alternative is in Woodbridge Bay at the commercial port. Some ships berth at Portsmouth in the north, but may have to tender in.

Martinique

Cruise ships dock in the capital, Fort-de-France, at two places: the old dock in Tourelles, 1.5 miles (2km) from the town center, around 15 minutes' walk, and at Pointe Simon, 600 yards (549 meters) from the nearest shops.

Guadeloupe

Cruise passengers arrive at centrally located Pointe-à-Pitre, which, along with Basse-Terre, is one of the island's two main towns. The Centre Saint-John Perse, a commercial area, is 5 minutes' walk from the town center. Small cruise ships visit Terre-de-Haut in Les Saintes.

St Lucia

Cruise ships dock either side of the harbor in Castries: on the north side at the efficient Pointe Seraphine cruise terminal, and on the south side at Place Carenage in downtown Castries, by the markets. Both reception areas have duty-free shopping.

Barbados

The cruise port is about 1 mile (1.6km) outside Bridgetown. Taxis wait at the terminal and there are shops and a tourist information booth directly outside.

St Vincent and The Grenadines

Cruise ships dock at the cruise terminal in Kingstown, the capital of St Vincent. The jetty is 5–10 minutes' walk from the town center. On the smaller islands they stay offshore and guests are tendered to land.

Grenada

Cruise ships dock in St George's Bay. Two vessels can berth at the Melville Street Cruise Terminal, with another at the north end of the main quay and four anchored in the outer harbor, from where passengers are brought ashore in tenders. The terminal has

full facilities for visitors and there are taxis and buses waiting outside.

Trinidad and Tobago

Cruise ships dock in the center of Port of Spain, the capital of Trinidad, within easy walking distance of the shops. On Tobago the cruise ship dock is right by the market area of Scarborough.

Aruba and Curaçao

Aruba: Cruise ships dock 5 minutes' walk from the center of Oranjestad, the capital, 5 minutes' drive from the nearest beaches. There are three terminals, each with tourist information offices, activities desks, car rental, souvenir stalls and communication centers.
Curaçao: There are two piers, both in Otrabanda – the Mega Pier, used by bigger ships, and the Mathey Wharf Cruise Terminal in the inner harbor. Both are a short walk from Willemstad shops.

CALENDAR OF EVENTS

British Virgin Islands

February/March: Billabong BVI Kite Jam
March: Annual Dark and Stormy Regatta
March/April: Easter Festival; Virgin Gorda Carnival; BVI Spring Regatta.
May: Annual Foxy's Wooden Boat Regatta; BVI Music Festival.
June: Swim the Sound and Water World
End June/beginning July: Highland Spring HIHO International windsurfing competition.
August: Festival – Tortola's week-long Carnival commemorating slave emancipation.

St-Barthélemy, Saba and Montserrat

St-Barths
January: St-Barths Music Festival
February/March: Carnival
April: St-Barths Film Festival; Les Voiles de St-Barth Regatta
May: West Indies Regatta
July: Anse des Cayes Festival; Bastille Day; Northern Neighborhoods Festival
August: Windward Festival, L'Orient; St-Louis Festival; St-Barthélemy Saint's Day

December: New Year's Eve Regatta

Saba
April: Coronation Day and Queen's Birthday
August: Carnival
December: Saba Day and Weekend; Kingdom Day

Montserrat
March: St Patrick's Day Festival
April: Local Fishing Tournament
June: Queen's Birthday Parade
July: Cudjoe Head Celebrations/ Calabash Festival
November: Alliouagana Festival of the Word (Literary Festival)
December: Christmas Festival (Carnival – ArrowFest)

Antigua
March/April: Easter
April: Kite Festival; Antigua Sailing Week and Classic Regatta
June: International cricket; Barbuda's Caribana
July/August: Carnival.
31 October: Heritage Day
November: Antigua and Barbuda Literary Festival; Jolly Harbour Yacht Club Regatta
December: Antigua Yacht Club – High Tide Series, Nelson's Pursuit

St Kitts and Nevis
April: Nevis Blues Festival
Mid-late June: St Kitts Music Festival
July–first Monday in August: Culturama – carnival and arts festival on Nevis
July: Mango Festival
September: Independence celebrations.
Mid-December–early January: Carnival

Dominica
February/March: Carnival/Mas Dominik
May/June: Domfesta and Giraudel-Eggleston Flower Show
June/July: Dive Fest, annual watersports festival, Kubuli Carib Canoe Race finale
August: Nature Island Literary Festival & Book Fair Festival
October (last weekend): World Creole Music Festival
November: Independence celebrations

Martinique

February/March: Carnival
March: International Sailing Week
April: Aqua Festival (Festival of the Sea)
1–30 May: Le Mai de St-Pierre (festivities in commemoration of the eruption of the Pelée volcano)
June: La Fête de la Musique
July: Fort-de-France Cultural Festival; International Bicycle Race; Crayfish Festival in Ajoupa Bouillon; sugar cane harvest festival
August: Yawl sailing race; Biguine Jazz Festival
November: International Fishing Tournament of Martinique; Biennial International Jazz Festival or the International guitar festival (alternate years)
December: Rum Festival, Musée du Rhum, St James Distillery

Guadeloupe

January: International Film Festival
February/March: Carnival
April: Crab Festival, Morne à l'Eau; Tour de Guadeloupe Regatta
May: Marie-Galante International Music Festival
July: Big Drum (Gwo-Ka) Festival, Sainte-Anne; Festival Guadeloupe
August: Traditional Music Festival in Le Moule; Fête des Cuisinières, festival of women cooks, Pointe-à-Pitre; Patron Saints' Days and Fishermen's Days around the islands
November: Music Day
December: Pointe-à-Pitre Jazz Festival

St Lucia

May: St Lucia Jazz and Arts Festival
29 June: Fishermen's Feast (Fête Pêche)
July: Carnival
1 August: Emancipation Day
30 August: Feast of St Rose De Lima (La Rose)
October: Thanksgiving Day
17 October: Feast of La Marguerite
25 October: Jounen Kwéyòl Entenasyonnal (International Creole Day)
December: Atlantic Rally for Cruisers
12 December: Festival of Lights
13 December: National Day

Barbados

January: Windsurfing championships; jazz festival; regional cricket series

February: The Holetown Festival
April: Oistins Fish Festival; Barbados Reggae Festival
May: Gospelfest; The Mount Gay Regatta; Celtic Festival
June: Harris Paints Sailing Regatta
July: Crop Over festival
August: Kadooment Day
November: Barbados Food and Wine and Rum festival

St Vincent and The Grenadines

February: Mustique Blues Festival
Easter: Bequia Regatta, boat races and festivities; Easterval, a weekend of music, culture and boat races on Union Island
June: Canouan Regatta
June/July: Carnival, Vincy Mas
Late July/early August: Canouan Carnival
August: Breadfruit festival
16–24 December: Nine Mornings – parades and dances in the days leading up to Christmas

Grenada

January: Spice Island Fishing Tournament; Annual La Source Grenada Sailing Festival
February: Carriacou Carnival
Late April: Pure Grenada Music Festival
May: Grenada Chocolate Festival
May/June: Spice Jazz Festival
June: Fisherman's Birthday is celebrated in Gouyave at the end of the month
July: Carriacou Regatta
August: the second weekend in August is Carnival time in Grenada; Rainbow City cultural festival, Grenville

Trinidad and Tobago

February/March: Hosay, the Muslim winter festival with processions, music and dance
March: Phagwa – Hindu New Year – is celebrated at March full moon
February/March: Carnival reaches a climax on the Monday and Tuesday before Ash Wednesday, and although not an official public holiday, everything is closed
March/April: the Tuesday after Easter is the goat race, Buccoo, an important social occasion in Tobago
April: Tobago Jazz Experience
Late July: Tobago Heritage Festival
Variable (according to lunar calendar): Eid-ul-Fitr is the Islamic new year festival which marks the end of Ramadan
October/November: Diwali, the Hindu Festival of Lights

Aruba

January–March: Carnival, including a torch parade and tumba contest. Grand Parade on last Sunday before Ash Wednesday
25 January: festivities and sports for GF Betico Croes Day
18 March: National Anthem and Flag Day
March/April: Easter
30 April: Queen's Birthday
Late May: Aruba Soul Beach Music Festival
June: Aruba Food and Wine Festival; Aruba International Film Festival
24 June: Dera Gai (St John's Day), Harvest Festival
June/July: Aruba Hi-Winds windsurfing and kitesurfing competition
August: Aruba Rembrandt Regatta
September: Aruba Piano Festival; Caribbean Sea Jazz Festival
November: Aruba Heineken Catamaran Regatta
27 December: Dande Festival

Curaçao

January–March: Carnival, including Tumba Festival, Kite Festival and Grand Parade, Sunday before Ash Wednesday
April: Curaçao Windsurfing Challenge
30 April: Queen's Birthday
May: Curacao International BlueSeas Festival
June: Sunfish Championship
2 July: Curaçao Flag Day
26 July: Curaçao Day
September: North Sea Jazz Festival
5 October: Banda Bou Day
November: Heineken Regatta
December: Hannukah, the Jewish Festival of Lights

EATING OUT

Eating out in **The British Virgin Islands** will bring your knife and fork into contact with American, European and Caribbean creations, such as *fungi* (cornmeal pudding) and *roti* (curry wrapped in a thin chapati). Seafood, tropical fruits and vegetables are fresh and plentiful.

Gourmet French and Créole cuisine is the norm on **St-Barths**, where seafood excels and ingredients are flown in from France and the French Antilles. Restaurants are decorated by top designers to match the standards set by the chefs and their wealthy customers. As a result, prices are very high. The top hotels have outstanding restaurants, among the best in the world. **Saba** is more down-to-earth, with its active diving and hiking visitors needing hearty food at reasonable prices. Much of the fruit and vegetables are locally grown on hillside plots. On **Montserrat**, the local cuisine is a mix of Caribbean and international. Goat water stew, commonly found on the menu, is believed to have originated from Irish settlers.

Antigua: There are some delicious local dishes worth trying, such as pepperpot (a stew of almost every possible ingredient), conch or chicken with rice and peas. Alternatively visitors can taste some of Antigua's international cuisine – French, Italian and Vietnamese.

St Kitts and **Nevis** have restaurants specializing in West Indian, Creole, French, Indian and Chinese food brought to the island by its many immigrants from around the world. In addition to the ubiquitous fresh seafood, the most distinctive feature of local cuisine is the abundance of fresh vegetables from the islands' volcanic soil. Breadfruit, eggplant (aubergine), sweet potatoes and okra all appear on island plates. The hotels offer fine dining but there are some excellent independent restaurants, particularly in Basseterre and the southeast peninsula.

Kittitians like to eat out on Saturdays at restaurants serving black pudding, souse, Johnny cakes, goat water and saltfish. On Nevis there are cookouts in most villages on Friday and Saturday nights starting from about 5pm, with local food, chicken, ribs, beer, music and dominoes.

Fresh fruit juices, made with tamarind, guava, sorrel and grapefruit, are one of the delights of the cuisine on **Dominica**, along with specialties such as 'mountain chicken' (a large frog endemic to Dominica), crab backs (land crabs) and *titiri* (tiny fish caught seasonally at river mouths). Other more rustic Dominican dishes include saltfish, ground provisions (*dasheen* – which is like spinach – yam, sweet potato, cous-cous), and *callaloo* (young shoots of the *dasheen*) soup.

Martinique: Creole cuisine is a blend of French, African and Indian influences; familiar French dishes are given a twist by the use of tropical fruits, vegetables and seafood. Visitors will find plenty of spicy Caribbean specialties. The local rum is best drunk at Ti Punch, mixed with a little cane syrup and a slice of lime.

The cuisine of **Guadeloupe** mirrors its many cultures. The local Creole specialties combine the finesse of French cuisine, the spice of African cookery and the exoticism of East Indian and Southeast Asian recipes. Fresh seafood appears on most menus. With its French Creole heritage, Guadeloupe is a great place to eat: You can sample crayfish, swordfish, stuffed crab and even sea oyster omelettes, as well as the local specialties, goat curry and blood sausage (*boudin*).

There is a colorful blend of African, Amerindian, French and British influences in the cuisine of **St Lucia**. The island enjoys a near endless bounty of nature, from cassava, sweet potato and dasheen to fragrant nutmeg, cinnamon and ginger. Bananas, pineapple, grapefruit, oranges and mangoes grow in abundance. There is also superb seafood from the surrounding Caribbean Sea and the Atlantic Ocean. Specialties include pumpkin soup and soufflé, flying fish, *poile dudon* (a chicken dish), pepperpot, green fig (banana) and saltfish, conch and *tablette* (a sweetmeat made of coconut).

Head for **Barbados**, and local specialties include flying fish cutters (breaded flying fish in a bun) for lunch; red snapper, hot saltfish cakes, pickled breadfruit and pepperpot, often accompanied by rice and peas, macaroni pie, plantain, sweet potato or yam. Among the usual fast food, look out for roti, a savoury pocket of curried chicken, prawn, beef or potato.

St Vincent and **The Grenadines:** Spicy Caribbean cuisine predominates, with continental and American fare also available. A variety of exotic fruits and vegetables and an abundance of lobster and other fresh seafood enrich St Vincent's cooking. Try something unusual, such as barbecued goat.

The colonial past of **Grenada** has endowed the island with an interesting mix of British and French influences. The emphasis tends to be on seafood, but there are many local delicacies

worth sampling. *Callaloo* soup made from *dasheen* leaves is excellent, as are traditional pepperpot, and *lambi* (conch). Game sometimes appears on tourist menus, although some may prefer not to experiment with armadillo, iguana or manicou. Spices, especially nutmeg, are another favorite, delicious in rum punches.

Trinidad and **Tobago** are multicultural societies with a broad range of culinary influences, including African, Indian, Chinese and French. You can find some of the best food in the region here, from a traditional Caribbean callaloo to pepper shrimp in a Chinese restaurant, or the Indian roti, a staple for lunch. Street food is good and cheap, always plentiful around lunchtime. On Maracas beach try shark-and-bake, a spicy fried bread sandwich of fried shark with a variety of sauces, while on Tobago seek out the tasty crab and dumplings. Staples are fresh seafood, vegetables and fruit, and non-meat-eaters will never go hungry. Mangoes come in all shapes and sizes, as do avocados, while coconut water makes a refreshing drink, sold around the Savannah in Port of Spain. There are lots of sweets to try too, usually of Indian or Chinese origin.

Aruba and **Curaçao** both have Indonesian, Chinese, French, Spanish and Italian restaurants. Their diverse populations, whose inhabitants are of Portuguese, Spanish, Venezuelan, Indian, Pakistani and African as well as Dutch descent, make them wonderful places to sample international cooking. Specialties include seafood dishes, as well as cornmeal bread, goat stew, hearty soups, grilled fish and filled patties (*pastechi*) – all popular local (*krioyo*) dishes. International options include Argentine *churrasco*, Middle Eastern *shoarma*, Japanese *sushi*, Spanish *tapas*, Indian curries and Jamaican jerk ribs. If you're in a group, splash out on a *rijstaffel* Indonesian banquet, where up to 40 small dishes are served.

GETTING AROUND

British Virgin Islands

By car
Driving is on the left. Advance booking is recommended in peak season.

Cars can be rented in Road Town, close to the docks. Car-rental firms include: **Avis**, tel: 284-340 5629, www.avis.com; and **Courtesy Car Rentals**, tel: 284-776 6650; www.courtesycar-rental.com.

By taxi

Taxis are easy to find on the BVI. They stop if hailed on the road, and wait at the cruise terminal. They have fixed prices, but check the fare before starting a journey. On Virgin Gorda, small lorries with benches run a reasonably priced shuttle service between the main tourist points.

Inter-island links

By Air: Small planes fly from Tortola to Virgin Gorda and Anegada. Day trips are possible with charter companies such as Air Sunshine, tel: 284-495 8900, www.airsunshine.com; or Fly BVI, tel: 284-340 1747, www.flybvi.com. There are good connecting flights from the international airports on St-Martin, Puerto Rico and the US Virgin Islands as well as other islands in the region with Cape Air, tel: 284-495 2100, www.capeair.com; LIAT, tel: 1-888-844 5428, www.liat.com; or VI Airlink, tel: 284-495 2271, www.viairlink.com.

By Ferry: Timetables are available in hotels, at the tourist board (www.bvitourism.com) and in *Welcome* magazine (www.bviwelcome.com).

There are regular services from: Road Town, Tortola, to Spanish Town, Virgin Gorda, and Peter Island; West End, Tortola, to Jost Van Dyke; Beef Island, Tortola, to North Sound; and Spanish Town, Virgin Gorda (North Sound Express); Road Town, Tortola, and West End to St Thomas and St John (both USVI, see page 339); Virgin Gorda to St Thomas (USVI). There is also a free ferry from Beef Island, Tortola, to Marina Cay (from Pusser's).

St-Barths, Saba and Montserrat

By car

St-Barths: Driving is on the right; French laws apply. Car rental should be organized in advance at busy times of the year. Many companies are at the airport. Roads are narrow and twisting in the hills and the smaller the car the better. Open-topped cars are popular. There is a chronic lack of parking space.

Saba: Driving is on the right. Limited car rental is available.

Montserrat: Several companies offer car rental. A local driving license must be purchased.

By taxi

St-Barths: Taxis are plentiful and efficient. They will do island tours or take you to a beach and pick you up later. There are two taxi stands, one at the airport and the other in Gustavia.

Saba: Taxis have fixed rates for destinations and for an island tour.

Montserrat: Taxis have green license plates beginning with H. They can be hailed on the street. They do island tours by negotiation.

By bus

St-Barths: There are no buses.

Saba: There are no buses.

Montserrat: Minibuses with green license plates beginning with H can be hailed as they pass. There are no scheduled times and no official stops.

Inter-Island Links

St-Barths

By Air: From St Maarten, Winair, tel: 1-721-545 4237, www.fly-winair.com; Air Caraïbes, www.aircaraibes.com; and St Barth Commuter, tel: 590-27 5454, www.stbarthcommuter.com, make the 10-minute shuttle flight to St-Barths (SBH). From Guadeloupe, Air Caraïbes offers a few direct flights (45 minutes). The airstrip in St Barths is small, 2,170 feet, and plagued by turbulence. Pilots have to be specially trained to negotiate a mountain, then drop sharply to land before they hit the sea at the end of the runway. For many passengers, the landing, especially on a windy day, is an adventure in itself.

By Ferry: See St-Martin/Sint Maarten, for ferry details.

Saba

By Air: Winair flies several times a day from Sint Maarten. Saba's Juancho E Yrausquin airport has the shortest commercial runway in the world at 1,300ft (400 meters) and, like St-Barths, suffers from turbulence, with a mountain on one side and the sea on the other (and at the end). Only small planes can fly in and flights are canceled if it is too windy. On landing, the runway looks so short it appears almost square. On takeoff the pilot puts on the brakes, then pushes the engines to full throttle until the plane vibrates,

before releasing the brakes and taking off as quickly as possible.

By Ferry: See St-Martin/Sint Maarten, for ferry details.

Montserrat

By Air: Montserrat has a new airport in the north after the original one in the east was covered with ash. Scheduled and charter flights are offered between Antigua and Montserrat by Fly Montserrat, tel: 664-491 3434, www.flymontserrat.com; and SVG Airline, tel: 784-457 5124, www.svgair.com. Fly Montserrat also offers connections with Anguilla, Guadeloupe, St Kitts, Tortola and some other islands. SVG Airline can be chartered for flights to neighboring islands and to St Vincent. Both airlines use nine-seater aircraft in to Montserrat. Caribbean Helicopters, in Antigua, tel: 268-460 5900, www.flychl.com, offer a charter helicopter service to Montserrat.

By Ferry: There is a ferry service 4 days a week between St John's, Antigua, and Little Bay; tel: 664-496 9912 in Montserrat and tel: 268-778 9786 in Antigua.

Antigua

By Car

Driving is on the left. Drivers require a local driving permit, available for a fee at any police station or car rental office if you present a valid driving license. Some roads outside St John's are narrow and potholed with no pavement. Rental agencies: Hertz, tel: 268-481 4440, www.hertz.com; Dollar Rent-a-Car, tel: 268-462 0362, www.dollar.com.

By Taxi

Taxis wait at the cruise terminals. Fares are posted at the cruise ship terminal, airport, tourist office, and in hotels. Agree a price before starting your journey. Many Antiguan taxi drivers are also qualified tour guides.

Inter-Island Links

By Air: Antigua has frequent links with most Caribbean islands. Try: LIAT, tel: 268-480 5601, www.liat.com; or Caribbean Airlines, tel: 800 744 2225, www.caribbean-airlines.com.

St Kitts and Nevis

By Car

Driving is on the left. Visitors must present a valid national or international license at the Traffic

Department or through the rental company. Car-rental agencies include: Avis, South Independence Square, Basseterre, St Kitts, tel: 869-465 6507, www.avis.com; Nevis Car Rental, Newcastle, Nevis, tel: 869-469 9837, http://neviscarrentals.com.

By Taxi

Taxis wait at the cruise terminal. On Nevis they wait at the airport or in Charlestown. Tariffs are fixed, but confirm the fare before starting out.

By Bus

Small minibuses are reliable and cheap. They do not run to Frigate Bay and the southeast peninsula, but you can get a bus from Basseterre up the coastal road to Old Road and on to Brimstone Hill Fortress. On Nevis, minibuses run on the road round the island all day. Stand on the side of the road and hail one in whichever direction you are going.

Inter-Island Links

By Air: St Kitts is linked by air with many islands including Puerto Rico, Antigua, Barbados, St Maarten, St Thomas, Anguilla, St-Barths, Saba, St Eustatius, BVI, Grenada and St Lucia.

Nevis is linked with Puerto Rico, Antigua and St Maarten.

Airlines serving the routes to and from St Kitts and Nevis include: Winair, tel: 721-545 4237, www.fly-winair.com; and LIAT, tel: 888-844 5428, www.liat.com.

By Ferry: an air taxi and a ferry run daily between Basseterre, St Kitts, and Charlestown, Nevis. Journey time is 30–45-minutes. Tickets can be purchased at the ferry terminal.

Dominica

By Car

Driving is on the left. The speed limit in built-up areas is 20 mph (32 kph). Roads in Dominica are twisting and narrow, with steep gradients, but the surface is generally very good.

Jeeps and cars can be rented at the cruise pier. You need a national or international driving license and a local visitor's permit, available from the police traffic department (High Street, Roseau), from the police station or airport, or from a car-rental company. Hire companies: Courtesy, tel: 767-448 7763, www.dominicacarrentals.com; Island Car Rentals, tel: 767-255 6844; www.islandcar.dm.

By Taxi

Taxis wait at the cruise terminal and will conduct private round-the-island tours. Official drivers should have number plates beginning with the letter H or HA. On fixed routes the fares are set by the government. Settle on a price before your journey.

By Bus

Minibuses are the local form of public transport, from early in the morning to nightfall. They run mainly to and from Roseau. There are no fixed timetables; buses leave when they are full. In Roseau there are various departure points depending on the destination. There are frequent services to villages around Roseau, but making a round trip in one day from Roseau to more remote communities can be a problem. Allow plenty of time to get back to the ship if you are using public transport.

Inter-island links

By Air: There are no direct flights from Europe to Dominica. Connections with Dominica are made with the regional airlines, LIAT (tel: 888-844 5428, www.liat.com) and Winair (tel: 866-466 0410, www.fly-winair.sx), from neighboring Caribbean islands, including Antigua, Barbados, BVI, Guadeloupe, Martinique, St Lucia and Sint Maarten. Seaborne Airlines (tel: 866-359 8784, www.seaborneairlines.com) flies daily from San Juan, Puerto Rico (with connections to the US). The main airport is Melville Hall. Light aircraft, including some Winair flights, also use the smaller Canefield Airport, close to Roseau.

By ferry: A regular, efficient ferry service connects Dominica with Guadeloupe (to the north), Martinique and St Lucia (to the south). For tickets contact: L'Express des Isles, Whitchurch Centre, Roseau. Tel: 590 519 520, www.express-des-isles.com. A new fast ferry, Val Ferry, operates between Dominica and Guadeloupe; www.val-ferry.fr.

Martinique

By car

A current driving license is required to rent a car for 20 days or fewer. Visiting drivers should have at least one year's driving experience. Budget Car Rental, 12 rue Félix Eboué, 97200 Fort-de-France, tel: 596-0-596-420 404, www.budget-martinique.com; Ciel Bleu rent-a-car, Fort-de-France, tel: 596-0-596-613 270, www.mn-location.fr.

By bus

There are bus stops along Boulevard Général de Gaulle for both urban and long-distance buses. Alternatively you can try the taxicos, shared taxis that leave from the terminal at Pointe Simon and run from early morning to 6pm all over the island, an inexpensive means of getting about.

By ferry

Small launches ply between Fort-de-France and Trois-Ilets, a quick and easy way of getting to the beach: Vedettes Madinina, tel: 596-0-596-630 646, www.vedettestropicales.com.

By taxi

Taxis wait at the cruise terminals; they are metered and expensive.

Inter-island links

By Air: airlines connecting Martinique to Antigua, Barbados, Dominica, Grenada, Guadeloupe, Puerto Rico, St Lucia, Sint Maarten, St Vincent and Trinidad include: Air Caraïbes, tel: 0820-835 835, www.aircaraibes.com; and LIAT, tel: 888-854 5428, www.liat.com

Air Antilles, tel: 0890 648 648, www.airantilles.com, shuttles between Martinique, Guadeloupe, St-Martin and St-Barthélemy and also flies to Santo Domingo.

By Ferry: ferries link Martinique to Dominica, Guadeloupe and St Lucia: L'Express Des Iles, Terminal Inter Iles, Quai Ouest, 97200 Fort-de-France, tel: 596-0-825-359 000, www.express-des-iles.com.

Guadeloupe

By car

A valid driving license is sufficient to rent a car for 20 days or fewer. Drivers need to be over 21 and require at least 1 year's experience. Car-rental agencies at Pointe-à-Pitre and Pôle Caraïbes airports are expensive. Mopeds, scooters, motorbikes and bicycles are also available for hire. Traffic is appalling around Pointe-à-Pitre. Drive on the right.

By taxi

Taxis are available at the cruise terminal but they are expensive; not all routes have pre-fixed rates. Drivers usually only speak French.

By bus

There are three main bus terminals in Pointe-à-Pitre, covering different areas of the country. Buses run to all towns and villages and are relatively cheap. During the week they run between 5.30am and 7pm, every 15 minutes or when full, but on Saturday afternoon and on Sunday there are very few buses anywhere.

By ferry

Ferries linking Guadeloupe with Les Saintes and Marie-Galante are operated by Express des Iles, tel: 590-0-590-911 105, www.express-des-iles.com.

Inter-island links

By Air: The airport at Les Abymes is in two parts: the older Le Raizet airport is used for regional flights, while the newer Pole Caraïbes airport next to it is for international flights. There are also airports on Marie Galante, Terre-de-Haut, La Désirade, at St-François and Baillif airport on the southern tip of Basse-Terre. LIAT, tel: 888-854 5428, www.liat.com; Air Caraïbes, tel: 590-0-590-824 747, www.aircaraibes.com; and Air Antilles Express, tel: 0890-648 648, www.airantilles.com; fly to neighboring Caribbean islands.

By ferry: Sea Express des Iles connects Guadeloupe, Les Saintes and Marie Galante with Martinique, Dominica and St Lucia several times a week.

St Lucia

By car

Driving is on the left. Visiting drivers must obtain a temporary driving permit, valid for three months, by presenting a current driving license at the police station (Bridge Street, Castries) or car-rental company, with a small fee. Cars and four-wheel-drive vehicles are available to rent at the port; a four-wheel-drive is best for places off the beaten track. Contact: Alexo Car/Avis, tel: 758-452 4554, www.avis.com; Cool Breeze Jeep-Car Rental, tel: 758-459 7729, www.coolbreezecarrental.com; Hertz, tel: 758-452 0680, www.hertz.com; West Coast Jeeps and Taxi Service, tel: 758-459 5457, www.westcoastjeeps.com.

By taxi

Taxis line up at the dock. The prices are fixed for set routes, but check the current rates at the tourist office booth close to the taxi rank. Negotiate a rate for island tours before setting out on your journey.

By bus

The public bus system in St Lucia operates from early in the morning until early evening. The frequency tends to tail off after the end of the working day. Castries and Vieux Fort have the best services, while the more remote rural areas aren't always as well served. If you go to Soufrière by bus, it is usually quicker and easier to return via Vieux Fort, where there are better connections.

Inter-island links

By air: Air Caraïbes, LIAT, Winair and SVG Air fly from neighboring islands. Local flights usually go from George F. L. Charles Airport, just outside the center of Castries.

By ferry: Express des Iles has a high-speed catamaran car ferry service linking St Lucia with Dominica and the French islands of Martinique, Guadeloupe, Les Saintes and Marie Galante, usually crossing three times a week. The agent in St Lucia, Cox & Company Ltd, has an office at the ferry terminal on La Toc Road in Castries (Mon–Fri 8am–4.15pm, tel: 758-456 5022, www.express-des-iles.com).

Barbados

By car

Driving is on the left and roads are generally good, if narrow outside Bridgetown.

A visitor's driving license is available from car-rental companies and most police stations for a fee. Rental companies have a choice of cars, including mini-mokes (beach-buggy-style vehicles): Courtesy Rent-a-Car, tel: 246-431 4179, www.courtesyrentacar.com; Top Class Car Rentals, tel: 246-228 7368, www.topclassrentals.com; Stoutes Car Rental, tel: 246-416 4456, www.stoutescar.com.

By taxi

Taxis wait at the cruise terminal and in town. Agree a fare before setting off.

Inter-island links

By air: There are frequent flights to nearly all the Caribbean islands

with LIAT, tel: 888-854 5428, www.liat.com. Other regional airlines include Caribbean Airlines, tel: 1 800 744 2225, www.caribbean-airlines.com; and SVG Air, tel: 784-457 5124, www.svgair.com.

By ferry: There is no ferry service to Barbados, but sailing tours are offered to nearby islands such as St Vincent and the Grenadines, St Lucia and Grenada.

St Vincent and The Grenadines

By car

Driving is on the left. You will need your home license and a local license (EC$65), which can be arranged at the police station in Bay Street, Kingstown, or the Licensing Authority in Halifax Street. Car rental is expensive and cars have limited access to some areas. A jeep is the best bet. Car-rental companies on St Vincent include Avis, tel: 784-456 6861, www.avis.com; and on Bequia: D&N (Noel's) Car Rental, tel: 784-458 3064, www.bequiarentalcars.com.

By taxi

Taxi fares are fixed, but check with the driver first to avoid misunderstandings. Taxis and minibuses are also available on Bequia and Union Island.

By bus

Local minibuses on St Vincent tend to be busy and noisy, but they are also cheap. Allow plenty of time to get back to port if using public transportation.

Inter-island links

By air: St Vincent is linked by air with other islands including Barbados, Trinidad, St Lucia, Martinique and Grenada. Petit St Vincent, Palm Island and Mustique, all private islands, are also accessible by permission. Airlines include LIAT, tel: 888-854 5428, www.liat.com; and SVG Air, tel: 784-457-5124, www.svgair.com.

By ferry: Inter-island ferries are cost-effective with regular services between the busier islands. Bequia Express (tel: 784-457 3539) and Admiral Express (tel: 784 458 3348) sail to Bequia. M/V Gem Star sails to Canouan, Mayreau and Union Island (tel: 784-526 1158) and M/V Endeavour sails to Mustique (tel: 784-457 1531). (

GRENADA

By car

Driving is on the left. Some roads are in poor condition, especially in the mountains. Drivers must be over 21, although most rental companies now want you to be over 25 and have a valid license as well as a local permit (available from the central police station). There is a good choice of rental firms, but cars can be difficult to obtain, particularly in high season and during Carnival. Rental companies include: Maitlands, tel: 473-444 4022, www.maitlandsrentals.com; McIntyre Bros Ltd, tel: 473-444 1555, www.caribbeanhorizons.com.

By taxi

Taxis are available at the cruise ship dock and on the Carenage in St George's. They are not metered and there are no fixed charges, so agree the fare with the driver before setting off. Taxi drivers can be hired by the hour or day for sightseeing tours. Allow a day for a tour of Grenada.

By bus

Grenada has an inexpensive and comprehensive bus network, but buses are normally crowded.

Inter-island links

By air: LIAT (tel: 888-854 5428, www.liat.com) and Caribbean Airlines (tel: 1 800 523 5585, www.caribbean-airlines.com) offer local flights.
By ferry: Osprey Lines offers a regular ferry service between Grenada and Carriacou and Petit Martinique (tel: 473-440 8126, www.ospreylines.com).

Trinidad and Tobago

By car

Driving is on the left. Visitors wishing to rent a car must be at least 21 years old and possess a valid driving license. Car rental companies National/Alamo, tel: 868-669 8393, www.alamo.com; and Budget (tel: 868-669 1635, www.budget.com).

By taxi and bus

Any form of public transportation is referred to as a 'taxi'. Taxis are available in the town center. Fares are fixed. Route taxis (minibuses) run along set routes and have fixed fares. Maxi-taxis (shared taxis) travel

greater distances than route taxis. All taxis are privately owned.

Buses are run by the state, PTSC (tel: 868-623 7872 Trinidad; tel: 868-639 2293 Tobago, www.ptsctt.com). The main bus station on Trinidad is City Gate, South Quay, Port of Spain, and is the hub for transport all over the island. On Tobago the bus station is at Sangster's Hill, Scarborough.

Inter-island links

By air: Caribbean Airlines runs the air bridge between the two islands with about 12 daily flights from 6am, taking 20 minutes. Flights get booked up on public holidays.
By ferry: The Port Authority of Trinidad and Tobago has two high-speed ferries, *T&T Express* and *T&T Spirit* running a daily service between Port of Spain and Scarborough, 30 minutes (tel: 868-625 3055, www.ttitferry.com) ;.

Aruba and Curaçao

By car

Driving is on the right. To rent a car you must be 21 years of age and in possession of a valid national driving license. Car-rental firms will deliver to and collect from the cruise terminals in Aruba and Curaçao. In Aruba, rent a four-wheel-drive vehicle if you want to explore the interior. Bicycles, scooters and motorbikes are also available for hire. Rental companies include: Ace Car Rental, Aruba, tel: 866-978 5191, www.acearuba.com; More 4 Less Jeep & Car Rental, Aruba; tel: 297-588 7255, www.more4less-aruba.com; Avis, Curaçao, tel: 5999-461 1255, www.aviscuracao.com; Budget, Curaçao, tel: 5999-868 3466, www.curacao-budgetcar.com.

By taxi

Taxis are available for hire at the cruise terminals and other central locations. In addition, on Aruba and Curaçao, public transport is provided by buses and taxis following fixed routes. Always agree the fare before beginning a taxi journey.

Inter-island links

By air: Insel Air, tel: 5999-737 0444, www.fly-inselair.com; and Tiara Air, tel: 297-528 2472, www.tiara-air.com; run scheduled flights between Aruba and Curaçao several times a day.
By ferry: There are no ferries.

MONEY MATTERS

British Virgin Islands

Currency is the US$. Banking hours are 9am–2pm, although some banks are open from 8.30am until 3 or 4pm and most until 5pm on Fridays. There are banks and ATMs in Road Town, Beef Island airport, Cane Garden Bay, Nanny Cay, Frenchman's Cay and Parham Town (Tortola) and Spanish Town (Virgin Gorda).

St-Barthélemy, Saba and Montserrat

St-Barths: The euro is the official currency but US dollars are accepted everywhere. There are banks (with ATMs) in Gustavia and St-Jean, open 8am–noon, 2–3.30pm. Credit cards are widely accepted.
Saba: The US dollar is the official currency. There is a bank in The Bottom, open Mon–Thu 3–5pm, Fri 1.30–3.30pm, and another in Windwardside, open Mon–Fri 8.30am–3.30pm, both with ATMs. Credit cards are widely accepted.
Montserrat: The official currency is the East Caribbean dollar (EC$). Banks with ATMs are in Brades. Credit cards are not widely accepted. Banks will cash travellers' checks.

Antigua

The currency is the Eastern Caribbean dollar; US dollars are also widely accepted. Major credit cards are accepted in most restaurants and shops. Most of the major banks are located in High Street, St John's. Banking hours vary but are generally 8am–1pm and 3–5pm Mon–Thu; 8am–noon, 3–5pm Fri; the Bank of Antigua opens 8am–noon Sat. Several banks have ATMs, located at Woods Shopping Center, St John's; the Royal Bank of Canada, Market Street and High Street, St John's. There is a branch of Antigua Commercial Bank in Codrington, Barbuda. There is also a branch of American Express at Antours, Long Street, St John's.

St Kitts and Nevis

The currency on both islands is the Eastern Caribbean dollar (EC$); US dollars are also widely accepted, but change will be given in EC$. Banks are open Mon–Thu 8am–2pm, Fri 8am–4pm and some on Sat 8.30am–11am. There are ATMs at all banks.

Dominica

The currency is the Eastern Caribbean dollar (EC$). US dollars are accepted in some places, although change will be given in EC$. Banking hours are usually Mon–Thu 8am–2pm, Fri 8am–4pm. First Caribbean, the Royal Bank of Canada and the Bank of Nova Scotia are the main commercial banks, all with branches in Roseau. There are ATMs, including one at the Royal Bank of Canada, Bay Street.

Martinique

The local currency on Martinique is the euro, but US dollars are also accepted. Most major credit cards are accepted throughout the island and there are banks with ATMs in town centers.

Guadeloupe

The local currency is the euro, and US dollars are rarely accepted. Most major credit cards are accepted. There are also banks with ATMs.

St Lucia

The currency is the EC dollar, although US dollars are also accepted in most places, as are credit cards and traveller's checks. There are foreign-exchange facilities and ATMs in Castries and Rodney Bay.

Barbados

The currency is the Barbados dollar (BDS$). US dollars are also widely accepted and goods are often labeled with a price in US dollars, so check which currency is being quoted before making a purchase. It is not permitted to export BDS dollars. Money can be changed at banks and hotels. Traveller's checks in US dollars and major credit cards are widely accepted. ATMs are available in most banks around the island. Banks are open 8am–2pm Mon–Thu; 8am–1pm, 3–5pm Fri.

St Vincent and The Grenadines

The currency is the EC dollar, which is tied to the US dollar. US dollars can be used in most places and major credit cards are accepted in most hotels and restaurants. There are several banks with ATMs in Kingstown. Banking facilities are also available on Bequia and Union Island.

Grenada

The currency is the East Caribbean dollar (EC$), tied to the US dollar. US dollars are also widely accepted. Banks open 8am–3pm Mon–Thu, 8am–5pm Fri. They close for lunch 1–2.30pm. Most banks are in St George's, but there are branches in Grenville, Gouyave, Sauteurs and Carriacou.

Trinidad and Tobago

The Trinidad and Tobago dollar (TT$) is the official currency on both islands, although some shops accept US dollars. Most hotels, restaurants and shops accept major credit cards. Banks in Port of Spain and on Tobago have ATMs and there are also ATMs in malls and at the airports. Banks are open Mon–Thu, 8am–2pm and Fri 9am–noon and 3–5pm. Banks in shopping plazas and malls are open 10am–6pm.

Aruba and Curaçao

The official currency on Aruba is the Aruba florin. Curaçao uses the Netherlands Antilles guilder (NAfl), also known as the florin. On both islands the US dollar is accepted nearly everywhere, as are credit cards issued abroad. ATMs are widely available.

POSTAL SERVICES

British Virgin Islands

The main post office on Tortola is on Main Street (take the lane off Waterfront Drive at the Ferry Dock).

St-Barthélemy, Saba and Montserrat

St-Barths: The main post office is in Gustavia on rue Centenaire, open 8am–3pm, closed Wed and Sat pm, and Sun. There are branches in Lorient and St-Jean Commercial Center, open in the mornings.

Saba: Post offices are in The Bottom and in Windwardside, open 8am–noon, 1–5pm.

Montserrat: The General Post Office is at Government Headquarters, Brades. Counter service 8.15am–4pm.

Antigua

The main post office in St John's is on Long Street.

St Kitts and Nevis

Two post offices are located on Bay Road in Basseterre and Main Street in Charlestown. Open: St Kitts: Mon–Tue 8am–4pm, Wed–Fri 8am–3.30pm. Nevis: Mon–Fri 8am–3.30pm.

Dominica

The main post office is at the Bay Front, Roseau (Mon–Fri 8am–4pm).

Martinique

There are post offices in all of the main towns. Hotels, tabacs and other shops also sell stamps.

Guadeloupe

In Pointe-à-Pitre, post offices are located on Boulevard Hanne and Boulevard Légitimus. There are post offices in all the main towns. Hotels, tabacs and other shops sell stamps.

St Lucia

The main post office in Castries is in Bridge Street, while most towns have a small post office. General opening hours are 8.30am–4.30pm Mon–Fri.

Barbados

The main post office is in Cheapside, Bridgetown (Mon–Fri 8am–5pm). Each parish has a post office and stamps are also sold in bookshops and hotels.

St Vincent and The Grenadines

The post office in Kingstown is on Halifax Street. Mon–Fri 8.30am–3pm, Sat 8.30–11.30am.

Grenada

The main post office is on Lagoon Road, south of Carenage, St George's. Mon–Fri 8am–3.30pm.

Trinidad and Tobago

There are post offices in most main towns. Surface mail can take several weeks to arrive. Opening hours are Mon–Fri 8am–4pm.

Aruba and Curaçao

The main post offices are in the center of Oranjestad and Willemstad.

PUBLIC HOLIDAYS

British Virgin Islands

1 January: New Year's Day
March: H. Lavity Stoutt's Birthday (1st Monday); Commonwealth Day (2nd Monday)
March/April: Easter; Good Friday; Easter Monday
May/June: Whit Monday
June: (2nd Monday) Queen's Birthday
1 July: Territory Day
August: (1st Monday and Tuesday) Festival Monday and Festival Tuesday
21 October: St Ursula's Day
25 December: Christmas Day
26 December: Boxing Day

St-Barthélemy, Saba and Montserrat

St-Barths

1 January: New Year's Day
March/April: Good Friday/Easter Sunday/Easter Monday
1 May: Labour Day
8 May: Armistice Day
June: Ascension Day
June: Whitsun
1 November: All Saints Day
11 November: Armistice Day
25 December: Christmas Day

Saba

1 January: New Year's Day
March/April: Good Friday/Easter Sunday/Easter Monday
30 April: Queen's Birthday
1 May: Labor Day
June: Ascension Day
December: Saba Day
25 December: Christmas Day
26 December: Boxing Day

Montserrat

1 January: New Year's Day
17 March: St Patrick's Day
March/April: Good Friday/Easter Sunday/Easter Monday

1 May: Labor Day
May/June: Whit Monday
June: Queen's Birthday
August: August Monday
25 December: Christmas Day
26 December: Boxing Day
31 December: Festival Day

Antigua

1 January: New Year's Day
2 January: Carnival Last Lap
March/April: Easter; Good Friday; Easter Monday
May: (1st Monday) Labor Day
May/June: Whit Monday
July: (1st Monday) Caricom Day.
August: (1st Monday and Tuesday) Carnival
1 November: Independence Day
9 December: National Heroes Day
25 December: Christmas Day
26 December: Boxing Day

St Kitts and Nevis

1 January: New Year's Day
March/April: Good Friday, Easter Monday
1 May: Labour Day
June: Whit Monday
August: (1st Monday) Emancipation Day; (2nd Monday) Culturama Last Lap
16 September: National Heroes Day
19 September: Independence Day
25 December: Christmas Day
26 December: Boxing Day

Dominica

1 January: New Year's Day
March/April: Good Friday; Easter Monday
1 May: Labour Day
May/June: Whit Monday
August: (1st Monday) August Monday
3 November: Independence Day
4 November: Community Service Day
25 December: Christmas Day
26 December: Boxing Day

Martinique

1 January: New Year's Day
February/March: Carnival
March: Mi-Carême (Mid-Lent)
March/April: Easter
1 May: Labor Day
8 May: VE Day
22 May: Slavery Abolition Day
May/June: Ascension Day
June: Whit Monday
14 July: Bastille Day/Fête Nationale

21 July: Schoelcher Day
15 August: Assumption Day
1 November: All Saints Day
11 November: Armistice Day
25 December: Christmas Day

Guadeloupe

1 January: New Year's Day
February/March: Carnival
March: Mi-Carême (Mid-Lent)
March/April: Easter
May 1: Labour Day
May 8: VE Day
May 27: Abolition Day
May (variable): Ascension Day
May (variable): Whit Monday
14 July: Bastille Day/Fête Nationale
21 July: Schoelcher Day (Emancipation)
15 August: Assumption Day
1 November: All Saints Day
11 November: Armistice Day
25 December: Christmas Day
26 December: Young Saints Day; Children's Parade
31 December: New Year's Eve

St Lucia

1 January: New Year's Day
2 January: New Year's Holiday
22 February: Independence Day
March/April (variable): Easter
1 May: Labour Day; Whitsun (variable); Corpus Christi (variable)
July: Carnival Monday
1 August: Emancipation Day
1 October: Thanksgiving
13 December: National Day
25 December: Christmas Day
26 December: Boxing Day

Barbados

1 January: New Year's Day
21 January: Errol Barrow Day
March/April: Easter
28 April: National Heroes Day
1 May: Labour Day
May/June: Whit Monday
August: (1st Monday) Emancipation Day; Kadooment Day
30 November: Independence Day
25 December: Christmas Day
26 December: Boxing Day

St Vincent and The Grenadines

1 January: New Year's Day
14 March: National Heroes Day
March/April: Easter
1 May: Labor Day
May/June: Whit Monday
7 July: Caricom Day

July (early): Carnival Monday/Tuesday
August: (1st Monday) Emancipation Day/August Monday
27 October: Independence Day
25 December: Christmas Day
26 December: Boxing Day

Grenada

1 January: New Year's Day
7 February: Independence Day
March/April: Easter; Good Friday; Easter Monday
1 May: Labour Day
May/June: Whit Monday
June: Corpus Christi
August: (1st Monday/Tuesday) Emancipation Days
August: Carnival
25 October: Thanksgiving Day
25 December: Christmas Day
26 December: Boxing Day

Trinidad and Tobago

1 January: New Year's Day
February/March: Carnival
30 March: Spiritual Baptist Liberation Day.
March/April: Easter
May: Indian Arrival Day
June (variable): Corpus Christi.
19 June: Labour Day
1 August: Emancipation Day
August: Eid al Fitr (end of Ramadan)
31 August: Independence Day
24 September: Republic Day
October/November (variable): Divali
25 December: Christmas Day
26 December: Boxing Day

Aruba and Curaçao

1 January: New Year's Day
25 January: G.F. Betico Croes Birthday
March: Carnival
18 March: Aruba Day
March/April: Easter
30 April: Rincon Day; Queen's Day
1 May: Labour Day
May/June: Ascension Day
June: Whit Sunday
2 July: Curaçao Flag Day
15 December: Kingdom Day
25 December: Christmas Day
26 December: Boxing Day

British Virgin Islands

An assortment of shops, including duty-free, line Tortola's Main Street in Road Town. The most famous of these is Pusser's Company Store, which in addition to its own rum, sells clothes, antiques and all things nautical. There are also branches in Soper's Hole Wharf in the west and Leverick Bay in Virgin Gorda. The waterfront Crafts Alive Market sells locally made products. BVI Apparel has factory outlets selling clothes and gifts at low prices at Soper's Hole, Baugher's Bay and Road Town. Dive BVI Ltd stocks diving equipment. On Anegada, Pat's Pottery & Art features items all made on the island. Don't miss the eccentric Sunny Caribbee Herb & Spice Company in Road Town for lotions, herbs and spices.

St-Barthélemy, Saba and Montserrat

St-Barths: In Gustavia and St-Jean you can find duty-free luxury goods such as designer wear (Hèrmes, Louis Vuitton, Chopard, Bulgari, Cartier etc.), perfume and quality local crafts. In the local supermarket, wine, cheese and other French goods are the same prices you'd find in France.
Saba: Saba Lace, the drawn-thread work, is also known as Spanish work because it originated from Venezuela. A Saban woman studied there in the 1870s, learned the skill and returned to share the craft with other local women. It is on sale in stores and from private houses. The Saba Artisan's Foundation sells locally designed and produced clothing and fabric. Saba Spice is the local liqueur, a 150° proof rum mixed with spices, particularly cloves and sugar. The best shops are in Windwardside, where there is a good art gallery and gift shop. At Jobean Glass Art Studio in Windwardside (www.jobean-glass.com) you can see the glass being blown and buy the artwork.
Montserrat: The Arts & Crafts Association in Brades sells handmade local souvenirs. Crafts include leather goods, hand-woven items from locally grown Sea Island cotton, T-shirts, volcanic souvenirs made of ash and volcanic rocks, handmade dolls and greeting cards, local preserves such as guava jelly and hot pepper sauce, local music CDs, and books and DVDs on Montserrat. The National Trust, on the Northern Main Road, has a gift shop with maps, photographs, crafts and other souvenirs. Postage stamps issued by the Montserrat Philatelic Bureau (in the same building as the National Trust) are collectors' items.

Antigua

Heritage Quay and Redcliffe Quay in St John's are popular because of their proximity to the cruise terminal. There are duty-free shops and a market. Harmony Hall art gallery exhibits the work of Caribbean artists at Brown's Bay, near Freetown (tel: 268-460 4120). The market in St John's is good for local produce, such as the Antigua black pineapple, reputed to be the sweetest in the world.

St Kitts and Nevis

For local color, don't miss the market in Basseterre (Saturday morning). There is a variety of shops in TDC Mall, Pelican Mall and at Port Zante. For colorful clothing, look for imaginative Caribelle Batik prints on Sea Island cotton or visit their workshop at Romney Manor (caribellebatikstkitts.com). Look out for the attractive local paintings and Giclee prints of Kate Spencer (www.katespencerfineart.com). Her studio can be visited at her house in the north, or visit her gallery at The Gallery Café in Basseterre. On Nevis, the market is in Charlestown near the ferry dock, open Mon–Sat, but busiest Fri–Sat, sells Caribbean produce, hot sauces and spices. Nevis Pottery, Newcastle, makes red-clay pots. The Nevis Craft Cooperative weaves rugs and makes wooden crafts and ceramics; it has a shop on Main Street, Charlestown.

Dominica

While Dominica cannot compete with other ports of call for the range of duty-free luxury goods, it has crafts that are unique to the island, such as Kalinago reed baskets, which provide a direct link to Venezuelan culture. These can be bought in the Carib Territory either at roadside stalls or at the model village, or from Tropicrafts on Turkey Lane in Roseau. Many natural products are made here with local ingredients, such as Coap Pot soaps and massage oils, and Heaven Scent soaps. You can find spices, vanilla, honey, coffee, teas, cocoa, bwa bandé (an local alternative to Viagra), rum and beer, all from the island.

Martinique

Many shops are outposts of French chains. Good buys include jewelry, cosmetics and French fashions. The main shopping streets are rue Victor Hugo and rue de la République, where there is a mall, Cour Perrinon. There is a larger mall, The Galleria, a short taxi ride from town on the way to the airport, with a French supermarket and fashion stores.

Guadeloupe

Best buys are bolts of fabric, arts and crafts, French designer clothing and perfume. There are shops at the Centre St-John Perse and the Cora Center in Bas-du-Fort. Good markets include the Marché de la Rotonde, Marché de la Darse and the Marche Nocturne night market in Saint Francois.

St Lucia

Pointe Seraphine on the waterfront in Castries is a duty-free complex selling perfume, china, crystal, designer-wear and locally made crafts. Castries Market is worth a look for the spices, fruit and vegetables, and crafts. The best places to shop for designer clothes are in Baywalk Mall, Rodney Bay, which also has a parking lot, supermarket and casino. There are art galleries showcasing works by world-class St Lucian artists in Pointe Seraphine, in Castries, in Rodney Bay and the marina. The studio of sculptor and woodcarver Vincent Joseph Eudovic can be visited on Morne Fortune.

Barbados

Look for local crafts, cigars, pottery and rum. Bridgetown has several art galleries. Visitors can shop duty-free in some outlets; always carry a cruise ID card. In Bridgetown, the main shopping area is Broad Street. The Chattel Village on St Lawrence Gap and Quayside Center in Hastings Plaza have stores selling a variety of souvenirs and local crafts. Earthworks Pottery, Edgehill Heights, St Thomas, tel: 246-425 0223, www.earthworks-pottery.com, make and sell colorful pots, trays, trinkets and dinnerware which is microwave- and dishwasher-safe. The company will ship it home for you if you can't carry it all and will even make individual items on request.

St Vincent and The Grenadines

St Vincent and Bequia are good places to find colorful batiks; locally made art and crafts, such as straw baskets and wood carvings; goatskin drums; stamps; and fresh fruit from the market in Kingstown.

Grenada

Cocoa is now the major crop on the island and it is grown organically. Look out for cocoa balls in the market, which you can use to make hot chocolate or grate into cakes. There is even locally produced chocolate, made by the Grenada Chocolate Company (grenadachocolate.com), which is also worth seeking out. Look out for packets of spice, jams, syrups, candy, rum, even jewelry made from nutmeg. Also batik and screen-printed items. Don't miss the Grande Anse Craft and Spice Market, 5 minutes from the harbor.

Trinidad and Tobago

Trinidad and Tobago are best for handicrafts, batik, rum, clothing and duty-free goods such as cigarettes and computers (carry your cruise ship ID to qualify for duty-free prices). Frederick Street, Queen Street, Charlotte Street and Henry Street are the main shopping areas. For a good selection of local calypso and soca music try Rhyner's record shop (www.rhyners.com), 54 Prince Street, Port of Spain.

Aruba and Curaçao

The ABC islands have a range of tax-free shopping outlets. Oranjestad in Aruba is goldmine of designer wear, jewelry, perfume and local art. There are several shopping malls offering a wide range of shops in the town center. Curaçao has great tax-free purchases, shopping malls and interesting boutiques in Willemstad. Look out for Dutch cheeses, flavored Curaçao liqueur and local art.

SHORE ACTIVITIES

British Virgin Islands

Excursions

Sailing, snorkeling, kayaking and beach day-trips are the best reasons to visit the BVI. Other excursions include shopping trips in Road Town; hikes in Sage Mountain National Park (Tortola); day-sailing trips to Virgin Gorda and Jost van Dyke; and mini-regattas.

Watersports

There is good snorkeling on the rocky edges of many beaches, such as Smuggler's Cove, Tortola, and Deadman's Beach, Peter Island. Norman Island, with the nearby rocks called 'the Indians', is worth a visit.

Apple Bay, Cane Garden Bay and Josiah's Bay are popular windsurfing beaches on Tortola; there are also good conditions in Trellis Bay. Island Surf and Sail has lessons for beginners and sailing classes (tel: 284 494-0123, www.bviwatertoys.com), best in November.

The wreck of the RMS *Rhone*, which lies west of Salt Island, is the most popular dive site in the BVI and is also a marine park. The reefs around Anegada have been badly damaged by too many divers and heavy anchoring. Anchoring has now been banned to allow the reef to recover and to establish a marine park there, although guided snorkeling and scuba diving tours are offered. Dive operators in the BVI include: Dive BVI with three locations, tel: 284-541 9818, www.divebvi.com; and Blue Water Divers, tel: 284-494 2847, www.bluewaterdiversbvi.com, with two locations.

Bonefish and marlin sport-fishing tours can be arranged through the Anegada Reef Hotel (tel: 284-495 8002, www.anegadareef.com).

St-Barthélemy, Saba and Montserrat

St-Barths

Excursions

Stroll round Gustavia to view the Swedish architecture, the Municipal Museum and the forts; take a taxi tour round the island; stop off at Corossol, a fishing village with the Inter Ocean Museum containing a shell collection from around the world; go shopping for designer goods; eat a long lunch in a restaurant; or drop in to the supermarket or deli to pick up supplies of French food for a picnic on the beach.

Best beaches

There are many lovely beaches on St-Barths, all of which allow topless sunbathing. Marigot is a good beach for snorkeling, with small patches of sand between rocky outcrops within the marine reserve. Motorized sports are not allowed, so it is very quiet. Anse du Grand Saline is a wide expanse of beach with cliffs and rocks at either end, and sand dunes behind. There is no hotel development here and the beach is totally unspoiled and beautiful. Another quiet, undeveloped bay is Gouverneur, down a steep road. Montbars the Exterminator, a 17th century pirate, apparently hid his treasure here.

Watersports
Windsurfing and kitesurfing are available at Grand Cul de Sac, a bay with shallow water protected from the sea by a peninsula and reef. Surfing is popular on Anse de Toiny and Anse du Grand Fond on the Atlantic coast, where swimming is not advised because of strong currents. Lorient offers good surfing or snorkeling depending on the mood of the sea. The combination of the marine reserve and lots of little rocks and islets around the island make St-Barths a very good diving destination. There is a good chance of seeing turtles, which nest on several beaches, including Colombier, and in May you can sometimes see sperm whales on their migration through the surrounding waters.

Saba

Hiking
The Saba Conservation Foundation preserves and marks the old trails used by people and donkeys until the road was built. Register at the Saba Trail Shop in Windwardside where you will be given a disk in return for your admission fee and you can pick up information and maps and hire a walking stick. You can then hike up Mount Scenery or tackle other trails

such as The Ladder, Crispeen Track, Sandy Cruz Track, Maskerhorne Hill Trail and the Sulphur Mine Track. Guides can be arranged at the Trail Shop in Windwardside if you wish, and are extremely informative on history, fauna and flora

Watersports
Most visitors come to Saba to dive and there are several dive shops offering a full range of activities and dive packages. The marine park around Saba was established in 1987 and all divers pay a fee for maintenance of the park. Mooring buoys have been provided for dive boats to prevent anchor damage. The best dive sites are off the west coast where there are interesting rock formations and a wealth of marine life with colorful fish, coral and sponges. The steep slopes of the volcano above water are replicated under the sea, so in the deep water you can also spot large pelagics, with migrating humpback whales, schools of porpoises, large tarpon, barracuda and sea turtles.

Montserrat

Excursions
Tours are offered around the north of the island to the Montserrat Volcano Observatory, the National Trust and to Little Bay, to see progress on construction of the new capital.

Best beaches
Rendezvous Bay in the north is the only white-sand beach, accessible on foot or by boat. The other beaches on the west coast, such as Carr's Bay, Woodlands, Old Road Bay, Foxes Bay Lime Kiln Bay and Bunkum Bay are all black, volcanic sand, but beautiful nonetheless.

Hiking
The Montserrat National Trust (www. montserratnationaltrust.ms) maintains

the trails in the north of the island and rangers are available to guide you. There are some excellent mountain walks and the rangers are very knowledgeable.

Watersports
Diving has improved since the south of the island and offshore waters were made a no-go area because of volcanic activity. Left alone for several years, marine life flourished and diving off the west coast is now very rewarding. There are a couple of dive operators offering lots of activities. Contact Scuba Montserrat, tel: 664-496 7807, www.scubamontserrat. com. Fishing charters are offered by dive operators and experienced fishermen, or you can just hire rods and fish from the shore. The same operators offer boat trips to see the former capital, Plymouth, from the sea, sunset cruises, round-the-island tours and transfers to Rendezvous Bay for a beach excursion.

Antigua

Excursions
The museum at Nelson's Dockyard; open air market on Saturdays in St John's; Harmony Hall art gallery; cricket matches; barbecue and steel band every Sunday at Shirley Heights Lookout Restaurant (from 4pm, not to be missed); day-trip to Barbuda; kayaking and hiking the inlets and mangroves of the east coast and offshore islets; zip-line canopy tour; trail horse riding at Spring Hill Riding Club (www.antiguaequestrian.com).

Best beaches
There is a beach for every day of the year on Antigua. Fort James, Dickenson Bay and Runaway Bay are only 5–10 minutes by taxi north from St John's; west of the capital are the four crescent-shaped Hawksbill beaches; south is the busy Jolly Beach with lots of activities and unspoiled Darkwood Beach with a beach bar. In the south, Carlisle Bay is pleasant, but much of it is taken up by a luxury hotel; Galleon Beach is the closest to Nelson's Dockyard. Half Moon Bay is the best beach on the eastern side.

Watersports
Sailing can be arranged through Nicholson Yacht Charters, tel: 268-460 1530, www.nicholson-charters.com. For windsurfing lessons

---

⊘ Sailing

The BVI is one of the best sailing areas in the Caribbean. Most cruise ship companies organize sailing trips or mini-regattas as excursions. There are lots of companies offering day-sails to islands around Tortola on yachts, schooners or catamarans. International yacht charters such as **The Moorings**

(www.moorings.com) or **Sunsail** (tel: 284-495 4740, www.sunsail. com) have branches on Tortola, for day hire, or a longer crewed or bareboat charter. Yachts are usually rented on a weekly basis. Check with the BVI tourist board, or see *Welcome* magazine for a comprehensive listing of local charter companies.

and equipment, contact Windsurf Antigua, tel: 268-461 9463, www.windsurfantigua.net. For kitesurfing, lessons and equipment, contact Kitesurf Antigua, tel: 268-720 5483, www.kitesurfantigua.com.

Several hotels have dive shops. Dive operators include: Dive Antigua, Rex Resorts' Halcyon Cove, Dickenson Bay, tel: 268-462 3483, www.diveantigua.com; Jolly Dive, Jolly Beach, tel: 268-462 8305, www.jollydiveantigua.com; Dockyard Divers, Nelson's Dockyard, tel: 268 729-3040, www.dockyard-divers.com.

Golf

There are golf courses at Cedar Valley Golf Club, tel: 268-462 0161, www.golfantigua.com (18-hole); and the Jolly Harbour Golf Club, Jolly Harbour, tel: 268-462 7771 (short 18-hole).

St Kitts and Nevis

Excursions

Historic tours of St Kitts; St Kitts Scenic Railway; Romney Manor Caribelle Batik workshops; Wingfield Estate sugar mill and Sky Rides zip-line tour; Black Rocks at Sandy Bay (lava formations); views and battlegrounds on Brimstone Hill; day-trips to nearby Nevis, 6 minutes by air or 45 minutes by ferry.

Best beaches

Banana Bay and Cockleshell Bay for peace and quiet; Turtle Beach and Frigate Beach for watersports; White House Bay for snorkeling.

Watersports

Strong currents make swimming on the Atlantic side of the islands dangerous, although hotels have built breakwaters to provide calmer water. Swim safely on the Caribbean side. For diving on St Kitts, try: Kenneth's Dive Center, with an operation at Port Zante, tel: 869-465 2670; Pro Divers, at Fisherman's Wharf, tel: 869-466 3483; www.prodiversstkitts.com). On Nevis there is Scuba Safaris, Oualie Beach, tel: 869 665-1516, www.divenevis.com.

Hiking

Both islands have lush rainforests and hilly terrain. A particular thrill is the hike down into the crater of an old volcano on Mount Liamuiga in St Kitts. Contact Greg's Safaris, tel: 869-465 4121, www.gregsafaris.com.

On Nevis, Sunrise Tours (tel: 869-469 2758, www.nevisnaturetours.com) organizes guided hikes of varying degrees of difficulty.

Golf

Royal St Kitts Golf Club is an 18-hole championship course on Frigate Bay Road (tel: 869-466 2700; www.royalstkittsgolfclub.com). Nevis has the 18-hole Robert Trent Jones II course attached to the Four Seasons Resort (tel: 869-469 1111, www.fourseasons.com) in Charlestown.

Dominica

Excursions

Excursions are offered from both Roseau and Portsmouth but, given the logistics, passengers are usually restricted to just one trip.

In Roseau you can visit the marketplace, Botanical Garden, cathedral and the Dominica Museum. Outside town there are trips to Trafalgar Falls followed by a visit to the botanic garden trail at Papillote Wilderness Retreat; rainforest aerial tram ride in Laudat; island tours; guided hiking trails of varying difficulty; the Morne Diablotin National Park, home to an endangered species of Amazonian parrot (access by four-wheel-drive vehicle); tours of the Carib Territory for traditional crafts and culture. Portsmouth provides easy access to the Carib territory, boat trips on the Indian River and the unspoilt Cabrits National Park.

Dominica has the only long-distance hiking trail in the Caribbean, the Waitukubuli National Trail. It stretches from north to south and runs for 115 miles through forest, national parks, old slave routes and villages where hikers can stop for sustenance (www.waitukubulitrail.com).

Best beaches

Hampstead Beach on the northern coast is one of the finest, with white sand and palms, and sheltered Macousheri Bay and Coconut Beach near Portsmouth; accessible by four-wheel-drive vehicle are Turtle Beach and Pointe Baptiste (unsafe for swimming due to Atlantic rollers and currents).

Watersports

Dominica has whale-watching trips organized by local operators, and some of the best diving in

the Caribbean, with steep, 1,000ft (300-meter) drop-offs, hot springs, pinnacles and walls. Dive sites are concentrated along the west coast. The deep waters make local expertise essential for diving excursions. Operators offer a variety of packages for beginners and experienced divers. An annual Dive Fest in July has diving, kayaking, swimming, fishing, snorkeling and sunset cruises; the grand finale is a Kubuli Carib canoe race. Approved dive operators who also provide snorkeling gear include: Anchorage Dive Center, tel: 767-448 2638, www.anchoragehotel.dm; and Dive Dominica (at Castle Comfort Lodge), tel: 767-448 218, www.divedominica.com).

River sports are also exciting and rewarding, including rappelling, abseiling, canyoning and tubing. Contact Extreme Dominica just outside Roseau, tel: 760-350 5780, www.extremedominica.com.

Martinique

Excursions

Shopping in Fort-de-France, markets and Galleria shopping mall for French designer outlets; Macouba fishing village; St-Pierre and Musée Volcanologique; hike the Route de la Trace or any of the 31 marked trails maintained by the National Forest Service; canyoning; quad-bike riding; butterfly garden at Anse Latouche; Balata Botanical Garden; Chateau Dubuc; the Orchid Farm, Route du Vauclin; Route des Rhums tour of distilleries; Musée du Rhum, Sainte-Marie; Maison de la Canne, sugar museum at Pointe Vatable.

Best beaches

For the southern, white-sand beaches take a ferry trip to Pointe du Bout (25 minutes). The closest to the ferry are Anse Mitan and Anse à l'Ane. The beaches are good all along the southern coast. Those to the north of Fort-de-France are black sand.

Watersports

Popular areas for watersports include Tartane (La Trinité), Le Robert, Schoelcher and St-Pierre. In the south, scuba diving, waterskiing, jet-skiing, surfing and windsurfing, sailing and canoeing are all available. The most popular dive sites

◎ Nightlife

Barbados is lively at night, especially on the south coast:
The Boatyard, Bay Street, Bridgetown. Tel: 246-826 4448, www.theboatyard.com. Live bands every evening except Monday and Wednesday.
Harbour Lights, Bay Street, Bridgetown. Tel: 246-436 7225, www.harbourlightsbarbados.com. An open-air nightclub on the beach. Top live bands at weekends.
Limegrove West Bar, Limegrove, Holetown. Tel: 246-571 7300 Cocktails, food and live local bands till late
The Cove, St Lawrence Gap, tel: 246-420 7612, www.coveclubbarbados.com Big nightclub with guest DJs.
The Waterfront Cafe, The Careenage, Bridgetown. Tel: 246-427 0093, www.waterfrontcafe.com.bb. Live music nightly with jazz on Thursday, Friday, and Saturday.

around Martinique include shelf diving off Diamond Rock (Le Rocher du Diamant) and exploring the wrecks in the bay at St-Pierre. The wrecks were sunk in 1902 during the eruption of the Mont Pelée volcano. Contact Acqua Sud, Pointe de la Cherry, Le Diamant, tel: 0-596-765 101. For surfing, contact Martinique Surfing, in Fort-de-France, www.martiniquesurfing.com.

Golf

Martinique Golf and Country Club, 97229 Les Trois-Ilets (tel: 596-68 32 81, www.golfmartinique.com), an 18-hole championship course designed by Robert Trent Jones.

Guadeloupe

Excursions

Shopping in Pointe-a-Pitre; trips along the dramatic coastline at Pointe des Chateaux; La Soufrière volcano and national park; diving and snorkeling at the Cousteau Underwater Park in Basse-Terre; day-trips to Marie-Galante island; water-scooter tours of the mangroves; deep-sea fishing; hiking; rock climbing and abseiling on Terre-de-Haut.

Best beaches

Anse Carot on Marie-Galante; Pompierre on Terre-de-Haut; Gosier and Ste-Anne; Pointe des Chateaux has snack bars and scenery, but rough seas. In town, try Plage du Bourg.

Watersports

For a list of day-sailing trips see www.caribya.com/martinique/sailing.and. boating, for scuba diving, contact the tourist office; there are dozens of

companies around all the islands. There is good snorkeling and diving around Pigeon Island in the Cousteau Marine Park on the Golden Corniche (a popular cruise excursion), with glass-bottomed boat trips.

St Lucia

Excursions

Sightseeing trips to the Pitons; Diamond Falls, Mineral Baths and Sulphur Springs; rainforest walks; Pigeon Island National Park; deep-sea fishing. If you're staying on, don't miss the weekly street party at Gros Islet – the Friday night jump-up – or the Friday fish fry at Anse La Raye for something a little less exuberant.

Best beaches

Anse Cochon and Anse Chastanet for snorkeling; Reduit Beach and Pigeon Island for white sandy beaches, good facilities, watersports and the ruins of Fort Rodney. A lot of cruise passengers go to Choc Bay, a short drive from the cruise terminal; Vigie, near Castries, is also clean and pretty, although it is near the airport and can be noisy.

Watersports

There are many places offering watersports on the island from sailing to diving and deep-sea fishing. Most sail charter companies are based in Marigot Bay and Rodney Bay. River and coastal kayaking is very popular.

For deep-sea fishing day and half-day trips, contact: Captain Mike's, Vigie Marina, Castries, tel: 758-452 7044, www.captmikes.com; Hackshaws Boat Charters, Vigie Marina, tel: 758-453 0553, www.hackshaws.com.

For diving and snorkeling, contact: Scuba St Lucia, Anse Chastanet

Resort, Soufrière, tel: 758-459 7755, www.scubastlucia.com; or Dive Fair Helen, Marigot Bay, tel: 758-451 7716, www.divefairhelen.com.

Windsurfing and kitesurfing are exceptionally good on the east coast and there are facilities at Cas-en-Bas in the north and Anse de Sables in the south. Contact The Reef Kite and Surf, Anse de Sables Beach, Vieux Fort, tel: 758-454 3418, www.stluciawindsurfing.com, Kitesurfing St Lucia, Cas-en-Bas, Gros Islet, tel: 758-714 9589, www.kitesurfingstlucia.com.

Golf

There is a good 18-hole public golf course at Cap Estate in the far north of the island that offers a special rate for cruise passengers: St Lucia Golf Club, Cap Estate, Rodney Bay, tel: 758-450 8523, www.stluciagolf.com.

Barbados

Excursions

Visit the art galleries and shop in Bridgetown; tour St Michael's cathedral; the Garrison; Mount Gay Rum tour; self-drive tours by mini-moke to the north and east coasts; Welchman Hall Gully nature reserve; Harrison's Cave; Andromeda Gardens; Earth Works Pottery; Animal Flower Cave in the north; Cherry Tree Hill for views of the Atlantic coast; Atlantic beaches; cricket matches at Kensington Oval; polo matches at Holders Hill, St James, Nov–May; horseracing at the Garrison, Jan–Mar, May–Oct, Nov–Dec; hike the old railway track from Bath to Bathsheba and on to Cattlewash; day-trips to the Grenadines.

Best beaches

Holetown for people-watching and great food; Brighton Beach next to the cruise terminal; Bathsheba for wild Atlantic scenery; Crane Beach; Bottom Bay.

Watersports

Most watersports are available at the hotels along the west and south coasts. Equipment can be hired at Brighton Beach.

There are several wrecks to explore and excellent visibility for divers and snorkelers. Try: Underwater Barbados, tel: 246-426 0655, www.funbarbados.com; West Side Scuba Centre, tel: 246-262 1029, www.westsidescuba.com; Hightide Watersports, tel: 246-432 0931, www.divehightide.com. Then there is the Atlantis submarine for those who don't want to get wet: Atlantis Adventures, tel: 246-436 8929, www.barbados.atlantissubmarines.com.

Mount Gay Regatta is the highlight of the yachting season in May or June. Small sailing boats, such as a Sunfish or Hobie Cat, can be rented by the hour along the south and west coast beaches. Sailing trips around the island can include lunch, snorkeling or a moonlight cruise; www.barbados.org; Cool Runnings, tel: 246-436 0911, www.coolrunningsbarbados.com. Barbados Black Pearl operates the infamous Jolly Roger booze cruises (tel: 246-826 7245, www.barbadosblackpearl-jollyroger1.com).

Body surfing is good along the southeast coast; you can rent boards on the beach at The Crane. The best surfing around the island is in an area known as the Soup Bowl at Bathsheba on the Atlantic Coast, but beware of the strong currents. Contact: the Barbados Surfing Association, Box 24, Barbados Olympic Association Inc., Olympic Centre, Garfield Sobers Sports Complex, Wildey, St Michael, BB15094, tel: 246-826 7661, www.barbadossurfingassociation.org.

There is excellent windsurfing and kitesurfing to be had at the southernmost point of the island at Silver Sands and Silver Rock.

St Vincent and The Grenadines

Excursions

Hiking La Soufrière volcano (a tough, full-day walk) or Mount St Andrew (gentler, with amazing views); Trinity Falls, Dark Wood Falls and Baleine (reach the waterfall, by boat); Montreal tropical gardens; Belmont Lookout, Cumberland Nature Trail, Vermont Nature Trail, Owia Salt Pond, day sailing trips; snorkeling in Tobago Cays; beaches and watersports on Canouan; eating out on Bequia.

Best beaches

Villa, just southeast of Kingstown; Young Island, offshore near Villa; Cumberland Bay; and smaller Grenadines islands. Small ships may tender off one of these.

Watersports

Divers will find a range of sponges, corals, fish, exciting marine life and a number of sunken wrecks. Operators include: Dive St Vincent, Young Island Dock, tel: 784-457 4714, www.divestvincent.com; Bequia Dive Adventures, Admiralty Bay, tel: 784-458 3826, www.bequiadiveadventures.com; Canouan Dive Center, Tamarind Beach Hotel, tel: 784-532 8073, www.canouandivecenter.com; and Grenadines Dive, Union Island, tel: 784-458 8138, www.grenadinesdive.com.

To organize bare-boat sailing or a yacht with a crew, contact: Barefoot Yacht Charters, tel: 784-456 9526, www.barefootyachts.com; Grenadine Escape, tel: 784-496 0654, www.grenadine-escape.com. For sport-fishing trips try: Crystal Blue Sportfishing, www.caribbeanedge.com.

Grenada

Excursions

Markets, shopping, Georgian architecture and three historic forts in St George's; Grand Etang National Park for hiking and nature trails; Dougaldston Spice Estate; Gouyave Nutmeg Processing Station (tours); Belmont Estate plantation tour; Sauters for Carib's Leap, where the Caribs leapt to their deaths rather than surrender to the French; Clabony Sulphur Pond, with healing properties; River Antoine Rum distillery.

Best beaches

Grand Anse is just outside St George's, a 2-mile (3km) stretch of soft white sand with bars, restaurants, shops and watersports. La Sagesse is quieter with good hiking in the area; good swimming again, fewer crowds at Levera Beach and Bathway Beach.

Watersports

Grenada and Carriacou have a good range of diving sites, including the Caribbean's biggest wreck, *Bianca C*, which sank outside St George's in 1961. There are spectacular reefs. Grand Anse beach has dive companies, as does Carriacou. Contact: Deefer Diving, tel: 473-443 7882, www. deeferdiving.com; Dive Grenada, tel: 473-444 1092, www.divegrenada.com.

Windsurfing and waterskiing facilities are available on Grand Anse beach. The Secret Harbour Hotel rents snorkeling equipment and also organizes windsurfing, yacht charters and speedboat outings. Tel: 473-444 4439, www.secretharbourgrenada.com.

Trinidad and Tobago

Excursions

Shopping; Botanic Gardens; stroll along Brian Lara Promenade in Port of Spain; Gasparee Caves (by boat); rum distillery tours; hiking at Blanchisseuse; manatee spotting at Navira Swamp; Pointe-a-Pierre Wildfowl Trust; Asa Wright Nature Centre; scarlet ibis roosting time at Caroni Bird Sanctuary; cricket matches at the Oval; Carnival celebrations; Little Tobago Bird Sanctuary with glass-bottom boat tour; hiking up Pigeon Peak; snorkeling and diving at Buccoo Reef; Nylon Pool boat trip; plantation tour with rum and chocolate tasting at Tobago Cocoa Estate.

Best beaches

Maracas on Trinidad for surfing; Las Cuevas (1 hour from Port of Spain) for peace and quiet. On Tobago: Pigeon Point, Store Bay, Mount Irvine, Castara, Englishman's Bay on the west side, Big Bacolet Bay on the east coast for surfing, and Speyside, where the reefs are less damaged than Buccoo.

Watersports

The best diving and snorkeling can be found among the exciting reefs around Tobago and its neighboring islands. Dive operators on the island work with beginners and experienced divers. For more details contact Tobago Dive Experience, Manta Lodge, Speyside and Arnos Vale

---

⊘ Hiking in Trinidad and Tobago

Walking is a good way to explore the islands and see the fabulous flora and fauna. Always travel with an experienced guide. For details contact: **The Forestry Division**, Long Circular Road, Port of Spain, tel: 628 4077; **Trinidad and Tobago Field Naturalists' Club**, tel: 624 8017, www.ttfnc.org; **Chaguaramas Development Authority Guided Tours**, tel: 634 4227, www.chaguaramas.com; **Pioneer Journeys**, Pat Turpin, Man-O-War Bay Cottages, Charlotteville, tel: 660 4327, pturpin@tstt.net.tt; Darren Henry, tel: 868-639 4559, darren_tours@yahoo.com.

Hotel, Plymouth, tel: 868-660 4888, www.tobagodiveexperience.com.

Aruba and Curaçao

Excursions

Aruba: Half-day jeep or ATV safaris into the desert-like interior; duty-free shopping in Oranjestad; snorkeling on the wreck *Antilla*; hiking in the Arikok National Park; visits to the Natural Bridge; catamaran snorkeling tours; butterfly farm tours (www.thebutterflyfarm.com).
Curaçao: Museum and synagogue tours; art galleries, the floating market in Willemstad; Ostrich Farm (www.curacaoostrichfarm.com); Landhuise Chobolobo (liqueur factory); Amstel Brewery tours; Seaquarium underwater observatory; hiking in Christoffel National Park.

Best beaches

Aruba: Palm Beach and Eagle Beach, 5 to 10 minutes by taxi from the port; Baby Beach in the south for soft sand and snorkeling. Dos Playa and Boca Prins in the east for sand dunes and body surfing.
Curaçao: Mambo Beach at the Seaquarium; Playa Porto Marie for snorkeling; Caracas Bay Island for activities from horse riding to kayaking. Knip is a large sandy beach, popular at weekends; Jeremi is sandy, protected by cliffs and is public. Some beaches are private and make a charge to visitors.

Watersports

Both islands have diving in clear water. Dive operators: Aruba Pro Dive, Oranjestad, tel: 297-582 5520, www.arubawavedancer.com/arubaprodive; The Dive Bus, Curaçao, tel: 5999-693 8305, www.the-dive-bus.com; Ocean Encounters, Lions Dive and Beach Resort, Curaçao, tel: 5999-461 8131, www.oceanencounters.com.

Snorkeling gear, windsurf boards and Hobie Cats can be rented at most beaches.

Cycling and hiking

The flat, but rugged terrain of the ABC Islands is ideal for cycling. For details of mountain bike rentals and tours contact: Bike Rental Aruba, tel: 297-630 8262, www.bikerentalaruba.com.

At a more leisurely pace, hiking is the best way of studying the islands' remarkable flora and fauna, especially through the national parks.

Golf

Courses include: Tierra del Sol, tel: 297-586 7800, www.tierradelsol.com, an 18-hole golf course in the north west of Aruba. On Curaçao there is the 9-hole course at the Curaçao Golf & Squash Club, tel: 5999-737 3590; an 18-hole course at Blue Bay Golf & Beach Resort, tel: 5999-868 1755; and an 18-hole championship course at the Santa Barbara Beach & Golf Resort, www.santabarbararesort curacao.com.

TELECOMMUNICATIONS

British Virgin Islands

The dialing code is **284**. International phone calls may be made from most phones, and some will take phone cards.

There are lots of places offering WiFi, including some shops in Road Town and marinas and many restaurants. Local SIM cards are available for purchase.

St-Barthélemy, Saba and Montserrat

St-Barths: all French phone numbers have 10 digits (nine when calling from abroad); those in St-Barths begin with 0-590-, or 0-690 for cell phones. In addition the country code is 590, so if dialing from the US, dial 011-590-590-123 456. Most public phones accept Télécartes, which can be bought in the post office or the gas station by the airport. Most hotels, cafés and bars offer Wi-Fi for guests. St Barts telecom offers a 'hotspot' covering Gustavia. A connection card can be purchased to surf without limit. Local SIM cards are available.
Saba: hotels usually offer internet access for guests, but connection can be poor. The international dialing code is 599.
Montserrat: the international dialing code is 664. High-speed internet access and cellular service are available and WiFi can be found in some public places.

Antigua

The international dialing code is **268**. You can buy phone cards for payphones, WiFi is extensively available and local SIM cards can be purchased.

St Kitts and Nevis

The dialing code is **869**. Many cafés and restaurants provide free WiFi and local SIM cards can be purchased.

Dominica

The dialing code is **767**. LIME provides pre paid SIM cards or cards can be purchased locally. High-speed broadband is available in practically every hotel and many cafés and restaurants.

Martinique

The dialing code for Martinique is **596**. Telephone numbers are prefixed with 0596 (0696 for cellphones). Drop the first zero when dialing from abroad. To call within Martinique dial 0596 followed by the six-digit number. Local SIM cards can be purchased.

Guadeloupe

The international dialing code is **590**. The local number is prefixed with 0590; drop the first zero when dialing from abroad. WiFi is available at most hotels and in many cafés and bars. Local SIM cards available for purchase

St Lucia

The dialing code for St Lucia is **758**. SIM cards can be purchased locally as can Pay As You Go phones. Most hotels and many cafés have WiFi available.

Barbados

The dialing code is **246**. Barbados is in the process of covering the entire island with WiFi internet access. Most current coverage is on the West and South coast. Most hotels and guesthouses provide free access. SIM cards can be purchased locally.

Grenada

The dialing code is **473**. Local SIM cards are available and WiFi is provided in many hotels and cafés.

Trinidad and Tobago

The dialing code is **868**. Internet access is free in public libraries and available in many cafés and most hotels. SIM cards can be purchased locally as can prepaid phones

Aruba and Curaçao

The dialing code for Aruba is **297** and for Curaçao **5999**. Both islands have modern telecommunications systems. WiFi is widely available in hotels and hotspots around the islands.

TOURIST OFFICES

British Virgin Islands

In the UK
British Virgin Islands Tourist Board, 15 Upper Grosvenor Street, London, W1K 7PJ
Tel: 020 7355 9585
Email: infouk@bvi.org.uk
In the US
British Virgin Islands Tourist Board, 1 West 34th Street, Suite 302, New York, NY 10001.
Tel: 212-563 3117, 800-835 8530
Email: info@bvitourism.com
In the British Virgin Islands
3rd floor, Eureka Geneva Building, Road Town, Tortola
Tel: 284-494 3134
Email: info@bvitourism.com
Also an office at:
Virgin Gorda Yacht Harbour, The Valley
Tel: 284-495 5181
Websites
www.britishvirginislands.com
www.bvitourism.com
www.bviwelcome.com

St-Barthélemy, Saba and Montserrat

St-Barths
In St-Barths
1 Quai du Général de Gaulle, Gustavia
Tel: 590-590-278 727
In the UK
Lincoln House, 300 High Holborn, London, WC1V 7JH
Tel: 020 7061 6631
In the US
444 Madison Ave. 16th floor, New York NY 10022
Tel: 212-838 7800

Saba
In Saba
PO Box 527, Windwardside
Tel: 599-416 2231/2322, www.saba tourism.com

Montserrat
In Montserrat
The Montserrat Tourism Division, E.K. Osbourne Building, Little Bay, Montserrat
Tel: 664-491 4700
Websites
www.st-barths.com
www.saintbarth-tourisme.com
www.sabatourism.com
www.visitmontserrat.com

Antigua
In Canada
60 St Clair Avenue East, Suite 304, Toronto, Ontario M4T 1N5
Tel: 416-961 3143
Email: info@antigua-barbuda-ca.com
In the UK
Victoria House, 4th Floor, Victoria Road, Chelmsford, Essex CM1 1JR
Tel: +01245-707 471
In the US
3 Dag Hammarskjold Plaza, 305 East 47th Street – 6A, New York, NY 10017
Tel: 212-541 4119
Email: info@antigua-barbuda.org
In Antigua
Antigua & Barbuda Tourism Authority, Government Complex, Queen Elizabeth Highway, St John's
Tel: 268-262 0480
Website
www.antigua-barbuda.org
www.visitantiguabarbuda.co.uk

St Kitts and Nevis
In Canada
St Kitts Tourism Authority, 133 Richmond St West, Suite 311, Toronto, Ontario M5H 2L3
Tel: 416-368 6707
In the UK
10 Kensington Court, London, W8 5DL
Tel: 020 7376 0881
In the US
7 Burgess Drive, Litchfield, New Hampshire 03052
Tel: 212-535 1234
Toll-free: 603-424 3665
In St Kitts and Nevis
Pelican Mall, Bay Road, Basseterre, St Kitts
Tel: 869-465 4040
Nevis Tourism Authority, Main Street, Charlestown, Nevis
Tel: 869-469 7550
Email: info@nevisisland.com
Websites
www.stkittstourism.kn
www.nevisisland.com

Dominica
In the UK
Discover Dominica
Tel: 020 7326 9880
In the US and Canada
Discover Dominica
Tel: 866-522 4057 (toll-free)
Email: dominicany@dominica.dm
In Dominica
Discover Dominica Authority, 5–7 Great Marlborough Street, Roseau, Commonwealth of Dominica
Tel: 767-448 2045
Email: tourism@dominica.dm
Website
www.dominica.dm

Martinique
In the US
Martinique Promotion Bureau, 825 Third Avenue, 29th Floor, New York, NY 10022
Tel: 212-838 6887
Email: info@martinique.org
In Martinique
Comité Martiniquais du Tourisme, 5 Avenue Loulou Boislaville, 97200 Fort-De-France
Tel: 596-0-596 61 61 77
Website
www.martinique.org

Guadeloupe
In France
8-10, rue Buffault, 75009 Paris
Tel: 33 1 40 62 99 07
Email: infoeurope@lesilesdeguade-loupe.com
In Guadeloupe
Office du Tourisme de la Guadeloupe, 5 Square de la Banque, BP 555, 97166 Pointe-à-Pitre
Tel: 590-0-590-820 930
Email: info@lesilesdeguadeloupe.com
Office Municipal de Tourisme Terre de Haut – Les Saintes, Rue Jean Calot, BP10 97137 Terre-de-Haut
Tel: 590-0-590-995 860
Websites
www.franceguide.com
www.lesilesdeguadeloupe.com

St Lucia
In Canada
60 St. Clair Avenue East, Suite 909 Toronto, Ontario M4T 1N5
Tel: 416-392 4242
Email: sltbcanada@aol.com
In the UK
1 Collingham Gardens, London, SW5 0HW

Tel: 020 7341 7005
Email: sltbinfo@stluciauk.org
In the US
St Lucia Tourist Board,
3645 Marketplace Blvd, Suite 130 #178, East Point, GA 30344
Tel: 1-800-456-3984 Email: stluciatourism@aol.com
In St Lucia
St Lucia Tourist Board, PO Box 221, Sureline Building, Vide Bouteille, Castries
Tel: 758-452 4094
Website
www.stlucia.org

Barbados

In Canada
110 Sheppard Avenue East, Suite 205, North York, Ontario M2N 6Y8
Tel: 416-214 9880
Email: canada@visitbarbados.org
In the UK
263 Tottenham Court Road, London, W1T 7LA
Tel: 020 7299 7175
Email: btauk@visitbarbados.org
In the US
800 2nd Avenue, 5th floor, New York, NY 10017
Tel: 212-986 6516
Email: btany@visitbarbados.org
In Barbados
1st Floor, Warrens Office Complex, Warrens, St. Michael, Barbados, W.I.
Tel: 246-427 2623
Email: btainfo@visitbarbados.org
There is an office at the cruise terminal (tel: 246-426 1718); and an information kiosk is at Cave Shepherd department store, Broad Street.
Websites
www.barbados.org
www.visitbarbados.org

St Vincent and The Grenadines

In Canada
55 Town Centre Court, Suite 624, Scarborough, Ontario M1P 4X4
Tel: 416-630 9292
Email: svgtourismtoronto@rogers.com
In the UK
10 Kensington Court, London, W8 5DL
Tel: 020 7937 6570
Email: svgtourismeurope@aol.com

In the US
801 Second Avenue, New York, NY 10017
Tel: 212-687 4981/800-729 1726
Email: svgtony@aol.com
In St Vincent and the Grenadines
Ministry of Tourism, NIS Building, Upper Bay Street, Kingstown
Tel: 784-456 6222
Email: tourism@vincysurf.com
There are also information desks at the cruise ship terminal, tel: 784-457 1592 and E. T. Joshua Airport, tel: 784-458 4685.
Websites
www.discoversvg.com
www.svghotels.com

Grenada

In Canada
Grenada Tourism Authority, 90 Eglington Ave East, Suite 605, Toronto, Ontario M4P 2Y3
Tel: 416-995 1581
Email: tourism@grenadaconsulate.com
In the UK
Grenada Board of Tourism, 26–28 Hammersmith Grove, 4th Floor, London, W6 7BA
Tel: 020 8328 0640
Email: grenada@eyes2market.co.uk
In the US
Grenada Tourism Authority, 685 Third Avenue, 11th Floor, Suite 1101, New York, NY 10017
Tel: 917-929 7892
Email: cnoel@grenadagrenadines.com
In Grenada
Grenada Board of Tourism, Burn's Point, PO Box 293, St George's
Tel: 473-440 2279
Email: info@puregrenada.com
There is also an information booth in the cruise terminal.
Website
www.puregrenada.com

Trinidad and Tobago

In Canada
Suite 606, 130 Spadina Avenue, Toronto, Ontario M5V 2L4
Tel: 416-561 8243
In the UK
Suite 200, Parkway House, Sheen Lane, London, SW14 8LS
Tel: 0844 846 0812

In the US
331 Almeria Avenue, Coral Gables, Florida FL33134
Tel: 305-444 4033
In Trinidad
TIDCO (Tourism Development Company of Trinidad and Tobago Limited), Maritime Centre, 29 Tenth Avenue, Barataria
Tel: 868-675 7035
Also an information booth at:
Piarco International Airport, Port of Spain
Tel: 868-669 5196
Websites
www.gotrinidadandtobago.com
www.tdc.co.tt

Aruba and Curaçao

Aruba

In Europe
Aruba Tourism Authority (UK)
Tel: 44 788 591 3860
Email j.walding@aruba.com
In the US
Tel: 1-800 862 7822
Email: support@aruba.com
In Aruba
Aruba Tourism Authority, 8 L.G. Smith Boulevard, Oranjestad
Tel: 297-582 3777
Websites
www.aruba.com
www.visitaruba.com

Curaçao

In Europe
Curaçao Toeristen Bureau Europa, Anna van Buerenplein 41, 2595 DA The Hague, The Netherlands
Tel: 31 070 891 6600
In the US
791 Brickell Avenue, Suite 860, Miami, FLA 33131
Tel: 800-328 7222
Email: northamerica@curacao.com
In Curaçao
Tourism Development Bureau, PO Box 3266, Pietermaai 19, Willemstad
Tel: 5999-434 8200
And also an information booth on the Punda side of Queen Emma Bridge, open 8am–6pm Mon–Fri, 8am–5pm Sat.
Website
www.curacao.com

PRIVATE CRUISE ISLANDS

Each major cruise line has a private island (in reality, usually one beach reserved exclusively for the cruise line on certain days, apart from Disney's Castaway Cay, which is wholly owned by the cruise line). These are used for private beach days and all facilities are provided, from a restaurant to restrooms, hammocks, watersports equipment and entertainment. Some have lavish water toys, slides, horses and attractions like ziplining.

The bonus of these enclaves is that local hawkers are usually prevented from hassling passengers (although most beaches do accommodate small, local craft markets) and the equipment is of a reliable standard. The disadvantage is that 2,000 passengers or more on one beach can stretch facilities and there is little chance of getting away from it all in a big group.

Most islands can be accessed by tender. There are usually extra charges for drinks and some services ashore, although passengers can use their ship's ID cards for making purchases. The exception to this is the craft markets that are a feature on most islands, where cash is required. Expect to sign waiver forms for any hired equipment, and strict safety controls on all sports, for example, passengers may not be allowed even to snorkel alone.

GREAT STIRRUP CAY

Norwegian Cruise Line

This was the first private island to be developed, located at Bertram's Cove in the Bahamas' Berry Island chain, with white sand, offshore coral reefs and shade from palm trees. Snorkeling equipment, foam floats, inflatable rafts, pedalos, kayaks and small sailing boats are available for day hire; hammocks are also available, as are beachfront cabanas. Limbo dancing, beach games, two bars and lunchtime barbecue in an 8,500 sq ft buffet area are all on offer to while away the hours, and there's also hiking (you can walk to the lighthouse) and beach volleyball, as well as snorkeling over an underwater sculpture garden. Excursions are offered to see and touch stingrays, and there's a well-equipped children's playground.

Zip-lining over the beach at Great Stirrup Cay.

PRINCESS CAYS

Princess Cruises and P&O Cruises

One and a half miles (2km) of beachfront at the tip of lovely Eleuthera, one of the Bahamas' Out Islands, closest to Nassau. The island has shade from palm trees and there are hammocks to lounge in, private cabanas to rent and a coral reef offshore, with superb snorkeling. Watersports equipment is available for hire and you'll find a beach barbecue, several bars and boutiques, and a small section where local vendors sell souvenirs and braid hair. There's a supervised playground for kids, too. As the beach is on Eleuthera, it's also possible to venture out and have a look at the island, although the vast majority of passengers stay put.

LABADEE, HAITI

Royal Caribbean and Celebrity Cruises

This is probably the most developed of the private islands, complete with a pier, where ships can dock, and facilities including a spectacular zipline, thrill rides, five bars and three restaurants. Labadee is, in fact, on a peninsula, with a pretty beach in a quiet corner of poverty-stricken Haiti, backed by trees that offer plenty of shade. The peninsula has undergone extensive development to keep pace with the growing size of Royal Caribbean's new ships.

Entertainment includes watersports, a children's aqua park with floating trampolines and inflatables, beach volleyball, 200-year-old ruins to explore (a short walk away) and local tradespeople selling crafts (with a degree of pushiness, to judge by reports on cruise review websites). There's a hillside spa for those who want a massage open to the sea breezes. Snorkeling expeditions to nearby Amiga Island reveal anchors, cannonballs, pottery and other 16th-century artifacts on the seabed.

COCO CAY

Royal Caribbean

Royal Caribbean's other island, shared with sister line Celebrity Cruises. Originally named Little Stirrup Cay, this strip of sand is located within the Berry Island chain of the Bahamas, about 50 miles (80km) from Nassau. There is a rumor that the grave of the pirate Blackbeard is located here.

Located here is a sunken plane and a shipwrecked replica of *Queen Anne's Revenge*, Blackbeard's flagship that sank off North Carolina in 1718. Activities include pirate hunting, beach volleyball, snorkeling and scuba diving, jet-skiing, parasailing and paddleboats. There's a water park for kids and deluxe cabanas to rent for adults, although almost everything here carries an extra charge. Although there are no restaurants on Coco Cay, food is served at the beach barbecue. Access is via tender.

HALF MOON CAY

Holland America Line and Carnival Cruise Line

This stunning private island, a former pirate hideout, is visited by Carnival's and Holland America's ships during most of their Caribbean and Panama Canal itineraries.

Only 45 of the island's 2,400 acres (971 hectares) are developed; the rest is kept as a nature reserve. Activities include a nature trail, volleyball, shuffleboard, basketball, swimming, snorkeling, scuba diving, kayaking, windsurfing, parasailing, paddleboarding, banana boating, sailing, jet-skiing, deep-sea fishing and trips on glass-bottom boats. There's even a small chapel for

Cruise ship off the coast at Half Moon Cay.

weddings or marriage vow renewals. Luxurious cabanas are available to rent, too. Children's activities take place on a special section of the beach and include treasure hunts and the ice cream parlor. One of the best excursions here is horse riding along the beach.

In addition, there are several bars and a food pavilion serving barbecue dishes. The most dramatic watering hole is Captain Morgan's On The Rocks Island Bar, resembling a wrecked schooner and bedecked with pirate memorabilia. The island has also been well adapted for wheelchair users, with ramps, an accessible tram and a wheelchair path to the beach.

CASTAWAY CAY

Disney Cruise Line

Located 175 miles (282km) east of Miami in the Abacos, Castaway Cay (formerly Gorda Cay), conveniently has its own pier. Passengers are transported around by tram, with Disney characters in abundance.

There are three beaches: one for families, one for teens and one for adults only. The latter includes a bar, hammocks, private cabanas and beach massages. The teen beach has volleyball.

Activities and facilities include paddleboats, kayaking, snorkeling for sunken treasure, tubes and rafts. The kids' facilities are superb, with a floating jungle gym, cycle trails, plenty of shade (including cabanas to rent) and a wreck: the *Flying Dutchman*, the ship used in the movie *Pirates of the Caribbean:*

Dead Man's Chest, is moored here for guests to admire.

Cookies Bar-B-Q serves up burgers, hotdogs, ribs, fries and salads. There's even a post office and a shop on this island, and at Christmas the whole place is transformed, including the addition of fake snow.

CATALINA ISLAND

Costa Cruises

Costa's UNESCO-protected private hideaway is just south of La Romana on the Dominican Republic. There's a barbecue, a shopping area for local craft vendors, and plenty of watersports equipment for hire. This is one of the few places, being Italian, where topless sunbathers can relax; the American-run beaches tend to take a more prudish view.

HARVEST CAYE

NCL

Harvest Caye is a new, $50 million development in Belize, which Norwegian, Regent Seven Seas Cruises and Oceania Cruises use as their private beach. The resort offers beautiful beaches, snorkeling, a watersports lagoon, an enormous pool with swim-up bar, a 'village' for shopping and eating, and a broad range of excursions covering all the usual Belize activities, from inner tubing to exploring Maya ruins. Ships can dock at the jetty here, making Harvest Caye easily accessible for the less mobile.

CRUISING PUBLICATIONS

Berlitz Cruising and Cruise Ships by Douglas Ward (2018, updated annually). The industry's bible, this bestseller contains detailed, candid reviews of 275 ships, plus impeccable advice.
Porthole, a US-based cruising/lifestyle magazine featuring ships and advice (www.porthole.com).
World of Cruising magazine, advice aimed mainly at the UK market (www.worldofcruising.co.uk).
Devils on the Deep Blue Sea by Kristoffer Garin (2006). An entertaining history of the cruise industry.

HISTORY, ECONOMICS AND CULTURE

America's Virgin Islands: A History of Human Rights and Wrongs by William H. Boyer (1983; second edition 2010).
A–Z of Caribbean Heritage by Brian Dyde (2011).
Barbados: A History from Amerindians to Independence by F.A. Hoyos (1978).
Caribbean Dispatches: Beyond the Tourist Dream, edited by Jane Bryce (2006).
The Dominica Story: A History of the Island by Lennox Honeychurch (1995).
Gardens of the Caribbean by Jill Collett and Patrick Bowe (1998).
Material Cultures of Slavery and Abolition in the British Caribbean by Christer Petley and Stephan Lenik (2018).
Islands, Forests and Gardens in the Caribbean: Conservation and Conflict in Environmental History, edited by Robert Anderson, Karis Hiebert & Richard Grove (2006).
The Oxford Book of Caribbean Short Stories, edited by Stewart Brown and John Wickham (1999; new edition 2002).
The Penguin Book of Caribbean Verse in English, edited by Paula Burnett (2005).

FURTHER READING

A Traveller's History of the Caribbean by James Ferguson (1998; revised edition 2012).
A Traveller's Literary Companion to the Caribbean by James Ferguson, with chapters on Cuba and Puerto Rico by Jason Wilson (1997).
Our Culture One People Poetry Anthology: Book of Poetry from West Indian Literature Students by Royette G. Williams James (2015), edited by

⊙ Send us your thoughts

We do our best to ensure the information in our books is as accurate and up-to-date as possible. The books are updated on a regular basis using local contacts, who painstakingly add, amend and correct as required. However, some details (such as telephone numbers and opening times) are liable to change, and we are ultimately reliant on our readers to put us in the picture.

We welcome your feedback, especially your experience of using the book "on the road". Maybe you came across a great bar or new attraction we missed.

We will acknowledge all contributions, and we'll offer an Insight Guide to the best letters received.

Please write to us at:
Insight Guides
PO Box 7910
London SE1 1WE

Or email us at:
hello@insightguides.com

Kenneth Ramchand and Cecil Gray (1989).
Caribbean Food Made Easy by Levi Roots (2013). West Indian recipes from reggae musician turned chef and TV personality.
Wild Caribbean: The hidden wonders of the world's most famous islands by Michael Bright (2007).

NATURAL HISTORY

Birds of the West Indies: A Guide to the species of birds that inhabit the Greater Antilles, Lesser Antilles and Bahama Islands by James Bond (2015).
Reef Fish Identification: Caribbean, Bahamas, South Florida by Paul Humann and Ned DeLoach (2014).
Exploring Tropical Isles and Seas: An Introduction for the Traveler and Amateur Naturalist by Frederic Martini (1984).
Wildlife of the Caribbean by Herbert A. Raffaele and James Wiley (2014).
Caribbean Birds: A Folding Pocket Guide to Familiar Species by James Kavanagh (Waterford Press, 2016).

OTHER INSIGHT GUIDES

Insight Guides also publishes several other titles in the series to the Caribbean region, including *Caribbean: The Lesser Antilles*; *Cuba*; *Puerto Rico*; *Belize*; *Guatemala, Belize and the Yucatan*; *Florida*; and *Mexico*. In addition, Insight Pocket Guides, a new series, feature brand new guides to *St Lucia* and *Antigua and Barbuda*, as well as the *Caribbean Ports of Call*.

CREDITS

PHOTO CREDITS

123RF 186
akg images 20, 22
Alamy 199
Alex Havret/Apa Publications 11B, 40, 55, 98, 117, 120T, 125T, 127, 137, 139B, 139T, 326, 328
Anse Chastanet Resort 268T
Antigua & Barbuda Tourism Authority 215
Antigua Tourist Board 346
Apa 223T, 232, 266T, 275T
Aruba/fotoseeker.com 235BL, 300, 302, 303T, 303B, 306/307
AWL Images 115, 128, 225, 237, 248, 278BL, 296BR
Bahamas Tourist Office 176T, 178
Barbados Tourism Authority 29R, 271, 275B, 276, 277
Blount Small Ship Adventures 316/317
BVI Tourist Board 218B, 218T
Carnival 67, 77, 78, 89, 93, 169
Cayman Islands Department Of Tourism 110, 114, 151B, 156B, 234BR
Celebrity Cruises 42, 44, 49L, 64, 83, 87, 92
Celebrity Cruises/Quentin Bacon 81
Chris Huxley 268B, 269T
Claude Cavalera/St Maarten Tourist Bureau 210
Corbis 7MR, 36, 38, 39
Corrie Wingate/Apa Publications 28, 53, 100/101, 102/103, 104/105, 106, 107B, 136, 141B, 141T, 142B, 142T, 143, 145, 206/207T, 206BR, 206BL, 234BL, 308, 322, 335
Courtesy Casa de Campo 190
Courtesy Fort Shirley 245
Cunard 46, 47, 66
Cunard/Indusfoto 49R
Cunard/Indusfoto Ltd 69
Curacao Tourist Board 107T, 234/235T, 235BR, 235TR, 301, 306T, 306B
Dave Gorham/Cayman Islands Department of Tourism 155
Dave Taylor/Cayman Islands Department of Tourism 112T, 152
David MacGillivary 228

Discover Dominica Authority 242, 243, 244, 247B
Disney Cruise Line 61, 79, 95, 116, 170B
Douglas Ward 56, 65, 318
Edwin Casado Baez 189
Eugen Lehle 192T
Fotolia 207BR
Getty Images 4, 6ML, 6BR, 7TR, 7BR, 11T, 18, 32/33, 34B, 74, 123, 126, 129, 146, 148/149, 157, 164B, 173, 176B, 177, 179, 193B, 200, 201, 208, 219, 231, 240/241, 252B, 253, 254, 259B, 270, 273, 279ML, 296/297T, 297BL, 297TR, 304/305B
Glyn Genin/Apa Publications 10T, 27, 99, 168, 194, 195, 197T, 197B, 198
Grenada Board of Tourism 112B, 284, 286, 287, 288T, 289T
Grenada Cocolate Company 289B
Guadaloupe Tourist Board 217B, 217T, 255
Hapag Lloyd 60
Holland America Line 34T
iStock 6MR, 7ML, 7BL, 8B, 9BR, 10B, 45, 58, 120B, 121T, 122, 144T, 144B, 151T, 166/167, 171, 172, 174, 191, 204, 207TR, 216, 220, 221, 223B, 224, 227T, 227B, 230, 236, 239T, 246, 247T, 249, 257, 260/261, 262, 264, 265B, 265T, 267, 274T, 279BR, 279BL, 279TR, 285, 288B, 292, 304T, 367
Jean-Marc Lecerf/Guadeloupe Island Tourist Board 259T
Kevin Cummins/Apa Publications 9ML, 29L, 111, 119, 125B, 158, 159, 161, 162, 163T, 164T, 165, 207BL, 278BR
Library of Congress 26
Luc Olivier/Martinique Tourist Board 250
Martinique Tourist Board 113, 214, 251
Mary Evans Picture Library 23, 24, 25
Ministry of Tourism of The Dominican Republic 188
Montserrat Volcano Observatory 6BL, 229
Nasa 132B

Norwegian Cruise Line 31, 80, 84, 88R, 366
Nowitz Photogrpahy/Apa Publications 54, 57, 124T, 124B, 131T, 131B, 132T, 134, 135
P&O Cruises 147
Phil Wood/Apa Publications 153, 154
Philippe Giraud/Guadeloupe Island Tourist Board 258
Pictures Colour Library 274B, 296BL
Princess Cruises 76, 121B
Public domain 21, 35, 252T
Regent Seven Seas Cruises 9TR, 97
Royal Caribbean Cruises 12/13, 14/15, 16/17, 19T, 19B, 30, 41, 50, 51, 52, 62, 68, 70, 71, 72, 73, 75, 82, 86, 88L, 91, 94, 365B, 365T
Saint Lucia Tourist Board 263, 266B, 269B
Scott Lowden/Aruba Tourism Authority 212/213, 298/299
Sea Cloud Cruises 43
Shutterstock 7TL, 8T, 85, 133, 156T, 163B, 175B, 175T, 205, 233, 239B, 297ML
Silversea Cruises 63
Silversea 59, 63, 90
St Maarten Tourist Bureau 170T, 209, 211
St Vincent & the Grenadines Tourist Office 280, 281, 283
Star Clippers 96
Sylvaine Poitau/Apa Publications 180/181, 182, 183, 184, 185, 187T, 187B, 207ML, 278/279T, 336
The Ministry of Tourism of The Dominican Republic 192B, 193T
TopFoto 37
Tourism Corporation Bonaire 118, 235ML
Trinidad & Tobago Tourism Development Company
Trinidad & Tobago Tourism Development Company 291, 293T, 293B, 294T, 294B, 295T, 295B, 297BR
U.S. Virgin Islands Department of Tourism 310
Windstar Cruises 1, 48

COVER CREDITS

Front cover: Cruiseship in Tortola, *AWL Images*
Back cover: Marina Cay, British Virgin Islands *iStock*
Front flap: (from top) Labadee Zipline *Royal Caribbean Cruises*; Willemstad, Curaçao *iStock*; Caribbean coral reefs *iStock*; Symphony of the Seas *Royal Caribbean Cruises*
Back flap: Allure of the Seas *Royal Caribbean Cruises*

INSIGHT GUIDE CREDITS

Distribution
UK, Ireland and Europe
Apa Publications (UK) Ltd;
sales@insightguides.com
United States and Canada
Ingram Publisher Services;
ips@ingramcontent.com
Australia and New Zealand
Woodslane; info@woodslane.com.au
Southeast Asia
Apa Publications (SN) Pte;
singaporeoffice@insightguides.com
Worldwide
Apa Publications (UK) Ltd;
sales@insightguides.com
Special Sales, Content Licensing and CoPublishing
Insight Guides can be purchased in bulk quantities at discounted prices. We can create special editions, personalised jackets and corporate imprints tailored to your needs.
sales@insightguides.com
www.insightguides.biz

Printed in China by CTPS
All Rights Reserved
© 2019 Apa Digital (CH) AG and
Apa Publications (UK) Ltd

First Edition 2003
Fourth Edition 2019

Editor: Siobhan Warwicker
Author: Sue Bryant
Head of DTP and Pre-Press:
Rebeka Davies
Managing Editor: Carine Tracanelli
Picture Editor: Tom Smyth
Cartography: original cartography Polyglott Kartographie, updated by Carte

CONTRIBUTORS

This thoroughly revised new edition of *Insight Guide Caribbean Cruises* was commissioned by **Sian Marsh** and copyedited by **Siobhan Warwicker**. It was updated by **Sue Bryant**, a London-based journalist who has specialized in cruising for more than 20 years. She is cruise editor of *The Sunday Times* newspaper and contributes to magazines and websites worldwide as well as commenting on the ever-changing cruise industry for TV and radio. Sue also wrote several of the features for the original book. She would like to thank **David Appleton**, who helped with the research for this update.

Some of the features in earlier editions of this book were written by Caribbean specialist **Sarah Cameron**, while the book's original introduction was written by **Douglas Ward**, the highly respected author of the cruise industry's 'bible,' the annual *Berlitz Cruising and Cruise Ships*.

ABOUT INSIGHT GUIDES

Insight Guides have more than 45 years' experience of publishing high-quality, visual travel guides. We produce 400 full-colour titles, in both print and digital form, covering more than 200 destinations across the globe, in a variety of formats to meet your different needs.

Insight Guides are written by local authors, whose expertise is evident in the extensive historical and cultural background features. Each destination is carefully researched by regional experts to ensure our guides provide the very latest information. All the reviews in **Insight Guides** are independent; we strive to maintain an impartial view. Our reviews are carefully selected to guide you to the best places to eat, go out and shop, so you can be confident that when we say a place is special, we really mean it.

INDEX

MAIN REFERENCES ARE IN BOLD TYPE

INSIGHT ⊙ GUIDES

OFF THE SHELF

Since 1970, INSIGHT GUIDES has provided a unique perspective on the world's best travel destinations by using specially commissioned photography and illuminating text written by local authors.

Whether you're planning a city break, a walking tour or the journey of a lifetime, our superb range of guidebooks and phrasebooks will inspire you to discover more about your chosen destination.

INSIGHT GUIDES

offer a unique combination of stunning photos, absorbing narrative and detailed maps, providing all the inspiration and information you need.

PHRASEBOOKS & DICTIONARIES

help users to feel at home, when away. Pocket-sized with a free app to download, they go where you do.

CITY GUIDES

pack hundreds of great photos into a smaller format with detailed practical information, so you can navigate the world's top cities with confidence.

EXPLORE GUIDES

feature easy-to-follow walks and itineraries in the world's most exciting destinations, with our choice of the best places to eat and drink along the way.

POCKET GUIDES

combine concise information on where to go and what to do in a handy compact format, ideal on the ground. Includes a full-colour, fold-out map.

EXPERIENCE GUIDES

feature offbeat perspectives and secret gems for experienced travellers, with a collection of over 100 ideas for a memorable stay in a city.

www.insightguides.com

Sailing Terms

Boarding a cruise ship is like entering a world with its own language. Learning a few nautical terms is not simply a case of impressing fellow passengers but a useful way of fitting into the rhythm of life on board. The following terms are part of the everyday language of cruising:

Aft: towards the rear of the ship.
Amidships: towards the center of the ship.
Astern: behind the ship.
Beam: the width of the ship at its widest point.
Bow: the front end of the vessel.

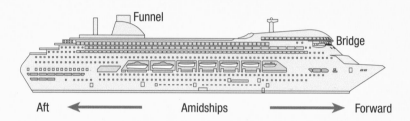

Bow thrusters: small propellers at the front of the ship, used when docking.
Captain's table: a special table reserved for the Captain and VIP guests in the dining room. If you are invited to join this table, it is good etiquette to accept.
Chart: a nautical map.
Cruise and stay: a holiday which combines a cruise with a hotel stay on land.
Draft: the measurement from the ship's waterline to the lowest point of its keel; a ship with a "deep draft" should be more stable in rough seas.
Dress code: not always what you might think. Generally speaking, "casual" means smart casual resort wear. "Informal" means cocktail dress or jacket and tie. "Formal" means black tie for gentlemen, long dress or best cocktail dress for ladies.
Fly-cruise: a vacation on which you buy a package including a flight to and from your ship, as opposed to buying a cruise-only deal, which includes no flights.
Force: the wind velocity according to the Beaufort Scale, ranging from 0 (flat, glassy water, no wind) to 12 (hurricane).
Forward: towards the front of the ship.
Galley: the ship's kitchen.
Hotel manager: the officer in charge of all accommodation and catering-related matters on board.
Hull: the main body of the ship.